8/00

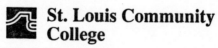

Emotions in Sport

Yuri L. Hanin, PhD, DSc
Research Institute for Olympic Sports
Jyväskylä, Finland

Editor

Human Kinetics

Library of Congress Cataloging-in-Publication Data

Emotions in sport / Yuri L. Hanin, editor.
    p. cm.
    Includes bibliographical references (p.   ) and index.
    ISBN 0-88011-879-2
    1. Sports--Psychological aspects. 2. Athletes--Psychology. I.
Khanin, IU. L. ((IUrii L'vovich)
    GV706.4 .E459 1999   99-16522
    796' .01--dc21   CIP

ISBN 0-88011-879-2

Acquisitions Editor: Steven W. Pope, PhD; **Developmental Editor:** Elaine Mustain; **Assistant Editor:** Melissa Feld; **Copyeditor:** Joyce Sexton; **Proofreader:** Erin Cler; **Indexer:** Nancy Ball; **Graphic Designer:** Stuart Cartwright; **Graphic Artist:** Yvonne Griffith; **Cover Designer:** Jack W. Davis; **Photographer** (interior): Tom Roberts; **Illustrator:** Sharon Smith; **Printer:** United Graphics/Dekker Bookbinding

Printed in the United States of America   10 9 8 7 6 5 4 3 2 1

Human Kinetics
Web site: http://www.humankinetics.com/

United States: Human Kinetics
P.O. Box 5076
Champaign, IL 61825-5076
1-800-747-4457
e-mail: humank@hkusa.com

Canada: Human Kinetics
475 Devonshire Road Unit 100
Windsor, ON N8Y 2L5
1-800-465-7301 (in Canada only)
e-mail: humank@hkcanada.com

Europe: Human Kinetics
P.O. Box IW14
Leeds LS16 6TR, United Kingdom
+44 (0)113-278 1708
e-mail: humank@hkeurope.com

Australia: Human Kinetics
57A Price Avenue
Lower Mitcham, South Australia 5062
(08) 82771555
e-mail: humank@hkaustralia.com

New Zealand: Human Kinetics
P.O. Box 105-231, Auckland Central
09-523-3462
e-mail: humank@hknewz.com

To my wife Muza and my son Alex

CONTENTS

Part III
Three Approaches to Training
and Emotional Exhaustion   189

Part IV
Additional Issues in Emotion and Sport   243

ACKNOWLEDGMENTS

I would like to acknowledge several people who provided me with outstanding help and support both personally and professionally at different stages of my career. They include my support team—my wife Muza and my son Alex. In fact, the idea to summarize my experiences in research and consultancy with elite athletes in book form came from Muza. Her feedback was especially invaluable in preparing the structure of the book and in the description of stepwise assessment procedures. I'd also like to express my appreciation to several people who are very special to me: A.C. Puni, E.S. Kuzmin, C.D. Spielberger, and W.P. Morgan.

My research and applied work resulting in the development of the extended IZOF model has been greatly facilitated in that since 1991 I have been privileged to work in one of the best research centers in Finland—the Research Institute for Olympic Sports (Director, Dr. Heikki Rusko). Finally, I would also like to thank all the contributors to this volume. It was indeed my pleasure to work with such dedicated professionals making the best shot at what they are really good at. Appreciation is also expressed to Rainer Martens for continuous support in this challenging task and to Elaine Mustain for her highly professional editorial work.

INTRODUCTION
An Individualized Approach
to Emotion in Sport

Yuri L. Hanin
Finland

Emotion is an important component of total human functioning—and critically important for understanding many core phenomena in virtually every major subdiscipline of psychology (Davidson & Cacioppo, 1992). Although emotions represent an important aspect of one's involvement in sport (Vallerand, 1983) and a critical factor in either enhancing or impairing individual or team performance, little systematic research has been conducted on positive and negative emotions. For instance, most sport psychology research during the last two decades has been negatively biased, focusing on anxiety-performance relationships and using models initially developed in non-sport settings (Gould & Krane, 1992; Hackfort & Schwenkmezger, 1993; Hanin 1986, 1993; Hardy, 1990; Jones, 1995a; Klavora, 1979; Kleine, 1990; Landers & Boutcher, 1986, 1993, 1998; Morgan & Ellickson, 1989; Raglin, 1992; Weinberg, 1990). Balance in the study of emotions and athletic performance is clearly missing at this point.

There are already a number of good reviews of research, especially on stress-related emotions, for researchers and practitioners in emotion-performance relationships (Gould & Tuffey, 1996; Jones, 1995a; Hardy, 1990; Morgan, 1997b; Raglin, 1992; Terry, 1995; Burton, 1998; Smith, Smoll, & Wiechman, 1998; Landers & Boutcher, 1998). Thus, we have chosen to undertake in this text the more focused task of describing new approaches and recent developments in the study of performance-related emotions in sport. This text concentrates on emotion problems from the idiographic (individualized) perspective, which is becoming more and more recognized and appreciated in sport as well as other areas of applied psychology. Therefore, the Individual Zones of Optimal Functioning (IZOF) model has been chosen as a major theoretical and methodological framework.

There are several reasons for this choice. Of course, the first reason relates to the field research and applications that I have been conducting with elite athletes and coaches during the last 30 years. My initial research focus on optimal communication in top-performance Russian teams (Hanin, 1980, 1992) was closely linked to optimal pre-performance emotional states. However, when Rainer Martens and Jack Cratty came to St. Petersburg (Leningrad) in 1974, as the first American sport psychologists to initiate closer cooperation with their Russian colleagues, I became interested in competitive anxiety. At that time, Rainer helped me establish contact with Charles Spielberger, and our joint project resulted in development of the Russian form of the State-Trait Anxiety Inventory. My work with this and several other self-report instruments developed or adapted for sport settings led me to realize that it was more important to assess each athlete's subjective emotional experiences than to describe how that athlete is different from (or similar to) other performers. Thus, it was my contention that to understand why and how outstanding performers achieve consistent excellency, one needs to focus primarily on their unique experiences. Interindividual differences in emotion in elite athletes were also observed but were less useful in predicting an athlete's performance and in interventions. Gradually, more research in field settings and practical work with athletes helped me to formulate several principles for accurately describing and predicting anxiety-performance relationships in individual athletes. International studies testing the basic predictions of the IZOF model, applied initially only to precompetition anxiety, were instrumental in extending the approach to positive and negative emotions conceptualized as a component of psychobiosocial states (Hanin, 1997a).

Therefore, this book does not attempt to review the state of the art in mainstream psychology or emotion research in sport in general. The aim instead is to provide an idiographic (individual-oriented) sport-specific approach to performance-related emotions. The core of the book is the IZOF model (Hanin, 1978, 1983a, 1986, 1989, 1995, 1996, 1997a) of positive and negative emotions related to individually successful and unsuccessful performance. The reader will see that the IZOF model suggests a multidimensional conception of subjective emotional experiences and provides reliable tools to assess positive and negative emotions. Furthermore, the IZOF model attempts to predict individually successful and less-than-successful performances based on current emotion states and previously established individualized criteria (zones).

It is essential to realize that in the area of performance-related emotion there are many different approaches. Thus conceptualizing emotion-performance relationships in sport from different perspectives leads to particularly useful insights—for instance, those on various aspects of emotional response to strenuous practices.

The book has four parts:

▶ **Part I** provides an overview of theoretical, conceptional, definitional, and general methodological foundations of the individualized approach to the study of performance-related emotions. In chapter 1, Robert Vallerand and Céline Blanchard provide a theoretical background for conceptualizing emotions and performance, as well as a broad overview of the current situation in research on emotion in sport. Chapter 2 reprints an earlier paper by Lazarus (1991c) on the cognitive-motivational-relational theory. In chapter 3, I discuss the theoretical underpinnings of the IZOF model, which I believe generates useful questions and can guide our efforts to better understand the impact of emotions as components of psychobiosocial states upon athletic performance.

▶ **Part II** deals with the basic emotions or emotion clusters such as competitive anxiety, anger, joy, and "flow" as they relate to athletic performance. In chapter 4, John S. Raglin and I show that traditional theories of anxiety and performance have fared poorly when applied to the realm of sport, and that research has supported the considerations and predictions of the ZOF model. We also present recent developments that have extended the model beyond anxiety to incorporate both positive and negative affect and to examine the influences of affect during as well as prior to performance. In chapter 5, Leif Isberg explores anger as one of many emotional states that can affect an athlete's performance. Susan Jackson addresses the positive side of sport experiences in chapter 6, bringing to the forefront the fact that sport has the potential to foster such experiences, and that we have much to learn about the factors leading sport participants to emotions such as joy. She highlights the concept of flow as a central and unifying phenomenon that can help explain what makes sport positive. In chapter 7, I review empirical evidence supporting the IZOF model by describing patterns of emotional experiences related to successful and poor performances of skilled athletes mainly in competitions. The major emphasis is on the balance (or imbalance) of positive and negative emotions that are either functionally optimal or dysfunctional for an individual's performance.

▶ **Part III** presents three different approaches to the same problem: patterns of acute and chronic emotional response to strenuous work in practices. The diversity of these approaches will hopefully set the stage for a more balanced view of emotions as crucial components of an athlete's working state and as an important predictor of individual performance from the short- and long-term perspectives. It appears that integrating these multiple perspectives to overtraining, staleness, and burnout in sport within the framework of one sport-specific model presents quite a challenge for future researchers. In chapter 8, John S. Raglin and Gregory S. Wilson review the literature on staleness and overtraining and provide new insights into the problem of staleness, including prevention and treatment. In chapter 9, Wolfgang Kallus and Michael Kellmann outline their approach to burnout and staleness via a stress-recovery balance-disbalance model, providing empirical evidence in support of these new conceptual and methodological ideas. In chapter 10, Keith Henschen presents the concept of maladaptive and adaptive fatigue syndrome, discussing the implications of emotion for the prevention and rehabilitation of this performance-induced psychobiosocial state.

▶ **Part IV** provides an overview of additional issues in which the role of emotions has special importance. These include injury-related and exercise-induced emotions. Chapter 11 is John Heil's examination of effective team-based emotional management of injury as an essential factor in efficient recovery. Heil describes patterns of emotional response in injured athletes from the perspective of psychobiosocial states and provides useful insights into remarkable and poor recovery. A need to examine emotions facilitating and impairing the healing process is clearly indicated. In chapter 12, Stuart Biddle provides a comprehensive overview of narrative and meta-analytic reviews, population surveys, and empirical studies of emotions related to exercise. Factors moderating the relationships between dysphoric mood and exercise, as well as mechanisms explaining exercise-induced emotion, are also discussed.

In concluding remarks, I briefly examine conceptual, methodological, and applied issues as future directions in emotion-performance research. These include

- ▶ terminology, multidimensionality, and optimal emotion patterns;
- ▶ individualized self-reports, emotion content relevancy, metaphoric description of emotions, and performance measures;
- ▶ predictions of burnout, staleness, maladaptive fatigue, and injury; and
- ▶ IZOF-based teaching of self-regulation skills and interventions.

As is the case with any framework or new orientation, it is important in IZOF-based research and consultancy to use a sound methodology to test the validity and practical utility of the model. Therefore in the appendix I have included brief instructions and an assessment form describing step-wise procedures to develop, validate, and refine individualized emotion scales and profiles. These forms have been used in applying the IZOF model to individual athletes and teams. You may copy them and use them as often as you like. In return, I would very much appreciate hearing of the experiences you have using the IZOF model, the assessment forms, and the results you achieved with them (the contact information is listed below).

Most chapters in the book represent the contributors' own areas of research, application, and expertise, emphasizing their work during the last decade. However, one can easily recognize two common elements in all their work on emotion-performance relationships. These are an individualized approach to subjective emotional experiences and a clear conclusion that nomothetic and idiographic perspectives can be combined.

Yuri L. Hanin, PhD, DSc
Professor and Senior Researcher
Research Institute for Olympic Sports
Rautpohjankatu 6, 40700 Jyväskylä, Finland
fax: 358-14-603-171
e-mail: yhanin@kihu.jyu.fi

PART

I

Foundations of the Individualized Approach to the Study of Performance-Related Emotions

CHAPTER

1

The Study of Emotion in Sport and Exercise

Historical, Definitional, and Conceptual Perspectives

Robert J. Vallerand and Céline M. Blanchard
Canada

Emotions are present in all aspects of human life, including sport and exercise. Athletes may be anxious before the game, coaches may be disgusted at an athlete for blowing an easy play, fans may be sad following the loss of the local team, or participants may feel embarrassed or incompetent during an exercise routine in a group setting. But such emotions are not merely interesting phenomena; they may also have important consequences that go beyond mere emotional experience. Athletes who are too anxious may not perform at an optimal level; the angry coach may scream at a clumsy player, making her more clumsy than ever; and the embarrassed exercise participant may stop going to exercise class altogether. Hence, emotional phenomena play an important part in sport and exercise from both an intra- and an interpersonal perspective.

Whereas in 1983 Vallerand noted that research on emotions in sport settings was sparse, in 1995 Crocker and Graham could say "There has been a surge of research activity" (p. 117). The purpose of this chapter is to evaluate progress in the field over the past 15 years, specifically:

1. To define emotion

2. To propose a sequence involving both the antecedents and consequences of emotion, distinguishing between theories about the production of emotions—that is, the antecedents—(e.g., Schachter & Singer, 1962;

Preparation of this chapter was facilitated through grants from the Social Sciences and Humanities Research Council of Canada (SSHRC), Le Fonds pour la Formation des Chercheurs et l'Aide à la Recherche (FCAR Québec), and the Université du Québec à Montréal to the first author and a fellowship from SSHRC to the second author. We would like to thank Pierre Provencher for his help in preparing the figures and Stéphane Perreault for his comments on a previous version of this chapter.

Smith, 1996; Vallerand, 1987; Weiner, 1979) and those dealing with emotional consequences (e.g., Forgas, 1995; Hanin, 1997a).

3. To review emotion theory and research in sport and exercise settings noting how the sequential framework proposed in number 2 allows us to integrate much of this theory and research

4. To suggest directions for future research

WHAT IS AN EMOTION?

Although we have learned much about emotion since William James asked this question in 1884, the concept remains undefined. Of dozens of suggested definitions (see Arnold, 1968; Carlson & Hatfield, 1992; Ekman & Davidson, 1994; Frijda, 1986; Oatley & Jenkins, 1996), none encompasses all the research. For now we sidestep the search for *the* definition in order to discuss some dimensions, categories, and components of emotion that researchers have studied; a later section will present a working definition. Finally, we address distinctions among various affective phenomena.

Dimensions of Emotion

Much research has focused on the dimensions of emotions in the hope of identifying the underlying properties common to all emotions. This research has primarily employed two distinct methodologies. With the first one, participants are asked to rate various words or adjectives on a number of scales (e.g., Mehrabian & Russell, 1974). Such ratings may also involve comparing the words and adjectives with one another in order to derive similarity ratings (e.g., Bush, 1973). With the second methodology, participants are asked to judge faces depicting emotions on a set of various scales. In both methodologies, participants' ratings are analyzed through "reduction" analyses, examples of which are factor analysis, cluster analysis, and multidimensional analysis.

Through such studies, researchers have identified a number of dimensions that seem to underlie most emotions. Most researchers have been able to agree at least on the two dimensions of pleasure/displeasure and activation (i.e., sleep/tension) (see Watson & Tellegen, 1985). For instance, interest can be seen as being high on the dimension of pleasure and low to moderate on the dimension of activation. On the other hand, anger is low on the dimension of pleasure and high on the dimension of activation. If one chooses to picture the basic dimensions of emotions on a graph, the number of dimensions theorized will obviously affect the type of geometrical representation chosen. Many theorists favor a two-dimensional approach. They propose using four quadrants, two representing high or low pleasure and two representing high or low activation (e.g., Watson & Tellegen, 1985). Presumably, all emotions can be placed in one of these four quadrants. Some researchers have proposed more complex geometrical representations, such as the circumplex model in which emotions are placed on a circle depending on their underlying properties (see

Russell, 1980). This model places various emotions on a 360° plane as a function of the relationships among them. Similar emotions are placed close to each other while opposite emotions are situated at 180° from one another, and so on. For instance, angry and upset would be placed in adjacent positions on the circle, and they both would be situated roughly 180° from bored. While there is empirical support for a diversity of models, it can be said that the two-dimension model has garnered more support at this point.

Discrete Emotions

Many theorists and researchers (e.g., Izard, 1993; Lazarus, 1991a, 1991b) believe that the richness of emotional life cannot be subsumed under a finite number of dimensions. Rather, they propose that there are a number of primary discrete emotions that vary in important ways and that cannot be explained by the underlying dimensions of pleasure and activation. Thus, anger at a referee is intrinsically different from fear at the sight of an opponent's high hockey stick. Both emotions involve high levels of activation and displeasure, yet they are experienced very differently. Cognitive theories (e.g., Arnold, 1960; Lazarus, 1991a; Smith & Lazarus, 1990), discussed later, explain the differences by specifying that these emotions result from different appraisals of the situation. Thus, the position that there are discrete emotions with certain boundaries between them may have some merit.

Research from this perspective, in which participants judge emotions displayed by people in photographs or videos (e.g., Ekman, Friesen, & Ellsworth, 1982), has uncovered at least seven basic emotions: anger, disgust/contempt, fear, happiness, interest, sadness, and surprise. (Note that others have proposed longer lists of emotions: for example, Izard [1977] would add guilt, shame, and distress to this list; Lazarus [1993] would add shame, envy, jealousy, pride, anxiety, relief, hope, love, and compassion, but does not include interest.) As people across cultures experience all these emotions, except interest (see Ekman, 1994; Ekman et al., 1982), emotions seem to be innate (as the nativity hypothesis states). Others, such as pride and confidence, seem to derive from primary emotions (see Plutchik, 1980, 1993).

Components of Emotion

Theorists (e.g., Deci, 1980; Young, 1973) have suggested that emotion consists of three main elements.

1. Physiological changes. The physiological alterations that occur during emotion include those in the autonomic system, such as increases in heart rate, blood pressure, and skin response. Psychophysiologists (e.g., Levenson, Ekman, & Friesen, 1990) have mainly focused on this aspect of emotion. Thus, seeing Shaquille O'Neal preparing to dunk on him, a defender might express fear through sudden increases in heart rate and skin conductance (e.g., Ekman, Levenson, & Friesen, 1983). Social psychophysiologists (e.g., Cacioppo, Klein, Berntson, & Hatfield, 1993; Ekman et al., 1982; Hess & Kirouac, in press) have studied physiological changes in the face, which are important because they may amplify emotional experience (e.g., Tomkins, 1962, 1963) as well as convey social messages (Ekman et al., 1982; Hess & Kirouac, in press). Thus our basketball player might display fear through wide-open eyes, raised eyebrows, and tensed lower lip (Ekman & Friesen, 1975).

2. **Action tendencies.** Some (e.g., Arnold & Gasson, 1954; Frijda, 1986) suggest that action tendencies represent the core element of emotions. For instance, fear may involve a tendency to run away, and sadness may render a person motionless. Accordingly, behaviorists (e.g., Millenson, 1967) have considered behavior an adequate representation of emotion. But because display rules (what seems to be the appropriate behavior in a situation; see Buck, 1985), as well as social and cultural forces (see Hess & Kirouac, in press), may moderate their impact on actual behavior, action tendencies do not always translate into observable behavior. At the sight of Shaq, the basketball player may have an urge to flee (because of fear) but will remain in a defensive stance in front of Shaq because of display rules (NBA players are not supposed to flee) and/or because he does not want the coach to bench him (a powerful social force).

3. **Subjective experience.** It refers to what an individual consciously experiences during the emotional episode. If we asked the basketball player how he feels at the sight of Shaq preparing to dunk on him, he would probably say he feels afraid, scared, frightened, and apprehensive (Watson & Clark, 1992). The subjective component of human emotion, probably the most studied, may be the most fundamental (e.g., Leventhal, 1974, 1982).

The three fundamental components may yield a working definition of emotion. Deci (1980) has proposed the following:

> An emotion is a reaction to a stimulus event (either actual or imagined). It involves change in the viscera and musculature of the person, is experienced subjectively in characteristic ways, is expressed through such means as facial changes and action tendencies, and may mediate and energize subsequent behaviors. (p. 85)

Although it does not represent all theories and research, this definition conveys the meaning of "emotion."

On Distinguishing Among Different Affective Phenomena

Researchers have distinguished between emotion and concepts such as mood, affect, feelings, emotional traits, and temperaments (see Batson, Shaw, & Oleson, 1992; Ekman, 1994; Frijda, 1993a; Oatley & Jenkins, 1996; Watson & Clark, 1994). Whereas authors often use the terms *feeling, affect,* and *emotion* interchangeably, *affect* can be understood as including emotion, feelings, and even mood (Oatley & Jenkins, 1996). Thus, it may be used as the generic term for affective phenomena. Emotion refers to a sudden reaction to a specific event leading to the physiological, experiential, and behavioral changes already described; feelings more specifically reflect the subjective experience of emotion and mood, without physiological or behavioral changes. Mood is more diffuse and longer lasting than emotion (Frijda, 1993a) and, unlike emotion, lacks a relationship with an object. Mood, though, can result from an emotion (Frijda, 1994). Thus, an athlete may be angry at her coach or disgusted with her teammates during a game and later feels "down" (a negative mood). Emotions may involve physiological and behavioral changes because they represent a stronger affective state than mood and feelings (Watson & Clark, 1994).

Emotional traits refer to stable individual differences in the tendency to experience a particular emotion or mood (Watson & Clark, 1994). While temperaments also represent individual differences in the tendency to experience certain emotions and moods, these tendencies originate, at least in part, from heredity (see Buss & Plomin, 1984). This is not necessarily the case for emotional traits that may also result from environmental influences (Watson & Clark, 1994).

Scales such as the Competitive Sport Anxiety Inventory-2 (CSAI-2; Martens, Vealey, & Burton, 1990) measure these constructs in sport and exercise settings. The CSAI-2 includes three subscales that assess state anxiety; two of these, on cognitive anxiety and somatic anxiety, more clearly relate to state anxiety in sport than does the third, which measures confidence. The CSAI-2 has shown high levels of reliability and validity (see Smith, Smoll, & Wiechman 1998). Most other scales on emotions in sport focus on the experiential component. The majority, following the lead of Weiner, Russell, and Lerman (1978, 1979), use affects relevant to achievement settings (e.g., feeling proud, competent, grateful); they refer more directly to feelings than to emotion per se, although some studies have assessed the "big seven" emotions (i.e., anger, fear, disgust, etc.).

Other instruments, such as the Exercise-Induced Feeling Inventory (Gauvin & Rejeski, 1993) and the Subjective Exercise Experience Scale (McAuley & Courneya, 1994) measure transient affective states that are not directed at specific objects. Thus, they are exercise-specific measures of mood (see Gauvin & Spence, 1998, for a discussion). Both these instruments have adequate psychometric properties. Researchers also use the Profile of Mood States (McNair, Lorr, & Droppleman, 1981), a non-sport-specific instrument assessing states such as anger, fatigue, and tension that has yielded interesting results with athletes (e.g., Morgan, Costill, Flynn, Raglin, & O'Connor, 1988). Other instruments focus on individual differences in emotions in the sport context— for example, the Sport Competition Anxiety Test (Martens, 1977) and the Sport Anxiety Scale (Smith, Smoll, & Schultz, 1990). As temperaments appear to influence emotionality in all aspects of life, there are no measures of temperament for sport settings (see chapter 12 for a fuller discussion of affect measures).

Oatley and Jenkins (1996) suggest that emotions, feelings, moods, emotional traits, and temperaments differ according to their time course—though this dimension does not explain all the differences (see also Frijda, 1993a). Figure 1.1 presents the time course for each. It shows that emotions (minutes

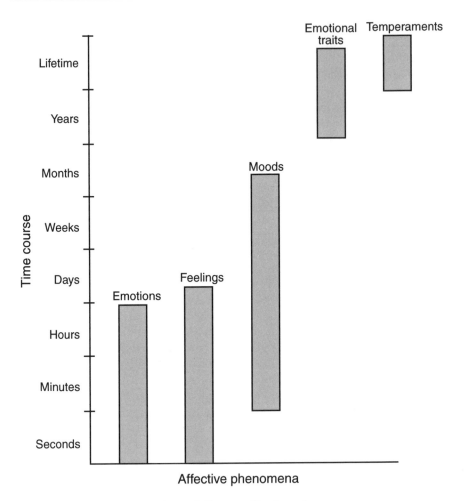

Figure 1.1 On distinguishing different affective phenomena.
Adapted from Oatley and Jenkins (1996, p. 124).

or hours), feelings (minutes, hours, and days), moods (hours, days, weeks, and even months), emotional traits (years), and temperaments (lifetime) differ on a temporal basis. After a loss, for example, a soccer player feels sad, and when she gets home, the feelings of sadness soak in. In time she is in a bad mood that lasts the remainder of the day. Both the tendency to experience sadness and the negative mood may stem from the emotional trait of negative affect (Tellegen, 1985, 1991). Negative affect, in turn, may stem from the broader, inborn temperament of neuroticism (McCrae & Costa, 1987).

In sum, the complex and varied concept of emotion includes the related constructs of feelings, mood, and affect, which researchers have measured in various ways. In the following review, we consider emotion theory and research in sport and exercise.

AN INTEGRATIVE ANALYSIS
OF EMOTION THEORY AND RESEARCH
IN SPORT AND EXERCISE

Modern research on the psychology of emotion dates back at least to Darwin (1872/1965) and perhaps even earlier (see Solomon, 1993). There are several excellent analyses of this vast literature (e.g., Carlson & Hatfield, 1992; Ekman & Davidson, 1994; Lewis & Haviland, 1993; Oatley & Jenkins, 1996). Our integrative analysis uses a sequence involving antecedents and consequences of emotion. The focus here is on theory and research in sport and exercise settings—specifically, theories on the antecedents or production of emotions (e.g., Schachter & Singer, 1962; Smith, 1996; Vallerand, 1987; Weiner, 1979) and theories dealing with emotional consequences (e.g., Forgas, 1995; Hanin, 1997a; chapters 3 and 7). Figure 1.2 presents this framework.

Theory and research (figure 1.2) on antecedents deal with psychological processes that elicit emotion. Such work includes that of Weiner (1979, 1981), Vallerand (1987), and Smith (1996) on the causal role of cognitive appraisals in emotion. More recent research has addressed how motivation and goals (e.g., Bandura, 1986; Deci & Ryan, 1985, 1991; Nicholls, 1984) impact emotion in sport and exercise. Lazarus's theory of emotion also addresses antecedents (chapter 2). The aim of these theories and models is to understand and predict how an individual will feel in a given sport situation.

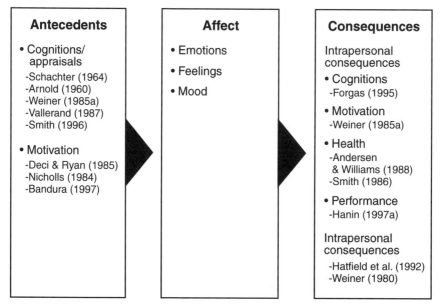

Figure 1.2 An integrative sequence involving emotional antecedents and consequences.

Other theories and models concern the consequences of emotion. For instance, Hanin (chapters 3 and 7) has proposed the Individual Zones of Optimal Functioning (IZOF) model for determining the consequences of emotions on sport performance. Forgas (1995) has proposed a model to explain how emotion affects cognitive judgments. Most research on consequences has dealt with intrapersonal consequences (i.e., those for the individual experiencing the emotion). For instance, authors of this volume have examined physical health (Heil, chapter 11; Henschen, chapter 10; Kallus & Kellmann, chapter 9) and sport performance (Hanin, chapters 3 and 7; Isberg, chapter 5; Jackson, chapter 6; Raglin & Hanin, chapter 4; Raglin & Wilson, chapter 8). Little research has addressed interpersonal consequences of emotion in sport. These few studies include investigations of interpersonal and intragroup anxiety (Hanin, 1977; Hanin & Bulanova, 1979; Hanin & Kopysov, 1977) and the impact of communication patterns within different sports upon emotional states (Hanin, 1992; see also chapter 3).

The present review is not meant to be exhaustive but rather to illustrate past research and recent trends. Much of the work has proceeded from a nomothetic perspective, with the aim of making predictions regarding athletes and exercise participants in general (Smith, 1996; Vallerand, 1987). Recent studies, however, have begun to reflect an idiographic perspective, with the aim of making predictions about individuals or subsets of athletes (e.g., Hanin, 1997a).

We will see that the proposed framework involving antecedents and consequences allows us to integrate a large portion of findings in emotion research. The first section deals with theory and research on the antecedents of emotion, while the second focuses on theory and research on emotional consequences.

THEORY AND RESEARCH ON THE ANTECEDENTS OF EMOTION IN SPORT

Most research on emotion has focused on identifying the psychological processes leading to emotion. Such studies have originated in various perspectives and dealt with various affective phenomena (see Lewis & Haviland, 1993). One can say that theorists and researchers belong to one of two camps. One camp posits that the necessary cause of emotion is cognition or at least appraisal (e.g., Frijda, 1986; Lazarus, 1991b; Ortony, Clore, & Collins, 1988; Roseman, 1984; Scherer, 1984a; Smith & Ellsworth, 1985). The second, while not denying that cognitive processing can determine emotions, argues for other sources of influence (e.g., Izard, 1992; Ledoux, 1993; Zajonc, Murphy, & McIntosh, 1993).

For instance, Izard (1992, 1994) suggests that information processing is mainly what elicits emotion. Of the four types of information processing that Izard posits, only one is solely cognitive. Cellular information processing involves information encoding and decoding that take place mostly in genes and influence mainly emotional traits and temperaments. Organismic information processing deals with genetically coded data that lead to emotion through involvement of interoceptors (sensory receptors that receive input from inside the organism—e.g., taste-elicited disgust), with little input from exteroceptors (sensory receptors that receive input from the organism's surface) and independently of cognition. Biopsychological information processing reflects interactions between genetic codes and acquired knowledge—for example, fear in response to stimuli such as snakes (Lanzetta & Orr, 1986). Finally, cognitive information processing includes appraisals and attributions that determine emotion.

Several theorists (e.g., Frijda, 1994; Lazarus, 1991a, 1991b; Scherer, 1984b) propose that while human emotion may at times be elicited with minimal cognitive processing, such instances are rare. Thus, the main task for emotion theories should be to determine the different types of cognition that determine various emotions (Lazarus, 1994). This position is based on more than 40 years of theory and research showing that cognitions (even in the most implicit form) play a causal role in emotion and, further, that they may represent the most fundamental antecedent of affective phenomena (Arnold & Gasson, 1954; Lazarus, 1966; Weiner, 1985a).

Accordingly, this section addresses cognitive theories and related research. Such theories have been selected on the grounds of sound theorizing as well as for their contribution to the understanding of emotion in the sport/exercise domain. Specifically, we discuss (1) theories that have paved the way to current emotion theories in the realm of sport and exercise; (2) three appraisal theories—those of Weiner (1979, 1981), Vallerand (1987), and Smith (1996); and (3) goal and motivation theory and research (Bandura, 1986; Deci & Ryan, 1985; Nicholls, 1984).

Forerunner Theories

Early contributions to theory on emotion include those of James (1884/1968), Cannon (1927), Schachter (1964; Schachter & Singer, 1962), and Arnold (1960).

James and Cannon

James (1884/1968) proposed a theory of emotion that underscored the role of peripheral bodily cues. Here, an event triggers autonomous responses (e.g., visceral changes) as well as skeletal muscle responses connected to internal receptors. These receptors send impulses to the brain that are then interpreted as the experience of emotion. Thus, for James, the sight of an event (an angry hockey player coming at you with a high stick) may lead to skeletal and autonomous reactions (fleeing, shaking) that you later interpret as the emotion (fear). See figure 1.3 for a schematic description of James's theory.

James's theory was severely criticized (e.g., Bard, 1928; Cannon, 1927; Lehmann, 1914/1968). Cannon, for instance, attacked it on the basis of experiments (e.g., Cannon, Lewis, & Britton, 1927) indicating that it is unlikely that the viscera play a causal role in producing emotion. This led Cannon (1927) to propose his own theory, which emphasized the role of central factors (especially the thalamus) in generating emotional experience and behavior. According to

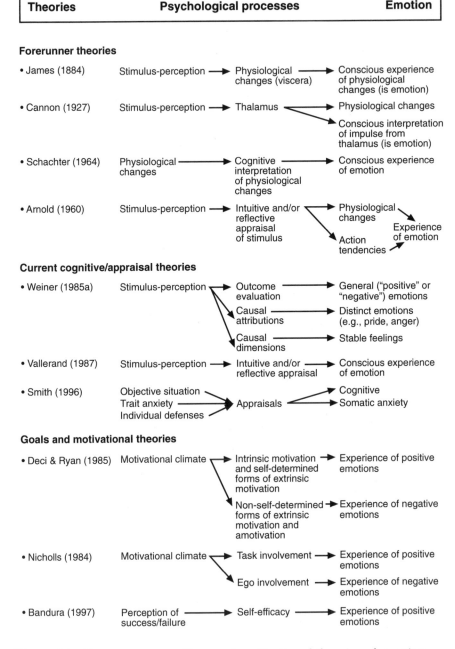

Figure 1.3 Forerunner, cognitive, and motivational theories of emotion.

Cannon, a perceived stimulus arouses the thalamus. An interpretation of the stimulus from the thalamus triggers impulses simultaneously to (1) internal organs (viscera) and skeletal muscles, thereby producing emotional behavior; and (2) the cerebral cortex, where impulses are interpreted as the emotional experience (see figure 1.3). Thus, the sight of the angry hockey player is interpreted by the thalamus and leads to both emotional behavior (moving away) and emotional experience (fear).

Schachter's Two-Factor Theory

James's theory (1884/1968) favored a peripheral perspective and Cannon's (1927) a central perspective. These frameworks remained unreconciled until Schachter (Schachter & Singer, 1962) developed his theory encompassing both positions. From the peripheral perspective, Schachter derived the fundamental role of physiological arousal; from the central position he borrowed cognitive evaluation of the current situation. His theory proposes that both arousal and cognition are necessary for the experience of emotion—specifically, emotion results from the labeling of *preexisting unexplained arousal*. What produces such labeling is the cognitive interpretation of the immediate social context.

Thus, it may have been that the hockey player in our example experienced increased arousal (e.g., high heart rate) because it was a high-paced game. But he may have doubted that exercise was the cause of the increased arousal because this was the beginning of a new shift on the ice. The sight of the angry opponent provided him with the explanation for his arousal, according to Schachter, thereby leading to the experience of fear. In sum, for Schachter, both arousal and cognition are necessary causes of emotion. Neither suffices to produce emotion on its own; it is their conjunction that produces emotion (see figure 1.3).

Research based on Schachter's theory has important implications for sport and exercise psychology. For example, Zillman, Johnson, and Day (1974) studied the impact of residual excitation (or arousal) from strenuous physical exercise on anger and aggressive behavior (retaliation). Participants were provoked, engaged in exercise, and given an opportunity to retaliate against the instigator either immediately after exercise or after a brief recovery period. As Schachter's theory would predict, participants retaliated much more after the recovery period than immediately after exercise. Why? Immediately after exercise, the cause of the arousal was clear (exercise), so the arousal did not lead to emotion. In the recovery condition, overt physiological manifestations of arousal had disappeared; thus participants could attribute their arousal to the instigator, which led them to feel anger and retaliate. Although Schachter's theory leads to intriguing hypotheses and should interest sport and exercise psychologists, few studies have pursued this line of research.

Schachter's theory has generated much criticism, often focused on the concept of arousal and its role. For instance, Zillman (1978) emphasized that Schachter does not specify the origin of arousal. Further, experiments by Zimbardo and colleagues (Marshall & Zimbardo, 1979; Maslach, 1979) have shown that unexplained arousal does not lead to a search for cognitions but rather to negative cognitions. Finally, the theory does not specify how arousal and cognition combine to lead to emotion (Leventhal, 1974). While Schachter and Singer (1979) convincingly rebutted some of these criticisms, these issues merit consideration.

Arnold's Appraisal Theory

Importantly, however, Schachter's theory may not apply to everyday situations. For instance, why does Schachter need to posit prior arousal in order for the hockey player to experience fear? Why not posit that the athlete has appraised the situation as dangerous? This is exactly Magda Arnold's position. In line with other cognitive theorists (e.g., Lazarus & Alfert, 1964), Arnold (1960, 1968, 1970a, 1970b; Arnold & Gasson, 1954) postulates that how one appraises the situation determines the emotion. She identifies two types of appraisal: an intuitive, quick, and almost automatic type that is sufficient and necessary for experiencing emotion, and a more reflective or rational type that is neither necessary nor sufficient to produce emotion but that modifies or reinforces the effects of the intuitive appraisal. For instance, seeing the angry opponent, the hockey player might appraise the situation as dangerous and experience fear; but if he then realizes that the opponent is skating by him to hit the board, he will reappraise the situation and feel relief.

Arnold's theory has built upon that of other theorists. Like Cannon, Arnold took a central position, suggesting that the brain plays a prominent part in emotion; she even proposed the existence of brain pathways leading to the experience of emotion. However, in contrast to Cannon, she suggested a psychological theory that would lead not only to the explanation of emotion but also to its prediction. In line with Schachter, she believed in the role of cognition; but contrary to Schachter's belief that arousal preceded cognition, her belief was that appraising a stimulus produces the physiological changes (and thus arousal). She proposed that physiological changes and action tendencies (also the result of appraisals) jointly lead to emotion (see figure 1.3).

Arnold's theory in turn has drawn criticism. For example, Strongman (1973) suggested that if the intuitive appraisal is almost automatic, then it may be more parsimonious scientifically to employ other explanatory constructs that do not involve higher cognitive functions such as conditioning. Also, the theory could not precisely predict specific emotions, since it did not spell out the content of appraisals. Nevertheless, Arnold's theory has proved influential. Although it has not led directly to emotion research, it has paved the way to other theories aimed at specifying the content of intuitive and or reflective appraisals. We now turn to such theories.

Current Cognitive/Appraisal Theories

Here we will consider three cognitive/appraisal theories relevant to sport and exercise settings: those of Weiner (1985a), Vallerand (1987), and Smith (1996).

Weiner's Attributional Theory of Emotion

Although appraisal theorists (e.g., Arnold, 1960; Lazarus, 1966) proposed that how one assesses an event determines the emotion, these theories did not include specific cognition-emotion linkages. In the first version of his attributional theory of achievement motivation, Weiner (1972) included pride and shame as determinants of motivated behavior but did not discuss other emotions. Subsequently, Weiner, Russell, and Lerman (1978, 1979) sought to identify the types of attributions that lead to more diversified types of emotions. In an initial study (Weiner et al., 1978), participants read hypothetical scenarios in which another person failed or succeeded at a task because of a specific attribution. In the next study (Weiner et al., 1979), participants recollected their own successes and failures as attributed to various causes. They indicated the emotions that the person in the situation would experience (Study 1) or that they themselves had experienced in the past (Study 2) as a function of the attributions. The findings of the two studies were almost identical and have led to Weiner's (1979, 1985a, 1986, 1995) theory of emotion.

Weiner's theory includes three sources of emotion:

1. The impact of an event: the event produces emotions such as joy following success and sadness following failure. These *outcome-dependent emotions* are the first emotions experienced, as well as the strongest.

2. Attributions for the outcome: these lead to more distinct emotions, such as anger when one attributes one's failure to others or pride when one attributes success to one's own ability. Emotions emerging from the attributional process are *attribution-dependent emotions*.

3. Causal dimensions: these mediate long-lasting feelings and underlie the types of attributions. The three causal dimensions leading to attributions are locus (the cause is internal or external to the person), stability (the cause is permanent or changing), and control (the cause is under the person's direct control or not). Each dimension produces distinct emotions. For example, internal attributions for success increase feelings of self-esteem, while controllable attributions for another person's insulting behavior may lead to hatred.

Thus, according to Weiner's theory, a squash player wins a tournament and feels "good" about it. She attributes her success to her ability and experiences pride and competence. A further causal analysis leads her to reinforce the role of internal factors in her success, thereby leading to enduring feelings of high self-esteem (see figure 1.3 for a schematic description of Weiner's theory).

Much support exists for Weiner's theory of emotion (see Weiner, 1985a, 1995), including in the sport domain. One line of research has addressed the link between the causal attributions and the emotions of winners and losers of sport events. For instance, McAuley, Russell, and Gross (1983) asked winners and losers in table tennis to complete the Causal Dimension Scale (Russell, 1982) and to respond to a list of affects derived from Weiner et al. (1978, 1979).

In the success condition, satisfaction was the only emotion predicted by all three types of attributions (locus, control, and stability). In addition as the authors had hypothesized, pride and confidence were positively predicted by controllable and stable attributions, and gratitude and surprise were predicted by controllable attributions. In the failure condition, although no results were statistically significant, depression and shame tended to be positively predicted by locus and negatively by control; and, as in the success condition, surprise was positively predicted by controllable attributions. Others have obtained similar results in an exercise setting: McAuley, Poag, Gleason, and Wraith (1990) investigated how attributions for dropping out of an exercise program determined participants' affective reactions. Guilt and shame were positively associated with the causal dimension of locus, while depression was associated with that of stability. Frustration was positively associated with stability and control.

People are more likely to make attributions when outcomes are unexpected (see Weiner, 1985b). Thus, McAuley and Duncan (1989) reasoned that people would be more likely to make attributions and consequently experience emotions following disconfirming outcomes. In a study using an ergometer bike race, they asked participants their expectations before competing. Those who expected to win were assigned to the losing condition, and those who expected to lose were assigned to the winning condition. After the race, participants completed the Causal Dimension Scale (Russell, 1982) and responded to a list of emotions (Weiner et al., 1978, 1979). In the success condition (expected to lose but won), only one relationship was significant: feelings of confidence were positively predicted by the locus, controllability, and stability dimensions. In the failure condition, significant results were obtained for several emotions. Depression was positively predicted by stability but negatively by locus, while displeasure was positively predicted by stability and locus. On the other hand, surprise and competence were negatively predicted by locus whereas guilt and shame were positively related to stability. Hence, it would appear that disconfirming outcomes are likely to generate an attributional search, and consequently, important attribution-affect relationships, especially after failure.

In sum, research in sport has provided some support for Weiner's theory of emotion. Some affects have been related to attributions in accordance with Weiner's theory: following failure, for instance, depression, shame, and guilt are associated with internal attributions (the locus dimension). However, surprisingly, researchers have found other emotions such as gratitude to be related to controllable attributions. In addition, no research in sport has shown that attributions do cause emotions—as no study, to our knowledge, has experimentally manipulated attributions and assessed their effects on emotions (see McFarland & Ross, 1982, for such research in an interpersonal setting). This represents an important future research direction. Further, attributions typically explain a limited amount of variance in emotions in sport and exercise settings (see Biddle, 1993; Biddle & Hanrahan, 1998; Willimczik & Rethorst, 1995, for similar conclusions). Clearly, while attributions are involved in the production of emotion, other constructs are needed in order to more fully understand the nature of the antecedents of emotion.

The Intuitive-Reflective Appraisal Model (Vallerand, 1987)

On the basis of appraisal theories, especially that of Arnold (1960; Arnold & Gasson, 1954), Vallerand (1987) proposed an intuitive-reflective appraisal model for self-related affects in achievement situations. Here it is not events per se that produce emotions, but the cognitive appraisal of events, which is both intuitive and reflective. Intuitive appraisal involves minimal cognition and is akin to one's almost automatic subjective assessment of performance, as when an athlete knows during a game that he or she is not playing well. Reflective appraisal involves deliberate cognitive processing of information dealing with the external and internal (e.g., memory) environment. It appears in several forms: intellectualization (Lazarus, 1966); comparison processes (Suls & Mullen, 1983); mastery-related cognitions (Markus & Zajonc, 1985); information-processing functions (Taylor, 1981); and causal attributions (Weiner, 1979, 1985a). See Vallerand (1987) for a fuller discussion of this model.

According to Vallerand (1987), the intuitive appraisal is always implicated in the enactment of an emotion, and this subjective assessment of performance is often a more important determinant of affect than the reflective appraisal, as the latter is not seen as being necessary to produce emotions. The latter modifies, minimizes, or augments the effects of the intuitive appraisal. The reflective appraisal surfaces when a mismatch occurs between the individual's expectations and the actual outcome (see also, McAuley & Duncan, 1989). If the outcome is different than expected, the individual will engage in more elaborated appraising of the situation (such as attributions), which will serve to modify the effects of the intuitive appraisal (Vallerand, 1987; see figure 1.3 for a schematic description of this model).

The intuitive-reflective appraisal model has led to several studies. Vallerand (1987, Study 1) examined the role of intuitive performance and reflective attributional appraisals in the experience of general (e.g., joy, sadness, satisfaction) and self-related affects (e.g., competence, pride) in both success and failure conditions. Immediately after an important playoff game, basketball players completed a questionnaire including measures of intuitive performance appraisal, reflective (attributional) appraisal, and affects. In the success condition, the intuitive performance appraisal in the form of perceived outcome was an important predictor of both types of affects. The reflective attributional appraisal was also an important predictor of self-related affects. In the failure condition, only the intuitive appraisal predicted self-related affects. The reflective attributional appraisal yielded nonsignificant results with self-related affects. With respect to general affects, no predictor yielded significant results.

Vallerand (1987, Study 2) further tested the model in a second study conducted in laboratory settings. Participants engaged in a motor maze task and were randomly assigned to conditions of success and failure. After performing the task, they completed a questionnaire assessing intuitive and reflective attributions (using the Causal Dimension Scale), appraisals, and general and self-related affects. The first of several interesting results was that the intuitive appraisal had a more important influence on affects than the objective conditions (i.e., success and failure). Thus, as Vallerand suggests, it is not the event per se, but rather its subjective interpretation that is important. Second, the intuitive appraisal was found to be a more important predictor of both general and self-related affects than the reflective appraisal (attributions). Third, the reflective attributional appraisal nevertheless did have an important impact on emotions. Further, in line with the model, stable and controllable attributions led to augmenting and minimizing effects: participants making controllable attributions in the success condition reported more positive self-related affects (augmenting effects) than participants making noncontrollable attributions. On the other hand, participants in the failure condition who made more controllable attributions reported less positive self-related affects (mini-mizing effects) than participants making more controllable attributions. Thus, perceiving oneself as responsible for a success increases feelings of pride and competence, while being responsible for a failure undermines such feelings. The stability dimension showed similar results. Thus, the Vallerand (1987) studies provided important support for the intuitive-reflective appraisal model.

Other studies have tested Vallerand's model in sport and exercise settings. For instance, McAuley and Duncan (1990) investigated relationships between the intuitive (performance) and reflective (attributional) appraisals and self-related and general affects after performance of a required gymnastic routine. The intuitive appraisal strongly predicted both types of affects. The impact from the reflective appraisal was much less important, as only stability attributions significantly influenced both types of affects. Similar findings were obtained with high school students in a team sport program (Robinson & Howe, 1989), participants in a regional squash league (Biddle & Hill, 1992a), and participants in an exercise program (Courneya & McAuley, 1996).

Another type of reflective appraisal, which can take several forms, is that of task/event importance (or value). After an event, task reappraisal refers to what Vallerand (1987) calls the intellectualization function. Thus, after a loss an athlete can decide that the event was not that important or after success can amplify its importance. This type of reflective appraisal may alter the intensity of the emotions. Before the event, the function may be different. Subjective importance may then reflect an overall subjective value for the event devoid of augmenting or minimizing effects. The impact on emotions is then likely to be indirect through effects on postparticipation reflective appraisals, such as attributions (a moderator effect).

Vallerand (1987, Study 1), assessing the role of task importance appraisal after participation, found no effect on emotions. However, studying how various appraisals related to mood, Crocker and Bouffard (1992) reported that the appraisal of task importance (or task value) following participation was the most important predictor of mood on the part of individuals with physical disabilities during challenging physical exercise. It thus appears that the role of task importance appraisal in affect is more complex than anticipated and warrants further research.

More recently Biddle and colleagues reported interesting findings on the perceived importance of winning. In an initial laboratory-based study using a one-versus-one fencing contest, Biddle and Hill (1992b) assessed the link between perceived importance of winning prior to the competition and affects (assessed by a list of 28 adjectives as in Weiner et al., 1978). The perceived importance of winning was the second most important predictor of self-related affects (after the intuitive appraisal, but before attributions).

In another study, Biddle and Hill (1988) assessed the moderating effects of the importance (of winning) appraisal in an ergometer bike race study. Before the race, participants rated the importance of winning; following the race, they completed a measure of causal attributions and responded to a list of affects. To test the moderating effects of perceived importance on the relationship between attributions and affects, the authors statistically "partialled out" the perceived importance of winning from the attribution-emotion correlations, and several moderating effects emerged. For example, effort attribution was related to feeling good, cheerful, proud, secure, contented, and thankful only when winning was deemed important. Similarly, winning because of one's personality (an internal and stable attribution) was associated with feeling good, proud, and happy only when it was important to win. However, attributing a win to mood was related to feeling cheerful and delighted independently of the importance of winning. Similarly, the ability attribution was correlated with feelings of confidence, competence, and contentment independently of outcome importance. However, attributing a win to one's own mood was associated with feeling proud and happy only when the win was important. These findings reveal that the importance appraisal has both a direct and a moderating influence on emotions.

In sum, research provides strong support for the intuitive-reflective appraisal model:

▶ Appraisals have a more important impact on emotion than the objective event.

▶ Reflective appraisals, especially attributions, seem to contribute significantly to emotions, although the intuitive appraisal is a better predictor (on this issue see Biddle & Hanrahan, 1998; Willimczik & Rethorst, 1995).

▶ The conjunction of the intuitive and reflective appraisals explains a rather large portion of the variance in emotions, with the intuitive appraisal explaining the most variance.

Future research should test the impact of the other types of reflective appraisals in Vallerand's model (1987). The role of comparison processes and intellectualization (e.g., task importance) appraisals, among others, deserves consideration. In addition, more research should address the complementary roles of intuitive and reflective appraisals, and not only their relative importance in predicting emotions. Finally, tests of the model should include emotions other than those typically assessed in achievement situations.

Smith's Sport Performance Anxiety Model

On the basis of the work of appraisal theorists such as Arnold (1960) and Lazarus (1966; Lazarus & Folkman, 1984), as well as of theories of anxiety (e.g., Spielberger, 1966b), Smith (1996) has proposed a model of sport anxiety. Although the model includes both determinants and consequences of anxiety, we consider only the determinants here.

Smith suggests that three factors influence the intensity and duration of cognitive and somatic state anxiety. These factors determine how the athlete will appraise a situation, and thus how anxious he or she will be in that situation:

▶ **The objective competitive sport situation.** The importance of the game may represent a key factor: one will probably react differently to an easy game than to a final playoff game. The situation also includes factors such as the strength of the opponent, presence of significant others, and degree of social support from coaches.

▶ **The sport-specific trait anxiety of the person.** Athletes with high levels of trait anxiety tend to experience high levels of state anxiety in competitive sport situations (e.g., Martens, Vealey, & Burton, 1990).

▶ **An athlete's psychological defenses for coping with anxiety-arousing competitive situations.** In line with Spielberger (1966b), Smith suggests that psychological defenses distort the perception of the situation. The more successful this defense process is, the less threatening the situation will seem and the less state anxiety will be present.

According to Smith, all three factors influence state anxiety through their impact on the athlete's appraisal processes. Four types of appraisal come into play:

1. Appraisal of situational demands
2. Appraisal of resources to deal with the immediate situation
3. Appraisal of the nature and likelihood of potential consequences if the demands are not met
4. The personal meanings attached to the consequences

For example, the athlete who appraises the situation as highly demanding, who believes his or her skills insufficient to deal with it, who expects failure, and who derives increases in self-esteem from performance is likely to perceive the competitive situation as highly threatening and thereby to experience high levels of physiological arousal. In turn the arousal will further influence the appraisal and reappraisal process (Lazarus & Folkman, 1984), leading to the experience of state anxiety (see figure 1.3 for a schematic representation of Smith's model).

Because it is so new, the model has not led to much research. In one recent study, Hall, Kerr, and Matthews (1998) assessed the effects on state anxiety of perfectionism and goals (task vs. ego orientations) as determinants of appraisal of the personal meaning of a competition. They reasoned that extreme perfectionists who display an ego orientation (those trying to beat others) should experience higher levels of cognitive anxiety. Results with 119 high school runners supported their hypotheses, providing preliminary evidence for Smith's model. Further research along those lines would be worthwhile. In addition, this study underscores the fact that motivation may be an important determinant of emotions. We now turn to this aspect.

Goal and Motivational Theories

Several theorists have suggested that goals and motivation play an important role in producing emotions (Frijda, 1988; Lazarus, 1991a, 1991b; Mandler, 1984; Ortony, Clore, & Collins, 1988). For instance, Mandler (1984) proposes that emotion results from goal blockages ("interrupts"). For Ortony et al. (1988), emotions result from appraisals of events with reference to some goal. Perhaps Frijda (1988) said it best: "Emotions arise in response to events that are important to the individual's goals, motives, or concerns" (p. 351).

Research on theories of motivation, such as self-determination theory (Deci & Ryan, 1985, 1991), achievement goal theory (Nicholls, 1984), and social cognitive theory of self-regulation (Bandura, 1991, 1997), has tested the relationship between motivation and emotion in sport and exercise.

Self-Determination Theory (Deci & Ryan, 1985, 1991)

Self-determination theory holds that individuals engage in sport and physical activity for a number of reasons (see Brière, Vallerand, Blais, & Pelletier, 1995; Pelletier, Vallerand, Green-Demers, Brière, & Blais, 1995; Vallerand, in press; Vallerand & Losier, in press). Some reasons are intrinsic, such as the simple pleasure of engaging in the activity. Other, extrinsic reasons derive from self-regulation. Self-regulation includes three types (Deci & Ryan, 1985, 1991): identified regulation, introjected regulation, and external regulation. (Note that Deci and Ryan [1985] discussed a fourth type of extrinsic motivation, termed integrated regulation; but as this type is present mainly in adults and as sport research typically focuses on younger age groups, it is not discussed here.) Identified regulation refers to engagement in an activity because the person has chosen it. Introjected regulation refers to engagement out of a sense of obligation or of self-imposed pressure. When externally regulated, people participate in activities because someone else (e.g., parents or a spouse) is pressuring them. Finally, amotivation refers to the relative absence of motivation of any type.

Deci and Ryan (1985, 1991) locate the various types of self-determination along a continuum. From high to low levels of self-determination we find intrinsic motivation, identified regulation, introjected regulation, external regulation, and amotivation. Several studies have supported this ordering (see Vallerand, 1997, for a review). The self-determination continuum helps predict affective consequences of motivations: because self-determination should enhance psychological functioning (Deci, 1980; Ryan, Deci, & Grolnick, 1995) and because we know the location of each type of motivation on the continuum, we can predict that various consequences—including affective ones—are decreasingly positive as we go down on the continuum. Research in various contexts (e.g., education, leisure, work) bears this out (see Vallerand, 1997, for a review; see also figure 1.3 for a schematic description of the theory).

Sport and exercise researchers have also examined the emotional consequences of the various types of motivation. In a study by Pelletier et al. (1995), participants from several sports completed the Sport Motivation Scale (Pelletier et al., 1995) and other scales measuring positive emotions. Intrinsic motivation, followed by identified and introjected regulation, produced the most positive correlations; amotivation, followed by external regulation, yielded the most negative correlations. Brière and colleagues (Brière et al., 1995) obtained similar results with French-Canadian athletes from various sports and ages, as did Blanchard and Vallerand (1996) with basketball players.

In a recent study (Blanchard & Vallerand, 1998), 274 individuals in a weight-loss program completed the Situational Motivation Scale (SIMS; Guay & Vallerand, 1998) and a scale assessing positive affect. The SIMS assesses intrinsic motivation, identified and external regulation, and amotivation at a precise moment. Again, intrinsic motivation, followed by identified regulation, produced the most positive correlations. Correlations with external regulation were either negative or close to zero, and correlations with amotivation were strongly negative.

Finally, with participants in weightlifting and cardiovascular activities, Rozniak, Blanchard, and Koestner (1998) tested the impact of identified and introjected regulation on mood as measured by the Exercise-Induced Feeling Inventory (Gauvin & Rejeski, 1993). Those who participated out of identified regulation experienced a more positive mood (higher levels of revitalization and positive engagement) following their training session than those participating out of introjected regulation. Moreover, the latter were more exhausted (negative mood) and relieved after the training session.

In sum, results from studies conducted in sport and exercise settings provide support for the self-determination theory. The more self-determined forms of motivation (intrinsic motivation and identified regulation) lead to positive affect, while those less self-determined forms of motivation (introjected and external regulation and amotivation) lead to less positive or even negative affect.

Goal Orientations

Work over the past 15 years has shown that individuals engage in athletic activities out of either ego or task involvement (Ames, 1992; Duda, 1992; Dweck & Leggett, 1988; Nicholls, 1984; Roberts, 1992). Athletes are ego involved when they engage in sport to demonstrate their level of competence to others; they are task-involved when they seek to master challenges for themselves. Much research in sport has shown the validity of these two types of goal orientations (see Duda, Chi, Newton, Walling, & Catley, 1995; Roberts & Treasure, 1995). Nicholls (1984) suggested that the two types of goals should have different consequences, including affective reactions. Task-involvement should lead the athlete to select competitive levels, opponents, and tasks conducive to maximal personal improvement and satisfaction. Ego-involved individuals are more likely to experience negative affect and a lack of interest (see figure 1.3 for a schematic description of the theory).

Research conducted in sport and exercise settings tends to support the theory. For example, Newton and Duda (1993) assessed the degree of task- and ego-involvement of bowlers across three games in a college-level physical education class. In addition, they measured feelings of enjoyment and anxiety. They then correlated the goal orientations with these affects. Results indicated that task orientation was positively related to enjoyment and negatively related to being worried about one's performance. Similar results were obtained in a study conducted by Duda and Nicholls (1992) in which the sport task orientation of high school students was positively associated with feelings of satisfaction and enjoyment. Conversely, ego orientation was positively related to feelings of boredom. White and Duda (1991) also conducted a study of intercollegiate skiers. The results showed that task orientation was negatively related to task-relevant worries and thoughts of escape. Finally, several studies have found that ego orientation is positively related to cognitive anxiety (Duda, Chi, & Newton, 1990; Hall et al., 1998; Lewthwaite, 1990; Vealey & Campbell, 1988). These investigations bear out Nicholls's (1984) hypothesis that task-involvement relates positively to positive affective states whereas ego-involvement relates positively to negative states such as anxiety.

Of particular interest is a study by Vlachopoulos, Biddle, and Fox (1996) on the impact of goal orientations and intuitive and reflective appraisals (attributions) on positive and negative affect. Prior to the study the authors assessed the goal orientations of the participants, students 11 to 14 years of age who engaged in either a track and field event or a health-related fitness test during physical education class. After completing the activities, participants indicated the goals they had adopted during the activities (i.e., task- and ego-involvement), their intuitive appraisal (perceptions of success), reflective appraisals (attributions for success or failure), and positive (e.g., confident, pleased) and negative affects (e.g., depressed, ashamed). Task-involvement and the intuitive appraisal emerged as significant predictors of positive affects. Internal attributions for success significantly predicted positive affects, although the effect was rather weak. Only the intuitive appraisal influenced (negatively) negative affect. Through structural equation modeling, the authors found support for a model in which goal orientation influenced goal involvement (the actual goals used in the event). In turn, goal involvement determined the intuitive appraisal. Only task-involvement influenced (positively) the intuitive appraisal of success. Finally, the intuitive appraisal positively influenced positive affects and negatively determined negative affects.

The results suggest that adopting a task goal enhanced the children's positive affect and, more importantly, that intuitive appraisal mediated such effects. These findings accord with propositions of theorists (e.g., Lazarus, 1991a, 1991b; Smith & Lazarus, 1990) that goals and motivation influence emotions through their influence on appraisals. Future research on this issue would appear fruitful.

Social Cognitive Theory of Self-Regulation (Bandura, 1991, 1997)

Another theory with important implications for emotion is Bandura's social cognitive theory, which holds that individuals are generally able to coordinate internal and external influences according to goals and standards they set for themselves (Bandura, 1991). If they regulate themselves efficiently and reach their goals, positive affect will be experienced; if they do not, losses in self-efficacy are reported and negative affect results. Thus, the self-regulatory process leads to either high or low perceptions of self-efficacy. In turn, perceptions of self-efficacy lead to positive or negative affect, depending on whether or not one perceives improvement toward the attainment of his or her goals. Thus, self-efficacy plays a mediating role between self-regulatory processes and emotions (see figure 1.3).

In studies on the social cognitive theory of self-regulation in exercise settings, researchers have typically related perceptions of self-efficacy to affective states. For instance, McAuley and Courneya (1992) examined the relationship between preexisting self-efficacy for exercise with the affect of pleasure/displeasure experienced during exercise by testing 88 sedentary, middle-aged adults (aged 45-64) participating in a submaximal cycle ergometer-graded exercise test. Perceptions of self-efficacy were assessed prior to exercise testing, while in-task affect were assessed at 70% of predicted maximum heart rate. Results revealed that highly efficacious participants reported more positive affect during exercise than did their less efficacious counterparts. On a similar note, Mihalko, McAuley, and Bane (1996) found that changes in self-efficacy predicted changes in positive well-being (mood) on the Subjective Exercise Experience Scale (McAuley & Courneya, 1994). However, no effects on negative affect were found.

Other researchers (e.g., Tate, Petruzello, & Lox, 1995; Treasure & Newbery, 1998) have shown that self-efficacy relates to positive mood most strongly at a level of exercise that is individually optimal. For sedentary persons, for example, exercise at 50% of capacity may represent the optimal challenge leading to the highest level of self-efficacy and the highest level of positive mood. On the other hand, such an effect may be experienced at 70% of maximal capacity for highly active individuals. These findings suggest that optimal levels of challenge during exercise are conducive to a flow state, self-efficacy, and positive mood (see chapter 6 for a discussion of flow).

Finally, McAuley (1991) examined how self-efficacy and causal attributions impacted the emotions of sedentary middle-aged individuals 10 weeks into an exercise program. On the basis of the work of Bandura (1986) and Weiner

(1985a), McAuley hypothesized that exercise efficacy would influence causal attributions and consequently affective responses to participation. Path analysis showed that greater exercise frequency resulted in more internal, somewhat stable, and personally controllable attributions for perceived exercise progress. Subjects higher in self-efficacy also attributed their progress to more personally controllable causes. All three causal dimensions related to positive affect, and efficacy had significant direct and indirect influences on affect. The findings reveal that perceptions of self-efficacy, as well as causal attributions, do influence emotions—thereby supporting the positions of Bandura (1997) and Weiner (1985a), respectively. Furthermore, in line with findings on goal orientations (Vlachopoulos et al., 1996), self-efficacy also appears to influence emotions indirectly through its impact on reflective appraisals such as causal attributions.

To summarize, exercise research supports Bandura's theory: self-efficacy is related to affect. However, further research should test the generalizability of the theory in sport settings. In addition, future research should focus on the determinants of self-efficacy as well as on its consequences for emotion. While it appears that different levels of exercise produce different levels of self-efficacy, and thus different emotions, we need additional research to substantiate these findings.

Future Directions

Overall, research on emotional antecedents underscores several points:

▶ As the intuitive-reflective appraisal model (Vallerand, 1987) proposes, intuitive appraisal of performance seems to be the most important predictor of affect in sport following success and failure outcomes.

▶ Attributions also produce emotions, although it appears that their role is more limited than that of the intuitive appraisal.

▶ Motivational concepts such as intrinsic and extrinsic motivation (Deci & Ryan, 1985), self-efficacy (Bandura, 1991), and task- and ego-involvement (Nicholls, 1984) also represent important antecedents of emotions.

▶ Additionally, motivation plays an indirect role in producing emotion through its impact on both intuitive (perceived outcome) and reflective (attributional) appraisals.

Several research directions would therefore appear fruitful:

▶ As several theorists suggest (e.g., Smith & Lazarus, 1990), sport psychologists must turn toward predicting specific types of emotions. Existing research has focused on testing the roles of different types of antecedents (e.g., the intuitive and reflective appraisals, self-efficacy, goal orientations) without clearly delineating which types of antecedents produce which types of emotions. For example, sport psychologists could attempt to determine which types of appraisals lead to anger, pride, and shame.

▶ We need to look at a more diverse set of appraisals than we have so far. Research has focused on one type of intuitive appraisal (perceived outcome) and one type of reflective appraisal (attributions). We need to broaden our knowledge of other types of interactive and reflective appraisals, such as those proposed by Vallerand (1987), Crocker and Bouffard (1992), and Smith and Lazarus (1990).

▶ We need to expand our knowledge beyond the typical achievement affects (e.g., competence, pride) by investigating other types of emotion. It would be valuable to have more work such as that of McAuley, Mihalko, and Rosengren (1997) on how self-efficacy influences the emotion of fear of falling during a balancing task.

▶ We need more research on the role of temperaments (e.g., Kagan, 1989) in emotion in sport and exercise. Would some temperaments predispose people to be more emotional in sport? Are some people more "cool" under pressure from birth? If so, what are these temperaments? Could and should screening packages as used by some Olympic and professional teams include temperament? Future research on this issue would appear exciting.

▶ Finally, future research should focus on the intriguing findings showing that the mere act of exercising produces changes in affect (see chapter 12 for a review). We need to determine whether the more cognitive/appraisal processes produce such effects or whether, as some suggest (e.g., Izard, 1993; Zajonc, 1998), affective changes can occur during exercise in the absence of appraisals. If this is the case, researchers should attempt to identify the mechanisms responsible for such effects (see Boutcher, 1993, on this issue).

THEORY AND RESEARCH ON THE CONSEQUENCES OF EMOTION IN SPORT AND EXERCISE

According to two prominent positions on the consequences of affect, affective phenomena are either disruptive (e.g., Hebb, 1949) or facilitative with respect to subsequent behavior (e.g., Frijda, 1994). Debilitating effects may result from arousal (see Young, 1973): at very high levels of arousal, certain emotions (e.g., anxiety, fear) may negatively affect behavior. At lower arousal levels, though, affective phenomena may be adaptive. Feelings of competence, for instance, energize subsequent motivation (Vallerand, 1981; Vallerand & Reid, 1988). And even at high levels of arousal, certain emotions may be facilitative for some individuals. As Hanin suggests (chapters 3 and 7), some people may perform best at high levels of anxiety and others at considerably lower levels (see Kerr, 1997, for an alternative explanation). Furthermore, high levels of emotional experience may facilitate some types of sport and exercise activities. As the Yerkes-Dodson law (Yerkes & Dodson, 1908) would suggest, high arousal levels facilitate performance on tasks demanding high physical effort such as weightlifting and the shot put (Oxendine, 1970).

On this basis we suggest that affective processes typically play an adaptive role in sport and exercise settings. This position is consistent with recent theories on the adaptive functions of emotions (e.g., Fisher & Tangney, 1995; Frijda, 1986, 1994; Izard, 1993; Oatley & Jenkins, 1992, 1996; Plutchik, 1980, 1993). According to Izard (1993), emotions have at least five such functions:

1. Emotions constitute the primary motivational system.

2. Each emotion serves distinct functions in the way it organizes perception, cognition, and behavior.

3. Emotions serve to develop personality.

4. Individual differences in emotion activation are major determinants of broad dimensions of personality.

5. Specific emotion-behavior links develop over time.

Thus, as Frijda (1986) states, "Emotions serve something, and presumably they serve it well" (p. 475).

Smith and Lazarus (1990), in accord with Izard (1993), propose that each emotion serves a specific purpose or adaptive function. Thus, anger is an attempt to remove a source of harm from the environment, anxiety an attempt to avoid potential harm, and guilt an attempt either to make reparation for harm to others or to motivate socially responsible behavior. Such functions can be either intrapersonal (e.g., avoiding potential harm to oneself) or interpersonal (e.g., motivating socially responsible behavior). This framework is useful for examining the functions of affect in sport (Vallerand, 1983). Therefore in this section we will consider research, still in its infancy, on intra- and interpersonal consequences of emotion in sport and exercise. Although new theories (in both psychology and sport psychology) are emerging, this work has typically been atheoretical. While this review is merely illustrative, it may serve as a useful blueprint for future research.

Intrapersonal Consequences

Intrapersonal consequences are the effects of an emotion on the person who has experienced it. Here we limit discussion to intrapersonal cognitive, motivational, health, and performance consequences.

Cognitive Consequences

Emotion can influence cognitions (see Forgas, 1992, 1995, for reviews), including perception. For instance, individuals tend to perceive stimuli in line with their emotion (e.g., Niedenthal & Setterlund, 1994). Thus, an overly anxious basketball player may be more attuned to information in keeping with her anxiety (e.g., "The crowd is ready to jump on us for not playing well") than to other types of information (e.g., the play that the coach has just outlined). Since focusing on cues consistent with one's emotion may exacerbate that emotion, this athlete may become even more anxious as a function of focusing on the crowd.

Another cognitive effect relates to the quantity of information a person can attend to. One effect of emotions involving high levels of arousal, such as anxiety, is that they reduce the field of attention (see Abernethy, 1993). Depending on the task, if the field of attention becomes too narrow, the athlete will not attend to important cues (Easterbrook, 1959). This may have negative consequences for decision making, as Bird and Horn (1990) showed in a study of high school softball players. Participants completed the Competitive State Anxiety Inventory (CSAI-2; Martens, Vealey, & Burton, 1990) before a game; after the game, coaches assessed the mental errors the athletes had made. Athletes were divided into two groups according to their level of mental errors. Athletes in the high mental error group scored significantly higher in cognitive state anxiety than the other group. Smith, Smoll, and Schultz (1990) also found that cognitive anxiety positively related to concentration disruption. These findings accord with those of Isen (1993), from the more general psychological literature, showing that positive mood facilitates decision making.

Emotions can also influence personal judgments. When making evaluative judgments about themselves, individuals use their affect as information (e.g., Schwarz, Strack, Kommer, & Wagner, 1987). This suggests that when basketball players report their level of life satisfaction after a win, they will use their positive affect to infer that things are going well and will report higher levels of life satisfaction than athletes who have just lost (for reviews see Clore, Schwarz, & Conway, 1994; Schwarz & Strack, 1991). Forgas (1995) has proposed the affect infusion model to explain the effects of affect on judgments. According to the model, four main cognitive processing strategies can be used when making evaluative judgments. These are

▶ the direct access strategy (i.e., retrieval of already existing evaluations),

▶ the motivated reasoning strategy (i.e., a partial and somewhat biased search of information),

▶ the heuristic strategy (i.e., judgments made with little effort), and

▶ the substantive strategy (e.g., a full-fledged search for information in the hope of attaining an accurate judgment).

Because the first two strategies involve relatively closed information search processes, they are posited to be rather insensitive to the influence of affect. The second two strategies allow for the influence of affect on judgment (Forgas, 1995).

Much research supports Forgas's model (for reviews see Forgas, 1992, 1995), including studies on how affect impacts sport fans' judgments. For example, Schwarz et al. (1987) examined the impact of affect on judgments of life satisfaction of male respondents before and after the live broadcast of two 1982 Soccer World Cup games. After their team had won, fans made more positive judgments of their life satisfaction than fans whose team had lost. Presumably, the win generated positive affect that in turn colored judgments of life satisfaction, although the authors did not measure affect and therefore could not ascertain its precise role. Subsequent research using path analysis has shown that affect does mediate how the win/loss event impacts fans' judgments (Hirt, Zillman, Erickson, & Kennedy, 1992). This research (Hirt et al., 1992) also showed that we should distinguish between two types of affect: general mood (e.g., feeling good) and self-related affect (e.g., pride, competence) as predictors of fans' judgments (Hirt et al., 1992). In addition, research by Wann, Dolan, McGeorge, and Allison (1994) has shown that fans with high levels of team identification experience higher levels of affect than those with low levels.

On the basis of these results, Perreault, Vallerand, Guay, Chantal, and Richer (1998) have proposed and tested a model specifying the antecedents as well as the consequences of both positive mood and self-related affects. In this model, people's mood depends mainly on their level of team identification and on their intrinsic motivation (as seen earlier), while self-related affect depends only on team identification. In turn, mood and self-related affect impact fans' judgments of life satisfaction. In a test of the model in Montreal during the 1993 Stanley Cup parade after the Montreal Canadiens' win, 217 male and female attendees at the parade completed scales assessing team identification, intrinsic motivation, positive mood, self-related affect, and life satisfaction. Structural equation modeling showed support for the proposed model. Thus both positive mood and self-related affects can influence fans' judgments of life satisfaction.

The research reviewed reveals that emotion does matter with respect to our judgments and cognitions, influencing decision-making processes as well as personal judgments. While much research on judgments has dealt with fans, further studies should focus on this issue in athletes, referees, and coaches.

Motivational Consequences

Several authors have proposed that emotions play a major role in motivation (e.g., Arnold, 1960; Deci, 1980; Frijda, 1986; Weiner, 1977). Arnold and Gasson (1954) and Frijda (1986) propose that action tendencies are inherent in emotions. These tendencies lead individuals toward an object (e.g., in the case of anger) or away from an object (e.g., in the case of fear). Izard (1993) goes so far as proposing that emotions represent the major motivational system dictating that the individual attend to immediate concerns and needs (see also Demos, 1995; Tomkins, 1970). Weiner (1977) proposed that emotions are major determinants of motives and that distinct emotions are linked to specific motives: anger leads to an aggressive motive, pity to the helping motive, and so on. But very few researchers have pursued Weiner's suggestion. An exception is the work of Vallerand and colleagues on self-related affects. In line with the work of Deci (1980) and Deci and Ryan (1985, 1991), these studies have shown that self-related affects of competence have important positive effects on intrinsic motivation (e.g., Vallerand, 1981; Vallerand & Reid, 1988).

Many research avenues in this area remain. Pursuing Weiner's (1977) suggestion and mapping the links between distinct emotions and specific motivations could spur both theoretical and applied advances. For instance, determining which affects lead to which motives could enable us to better predict behavior in sport, although to do this we should consider not only emotions and motives but also situational factors and display rules (see Buck, 1985). Such social forces may interact with the initial action tenderly in shaping subsequent motivational behavior. Being able to predict behavior in sport could help us design better programs focusing on the welfare of participants such that aggression and violent acts would be things of the past.

Health Consequences

Health represents another important type of emotional consequence, and health psychology is an important research domain (for reviews see Adler & Matthews, 1994; Biddle & Fox, 1989; Cohen & Herbert, 1996; Taylor, Repetti, & Seeman, 1997). The relationship between emotions and disease has long captured the attention of researchers in health psychology, who have developed at least three traditions (Oatley & Jenkins, 1996) centering on the following principles:

▶ **Inner conflict leads to illness.** Based on psychoanalytic perspectives (see Alexander, 1950), this tradition holds that unresolved emotional conflict can produce physical problems. For example, the athlete who is experiencing (unconscious) conflict between quitting sport, which will disappoint his father, and continuing and experiencing repeated failures may experience chronic stress and eventually develop health problems such as chronic fatigue (see chapter 10).

▶ **Individuals who express their emotions are less inclined to develop illnesses** (see Pennebaker, 1995). For example, Pennebaker showed that people who wrote about traumatic experiences for three to five days, for as little as 10 min per day, experienced health benefits such as fewer visits to physicians (Pennebaker & Beall, 1986) in comparison to individuals who wrote about other topics. This research suggests that athletes who share the experience of a bad game with others, or express their feelings through writing (e.g., a diary), may preserve their physical health (see Pennebaker, 1995, for a review).

▶ **The immune system mediates between life stresses and illness.** Within this highly active tradition, Tessier and colleagues (Fillion, Tessier, Tawadros, & Mouton, 1989; Lemyre & Tessier, 1988; Tessier, Fillion, Muckle, & Gendron, 1990) have shown that life stresses (e.g., Holmes & Rahe, 1967) lead to the experience of being stressed out. In turn, being stressed out leads to immunological deficiencies and health problems. It follows that over a long season, professional and collegiate athletes may experience stress and anxiety, and eventually physical symptoms and perhaps injuries, because of lowered immunological functions.

Although sport research has not yet addressed the immune system as a mediator of the impact of negative affect (i.e., stress) on health, it has assessed the link between affect and health, including two issues to which we now turn: athletic injury and burnout. In the injury model of Andersen and Williams (1988), personality (e.g., trait anxiety), history of stressors (stressful life events), and coping resources (e.g., stress management) influence an athlete's appraisal of a situation as stressful and lead to negative physiological and attentional consequences. These consequences in turn increase the risk of athletic injury. Research supports some aspects of the model; for instance, studies have found links between life stressors and athletic injuries (e.g., Bramwell, Masuda, Wagner, & Holmes, 1975; Cryan & Alles, 1983; Hardy & Riehl, 1988). Unfortunately, these studies have not measured affect per se. However, research by Hanson, McCullagh, and Tonymon (1992) showed that sport competitive anxiety adequately predicted the severity of injuries of National Collegiate Athletic Association Division I and II athletes. In addition, in line with some of the health research presented earlier, the stress-injury relation seems to be especially strong for athletes whose poor coping skills *and* low social support prevent them from dealing effectively with the experience of stress (Smith, Smoll, & Ptacek, 1990).

Finally, emotion can not only determine athletic injury but can also influence recovery (see Pargman, 1993). In Heil's model (chapter 11), emotions such as fear and culpability (or guilt) affect the athlete's response to the injury. The model also offers insights into the psychological management of an injured athlete. Although there is little research on this model at this point, it appears promising.

Burnout affects a significant percentage of athletes (as high as 47%; Silva, 1990) and coaches (as high as 63%; Vealey, Udry, Zimmerman, & Soliday, 1992). According to one accepted definition (see chapter 10), burnout is a multidimensional syndrome characterized by feelings of emotional exhaustion and depersonalization and a reduced sense of personal accomplishment (Maslach & Jackson, 1986). Apparently the syndrome is not a reaction to short-term stress but rather long-term or chronic stress (Dale & Weinberg, 1990).

Smith (1986) has proposed a model of burnout, not unlike his anxiety model, emphasizing that appraisal processes of the situation determine perceived stress. Cognitive appraisals are themselves influenced by personality (e.g., trait anxiety) and motivational factors (high need for achievement) and lead to cognitive (ruminations), physiological (e.g., arousal), affective (anxiety, anger), and behavioral (e.g., staleness, withdrawal) consequences that together make up the burnout syndrome. Although researchers have not tested Smith's model in its entirety, it has served as a blueprint for fragmented research. Such research reveals that emotions, and especially stress, seem to play causal roles in predicting burnout (Kelley & Gill, 1993; Taylor, Daniel, Leith, & Burke, 1990; Vealey et al., 1992).

Other researchers, addressing athletes' training regimens and associated mental states, have sought to demonstrate that overtraining creates a negative affective state that may eventually lead to athletic burnout (e.g., Morgan, Brown, Raglin, O'Connor, & Ellickson, 1987). For instance, as Kallus and Kellmann (chapter 9) report, a study with German rowers showed that increases in heavy training led to mood disturbance whereas reduced training led to mood improvement. Although case studies reported by Kallus and Kellmann suggest that overtraining may eventually lead to burnout, there is at present no clear empirical evidence for this hypothesis.

Murphy, Fleck, Dudley, and Callister (1990) showed that over time during a training program, elite judo athletes became more angry and fatigued and by the end of the regimen experienced objective decreases in anaerobic endurance and strength. These findings underscore the double bind elite athletes may face. As participation at high training levels produces negative affect as well as reduced physiological benefits, the result may be to intensify an athlete's determination to continue. The athlete then continues to experience negative affect and diminished physical returns. Eventually the negative effects may lead to amotivation (Deci & Ryan, 1985; Vallerand, in press) and burnout.

To summarize, while the research area of emotions and health in sport participants is relatively recent, valuable findings include those on the role of emotions in the etiology of athletic injuries and burnout of athletes, coaches, and officials. Future research in this area would appear promising.

Sport Performance

Performance—one of the most interesting emotional consequences in sport—is not easy to predict, because it partly depends on the competition and is thus beyond one's complete control. But prediction of performance is important both theoretically and practically. From a theoretical standpoint, research should allow us to identify the emotional processes responsible for optimal performance and thus improve our knowledge of the consequences of emotional processes. From a practical standpoint, a better understanding of the determinants of performance will allow sport psychologists to help athletes in their quest for self-improvement.

Much research in this area has dealt with how state anxiety relates to performance (for reviews see Smith, Smoll, & Wiechman, 1998; Hackfort & Schwenkmezger, 1993); typically the aim has been to test for an inverted-U relationship between the two constructs. As we saw earlier, this position, based on the Yerkes-Dodson law (Yerkes & Dodson, 1908), suggests that (1) an optimal level of arousal exists for any task and (2) lower levels of arousal are more conducive to optimal performance on complex than on easy tasks. Thus, an optimal level of arousal exists for baseball hitting—any arousal below or beyond this optimal level should lead to subpar performance; and the optimal level of arousal for baseball hitting would be lower than for a tackling task in football. While initial sport studies presented support for the inverted-U relationship between performance and state anxiety (e.g., Klavora, 1978; Martens & Landers, 1970), others did not (e.g., Caruso, Gill, Dzewaltowski, & McElroy, 1990; Gould, Pelitchkoff, & Weinberg, 1984; McAuley, 1985).

In addressing this topic, researchers recently have taken individual differences into account (e.g., Burton, 1988; Sonstroem & Bernardo, 1982). For instance, Sonstroem and Bernardo (1982) showed that athletes performed better at their own moderate level of state anxiety. Hanin (chapters 3, 4, and 7) has pursued the intraindividual analysis further in proposing *individual* zones of optimal functioning (the IZOF model). The IZOF model emphasizes that each athlete has individualized levels of optimal intensity, but it does not predict the shape of the relationships along the entire range of intensity (see chapter 7). The zone ranges derived from the individualized levels ± SD and based on the interquartile range (which includes the range of scores from the 25th percentile to the 75th percentile) attempt to account for the measurement error and interactive effects of different emotions (see appendixes). Through this idiographic approach, Hanin has each athlete determine which types of positive and negative affect he or she experiences when performing dysfunctionally and optimally. He then uses this pattern to predict each athlete's future performance (see chapters 3 and 7 for fuller discussion).

Recent research has provided support for the IZOF model with state anxiety as a precompetitive measure (for reviews see Gould & Tuffey, 1996; Hanin, 1995, 1997a; Raglin, 1992). Specifically, athletes who were close to or within their optimal zones of anxiety performed better than those outside their zones (e.g., Gould, Tuffey, Hardy, & Lochbaum, 1993; Krane, 1993; Turner & Raglin, 1996). Significantly, some researchers have compared the IZOF model to other theoretical positions and obtained support for the IZOF model (e.g., Gould et al., 1993; Raglin & Turner, 1993; Turner & Raglin, 1996). The IZOF model offers an interesting method for predicting sport performance from state anxiety.

It should be noted that the IZOF model takes into account not only anxiety but a host of other emotions that the athletes themselves report. Hanin and colleagues have shown, with athletes of different sports and ages, that both positive and negative affect (not only anxiety) can predict positive performance (see Hanin, 1997a, for a review).

While the IZOF model is fundamentally an idiographic system couched in an intraindividual perspective, it also lends itself to a nomothetic approach that can uncover general principles relevant to most athletes. Because they have determined across athletes and sports which emotions are optimal and which are disruptive for performance, Hanin and colleagues can evaluate the overall effectiveness of various emotions. Hanin (1997a) has recently reported several noteworthy findings. The top nine functionally optimal affects appear to be energetic, charged, motivated, certain, confident, purposeful, willing, resolute, and alert; the top nine dysfunctional positive affects are easygoing, excited, composed, relaxed, overjoyed, fearless, satisfied, exalted, and pleasant. The top nine functionally optimal negative affects are tense, charged, dissatisfied, attacking, vehement, intense, nervous, irritated, and provoked; and the top nine dysfunctional negative affects are tired, unwilling, uncertain, sluggish, depressed, lazy, distressed, sorrowful, and afraid. This list of affects should help sport psychologists focus their efforts to predict sport performance.

Future Directions

Research reveals that emotion leads to important intrapersonal consequences in sport and exercise settings, notably on cognitions, motivation, health, and performance. Typically, positive affect produces positive effects, while negative affect yields negative consequences, although the work of Hanin suggests that both types of affect may have positive and negative effects on performance. We believe that a number of future research directions can be pursued in this area.

First, the impact of affect on the decision-making processes of both athletes and coaches appears to be a fruitful area to investigate. Based on the work of Isen (1993) and Forgas (1995), it would be predicted that positive affect leads to better decision making and personal judgments than negative affect. Second, we need to know more about the role of emotions in motivation. The suggestion of Weiner (1977) to identify specific emotion-motivation linkages deserves consideration. In addition, the role of negative affect merits further attention. While research typically reveals that negative affect leads to negative effects on motivation, common sense suggests that this may not always be the case. For example, it would be expected that athletes unsatisfied with their performance may at times be even more motivated in order to reach their objectives. Thus, negative affect may at times positively influence motivation. It is important to determine the situations and processes likely to trigger such effects. Third, we have seen in the previous section that cognitions (and appraisals) and motivation represent important determinants of emotion, and we have seen in this section that they are also affected by emotions. Thus, a reciprocal relationship seems to exist between these constructs. Future research should attempt to verify the existence of such a reciprocal relationship. Fourth, in light of the prevalence of health problems among athletes, more research is needed in this area. Of particular interest is the potential mediational role the immune system can play in the affect-health relationship.

Lastly, the nature of the emotional processes responsible for sport performance needs attention. Most theories use either the Yerkes-Dodson (1908) law on arousal or Easterbrook's (1959) position on attention to explain the impact of emotions on performance. Yet little research has demonstrated how these processes mediate the emotion-performance relationship. More parsimonious explanations are also possible. For instance, Crews (1992) has reported that negative mood (especially tension) leads to higher levels of oxygen consumption than positive mood; possibly such affective states cause athletes to use more oxygen, to fatigue more easily, and eventually to perform less well than athletes with more positive affective states. This hypothesis merits further attention. Finally, we need to consider the role of emotions other than anxiety in athletic performance; the preliminary work of Hanin may prove influential in this regard.

Interpersonal Consequences

It has long been recognized that emotion produces important interpersonal consequences (e.g., Darwin, 1872/1965), and a number of researchers (e.g., Frijda & Mesquita, 1994; Parkinson, 1997; Weiner, Amirkhan, Folkes, & Verette, 1987) have underscored the fundamental social role of emotions. As Frijda and Mesquita (1994), for example, suggest:

> In our analysis, emotions are not only intraindividual states but also forms of subject-environment interaction. This interaction may remain latent when the emotion is only a state of readiness; but even then, it is readiness for engaging in or breaking off interaction. By this very nature of readiness for and actual form of interaction, emotions exert influence on social interaction. In addition, many emotions are social events because they tend to occur in a context of socially shared meanings. They are recognized by others, they shed light upon the emotional relevance of the environment, they affect interpersonal relationships, and they in turn evoke responses from others that also affect the relationship from their side. (p. 73)

On this view, emotions play a crucial role in much social functioning. Although Vallerand (1983, 1984) underscored the importance of research on interpersonal consequences of emotion in sport settings, very little has appeared since 1983 (see Hackfort, 1996, for a notable exception). As Vallerand (1983) suggested, work on at least three issues of interpersonal consequences might have value:

1. An emotional display of one individual has consequences on the behavior of others, including emotional behavior. For instance, simply seeing a teammate smile may cause other players to smile and feel happier. This emotional contagion, "the tendency to 'catch' (experience/express) another person's emotion" (Hatfield, Cacioppo, & Rapson, 1992, p. 153; 1994), is common in sport. Although it appears that researchers have not investigated the topic in this setting, it should be of interest, since participants in sport freely express emotions and often share them (see Snyder, 1990). Possibly cohesive teams share emotions more fully and manifest emotional contagion more readily—or possibly the trigger comes not from athletes but from the fans. For instance, Greer (1983) has demonstrated that sustained displays of anger such as booing in basketball games increased rule violations called against the visiting team. Angry behavior from fans possibly produces fear or at least apprehension in referees, who may then feel the need to repair previous mistakes (the well-known "make-up call"). Of interest is that the trigger for the

referee's apprehension may come from interpersonal anger displayed by the fans. This represents an interesting research avenue.

2. A second process whereby one person's emotion may influence another's is the appraisal of the emotional message (Weiner et al., 1987). For instance, a coach might display anger at a player for poorly executing a play. The athlete's attributional search regarding the display might lead him or her to conclude that the poor play resulted from lack of effort. The athlete would then experience shame and consequently work harder to get the play right next time. On the other hand, had the coach displayed sympathy, the message would have been that the player failed because of lack of skills. The athlete would then experience feelings of incompetence and poor motivation. Much research in social psychology now supports this analysis (see Graham, 1984; Weiner, 1995; Weiner et al., 1987). It should be stated that emotion need not be displayed specifically toward a person in order to affect that person's emotion and behavior. Hackfort (1996) has demonstrated that merely watching videos highlighting emotional quality in various sports enhances athletes' levels of arousal and aspiration, as well as their motor performance on an endurance task. This too represents an interesting direction for future work.

3. Thus others' emotions can influence our own emotions and behavior. But as Vallerand (1983, 1984) observed, a third phenomenon warranting scrutiny is the interpersonal behavior that follows the experience of an interpersonal emotion. For example, how will a referee behave toward a coach who just yelled at him and made him angry? As social psychological research suggests, the referee is unlikely to favor the coach on future ambiguous calls. Weiner and colleagues (e.g., Schmidt & Weiner, 1988; Weiner, 1980) reported that when people feel anger toward someone they are less likely to help the person than if they experience sympathy. Other studies have yielded similar results (e.g., Betancourt, 1990; Meyer & Mulherin, 1980; Reisenzein, 1986). To our knowledge, no sport research has addressed this type of effect.

In sum, emotion can produce important interpersonal consequences. It is hoped that the present discussion will help kindle research in this important area.

SUMMARY

The major goal of this chapter was to evaluate the progress of theory and research in the field of emotion in sport and exercise over the past 15 years. The chapter included

- ▶ definitional issues,
- ▶ a framework integrating the antecedents and consequences of emotion, and
- ▶ a review of theory and research in sport and exercise according to the antecedents → emotions → consequences sequence.

Discussion of antecedents focused on theories that deal with the production of emotion; cognitive/appraisal theories (e.g., Arnold, 1960; Schachter, 1964; Smith, 1996; Vallerand, 1987; Weiner, 1985a) and motivational formulations (e.g., Bandura, 1997; Deci & Ryan, 1985; Nicholls, 1984) predominate in the field, and account for how people experience emotion in sport and exercise settings. The review also showed that emotions have profound influences on a number of processes, including cognition, motivation, health, performance, and interpersonal functioning. Throughout, the chapter included suggestions for future research. Here we emphasize that research needs to explore emotions other than anxiety and achievement affects in order to broaden our knowledge of both the antecedents and the consequences of emotion.

In sum, emotion in sport and exercise represents a vibrant and exciting research area. Although the past 15 years have witnessed substantial research, much remains unknown about the intricate psychological processes that produce emotion as well as its consequences. The authors hope that this chapter will help researchers progress on their journey of discovery and understanding of this pervasive and crucial phenomenon.

CHAPTER 2

Cognitive-Motivational-Relational Theory of Emotion

Richard S. Lazarus
United States

The first aim of this chapter is to examine what a theory of emotion must do and the basic issues it must address. These include how to define emotion; whether to include physiological activity as a defining attribute; whether to dimensionalize or categorize emotions; how cognition, motivation, and emotion interrelate functionally; how to reconcile biological universals with sociocultural sources of variability; and how to classify the emotions. The second major aim is to analyze several emotions in terms of appraisal patterns and their core relational themes, in order to show how a cognitive-motivational-relational theory can explain and predict the emotions. The role of coping in emotion is also discussed, and the chapter ends with a response to criticisms of a phenomenological, folk theory outlook.

After having been relegated to the doghouse for decades, written off as unscientific, and sometimes treated as a unidimensional intervening variable (Brown & Farber, 1951; Duffy, 1941, 1962; Malmo, 1959), emotion in both the social and biological sciences has had a sudden and dramatic change of fortune. From 1920 to 1960, only an occasional monograph appeared; but the 1960s saw renewed interest, especially in psychological stress (Janis, 1958; Lazarus, 1966; Mechanic, 1962) and its psychophysiology (Selye, 1956/1976), an important segment of the larger rubric of emotion. There are many new publications on emotion, including one of my own (Lazarus, 1991b; see also Smith & Lazarus, 1990).

Richard S. Lazarus, 1991, "Progress on a cognitive-motivational-relational theory of emotion," *American Psychologist, 46* (8), 819-834. Copyright © 1991 by American Psychological Association. Reprinted with permission.

As I interpret this revival, the cognitive movement in social science (Dember, 1974), as well as the more open epistemology following loss of influence of radical behaviorism, helped to open the floodgates. It became possible, indeed commonplace, to consider the cognitive mediators of psychological stress and emotion and even to take seriously the use of folk theory language.

There is also renewed interest in motivation, a long neglected topic. The motivational concepts used today (e.g., values, goals, commitments, intentions, and plans) are fused with cognitive activity, unlike earlier concepts such as instincts, drives, and needs, which implied purely innate biological forces. I believe that this renewal occurred because individual differences in stress and emotion could not be adequately understood without reference to what is personally important. We become emotional only about values and goals to which we are committed.

I begin by briefly exploring the main tasks of a theory of emotion and proceed to some of the issues a theory must resolve. I will then discuss the core relational themes and appraisal patterns for several emotions, the coping process in emotion, and finally criticisms of phenomenology and folk theory.

MAIN TASKS OF A THEORY OF EMOTION

To provide a reasonably complete and researchable analysis, a theory of emotion must include two main ingredients. First, it must offer general propositions about the emotion process, including setting forth the key variables and the ways they operate. An emotion theory should be a systems theory, encompassing a number of interdependent cause-and-effect variables and processes that follow the principle of reciprocal determinism (Bandura, 1978, 1983), in which an antecedent can be an outcome and vice versa. In recent years, however, I have become disenchanted with the practical use of systems analysis in research, and have come to favor narrative theories and methods as a better option (see Lazarus, 1999).

Secondly, an emotion theory must offer propositions about each emotion (e.g., anger, anxiety, sadness, pride), stating how the emotion is elicited and how it influences subsequent actions and reactions. These propositions should be consistent with the general propositions but also should offer, in a sense, separate subtheories specifying how the process differs for each emotion.

The theory is relational, motivational, and cognitive. *Relational* means that emotions are always about person-environment relationships involving harms or benefits. Psychological stress and emotion are not generated by factors in the environment *or* by intrapsychic processes, but by person-environment relationships that change over time and circumstances (Lazarus, 1966; Lazarus & Folkman, 1984, 1987).

A central premise is that each emotion involves a distinctive core relational theme, which is a molar way of describing the essence of that emotion's person-environment relationship. These themes are universals in human experience, are inherently capable of eliciting the appropriate emotions, are the same across eras, and reflect a kind of wisdom of the ages. Although authors often do not explicitly state that emotions have particular person-environment relationships, and although there are disagreements, there is also remarkable historical and contemporary consensus about the relational themes for many emotions.

Motivational means that acute emotions and moods are reactions to the status of goals in everyday adaptational encounters and in our lives overall. The concept of motivation helps us understand what makes an adaptational encounter personally relevant and a source of harm or benefit, hence emotional.

Motivation here has two interrelated senses. First, it is a characteristic of a person—a dispositional variable that one brings to every encounter, in the form of goal hierarchies. Second, the disposition to attain a goal must be activated in any encounter by the demands, constraints, and resources the environment presents. In other words, motivation is transactional as well as dispositional in that it depends on the juxtaposition of a motive trait and a suitable environment. These ideas have been around a long time.

Cognitive refers to knowledge and appraisal of what is happening in adaptational encounters (see Lazarus & Smith, 1988). Knowledge consists of situational and generalized beliefs about how things work; impersonal knowledge is apt to be cold rather than hot or emotional. Appraisal consists of an evaluation of the personal significance of an encounter with the environment.

Although core relational themes summarize the key, emotion-producing feature of the person-environment relationship, they do not adequately describe an emotion's cognitive determinants. In a further analytic step, one specifies the personal meanings, expressed as appraisal components whose pattern is causal for each emotion. In adults, these appraisal components are heavily influenced by sociocultural variables and individual development. To say how a specific emotion is generated, one needs to know the appraisal pattern for each emotion family. I will say more about this later.

DIFFICULT ISSUES FOR EMOTION THEORY

Five issues seem to have overriding importance: (a) What are the emotions? (b) Should physiological changes be a defining attribute? (c) Should emotion meanings be dimensionalized into a few basic factors or treated as discrete categories? (d) What are the functional relations among cognition, motivation, and emotion? (e) How can emotion theory reconcile biological universals with sociocultural, developmental sources of variability?

Definitional Problems: What Are the Emotions?

There has never been consensus about the list of emotions, in part because the typical response definitions of emotion (e.g., Drever, 1952) emphasize action or action tendencies, physiological changes, and subjective cognitive-affective states without the guidance of theory to portray the emotion process and the boundaries of emotion and nonemotion. This has led Shaver, Schwartz, Kirson, and O'Connor (1987) among others to suggest that emotions are fuzzy sets, with some being more or less prototypical, and that any effort to define emotions in terms of necessary and sufficient conditions will fail.

Ortony, Clore, and colleagues (Clore, Ortony, & Foss, 1987; Ortony & Clore, 1981; Ortony, Clore, & Collins, 1988; Ortony, Clore, & Foss, 1987; see also Johnson-Laird & Oatley, 1989; Ortony & Clore, 1989) have suggested several lexical tests of what is and is not an emotion. They have distinguished, for example, between entities that are merely emotional (e.g., distress, excitement, and arousal) and true emotions (e.g., anger). They also make the standard distinction between traits (dispositions) and states (emotions). Nevertheless, many questions about the definition remain, and resolutions require theory as well as evidence. For example, is startle an emotion? Is pain or pleasure? Is empathy? Is an aesthetic emotion?

Smith and Lazarus (1990) recently elaborated on an idea, proposed earlier by Tomkins (1962, 1963), that while sensory-motor reflexes, physiological drives, and emotions are fundamental adaptational resources for all animals, advanced species have evolved toward less dependence, adaptationally speaking, on innate reflexes and drives and greater dependence on emotions. I think that startle, pain, and pleasure are best thought of as reflexes rather than emotions (Lazarus, Averill, & Opton, 1970). These reactions are automatic and fairly rigid consequences of our physiological makeup; and specific, concrete stimuli are capable of eliciting each. In contrast, no single stimulus is capable of eliciting any emotion regularly in all intact persons (cf. Ekman, 1984).

Ekman, Friesen, and Simons (1985) studied the startle reaction under four conditions: a gunshot with no warning, a gunshot with a warning, instructions to inhibit the startle reaction, and instructions to simulate being startled in the absence of a gunshot. The timing of the expression of startle under the cognitive manipulations differed little, but the magnitude differed. Startle could not be totally inhibited. When it was simulated—although there were differences in morphology, timing, and magnitude compared with the real thing—it was correctly distinguished by observers only 60% of the time, statistically a little better than chance.

Startle, therefore, seems to be automatic and stereotypical—a reflex rather than an emotion. One might regard it as a pre-emotion, analogous to surprise (cf. Meyer, 1988; Meyer, Niepel, Rudolph, & Schützwohl, in press), curiosity, and the orienting reflex (cf. Kreitler & Kreitler, 1976). All these prepare us to evaluate the meaning of an environmental condition for our well-being. Startle is not fear, but it can lead to fear if one interprets the encounter as danger; nor is it anger, but it can lead to anger if one regards the stimulus as offensive and unjustified.

Pain and pleasure likewise result from concrete, specific physical stimuli whose capacity to produce these sensory reactions is determined physiologically. A complication, however, is that pain tolerance and possibly pain thresholds can be influenced by appraisal and the resultant anxiety about pain (cf. Beecher, 1956-1957), thereby dampening or enhancing both pain and pleasure. Although they are reflexes rather than emotions, pleasure and pain figure prominently in the development of the motivational structure on which appraisal and emotion depend. The young child learns to avoid pain and to seek pleasure. This idea has been central to emotion theory for centuries.

Emotions and reflexes constitute very different kinds of adaptational processes. As intelligent species evolved and their adaption came to depend on their ability to learn from experience, emotions allowed much greater variability and flexibility than either reflexes or physiological drives. Moreover, because human emotions are often predicated on complex social structures and meanings that define what is harmful or beneficial, they require judgment, the ability to learn from experience, and the ability to distinguish subtle differences signifying different consequences for well-being. Appraisal is thus a key factor in the evolution of adaptational processes, including emotion.

Pain and pleasure become emotional distress or satisfaction only as a result of appraisals of their significance. For example, in a close race, runners experiencing painful fatigue on the way to the finish line will probably react with distress because the pain means they are running out of steam. But during training, the same painful fatigue is likely to elicit satisfaction, because now the pain signifies improving strength, and not much is at stake. Similarly, sexual stimulation may lead to satisfaction or to distress, anger, or fear, depending on one's interpretation of its significance.

Empathy and aesthetic reactions, in contrast, are clearly emotional rather than reflexive. However, if we define empathy as sharing another's feelings (Hoffman, 1985), then it cannot be a single emotion because its response characteristics depend on the other person's emotion. The shared emotion could be joy, grief, anguish, envy, jealousy, guilt, shame, sadness, depression, and so on. It is therefore better to regard empathy as a capacity and a process rather than an emotional state. I prefer to consider compassion an emotion that can be specified in advance rather than a hodgepodge of shared reactions. It is experienced when one comprehends and reacts to someone else in trouble by wanting to ameliorate the suffering.

A similar problem applies to aesthetic emotions, which arise in response to a work of art, a religious experience, or a sudden illumination about nature. The emotion could be awe, fear, sadness, guilt, pride, joy, or whatever—again depending on the meaning. A painting of a man on a raft on a violent, windswept ocean might elicit anxiety, sadness, or awe. The statue of agonized Laocoön and his sons being strangled by serpents—presumably sent by a vengeful, punitive god—will elicit despair in some people and anger in others.

The rules relating to aesthetic emotions remain to be formulated. Why do we experience various reactions to music and painting? To what extent are our responses to universal forms and musical tones or rhythms innate as compared to learned, and how do innate and learned influences interact? Why do we react emotionally to a drama even though we are seated securely in a theater? For these profound and complicated questions our answers are inadequate and fragmentary.

It seems remarkable that psychologists have shown so little interest in the human capacity to experience emotions vicariously in drama and film (see also interchange in *American Psychologist* between Walters [1989] and Frijda [1989]). I think we react not because we suspend the reality of being in a theater, but because the story is believable and personally real, expressing active emotional struggles in our lives. I believe that although the so-called aesthetic emotions are real emotions, they do not constitute a single emotion family but, like empathy, include diverse emotions.

After I have eliminated some emotion-related terms for linguistic or other conceptual reasons (e.g., because they refer to traits rather than states), the basic, theoretically derived tests I use to distinguish a true emotion family should come as no surprise. These tests concern whether there is a clear, personally significant, relational content; an appraisal of personal harm, threat, challenge, or benefit; the potential for action readiness; and physiological changes.

Should Physiological Change Be a Defining Attribute?

This question implies two others: *whether* physiological activity should be a criterion of emotion, and *why* an affirmative answer has theoretical value. As to the first, the adaptational function of anger and fear and other so-called negative emotions implies mobilization to modify a harmful or threatening person-environment relationship. Cannon's (1932/1939) fight-flight reaction and Selye's (1956/1976) general adaptation syndrome draw on this idea. But although mobilization makes sense for anger and fear, it poses a problem for sadness, which seems to involve inaction, as well as for the so-called positive emotions, which arise in a person-environment relationship that does not require mobilization to act.

We can solve the problem for negative emotions such as sadness by speaking of physiological change rather than arousal; this also allows us to include relief in the list of emotions. One might say that relief involves the subsidence of activation in the form, say, of lowered sympathetic and raised parasympathetic discharge (Kemper, 1987; see also Davidson, Ekman, Saron, Senulis, & Friesen, 1990, for evidence of central nervous system differences in positive emotions).

However, for positive emotions such as contentment, pride, and happiness, the function underlying the physiological change is difficult to specify. We can propose that these emotions sustain or even enhance a benign or beneficial relationship with the environment (Lazarus, Kanner, & Folkman, 1980) or signal the possibility of a change to a negative one. Positive emotions and the conditions that produce them are evanescent, rapidly giving way to new commitments predicated on previous goal attainment. For example, after working for years toward a degree, one is briefly happy to graduate but soon must move on to the next phase of life and its obligations.

Second, why should I want to make physiological change a hallmark of emotion anyway? Why not postulate two kinds of emotion, one that involves physiological change and one that does not? Or, perhaps I should say that some emotions are characterized by physiological arousal, others by change, and still by others no change. The main reason for holding to the position that physiological change (autonomic nervous system activity and also hormonal and central nervous system activity) is a hallmark of emotion is to distinguish emotional processes from nonemotional ones such as cold cognitions, homeostatic processes, and reflex or automatized adaptations. The metaphor of temperature helps here: emotions are personally involving, whereas impersonal thoughts are cold. One usually thinks of emotions as organismic or embodied. It is an anathema to think of an emotion as an automatic pattern of thoughts without commitments, impulses, and bodily involvement.

If, on the other hand, one regarded all behavior and mental activity as organismic one would have to argue that the dichotomy of emotion and nonemotion is false or misleading. This would leave one without a clear distinction between emotional and nonemotional phenomena—which tends to be nihilistic with respect to the concept of emotion itself (cf. Duffy, 1941). If emotion and nonemotion are not different, why have the concept of emotion in the first place? And so I prefer to accept the concept of emotion as more organismic than other processes and states, its intensity reflecting the extent of commitment to a goal or stake in the encounter. When evoked, an emotion is its own system with its own rules of operation. For justification, I make three additional working assumptions.

1. Each emotion, which is defined by its core relational theme and pattern of appraisal, involves its own innate action tendency (see Frijda, 1986; Frijda, Kuipers, & ter Schure, 1989); this can be concealed or overridden by the process of coping. The action tendency in anger is attack, but it is often inhibited or transformed (cf. Averill, 1983). The action tendency in fear is avoidance or escape, but it too can be inhibited or transformed by counterphobic coping. This proposal contrasts with the position of Ortony et al. (1988) that it is awkward and unnecessary to identify an action tendency for all emotions.

2. Each emotion has its own pattern of physiological change, even in the difficult instances I have noted—a form of physiological specificity (e.g., Arnold, 1960; Ax, 1953; Engel & Bickford, 1961; Funkenstein, King, & Drolette, 1957; Lacey, 1959; Lacey, Bateman, & Van Lehn, 1952; Lacey & Lacey, 1958). Autonomic nervous system specificity has been staunchly defended by Levenson (1988), and this defense should be extended to other neurophysiological systems such as the neurohumoral (Mason, 1975; Mason et al., 1976). The relevant findings are sparse, given the importance of the issue, and weak for methodological and theoretical reasons. Nevertheless, a concerted effort to study the psychophysiology of the emotions would produce worthwhile data to help evaluate the proposition.

3. The physiological response specificity results in part from the action tendency generated in each emotion, providing one of the main explanatory links between emotion and physiological change (see Frijda, 1986; Frijda et al., 1989). The action tendency provokes a psychophysiological response pattern as preparation and sustenance for what must be done about the person-environment relationship. Our bodies also respond to much else—for example, inhibition and controlled timing, which are part of the coping process, and the complex, changing demands of the encounter. Therefore, much psychophysiological noise obscures an emotion's basic pattern.

Is this reasoning procrustean in difficult cases such as sadness, happiness, and pride? One is not constrained by data, because to my knowledge psychophysiological study of these emotions is virtually nonexistent. The dilemma for sadness is that its core relational theme, irrevocable loss, leads to inaction and withdrawal. I tend to think of inaction and this withdrawal as action tendencies, as I will explain later.

And what about happiness and pride? One could say that the action tendency is expansiveness and the approach is to share one's good fortune. Pride, though closely related to happiness, is distinct in its sense of enhancement of personal worth; but the action tendencies and motor expressions are similar. One thinks of Gilbert and Sullivan's *H.M.S. Pinafore*, in which the First Lord of the Admiralty, the Right Honorable Sir Joseph Porter, K.C.B., sings, "When at anchor here I ride, my bosom swells with pride."

Although the literature does not provide substantiation, perhaps our sense of the rightness of this imagery supports the hunch that it expresses a unique bodily feature of pride. We will not know with certainty until we make the observations. If the idea turns out to be untenable, we could still shift to the less parsimonious and internally consistent position that some emotions have action tendencies with corresponding physiological changes and others do not. On the other hand, it may be best to regard happiness, along with sadness and dysphoria, as a mood rather than an acute emotion. Because mood states unlike acute emotions have no specific focus, an action tendency could be irrelevant if we thought of happiness and sadness, too, as moods. I am not sure whether pride fits here at all. In any case, I find this solution tempting.

Should Emotion Meanings Be Dimensionalized Into a Few Basic Factors or Treated as Discrete Categories?

There is long-standing tension between two conceptions of emotion—one based on dimensions, and the other based on discrete categories such as anger, anxiety, guilt, and pride. In the former, one reduces the categorical variations by combining them on the basis of shared and divergent properties, usually by factor analysis, and then portraying the resulting factor structure in dimensional space. In the latter, one first indicates the categories and then considers each as varying along a dimension of intensity.

Efforts to identify the dimensional structure of emotion began with Spencer (1855/1890) and Wundt (1905) but are more familiar in Woodworth and Schlosberg (1954). Modern expression is found in Davitz's (1969) research and more recent work by Watson and Tellegen (1985), Russell (1980), Shaver et al. (1987), Storm and Storm (1987), and others.

Typically, factor-analytic strategies yield two or four dimensions, as in Watson and Tellegen (1985) with two (positive and negative affect) and Davitz (1969) with four (activation, relatedness, hedonic tone, and competence). In these studies, respondents matched facial or vocal emotional expressions to emotion terms, rated verbally or visually depicted social scenes, or rated similarities of the meanings of emotion words.

Dimensional analysis typically assumes an invariant structure of emotion. However, the patterns obtained depend on the circumstances and even on the stages of the emotion process, although this has generated little interest. In my research (Folkman & Lazarus, 1985) using a process formulation, subjects rated their emotions at three stages of a college examination: anticipation; right after the exam; and right after announcement of grades. Correlations between positive and negative emotions in the first stage were nearly zero, rising to −.25 after the exam and to −.50 after grades were announced. The explanation was that before the exam the situation was ambiguous, so it was reasonable to be both happy and disappointed. As the situation was clarified after the exam, the correlation rose; then to the extent people felt happy, they were less likely to feel disappointed. And when students knew their grades, there was a much stronger negative correlation between positive and negative emotions. In effect, unless one considers the context, in this case the stages of the emotion process, one will miss the variations in the dimensional structure.

There is value in generalizations that can suggest which emotions are closer to each other psychologically or are farther apart on meaning dimensions—and value even in merely reducing redundancy. In the opposing view, which favors categories, simplifying generalizations obscure important psychological meanings that the many emotion words in our language are intended to express.

An example of the latter problem is the two-factor solution of Watson and Tellegen (1985, p. 221), which places four response terms—drowsy, dull, sleepy, and sluggish—in the same position, presumably all sharing the property of low positive affect. Although the terms "drowsy" and "sleepy" probably should not be referred to as emotions, it is even more important to consider that when one is lying in bed with nothing pressing to do, being drowsy is pleasant—but when one is sitting in a meeting, being drowsy is distressing. Important relational meanings are obscured and even distorted by squashing different states into the same point of dimensional space.

One could argue that there are as many emotions as there are harms and benefits inherent in any person-environment relationship. Therefore, a categorical scheme leads to the same dilemma as factor-analyzing a correlational matrix. How many categories should be created, or how many factors should be extracted? The answers, in part arbitrary, depend on the purposes, clarity, internal consistency, and utility of the resulting categories or factor sets.

Thus to identify anger as an emotion is also to moot many relational meanings by combining them within the single emotion family. Are rage and annoyance different only in intensity, or also in quality? Is pouting a form of anger? Is gloating? Although these both contain anger, they are different ways of coping with a demeaning social relationship; and for some theoretical and research purposes these differences should be conserved. There is no absolute answer, inasmuch as the argument between the dimensional and the categorical approach is about conceptual or practical utility. One cannot be considered more right or wrong than the other, and their respective value depends on the kinds of questions one is pursuing.

Nevertheless, if the aim is to find out what makes people angry, the task is undermined by a preoccupation with reducing the basic response dimensions to a minimum. Anger then becomes a type of unpleasant activation when in reality it is a complex, rich, and varied relational pattern, even at times pleasant and distinctive in its effects as compared with other emotion categories (see also Clore et al., 1987, pp. 751-752, for a strong statement of this point of view).

What Are the Functional Relations Between Cognition, Motivation, and Emotion?

I have recently discussed the functional relations between cognition, motivation, and emotion (Lazarus, 1991a, 1991b). To summarize, I argued first that the behavioral flow between cognition and emotion goes both ways: although emotion is always a response to meaning, it can also influence subsequent thoughts and emotions.

Second, cognition, which is causal, also continues into the response state—a disturbing idea to those who follow the Aristotelian dictum that a concept, A (e.g., an appraisal), cannot also be B (part of an emotion). However, emotion is a complex state—an AB—with A as cause and B as a combination of an action tendency, physiological change, and subjective affect, which includes the appraisal. The germ theory of disease offers an analogy. The germ causes the disease, and its presence is essential while the person is sick. If overcome by the body's defenses, it disappears along with the disease, although it sometimes remains dormant in the body. The situation is the same for appraisal and the emotional response. Remove the provocation—say, the demeaning offense in anger—and the emotion no longer exists.

Third, in the absence of a goal and personal stake, an encounter will not generate an emotion. Appraisal is an evaluation of the significance of a transaction for personal well-being: a personal stake is involved. Knowledge, in contrast, may be impersonal. Therefore, knowledge is a necessary but not a sufficient condition of emotion, whereas appraisal is both necessary and sufficient (see also Lazarus & Smith, 1988)—clearly a controversial stand.

Fourth, neither the speed of emotion generation nor its presence in very young children and infrahuman animals, nor the fact that conditions such as fatigue, illness, and presence of drugs affect acute emotions and moods, militates against the proposition that appraisal is necessary for an emotion to occur. Because appraisal, which is always taking place in a conscious being, is confounded with the effects of these conditions, including drugs, the two antecedent levels of analysis (appraisal and direct physical effects on the nervous system) cannot readily be separated as causes. Therefore, one cannot say that appraisal is not a necessary factor in emotion.

Fifth, there is more than one way of knowing, and we need to give more attention to less articulate processes of emotion generation, such as resonances (see Shepard, 1984; Trevarthen, 1979; Trevarthen & Hubley, 1978) between wishes or fantasies and actual encounters, as opposed to more advanced forms of cognitive activity. *Resonances* refer to an ineffable sense of compatibility or incompatibility between our personal identity and the outer world.

Cognitive psychologists are beginning to examine at least two modes of meaning generation: one is deliberate and volitional, and the other operates automatically and without volitional control. Many are addressing this distinction and its implications about social attitudes and the emotion process, including several contemporary emotion theorists (e.g., Buck, 1985; Leventhal, 1984; Scherer, 1984b). And the work of neurophysiologists such as LeDoux (1986, 1989) is consistent with the theme of different levels at which meaning is achieved.

The distinction also makes more tenable my position that cognitive activity is necessary to emotion, inasmuch as hasty and developmentally immature appraisals may occur in young children—even in the absence of the ability to verbalize their insights about feeling rules—and across animal species. Furthermore, appraisal theory, which often seems to refer only to conscious evaluative processes, needs to coexist with depth psychology and an emphasis on the unconscious (see Lazarus, 1991a, 1991b).

How Can Emotion Theory Reconcile Biological Universals With Sociocultural Sources of Variability?

Emotion research and theory encompass two major field-related positions. One, phylogenetic and centered on biological universals, assumes the existence of underlying and peremptory neurophysiological mechanisms. The other, ontogenetic and sociocultural, assumes the existence of learned variations in the emotion process, which emerge in psychological development.

Neuropsychologists, and those committed to the Darwinian tradition of natural selection and evolution, including those doing programmatic research on the universals of facial expression (e.g., Ekman, 1977, 1984, 1989; Izard, 1971, 1977, 1984), have emphasized what is inherited by species. Sociologists (e.g., Kemper, 1981) and social psychologists (e.g., Averill, 1980, 1982) focusing on social structure, as well as anthropologists focusing on cultural meanings (e.g., D'Andrade, 1984; see also Shweder & LeVine, 1984), have emphasized what is acquired from the social system and from individual experience. I do not mean to perpetuate a false dichotomy; both Ekman and Izard acknowledge cultural variation, and Kemper speaks of biological universals. The differences are largely matters of emphasis and the central focus of the research.

Although the biological and the sociocultural are usually placed in apposition, even opposition, an adequate theory of emotion—especially one that claims to be cognitive, motivational, and relational—must find ways of reconciling the two perspectives. To this end I propose the following, cast in the form of "if . . . then" statements centering on the concept of appraisal, with one fundamental premise and two subpremises.

The fundamental premise is that owing to their biological construction and in order to survive and flourish, animals (humans particularly) are constantly evaluating (appraising) their relationships with the environment with respect to significance for well-being.

One subpremise concerns biological universals. One can understand these universals in the following way: *if* a person (or animal) appraises his or her relationship to the environment in a particular way, *then* a specific emotion, which is tied to the appraisal, always results; and *if* two persons make the same appraisal, *then* they will experience the same emotion regardless of the circumstances. We are built this way, and presumably because of our neural makeup these appraisals and the attendant emotions inhere in our collective mind. This suggestion is analogous to the concept of affect program that Ekman (1977, 1984) has proposed but not discussed fully.

A second subpremise concerns sociocultural sources of variation. Two conceptual steps make this clear: (a) a personality, which includes a person's goal hierarchy and beliefs, is forged by living in a particular society and culture and selectively internalizing its values, meanings, and social rules; and (b) individual variability in the emotion process, which is manifest first in divergent motives and beliefs and second in individual differences in appraisal and coping, contributes to the "if" part of the "if . . . then" statement. This is evident in the divergent ways people appraise the personal significance of occurrences and the ways they cope with the encounter and the emotions generated. This formula accommodates not only the biological universals in emotion, but also the variations based on sociocultural influences that shape the personalities of the members of a society whose experiences are both common and variable.

The "if . . . then" formula gives rise to a difficult question about the role of cultural meanings and language in the emotion process. If a culture has no term or concept for a given emotion, will the people of that culture fail to experience that emotion? Briggs (1970) suggested, for example, that certain Eskimo tribes do not feel, much less express, anger. Levy (1973, 1984) assumed that emotions are largely biological reactions, yet he observed that Tahitians have few words for sadness, longing, or loneliness. Levy referred to these scarcely recognized terms as *hypocognized;* although the Tahitians recognize severe grief and lamentation, they describe sadness and loss as fatigue, sickness, or other kinds of bodily distress. Guilt too is hypocognized. Shame and anger are hypercognized, and there are many terms for these in the Tahitian language.

To solve the problem this poses, one must choose among several alternatives. For example, when Tahitians react with sadness but label the reaction with a distinctive, culturally based word, are they experiencing but denying sadness, reacting with no emotion (which seems to be belied by their bodily distress), reacting with another emotion, or responding to different circumstances than do people in other cultures who commonly experience sadness? Presuming that their state is not sadness would imply that emotions are nothing but verbal tricks, labeled in whatever way the culture provides for—in a broad expansion of the Whorfian hypothesis that words define meanings, or as a variant of the Schachter and Singer (1962) thesis that we label diffuse arousal by whatever concept characterizes the social context.

In contrast, to claim that the Tahitians are actually experiencing sadness (which they can verbalize only as a metaphorical pain) would be to adopt the position that emotional meanings are fundamental and that words provide only an approximation of these meanings—the solution I prefer. I favor the proposition that over the course of living, people everywhere are likely to have all the basic relational experiences, that is, all the *core relational themes* for the emotions characteristic of human social life.

With or without a label or a consensually correct word for the person-environment relationship and attendant emotion, most of us have (a) been slighted or demeaned (for anger); (b) faced existential threats (for anxiety); (c) experienced irrevocable loss (for sadness); (d) transgressed a moral imperative (for guilt); (e) failed to live up to an ego ideal (for shame); (f) wanted something another has (for envy); (g) resented someone for having, seeming to have, or threatening what we want (for jealousy); (h) taken in or stood too close to—metaphorically speaking—an indigestible object or idea (for disgust); (i) feared the worst but yearned for better (for hope); (j) progressed toward achieving a goal (for happiness); (k) felt enhancement of our self or our social worth through a valued object or accomplishment (for pride); (l) credited another with an altruistic gift (for gratitude); (m) desired reciprocated affection from a valued person (for love); and (n) been moved by another's suffering (for compassion). These are my proposals for core relational themes for the main emotion families.

In effect, owing to our biological construction, if we experience any of these person-environment relationships and appraise them as such, regardless of their labels, we will experience the emotion linked to the appraised meaning. Neurologically intact persons are able to experience all the emotions. Although words help us define events, they are not necessary: children can experience emotions and grasp their rules without being able to verbalize them (cf. Dunn, 1988). The biological principle in the first subpremise operates regardless of our ability to label the experience or to judge our formulation of it. Emotions are not mere verbal tricks or labels, but reactions to fundamental relational meanings that have adaptive significance in our lives.

Nevertheless, if my idea about how sociocultural factors influence the "if" of the "if . . . then" formulation is valid, then language and cultural values must also affect the signs and significances carried by social events. How might we think about this? Diverse cultures make different sense of life's events. One way they do this is by emphasizing different aspects of general problems. For example, Lutz and White (1986) pointed to the situation in which one's cultural codes have been violated:

> The Japanese focus on the audience for their errors (Lebra, 1983) while the Ilongot adolescent experiences his inadequacy as a challenge to be overcome (Rosaldo, 1983) and the American might tend to focus on the damage done by the error or on what the error says about one's character. In addition, there is cultural variation in how much emphasis is given overall to each problem type. (p. 428)

Cultures also make different sense of life's events by interpreting them differently. In this connection, Lutz and White (1986) listed the following:

> What is considered dangerous, a thing worth having, or a loss? . . . Are many children a resource or drain? Is attachment to others at the center of life or life's illusion? . . . What risks are worth taking? . . . Who ought to take them, what causes or may be held accountable for them? (p. 428).

To summarize, culture helps define the conditions of appraisal of core relational themes—for example, indicating what the signs of love are, which objects of pride are suitable, what an appropriate stake is. All these meanings and more shape the appraisal process. Levy (1973) spoke of *constitutive rules*, whereby cultural meanings shape the emotion process between the event and the reaction, and *regulative rules*, which operate between the inner emotional state and the observable outcome in expression, as in display rules (e.g., Ekman, 1977).

The biological principle says only that certain fundamental meanings—subject to how the culture defines them—can be found in emotional social relationships, regardless of the fuzziness or obfuscations that verbal language permits. If we recognize that someone has slighted us, we will react with anger because we are built to, even if the interpersonal scenario is smoothed over, reinterpreted, or qualified. It is anybody's guess whether the process of anger generation is completely obscured by ego defenses that distort meaning, or whether instead the anger-generating process remains active in the mind, as illustrated by Freud's concept of the return of the repressed. Interested readers might consult Lazarus (1991b) for a fuller treatment of the role of culture and of the unconscious.

CLASSIFICATION OF THE EMOTIONS

Later I will comment on the reasons for excluding some states from my classification of the emotions.

There are four categories of emotion:

1. *Emotions resulting from harms, losses, and threats,* including anger, anxiety, fear, guilt, shame, sadness, envy, jealousy, and disgust. These are also referred to as negative or stress emotions because the cognitive-motivational-relational process involved is based on thwarting.

2. *Emotions resulting from benefits,* defined as attainment of a goal or subjectively reasonable movement toward it, including happiness and joy, pride, gratitude, and love. These emotions are considered positive.

3. *Borderline cases* such as hope, contentment, relief, compassion, and aesthetic emotions.

4. *Nonemotions,* which although often emotional in the sense of Ortony et al. (1988), should not be regarded as discrete emotions. They fall into several subcategories:

   a. Complex states including grief and depression

   b. Ambiguous positive states such as expansiveness, challenge, confidence, and determination

   c. Ambiguous negative states such as frustration, disappointment, and meaninglessness

   d. Mental confusion or bewilderment

   e. Contentless excitement or arousal such as upset, distress, nervousness, tension, and agitation

   f. Pre-emotions such as interest, curiosity, anticipation, alertness, surprise, and amazement

The first two categories are pretty standard. The third, borderline emotions, is more controversial, and I argued earlier against treating empathy or aesthetic emotions as emotion families. The nonemotions are the most controversial, inasmuch as grief and depression are commonly considered emotions. I now believe that it is best to regard challenge, like threat, as a mediating appraisal that may give rise to emotions such as hope or problematic states such as enthusiasm. Many treat frustration as an emotion, but I regard it as an appraisal—as also for disappointment and meaninglessness. Finally, although they are emotional, upset, distress, and the like refer only to a generalized arousal without any relational content. Terms such as these single out one facet of a complex emotional configuration; we cannot discern the precise person-environment relationship and appraisal pattern without reference to the whole configuration.

APPRAISAL PATTERNS

Because molar summaries, that is, the core relational themes, do not allow a detailed cognitive-motivational-relational analysis of each emotion, this section presents a more molecular analysis of the appraisal pattern for several emotions. First, however, we need a definition of each appraisal component in the system.

Primary Appraisal

Primary appraisal concerns one's stake in the outcome of an encounter. It is primary because without a stake there is no potential for an emotion. The three primary appraisals are *goal relevance, goal congruence,* and *goal content.* In a previous discussion (Lazarus, 1991b), I changed goal content to *type of ego-involvement.*

Goal relevance concerns whether anything is at stake; this determines whether the encounter holds the potential for any emotion. If something is at stake, then the outcome will result in an emotion whose intensity is tied mainly to the importance of the goal.

Goal congruence or incongruence concerns whether the encounter is appraised as beneficial or harmful (or threatening). This conflict-centered principle determines whether the resulting emotion will be positive or negative in affective tone.

Type of ego-involvement is needed to distinguish among several emotions, for example, anger, guilt, and shame. It concerns the kind of goal at stake, such as preservation or enhancement of one's ego identity (for anger), a moral value (for guilt), or living up to an ego ideal (for shame).

Secondary Appraisal

Secondary appraisal concerns the options and prospects for coping. The three secondary appraisal decisions are blame or credit, coping potential, and future expectations.

Blame or credit depends on whether an attribution of accountability or responsibility for the harm or benefit can be made, and also on how much control accountable persons have over their actions. The combination of these attributions is essential for a hot or emotional appraisal of blame or credit. The direction—inward or outward—influences whether there will be anger, guilt, shame, or pride. Note the interdependence between two distinct kinds of cognitive activity—knowledge (or attribution) and appraisal (Lazarus & Smith, 1988).

Coping potential relates to whether and how we can influence the person-environment relationship for the better. Future expectations concern what we think may change—whether things will improve or will worsen for any reason, including effective or ineffective coping.

Note the intimate relationship between core relational themes and the patterns of appraisal that discriminate among the emotions. Appraisal patterns provide the detailed evaluative decisions that sum up to each core relational theme, which captures the essence of the relationship. For example, relationally, anger signifies being unfairly demeaned, which in turn signifies the presence of a blameworthy external agent, as will be seen later. There is no contradiction or competition between these two levels of abstraction. One should be able to go from the more detailed appraisal components to the core relational theme and vice versa.

I said at the outset that a main task of a cognitive-motivational-relational theory of emotion is to show how the pattern of appraisal differs for each emotion. We need all six appraisal components in order to move beyond simple characterizations of each emotion family and consider the shades of meaning in variations within a family. For example, to distinguish pouting anger from gloating anger, one would need to consider secondary appraisals such as coping potential, in addition to blame. Pouting, a weak reproach, occurs when a dependent and needy person feels threatened by a loss of interest and support. If the threatened person were fully self-sufficient, he or she would not need to use a weak reproach to obtain more psychic supplies but might attack or even gloat instead. Coping potential contributes to this difference. Pouters see themselves as limited in power, whereas gloaters feel in much greater control, at least on the surface.

But we can understand much by using only four appraisal components—goal relevance, goal congruence or incongruence, goal content, and blame or credit. To illustrate appraisal-centered analysis, I will use only these four components to examine four emotions—anger, anxiety, sadness, and pride. I make no claim, as did Scherer (1984b), of any temporal order to the appraisal components in the appraisal decisions.

Anger

Anger is especially interesting and controversial. I propose that anger depends on an appraisal that one's ego identity, the active goal content, is at stake, which also implies goal relevance. When this identity has been threatened or harmed by an unfair slight or insult, there is goal incongruence (cf. Aristotle, 1941). Anger also necessitates blame, which depends on the attributions that someone is accountable and in control. If the person who thwarts us has no choice, anger is absent, muted, or directed elsewhere (cf. Berkowitz, 1989, for a different account).

In a prototypical anger scenario, you seek assistance in a store only to find the clerk engaged in an interminable personal phone call. In contrast, if the clerk is busy but seems to be doing his or her best, you are not as likely to get angry. You may instead direct anger toward the store management, or society, or inward. Finding a suitable external object to blame depends on how one construes accountability and control as defined by social rules and obligations.

This cognitive-motivational-relational view may seem to imply that one becomes angry only when there is direct harm to oneself, which is not so. This analysis also covers concern for the well-being of other persons and ideas. What of the anger we feel on seeing a personal, societal, or political assault on someone who is helpless? Why do we feel anger here if anger generation always involves a slight to our personal identity? In this situation, one's basic values, including fairness and justice, and hence one's ego identity, have indeed been assaulted. We react vicariously. Our goal commitments extend readily to people we love or persons and social groups with whom we identify, and also to ideas. Therefore, we react as though we had a personal stake in the encounter.

Whether or not one accepts this argument, many anger scenarios involve an attack on our ego identities, leading to appraisal of a personal slight or insult. I believe this is a major, if not *the* major, variant of the psychodynamics of anger. I prefer not to treat this anger scenario as a special case but rather as representative of the core relational theme of anger, in effect, of a sense that we have not been treated as we should, regardless of the intent. This may be why retaliation and vengeance are so much a part of anger; vengeance is a way of repairing damage to one's demeaned, hence damaged, ego identity.

At this point it may be useful to deal briefly with the development of the emotions. Earlier in this chapter, and elsewhere (Lazarus, 1991a, 1991b), I distinguished deliberate and volitional ways of achieving meaning from automatic and involuntary modes. The emotion process in infants and young children (or in infrahuman animals) is not necessarily the same as in adults. It might appear that I am presenting an exclusively adult version of appraisal, as deliberate and reflective. Is the emotion process in children, say, for anger, different from the adult version?

Striking evidence is emerging about the cognitive capabilities of infants and young children. For example, Stenberg and Campos (1990) observed evidence of anger in infants in response to physical restraint. At three months of age the babies showed only distress, not anger; at four months they showed anger and looked at the source of the restraint, which was a hand on their wrist; at seven months, they looked at the face of the person holding their wrist, or at the mother if she was present.

What does this mean for the appraisals relevant to anger? Is the baby capable of a primitive sense of identity? Probably yes if we take seriously the observations of Bahrick and Watson (1985) that five-month-old babies recognize the contingency between their own body movement and its playback on a video monitor (see also Papousek & Papousek, 1974). Distinguishing self from other seems to be a universal psychobiological principle. Even the tissues of animals and plants differentiate their own from foreign protein, and we die from autoimmune diseases if our bodies respond excessively and inappropriately to the distinction—a kind of rudimentary self and non-self.

Does the baby appraise the restraint as an unwarranted offense? Probably yes, in some sense. Does the baby view the agent of restraint as external and therefore show the capability to judge accountability? The reactions of the babies studied by Stenberg and Campos (1990) suggest that they were distinguishing the external source of the offense and gradually evolving greater understanding about it. Does the baby impute control to that source? It seems unlikely, but I know of no relevant evidence.

Whether and how an infant or young child arrives at the essential meanings inherent in appraisal components and patterns are crucial to how and when particular emotions emerge developmentally. We can say that very early there is an elemental sense of goal relevance, goal incongruence, ego identity, and a basis for the attribution of external accountability important in anger. Attributed control is problematic; perhaps blame is essential only in adult anger, although without solid evidence this question remains open. A major task for a cognitive-motivational-relational theory is the developmental study of appraisal and its role in individual emotions.

Anxiety

Along with others, I suggest that the goal content relevant to anxiety is existential—centered on meanings and a sense of individually constructed identity (see Lazarus & Averill, 1972). The threat to these meanings provides the goal incongruence in the appraisal. The goal content overlaps with that in anger, but in anxiety, the threat and the possible responses are quite different.

Although an uncertain threat that makes us anxious may be concretized as an upcoming exam or a social confrontation, the basic threat is to vague and symbolic existential meanings, so that we cannot tell what will happen, when, and what should be done about it unless we pin the threat down to a concrete event. Perhaps this is why anxiety has so often been treated as *the* basis of psychopathology. In anxiety, the threat is not an insult that we might retaliate against, but the potential loss of personal meaning, which makes us feel more or less powerless. And whereas anger centers on a damaging confrontation in the past, anxiety is future oriented—an anticipatory emotion par excellence.

In anxiety there is no obvious agent of threat, so there is no blame: if there were, and control were attributed to that agent, anxiety would be transformed into anger, guilt, or shame. Of the negative emotions, only sadness shares with anxiety the absence of blame and of a clear possible ameliorating action. In anxiety the action tendency, as in fright, is avoidance or escape, whereas in sadness it is inaction and withdrawal. Because in anxiety there is often nothing specific to avoid, the person also has a strong urge to concretize and externalize its source, inasmuch as it is easier to deal with a known danger than an unknown one. This urge to locate an external agent also applies to anger, especially when it is a defense against self-blame or when one is uncertain about the agent.

Sadness

The goal relevance in sadness is not content specific as with anger, anxiety, guilt, and shame, but consists of any commitment important to the individual—for example, one's social role, job, reputation, or a loved one. An irrevocable loss of this commitment, which implies helplessness or lack of control, is the goal-incongruent event that produces sadness. The person believes the loss cannot be restored, and as in the case of anxiety, does not hold an agent accountable. If an external agent is located, the emotion is more likely to be anger; if internalized, it will be guilt or shame. Attributions of accountability and control, and therefore appraisals of blame, can change during grieving; the emotion then changes from sadness to anger, anxiety, guilt, or shame.

This is why in depression, which is usually a mixture of anger, guilt, anxiety, and sadness, the sadness is often overwhelmed by these other active emotions, which require that the loss not be construed as irrevocable. People can (a) feel anger at a deceased loved one for desertion, (b) feel anxiety when attempting to restore the lost meaning (Marris, 1975), (c) disbelieve or deny the loss, or (d) struggle with its existential significance. Sadness requires an unusual combination of appraisals centered on irrevocability of loss and the absence of an agent to blame.

Sadness seems unique among the emotions in coming at the end of a chain of struggles to cope with loss. Early on, the person reacts mainly with other emotions such as anger, anxiety, guilt, and shame—active emotions focused on trying to restore what was. Only slowly does the person facing loss accept its irrevocability, and with this come a loosening of the commitment and an openness to new ones. In successful grieving, depression ultimately gives way to wistful sadness and occasional distress.

Sadness has two other distinctive features. First, its action impulse is inaction or withdrawal from involvement in the world; second, it tends to evolve slowly with the gradual struggle to accept the loss—a process that can be lengthy. For these reasons and because of its existential characteristics, it might be better to treat sadness as a mood rather than as an acute emotion.

Pride

The analysis draws on the same appraisal components for positive emotions such as pride as I have suggested for negative emotions. The goal relevance in this case involves a highly valued object or accomplishment. Goal congruence involves the attainment of a valued object or accomplishment in a pride-generating encounter. Accountability and control attributions, in this case credit, are directed to oneself. To draw on Hume (1957), receiving credit results in the enhancement of self-worth, which is the special theme distinguishing pride from happiness.

COPING PROCESS IN EMOTION

Coping is the psychological analogue of action tendencies. Where action tendencies are biologically given and therefore relatively rigid and automatic (although capable of suppression and transformation), coping is more psychological, complex, deliberate, and planful.

As noted elsewhere (Folkman & Lazarus, 1988a, 1988b; Lazarus, 1990; Lazarus & Folkman, 1984, 1987), coping is a key variable in the emotions, especially the negative ones. Not only does coping follow emotion, as in emotion-focused coping (which is designed to regulate emotional distress), but it also shapes emotion—a direction of effect underemphasized in traditional coping theory.

Coping shapes emotions in one of two ways. Problem-focused coping often involves planful, direct actions to change the person-environment relationship or oneself. Emotion-focused coping alters only what is in the mind, either through attention deployment (e.g., avoidance) or through reinterpretation of the relationship—for example, by denial or distancing. For this reason I have used the phrase *cognitive coping* as a synonym.

The fundamental mechanism of these effects is appraisal. Changes in the actual person-environment relationship change the way it is appraised, just as changes in attention deployment or in the meaning of the relationship through cognitive coping are based on appraisal. Emotion is a reaction to meaning, and if the meaning is changed the subsequent emotion will also change.

Laux and Weber (1991) have argued convincingly that coping is a way of dealing with a changed, hence newly motivated, person-environment relationship. However, if one takes seriously that coping is an effort to accomplish something or if one speaks of coping functions, intentions or goals are implied, whether or not the person is certain what they are. For example, if avoidance is a way of not paying attention to whatever troubles us, then it clearly has the intention, or function, of keeping our attention misdirected. In effect, when we use the terms *avoidance, denial,* and *distancing,* we are implying goals or intentions.

To explore the relationships among intentions underlying coping, Laux and Weber (1991) have studied anger and anxiety in married couples. For example, if one spouse slights the other, the resulting anger can lead to two kinds of intention: that of preserving the relationship or that of restoring the damaged ego identity. The coping strategies for these should differ. If the intention is to preserve the relationship, a likely coping strategy would be to stay away from the partner or find good reasons for the partner's behavior. However, if the intention is to preserve self-esteem, escalating the anger might be more suitable. In brief, intentions or goals should greatly affect the coping process.

One way to think of the coping process is as a set of lower-order goals (or intentions) that serve as methods of achieving higher-order goals, as in means-ends relationships. The intent of preserving the relationship, for example, or preserving or enhancing one's identity might be thought of as a higher-order goal for which lower-order goals serve as the means. The psychology of motivation has dealt with this important theoretical issue mainly in passing.

Small coping steps are like the twigs and small branches of a tree, and higher-order goals the larger branches and the trunk. Larger-order, more abstract goals such as living usefully and being a professional psychologist or university professor depend on lower-order goals such as going to college. The latter goals are, in a sense, steps that must be negotiated to reach the higher-order goal (see also Ortony & Clore, 1981).

The terms *coping, means to ends, goals,* and *intentions* relate less to kinds of behavior than to their place in the hierarchy—their scope or level of abstraction. From this point of view, coping is a part of motivational psychology as well as of decision processes (appraisal) and strategies or methods of attainment. It is artificial to separate these concepts when in nature they operate interdependently and in an overlapping way.

PHENOMENOLOGY, FOLK THEORY, AND EMOTION THEORY AND RESEARCH

In concluding, I address an issue often raised about appraisal theory: whether it can lead to empirical research. My approach to appraisal has some characteristics of a subjective or phenomenological system but other features contrary to the idea that "thinking makes it so." For example, I assume that people usually appraise encounters with the environment more or less realistically in keeping with the relational requirements it presents. Otherwise there would be a poor fit between appraisals and the adaptational requirements of the environment, as well as between the process of coping and those requirements, which should result in dysfunction (Lazarus, 1990, 1999; Lazarus & Folkman, 1984).

Nevertheless, there are often discrepancies between a person's appraisal/ coping and the objective realities of the person-environment relationship, at least as these are judged consensually. These discrepancies dictate that we not base theories of psychological stress and emotion solely on the objective characteristics of the environment or on personality, and that such theories take into account the person-environment relationship as this is understood and appraised.

Note, however, that discrepancies between the subjective and objective world do not necessarily imply distortion of reality, pathology, or dysfunction. For example, because goal commitments and beliefs vary both across people and within persons over time, people's pictures of the environment and their relationships with it will often differ, as will one person's picture over time. Thus, while divergent perceptions and appraisals sometimes originate from ego defenses, they often do not.

I tend to question whether it is methodologically possible to construct a picture of the objective environment that is suitable to the emotions, and have suggested elsewhere (Lazarus, 1990) that psychologists who inveigh against subjectivism as methodologically unsound have not themselves resolved these methodological issues. Two issues are particularly difficult. One is that a consensual definition of the objective environment may simply not apply to particular individuals from the standpoint of their personal beliefs and goal commitments. These individuals are, in a sense, looking at different worlds, and we will never understand them from a normative perspective.

An even more difficult problem is that the objective world is easy to describe physically but not so easy to describe in terms of its emotional meanings, which are not monolithic or universal. As Watzlawick (1976) pointed out, the physical properties of gold are not contested, but its symbolic meanings constitute its emotional significances. Even its material value changes consensually as a result of many variables leading to valuations by persons charged with making this decision each day in London, New York, Zurich, or wherever. It is not the physical properties of the environment that count in the emotion process, but its subjective meanings; and it is these we need to understand. Not that psychologists should not study the objective world, but they should not do so merely to castigate theories predicated on subjective appraisals.

From a larger epistemological viewpoint, the denigration of folk theory, or naive psychology, as it is sometimes called, has been common. This rests on a hidden position that theory in psychology, as in the physical sciences, should not be intuitively sensible but should involve reductive concepts that have no necessary connection with how the world of the mind appears to operate. To these critics, folk theory is another name for armchair blather having little scientific value.

I offer two replies to this canard. First, if we believe that emotions result from the way people construe and evaluate events, the most useful theory will be based on those construals and evaluations. Second, if formulated appropriately, folk theory can be evaluated by observation, which is the hallmark of science, just as readily as can any other kind of theory.

A deterministic folk theory faces the potential obstacle that if we are unable to predict appraisals on the basis of measurable causal variables, the conceptual system will remain entirely descriptive and circular because appraisal then could be known only after the fact. The solution, I think, lies in an epistemological blend of descriptive and causal analysis, which one can apply in a systems theory fashion by postulating and examining the appraisal consequences of the antecedent variables. As I have suggested elsewhere (Lazarus, DeLongis, Folkman, & Gruen, 1985; Lazarus & Folkman, 1986), using the flexibility about cause-and-effect variables provided by the concept of reciprocal determinism, personality variables such as motivation and beliefs in interaction with environmental conditions can explain and serve as predictors of appraisal and coping processes.

I used the qualifying phrase, "more or less," to point up the dilemma posed by a poorly understood distinction between moderator and mediator variables (see Baron & Kenny, 1986; Folkman & Lazarus, 1988a, 1988b; Frese, 1986; Zedeck, 1971). A moderator variable is present in the person or environment at the outset and can be measured prior to an emotional encounter. It affects the reactions of the person in somewhat statistically predictable ways. A mediator variable is not present at the outset but arises de novo out of the transaction between the person, whose characteristics are to some extent knowable in advance, and an environment whose characteristics are not likely to be so known. Thus, although we can make predictions about someone we know well, much that this person will do is not predictable in typical social transactions.

Appraisal and coping are mediational concepts because they are not completely predictable but depend on how the environment, as perceived and evaluated by an individual person, behaves.

When all is said and done, a cognitive-motivational-relational theory of emotion has great power to help us reason forward about how emotion is generated and how it shapes subsequent adaptations. In turn, it helps us to reason backward from any given pattern of emotion to its causation. This sort of knowledge can aid us in trying to change emotional patterns resulting from faulty appraisal and coping that are clinically dysfunctional or potentially damaging to health. I believe that the prospects for better understanding and intervention have also contributed to the recent surge of interest in the emotions and in programmatic research on the appraisals and coping processes underlying the emotions. The next few decades will indicate whether this interest is just another flash in the pan, as Averill (1983) suggested, or a new beginning to an old problem of great importance for human existence and adaptation.

SUMMARY

The 1960s saw a resurgence of interest in the long-neglected topic of emotion. An adequate theory of emotion is relational, motivational, and cognitive: emotional, because emotion is generated by relationships between the person and the environment, and each emotion has its own unique person-environment relationship or core relational theme; motivational, because as emotions are responses to the status of goals in a person's encounters with the environment; and cognitive, because emotions issue from knowledge and appraisal of an encounter with the environment and from the person's perception of its significance.

The cognitive-motivational-relational theory distinguishes emotions from nonemotions according to the presence (or absence) of a clear, personally significant, relational content; an appraisal of personal harm or benefit; the potential for action readiness; and physiological changes. Representing emotions along a limited number of dimensions obscures their core relational themes, whereas categorization brings out unique psychological meanings within each emotion family. The theory also addresses the functional relationships between cognition, motivation, and emotion, and deals with the divide in emotion research and theory between biological universals and sociocultural sources of variability. Cognition influences emotions, but emotion can also influence subsequent thoughts and emotions. Cognition is also a part of emotion. Goals and motivations influence appraisal and thus influence emotion. Appraisals and therefore emotion are shaped by both our biological makeup and cultural conditions.

There are four categories of emotion: those resulting from harms (e.g., anger), those resulting from benefits (e.g., joy), borderline cases (e.g., hope), and nonemotions of several types. Appraisals are of two kinds: primary appraisal concerns one's stake in the outcome of an encounter (including goal relevance, goal congruence or incongruence, and goal content), and secondary appraisal concerns the options and prospects for coping (including blame or credit). What makes each emotion unique is the appraisal pattern. An appraisal-centered analysis shows, for example, that anger depends on the appraisal that what one has to lose in an encounter is one's ego identity and on the attribution that someone is accountable.

Coping—which might be viewed as a psychological action tendency—is a key variable, based on appraisal. It ensues from but also shapes emotion. Problem-focused coping involves plans to change the person-environment relationship or oneself; emotion-focused coping entails changing the meaning of the relationship.

The cognitive-motivational-relational theory should enable one to postulate and examine how antecedent variables predict appraisal and coping, and also to reason backward from a particular pattern of emotion to its causation.

Individual Zones of Optimal Functioning (IZOF) Model
Emotion-Performance Relationships in Sport

Yuri L. Hanin
Finland

Chapters 1 and 2 provided an overview of current approaches to emotion and performance in mainstream and sport psychology, and also presented basic concepts, terminology, and a description of emotion as an unfolding process. This chapter focuses on the key factors in emotion-performance relationships by describing a reality-grounded, individual-oriented, motivational model that reflects conditions of sport settings and athletic performance. The Individual Zones of Optimal Functioning (IZOF) model serves as a framework for qualitative and quantitative analysis of the structure and function of emotional experiences related to a successful or poor performance.

The first aim of the chapter is to describe the development of the IZOF model and the theoretical underpinnings of the approach, including concepts from various branches of psychology. Subsequent sections propose a multidimensional description of performance-related psychobiosocial states, examine IZOF-based predictions of emotion-performance relationships, and suggest tentative functional interpretations of emotion-performance relationships with an emphasis on their bi-directionality and interaction effects. A concluding section contrasts the IZOF model with other approaches used in sport psychology during the two last decades. The emphasis of the chapter is on a detailed explanation of the IZOF framework as tested in elite sports.

OVERVIEW OF THE IZOF MODEL

General ideas about the function of theory of emotion, and an illustrative cognitive-motivational-relational theory (see chapter 2), offer a starting point for examining the key issues of emotion-performance relationships in sport. The aim in this section is to

▶ describe and substantiate an individual-oriented (idiographic), sport-specific approach to performance emotions with special reference to elite sport;

▶ show how certain key issues have been addressed in this particular setting; and

▶ discuss how the IZOF model attempts to predict individually successful and less-than-successful performances based on current emotion states and previously established individualized criteria (optimal and dysfunctional zones).

What Does "IZOF" Mean?

The IZOF model (Hanin, 1978, 1983a, 1986, 1989, 1995, 1997a, 1997b) focuses on describing, predicting, explaining, and regulating performance-related psychobiosocial states affecting individual and team activity. At present, however, its major emphasis is on subjective emotional experiences (emotions, feelings, mood, affect) as a critical component of such states (Hanin, 1993, 1995, 1997a). The following sections present features of the model as reflected in its acronym.

Individual

As an idiographic approach, the IZOF model focuses on patterns, structure, and functions of idiosyncratic emotional experiences of athletes (or teams) in various performance situations (Hanin, 1978, 1986, 1989, 1991). Therefore it emphasizes primarily the within-individual dynamics of subjective emotional experiences accompanying successful, average, and poor performances. Hence, the unit of analysis is the individual within the context of a high-achievement (competitive) sport. But although the idiographic orientation predominates, the model also attempts to generalize data across individuals, teams, and larger groups. Recently this emphasis on the individual athlete has been gaining ground in sport psychology (Gould & Krane, 1992; Weinberg, 1990; Vanden Auweele, Cuyper, Mele, & Rzewnicki, 1993).

Zones

The notion of zone (range) in the IZOF model is central for understanding, assessing, and optimizing an individual's emotional state and performance process. The zone principle implies a specific relationship between the perceived intensity of optimal and dysfunctional emotional states and the quality of a performance. Borg's range model of perceived exertion (see Borg, 1998, pp. 27-28) holds that people perceive the world in approximately the same way and that when performing maximally, experience similar sensations. The IZOF model focuses on intraindividual dynamics and interindividual differences in the intensities of subjective emotional experiences related to performances.

Methodologically, individually optimal (and dysfunctional) zones serve as empirically established criteria of an optimal performance state reflecting an individual's performance history. The zones are used to evaluate the degree of similarity (or discrepancy) between actually experienced (current, recalled, or anticipated) emotional states and this optimal state. The zone ranges were derived from research involving several hundred athletes in a variety of sports with precompetition anxiety levels manifested prior to performance (Hanin, 1978, 1983a). A large inter- and intraindividual variability in anxiety scores was consistently associated with optimal and dysfunctional performance under competitive stress. Thus, the model indicates that there is unlikely to be a single, specific optimal level of anxiety resulting in best or poor performance in athletes in the same sport activity.

A further assumption is an individual's best and worst performance anxiety at a given skill level is usually confined to a relatively narrow range. The in-out of the zone concept is used to evaluate deviations of currently experienced (or anticipatory, or recalled) levels of emotion from an individual's optimal and dysfunctional zones. Thus, the concept of zone resembles the range principle used in assessments of thresholds in perceptions and evaluations. The probability of individually successful or poor performance is predicted based on analysis of an athlete's performance history and patterns of emotional experiences. Additionally, these predictions are based on the interaction effects of both optimal and dysfunctional emotions varying in content and intensity.

Optimal

Optimal emotions are defined as those most relevant and appropriate for a particular athlete under specific conditions. Optimal performance state usually provides the best internal conditions, resulting in a total involvement in the task and the best possible recruitment of resources. This typically results in a high-quality performance process and achievement of individually successful performance outcomes (although not necessarily "peak or best ever"). The optimal performance state in the IZOF model is different from the "ideal performance state" (see chapter 6; Csikszentmihalyi, 1990; Loehr, 1982a, 1994; Unestâhl, 1986). Whereas "ideal performance state" includes only positive characteristics of a "dream" or "flow" state with emphasis on exceptional experiences, optimal performance state includes both positive and negative emotions reflecting idiosyncratic strategies and skills an individual athlete might use in recruiting and utilizing resources.

The concept of *optimal* in the IZOF model is multidimensional, thus relating not only to emotion intensity or content but also to dimensions such as form, time, and context. For example, emotional state can be optimal for practices but not for competitions (context); or what is optimal before performance may be not optimal during performance (time). Nonoptimal or dysfunctional emotions reflect situational maladjustment in individual-environment interactions. Thus, the notions of optimality and dysfunctionality refer to both the content of emotion experiences and their impact upon performance.

Functioning

The IZOF model focuses mainly on the structure of emotion content and on description of the emotion function (and dysfunction) in the performance process. The model is based on the results of systematic observation of top performers in real-life situations. The research has emphasized how and why athletes experiencing different levels of emotion intensity (e.g., high, moderate, or low precompetition anxiety) are consistently successful or unsuccessful. The term *functioning* refers to the specific optimal (or dysfunctional) effect of emotion (or its components) upon the quality of performance process. Functionally, task involvement is manifested in an athlete's recruitment of resources through generating the appropriate amount of energy, as well as in efficient utilization of available resources. Additionally, effective recovery on-the-task (or between-the-tasks) over time is critical to consistent performance. In contrast, emotion dysfunction typically results in failure to recruit the appropriate amount of resources, erroneous or inappropriate use of resources, and failure to recover.

The IZOF model examines two major functional aspects in emotion-performance relationships: energizing (de-energizing) and organizing (disorganizing) effects of emotion upon performance. Additionally, since it is important to describe and understand how changes in performance affect emotion, the model emphasizes how emotion influences performance and in turn performance process affects emotion content and intensity. From the applied perspective, it is a motivational model that aims to help top performers cope with extreme stressors of high-level competition and exceptionally intensive training. This is done through understanding and applying the best patterns based on analysis and cognitive restructuring (reconceptualizing) of athletes' own experiences related to successful and unsuccessful performances.

From Zones of Optimal Functioning Anxiety to IZOF Emotion

The IZOF model extends earlier research and theoretical statements by Hanin (1978, 1986, 1989) describing the functional relationship between individually optimal intensity of anxiety (level and zones) and performance in top Russian athletes (for review see Hanin, 1989, 1995, 1996; Jokela & Hanin, 1997). During the last decade, the IZOF approach has been extensively tested and validated across cultures, sports, and ages, and between genders (Gould, Tuffey, Hardy, & Lochbaum, 1993; Hyvönen, 1992; Krane, 1993; Morgan, O'Connor, Ellickson, & Bradley, 1988; Pons, 1994; Prapavessis & Grove, 1991; Raglin, Morgan, & Wise, 1990; Salminen, Liukkonen, Hanin, & Hyvönen, 1995; Turner & Raglin, 1996).

Although this work emphasized precompetition anxiety (see chapter 4; Jokela and Hanin, 1997), anxiety is only one emotion that can influence performance. Researchers and practitioners in mainstream and sport psychology increasingly concur that the emotions of elite, pre-elite, and even nonelite athletes are not limited to stress-related anxiety, anger, or depression, for example (Crocker, 1995; Gould & Tuffey, 1996; Hardy, 1996; Hanin, 1993, 1995, 1996, 1997a, 1997b; Lazarus, 1993; Terry, 1995).

Since sport participation at any skill level is often a challenge, athletes are highly unlikely to perceive competitive sport situations exclusively in terms of threats generating an anxiety response. Thus, the need for a more balanced view of emotions, both positive and negative, has been clear (Lazarus, 1991a, 1993). To meet this need, an earlier version of the concept of zones of optimal functioning (ZOF), dealing only with precompetition anxiety, was refined and extended. The IZOF model deals with functionally optimal and dysfunctional patterns of positive and negative emotions in elite athletes representing various sports (Hamill, 1996; Hanin, 1993, 1994, 1995; Hanin & Syrjä, 1995a, 1995b, 1996; Johnson, Anderson, AhYee, & Makua, 1995; Liukkonen, 1995; Pesonen, 1995; Saarnio, 1995; Syrjä, 1993; Syrjä, Hanin, & Pesonen, 1995; Syrjä, Hanin, & Tarvonen, 1995; Tarvonen, 1995).

The IZOF emotion model, developed in the naturalistic setting of elite sport, combines within- and between-individual analysis of the structure (content) and function of subjective experiences affecting performance. The ultimate goal, however, is to describe, predict, better understand, and explain the dynamics of emotion-performance relationships so that IZOF-based interventions and self-regulation strategies can be developed for sport psychology practice. Although the IZOF model is most relevant to the elite sport setting, it is hoped that its basic assumptions and methodological tools have more general applicability (see chapter 7 and "Concluding Remarks" in this volume). Most clinicians and educators agree that positive emotions as indicators of total well-being almost always produce optimal effect whereas negative emotions are typically dysfunctional. In contrast, the IZOF emotion model emphasizes the effect of both pleasant and unpleasant emotions on an individual's best and poor performance patterns. However, at present the model focuses mainly on the emotion-performance relationships as a first step in describing the role of the psychobiosocial state in performance process.

THEORETICAL UNDERPINNINGS OF THE IZOF MODEL

The IZOF model is based on ideas and principles developed in general, social, educational, and sport psychology. These include

- ▶ the unity of consciousness, psyche, and activity (Rubinstein, 1946);

- ▶ the person-environment interaction (balance/imbalance) as a source of emotional experience, and emotional experience as a conceptual unit (Vygotsky, 1926);

- ▶ the role of cognitive appraisals in person-environment interactions (Lazarus, 1991a, 1993; Endler, 1975);

► idiographic versus nomothetic views of personality and total human functioning (Allport, 1960);

► the systems approach to describing emotions and conceptualizing the relationships between functional states and human activity (Ananjev, 1968; Ganzen, 1984; Lomov, 1984);

► state-trait distinctions (Spielberger, 1966b); and

► psychological readiness for competition (Puni, 1969).

The following sections overview some of these ideas.

The IZOF model is readily testable. This is important since any model must be tested simply to see whether or not it works (Morgan, 1985), but especially important for the IZOF model in that one of its main purposes is as a motivational tool. Thus the conceptualization, measurement system, and developmental application focus are quite different from those of nomothetic or purely descriptive frameworks, for example.

The IZOF approach accords with work by Pritchard and associates on organizational productivity. Pritchard, Jones, Roth, Stuebing, and Ekeberg (1989) identified four purposes for measuring productivity in organizational settings:

1. To compare large aggregations of organizations

2. To evaluate individual organizations for comparison with other organizations or with some standard

3. To focus on a single organization

4. To use the measurement system as a motivational tool to produce changes in behavior productivity

These approaches have different goals and emphases. For instance, nomothetic anxiety models used in sport psychology usually stress anxiety-performance relationships at the intergroup, intragroup, and interindividual levels. Pritchard et al. (1989) contend that since the purposes of measurement are different, interindividual and intra- and intergroup comparisons cannot be directly applied to individuals. What is required is an individually oriented examination of the intraindividual dynamics of subjective emotional experiences and individual performance. The IZOF model, an attempt to meet this need, clearly emphasizes idiographic analysis.

Emotion States Within the Context of Sport Activity

The study of emotion-performance relationships in sport presents two options:

1. To regard emotion and performance as two separate entities, and an emotional response as a factor influencing athletic performance (implied

unidirectional causality). This is a quite common but relatively narrow approach in both mainstream and sport psychology.

2. To consider emotion within a broader context as an integral component of performance process, implying a special functional significance of emotion in performance and a bi-directionality in emotion-performance relationships. This approach is rooted in activity theory (Rubinstein, 1946; Leontjev, 1975; Ananjev, 1968), as well as in the dynamical systems theory developed in mathematics and physics and recently applied to social psychological phenomena (Vallacher & Nowak, 1997). Activity theory (to be distinguished from sports action model [Nitsch, 1975]) holds that

- ▶ activity is a part of human life and directed toward satisfying basic human needs;

- ▶ activity is a series of repeatedly performed tasks;

- ▶ task-execution process involves a sequence of actions (operations, movements, motor acts) under certain conditions of activity; and

- ▶ performance-related states are part of performance process, whereas emotion is a major component of the psychobiosocial state (Hanin, 1997a, 1997b).

Performance involves three stages: preparation (pre-performance), execution (during performance), and evaluation (post-performance).

Therefore, the study of emotions within the activity theory framework should aim at understanding the role of emotion as a component of the total working state related to performance process (pre-, during, and post-performance). Most earlier research on precompetition anxiety focused on the preparatory stage. Additionally, an activity theory orientation considers an athlete's performance history and patterns of subjective emotional experiences over the short and long term. Since athletes regularly evaluate their own performance, skilled athletes are usually well aware of their subjective experiences and performance patterns; and this knowledge can aid in the pursuit of consistent excellence.

Person-Environment Interactions and Emotional Experience

Vygotsky was among the first to suggest a functional relationship between the types of person-environment (P-E) interactions and an individual's emotional experiences. Vygotsky (1926) held that emotional experience reflects at least three types of such interactions (see Hanin, 1989, for a review):

1. Predominance of the organism (person) over the environment (P > E), resulting in a relatively easy task performance and a positive emotional disbalance (or a negative one, if the environment is perceived as deficient, for instance, requiring too little work)

2. A perceived balance between the person's resources and environmental demands (P = E), typically accompanied by positive emotions

3. Too much pressure in the environment in relation to resources (P < E), resulting in an imbalance between task demands and the individual's resources

Vygotsky further argued that emotion is inseparable from total human functioning and as such reflects the nature of future P-E interactions (a fit or a misfit) within the framework of past experiences and future consequences. One cannot understand the unity of something by dividing it into parts, studying them separately, and then trying to integrate the results. Hence, Vygotsky proposed emotional experiences (subjective feelings) as a basic unit of analysis of P-E interactions. The IZOF model includes these concepts as especially relevant for studying social psychological determinants of emotional experiences and response patterns in sport activity.

Lazarus's cognitive-relational-motivational theory of emotion (see chapter 2) elaborates on these ideas as applied to emotions. Specifically, appraisal patterns prior to performance (challenge and threat) as well as during or post-performance (gain and loss) are seen as triggers of specific emotional responses. These conceptualizations, critical for understanding the functional meaning of various emotions, will be elaborated later (see chapters 4 and 7).

Basic Assumptions of the IZOF Model

The basic assumptions of the IZOF model (Hanin, 1994, 1995, 1997a, 1997b) are that emotion is

▶ a component of adaptive or maladaptive response in person-environment interactions;

▶ an integral part of a person's psychobiosocial state, performance process, and total functioning;

▶ triggered by appraisals of a person's relationships with the environment; and

▶ a reflection of critical moments of imbalance in person-environment interactions.

These assumptions are conceptually and empirically substantiated in this chapter and in chapter 7.

The emotion-performance relationships in the IZOF model can be specified in the form of several assumptions that are later empirically tested.

▶ Emotions are triggered by a person's cognitive appraisal of the probability of achieving expected individually relevant goals.

▶ Because sport activity and related emotional experiences are repetitive, performance and emotion patterns develop gradually.

▶ Emotion patterns are specific to the individual, task, and setting, and their specificity is manifested in various dimensions of the psychobiosocial state such as form, content, intensity, time, and context (see later in the chapter).

▶ Emotion-performance relationships are reciprocal. Emotions affect performance; however, changes in the ongoing performance process and intermediate (and final) outcomes produce a shift in emotion content and intensity and thus affect performance. Reversal of the direction of impact (causality) is determined by ongoing appraisals of the performance process (Apter, 1982; Kerr, 1989, 1993, 1997; Lazarus, 1991a, 1993).

▶ Since different emotions can produce optimal or dysfunctional effects, or both, on performance process (Hanin, 1993, 1997a), prediction of performance is based on assessment of the interaction effect of these emotions (Gill, 1994; Gould & Tuffey, 1996; Hanin, 1997a, 1997b; Hardy, 1996; Syrjä, Hanin, & Pesonen, 1995; Syrjä, Hanin, & Tarvonen, 1995).

MULTIDIMENSIONAL DESCRIPTION OF PERFORMANCE-RELATED STATES

To understand emotion-performance relationships in sport requires, first, accurate description of the key emotion and performance parameters. *Therefore, specifying these parameters and dimensions is important both conceptually and methodologically.* The following sections outline current views regarding multidimensionality in sport psychology, and present one approach to describing emotions as components of performance-related states.

Issues of Multidimensionality in Research on Stress-Related Emotions

Sport psychologists increasingly agree that the unidimensional approach to the arousal- or anxiety-performance relationship is ineffective and simplistic (Fazey & Hardy, 1988; Gould & Krane, 1992; Hackfort & Schwenkmezger, 1993; Hanin, 1989; Hardy, 1990; Jones, 1995a; Landers, 1994; Neiss, 1988; Weinberg, 1990). This conclusion comes from a critique of the inverted-U hypothesis, as well as general dissatisfaction with global undifferentiated measures of arousal and use of a single total score of anxiety. Thus, early investigators addressed multidimensionality by examining components of anxiety response, for example. These first attempts focused on empirically derived concepts and produced different labels for anxiety components such as worry and emotionality (Liebert & Morris, 1967); cognitive and somatic anxiety (Schwartz, Davidson, & Goleman, 1978; Smith, Smoll, & Schultz, 1990); and cognitive and somatic anxiety and self-confidence (Martens, Vealey, & Burton, 1990). Furthermore, in conceptualizing situational determinants of anxiety, Endler and

Magnusson (1976), for instance, proposed five types of stressors: interpersonal, physical danger, ambiguity, novelty, and daily routines.

There are limitations to approaching multidimensionality by attempting to empirically derive additional elements of emotional response. For instance, one does not know whether all the important components of emotion have been identified. Moreover, there could be unexamined assumptions about the unidimensionality of a single-score instrument. An example is the State-Trait-Anxiety Inventory (STAI; Spielberger, Gorsuch, & Lushene, 1970), widely used in sport settings to measure both trait and state anxiety (already two dimensions). That the STAI uses a single combined score of state anxiety, derived by adding anxiety-present (negative affect) and anxiety-absent (positive affect) items (Hanin, 1995, 1996; Mook, Van der Ploeg, & Kleijn, 1992), led to the mistaken view that the scale *was* unidimensional (Gould & Krane, 1992; Jones, 1991). However, one could argue that this combined score is an index of interaction effects of negative (anxiety) and positive (complacency) emotions. Additionally, the STAI state anxiety subscale includes both worry items and emotionality items.

A second direction in conceptualizing unidimensionality versus multidimensionality evolved from discussion of emotion measures. Historically, three distinct and measurable parameters have been used to characterize emotions: physiological concomitants, verbally reported subjective affective experiences (feelings), and observed behaviors (Eysenck, 1975; Lazarus, 1968; Schlosberg, 1954). However, here the conceptualization of emotion dimensions is missing.

As another limitation of approaches to multidimensionality, existing methods and scales already have explicitly "fixed" or implied dimensions, reflected in inconsistent and confusing concepts and terms (Gould & Krane, 1992; Raglin, 1992). Attempting to integrate the current arousal-related construct terminology, for example, Gould and Krane (1992) fitted the terms and concepts used by various researchers into a three-level (physiological, cognitive, and affective) structure. The need for a conceptual framework that would help identify the dimensions necessary and sufficient to describe anxiety, or any other performance-related emotion, became clear. Thus, reexamining existing empirical evidence and available measures may be useful but does not provide a solution to multidimensionality. In the IZOF model, a systems theory approach was used to conceptualize and measure performance-related emotions. The next sections outline these assumptions.

The Systems Approach to Multidimensional Description of Emotions

One difficulty in conceptualizing and measuring performance-related psychobiosocial states is the complexity of these phenomena. Attempting to provide a new perspective on the complexity and dynamics of emotion, researchers have applied the systems approach and the dynamical systems theory to psychology (Allport, 1960; Ananjev, 1968; Lomov, 1984; Schedrovitsky, 1964; von Bertalanffy, 1952).

A dynamical system is a set of interconnected and changing elements. The systems approach describes these elements, whereas dynamical systems theory describes the connections among the elements and the changes in the system's behavior produced by these connections (Vallacher & Nowak, 1997). The first step in applying the framework is to identify the key elements of the system—the components of psychobiosocial state. The method of bases, which was instrumental in tackling this problem (Ganzen, 1984), emphasizes completeness of description in relation to the previously established logical foundation (basis). For a systems description of a phenomenon, one must select the basis and its elements before identifying key components of the phenomenon. One can also compare the components of anxiety, for instance, with the elements of the basis in order to identify missing elements or their interrelationships.

The bases for a systems description could differ and could include various numbers of elements. Ganzen (1984) suggested that "spatiality, time, information and energy were the basic characteristics of any object that typically functions as their integrator" (p. 44). He then suggested these concepts (space, time, energy, information, and a substrate) as a conceptual basis (a five-element foundation or a penta-basis) for integrating existing concepts and research findings in psychology. The penta-basis makes it possible to evaluate the completeness of the description of a phenomenon and also to better organize components, compare various descriptions, and thus to discover similarities among phenomena (Ganzen, 1984, pp. 41-42).

This approach to multidimensionality has been theoretically substantiated and empirically validated in psychology. It has been applied to systems descriptions of psychological phenomena, the nervous system, and the human personality (Ganzen, 1984). In the sport setting, the idea of systems description has been used in longitudinal studies of communication patterns in top teams (Hanin, 1985, 1992), in sport career research (Stambulova, 1994), and in the investigation of performance-induced emotions (Hanin, 1993, 1994, 1995, 1997a).

IZOF-Based Multidimensional Description of Psychobiosocial States

The IZOF model includes five basic dimensions as a foundation for the systems description of performance psychobiosocial states and emotion-performance relationships: form (substrate), intensity (energy), content (information), time, and context (space) (figure 3.1).

The Form Dimension

Basic to emotion-performance relationships is the form dimension—the way a phenomenon is manifested. The form (modality) dimension is well substantiated in the literature on measurement of emotion components (Eysenck, 1975; Krause, 1961) and in conceptualizations of a multimodal approach to interventions (Burton, 1990; Davis & West, 1991). The IZOF model includes seven basic form components of total human functioning (Hanin, 1993, 1995,

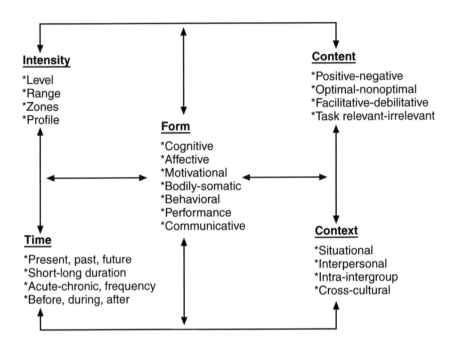

Figure 3.1 The five dimensions of a systems description for performance psychobiosocial states and emotion-performance relationships.
Adapted, by permission, from Y.L. Hanin, 1993, *IZOF Level 1 Certification Course: A Handbook and Materials* (Jyväskylä, Finland: Practical Psychology), p. 17a.

1997a, 1997b) that provide a relatively complete description of a performance state: *cognitive, affective,* and *motivational* components represent psychological aspects of a state; *bodily-somatic* and *motor-behavioral* components represent biological or psychophysiological aspects; and *performance* and *communicative* components reflect a person's observable social interactions with the environment. The seven components constitute the person's psychobiosocial performance-related state (Hanin, 1997a, 1997b), providing a framework for describing the factors affecting individual performance.

In this model, emotion is a component of the psychobiosocial state and is characterized by a specific constellation of subjective affective experiences. Emotion also has correlates or representations in other modalities (cognitive, motivational, etc.). Therefore, an analysis of emotion from this perspective should focus on the individual's subjective emotional experiences and his or her relationship with other modalities of the psychobiosocial state. Most existing sport psychology research examines either cognitive or affective and somatic components using standardized scales. There has been more progress in measuring the somatic (Collins, 1995; Landers, 1985; Lang, 1984; Malmo, 1959; Thayer, 1978) and cognitive (Nideffer, 1978) components. The motor-behavioral components (Beuter & Duda, 1985; Beuter, Duda, & Widule, 1989;

Ferrario, Storza, Michielon, Mauro, & Miani, 1995; Rushall, 1978; Weinberg & Hunt, 1976; Weinberg, 1978) and especially the performance process (Butler & Hardy, 1992; Courneya & Chelladurai, 1991; Doyle & Parfitt, 1996; Gould & Krane, 1992) and communication (Hanin, 1980, 1992) components, until quite recently, have been largely ignored.

The form dimension provides a framework for selecting the components of the psychobiosocial state, enables one to see what modalities may be missing or may require further study, and provides a tentative framework for integrating previous research into a coherent model.

The Content Dimension

In the IZOF model the content dimension is a qualitative (informational) characteristic of the performance state. Each component in the form dimension has its own qualitative characteristics. Thus, if we want to compare modalities or examine their interrelationships, we need to conceptualize and describe each component's content. This presents a major conceptual and methodological problem.

There are two major approaches to conceptualizing the content of emotion:

1. A primary, single-emotion approach focusing on such "basic" emotion constellations as anxiety, anger, joy, depression, etc. (Izard, 1977; Johnson-Laird & Oatley, 1989).

2. A global affect approach conceptualizing the content of emotional experiences in terms of hedonic tone or positivity-negativity (Lorr, McNair, & Fisher, 1982; Russell, 1979; Russell, Weiss, & Mendelsohn, 1989; Watson & Tellegen, 1985; Young, 1959).

The latter approach includes categorizing emotion content in terms of facilitative/debilitative effects of anxiety in test and sport situations (Alpert & Haber, 1960; Jones, 1991, 1995a) and conceptualizing differences between anxiety, excitement, boredom, and relaxation through an interaction of hedonic tone (positive-negative) and arousal intensity (high-low) (Apter, 1982). Note that arousal level here is not the content of the bodily-somatic component, but rather its intensity.

Although emotion content is critical for the functional interpretation of performance-emotion relationships, it is still the least studied dimension in sport psychology (Bejek & Hagtvet, 1996; Hanin, 1992, 1993). One reason may be the predominance of the nomothetic approach to the study of emotions. For instance, when standardized mood scales (STAI; Competitive Sport Anxiety Inventory-2 [CSAI-2]; Profile of Mood States [POMS]; Positive and Negative Affect Schedule [PANAS]) with researcher-generated items are used, their "fixed" emotion content (single or global affect) is almost never questioned (see chapters 4, 5, 9, and 10; Crocker, 1995; Hassmén & Blomstrand, 1995; Rowley, Landers, Kyllo, & Etnier, 1995; Terry, 1995).

Since the IZOF model emphasizes performance-induced idiosyncratic emotional experiences, the content of emotion is conceptualized within a framework that combines a global affect distinction, an individualized prototype approach, and a primary emotion approach (figure 3.2).

In a global affect approach, emotion content is first categorized within the framework of two closely related but independent factors: hedonic tone (pleasure-displeasure or positivity-negativity) and functional impact of emotion upon athletic performance (optimal-dysfunctional). Many have discussed the relevance of hedonic tone (Diener & Emmons, 1984; Diener & Iran-Nejad, 1986; Lazarus & Folkman, 1984; Russell et al., 1989; Watson & Tellegen, 1985; Young, 1959) and functional impact in categorizing emotion content (Hanin, 1993, 1997a, 1997b). One should note, however, that both factors reflect qualitatively different experiences related to successful and poor performances (Hanin, 1991, 1993, 1997a; Kelmar, 1990; Warr, Barter, & Brownbridge, 1983). The four global affect categories derived from the hedonic tone and impact factors are pleasant and functionally optimal emotions (P+); unpleasant and functionally optimal emotions (N+); pleasant and dysfunctional emotions (P–); and unpleasant and dysfunctional (N–) emotions. These four categories appear to provide a robust and broad structure allowing inclusion of a wide range of individually relevant and task-specific emotions in athletes prior to, during, and after performance (Hanin, 1993, 1995).

The IZOF model attempts, first, to identify the emotion content relevant to performance from an athlete's perspective (Fehr & Russell, 1984; Cantor, Mischel, & Schwartz, 1982). The four-category framework generates idiosyncratic emotion descriptors (prototypes) reflecting an individual's performance-related emotional experiences. Then idiosyncratic emotions are aggregated across athletes, tasks, and sports and content analyzed based on their functional impact upon performance process elements. Consequently, the individual athletes' emotion descriptors can be content analyzed, clustered into more basic categories, and compared with existing classifications of single (primary) emotions.

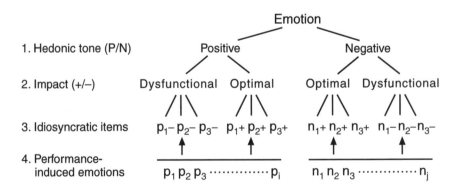

Figure 3.2   IZOF-based conceptualization of emotion content.

The Intensity Dimension: In-Out of the Zone Notion

Intensity is a quantitative characteristic of affect or any other modality of psychobiosocial state. Functionally it is related, for instance, to perceived effort (Borg, 1998) and to energizing (de-energizing) and organizing (disorganizing) aspects of performance process. Intensity is typically represented by scores on a selected parameter of a particular modality. Intensity of subjective experiences (mainly negative affect such as anxiety) is assessed by self-report ratings and is perhaps the dimension most studied in sport psychology. Until quite recently, however, all assessments of intensity were limited to attempts to identify intensity cross-sectionally on a single (arousal) or several parameters (e.g., cognitive and somatic components of anxiety). Assessments were typically contrasted across athletes and samples at the group level. A great range of intensity of separate emotions in athletes has not yet been investigated, nor have the separate and interactive effects of different emotion intensities, except for two components of anxiety (Hardy, 1996; Hardy, Jones, & Gould, 1997).

The IZOF model conceptualizes the intensity dimension at the individual level using the in-out of the zone notion. The zone of optimal functioning concept was derived from data that consistently demonstrated high interindividual variability in optimal precompetition anxiety among different samples of elite and competitive athletes (see chapter 4; Hanin, 1978, 1995, 1996; Raglin, 1992; Raglin & Turner, 1993), arguing for an individualized approach to evaluating intensity. In contrast to nomothetic orientations suggesting that a specific level of optimal emotion is characteristic of most athletes, the IZOF model is based on observations of real emotional experiences that are optimal (or dysfunctional) in individual athletes. Specifically, the in-out of the zone concept serves as a guiding principle in assessing, predicting, and optimizing an individual's performance. As initially applied to precompetition anxiety, it was assumed that each athlete has an individually optimal intensity level (high, moderate, or low) and a range or zone of optimal anxiety. Thus, particularly in short-duration tasks, performance success relates to whether the precompetition anxiety is near to, within, or outside this zone. The zone concept reflects the fact that each athlete has a unique set of resources that may or may not be situationally available for coping with current demands.

This approach is generally consistent with the range principle of Borg (1998) for interindividual comparisons of perceived exertion. However, Borg used the whole range from zero (at threshold or at rest) to maximal intensity as a frame of reference for ratings. The IZOF model has a different and broader focus in that it examines the qualitatively significant and performance-related intensities (optimal and dysfunctional zones); intraindividual consistency of intensity patterns; and interindividual variability in the zone intensity ratings.

At present, with the development of individualized emotion or positive and negative affect (PNA) scales (Hanin, 1993, 1994, 1995, 1997a; Hanin & Syrjä, 1996), the extended in-out of the zone concept is used to describe separate and joint effects of both positive and negative emotions using athlete-generated items. Individual zones of optimal and dysfunctional intensity are identified for each functionally optimal and dysfunctional emotion, respectively. Zones of optimal function are assumed in some emotions (P+N+) within which the probability of successful performance is highest, and dysfunctional zones in other emotions (P–N–) within which the probability of poor performance is highest. Low, moderate, or high optimal and dysfunctional intensity levels vary for the same emotion and different emotions across athletes (Hanin & Syrjä, 1995a, 1995b; Syrjä, Hanin, & Pesonen, 1995; Syrjä, Hanin, & Tarvonen, 1995). Functionally optimal and dysfunctional effects occur separately and jointly only when these emotions are near or within the previously established individual zones: the total effect of positive and negative emotions on performance appears to be determined by the interaction of optimal and dysfunctional effects.

In summary, although functionally optimal emotions are important predictors of successful performance, detrimental effects of dysfunctional emotions should also be considered. The notion of a zone provides individualized criteria to evaluate both optimal and dysfunctional effects, separately and jointly. Figure 3.3 illustrates how the in-out of the zone notion is applied for assessment and feedback to an athlete in the form of individualized emotion "iceberg" profile.

Recalls of a top Finnish cross-country skier were used to develop an individualized PNA scale. Optimal and dysfunctional intensity zones for the three most important emotions were identified using a modification of Borg's (1982, 1998) Category Ratio (CR-10) scale. (In our research on emotion [Hanin and Syrjä, 1995a, 1996], we have used the words "little" and "much" rather than "weak" and "strong." In this text, "CR-10 scale" refers to this modified version rather than to the original Borg CR10 scale [Borg, 1998, p. 41].) This athlete's emotion items, as well as the optimal and dysfunctional zones (P+, N+, P–, N–), are idiosyncratic: for example, his optimal positive emotions were

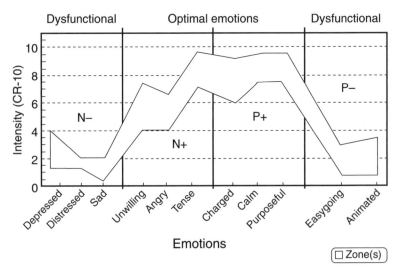

Figure 3.3 Emotion profile of a top Finnish cross-country skier.

charged, calm, and *purposeful.* This profile was given an "iceberg" shape to emphasize visually the optimal interaction effects between the maximum intensity of strong optimal (P+N+) emotions, placed in the middle, and the minimum intensity of weak dysfunctional (P–N–) emotions, placed at the sides (see appendixes). This idiosyncratic profile contrasts with Morgan's iceberg profile using the POMS, which includes fixed emotion content within positive and negative subscales. In the POMS iceberg, interaction between positive and negative affect is only implied. Deviations from the optimal "iceberg" profile immediately indicate a need for coping with the current situation, which is important when IZOF-iceberg profiles are constructed deliberately (appendix B). It also makes sense to identify what is beyond the optimal zones, since there are optimal, less-than optimal, and dysfunctional zones within an emotion's entire working intensity range (see chapter 7; Hanin, 1997c).

The Time Dimension

The temporal dimension reflects the dynamics of emotional experiences before, during, and after performance of a single or repeated short- or long-duration task (Fenz & Epstein, 1967; Gould, Pelitchkoff, & Weinberg, 1984; Hanin, 1978, 1983a, 1993; Jones, 1991; Karteroliotis & Gill, 1987). Research should also address the dynamics of emotion-performance relationships (bi-directionality) within and across tasks during longer time frames (weeks, months, season, championships, and Olympic cycles, or across an athletic career). Most current sport psychology research has focused on precompetition affect, mainly situational anxiety. Such studies (for example, Randle & Weinberg, 1997) do not address patterns of change in emotion, but compare precompetition anxiety with total performance scores; this could be a serious concern, especially in long-duration events and team sports (Raglin & Morris, 1994). Precompetition emotions are not sufficient for predicting performance process and outcomes. Furthermore, most studies use a cross-sectional between-subjects design; longitudinal within-subject designs are still rare (Bortoli, Robazza, & Nougier, 1999a, 1999b; Hanin, 1997a, 1997b; Woodman, Albinson, & Hardy, 1997). Research on the dynamics of emotional experiences during performance is limited to "flow" state studies (see chapter 6; Csikszentmihalyi, 1990; Jackson, 1995). Additional research on temporal patterns of recall and anticipatory measures is also warranted in view of the difficulties in assessing actual emotions, especially during performance.

The Context Dimension

The context dimension is an environmental characteristic including situational (practices vs. competitions), interpersonal, and intragroup antecedents or consequences that determine emotion intensity and content (Hanin, 1977, 1980, 1985, 1989, 1992; Hanin & Bulanova, 1979; Hanin & Kopysov, 1977; Iso-Ahola, 1995; McCann, Murphy, & Raedeke, 1992; Prapavessis & Carron, 1996). For example, context includes interpersonal and intragroup anxiety (Hanin, 1977, 1983a, 1983b, 1989, 1991, 1992) as experienced in actual, recalled, or anticipated interactions with significant others; or emotion content and intensity across practices and competitions in the same or different samples of athletes (Hanin & Syrjä, 1997). Data based on this dimension in sport are virtually nonexistent; a study of emotional responses to environmental factors would be highly desirable, not only for elite and pre-elite sport, but also for health and educational psychology (Hanin & Bulanova, 1979, 1981).

IZOF-BASED PREDICTIONS OF EMOTION-PERFORMANCE RELATIONSHIPS

The IZOF model includes predictions about emotion-performance relationships. Some have been empirically tested, and others are being investigated (see chapter 7). The following sections overview the basic predictions, grouped around the dimensions of the performance-related psychobiosocial state.

Patterns of Emotion Content and Performance

Since each athlete has his or her own emotion vocabulary for subjective emotional experiences, emotion content in athlete-generated items is idiosyncratic. Moreover, the same athlete may experience emotions of differing content at different stages of a task-execution process, as well as in different tasks and events. Stability of emotion content over time is determined by awareness level: athletes with characteristically high self-awareness have clearer and more stable patterns of emotion content than do others.

One expects that if emotion patterns reflect available resources, emotion profiles might be similar for tasks requiring comparable effort and skill. However, successful performance almost always means that an athlete has used his or her best performance patterns based on cognitive, emotional, motivational, bodily-somatic, and psychomotor resources.

Emotion Intensity and Performance: The In-Out of the Zone Notion

One expects a high degree of interindividual variability in the intensity of emotions that accompany individually successful and poor performances. This is manifested in between-subject differences in optimal (dysfunctional) levels and zones of intensities for emotions—similar and different in content—within and across sports.

The in-out of the zone notion suggests that to predict performance, we should evaluate how close an athlete's current (or anticipated) emotional state is in its intensity to the previously established individual zones. A large discrepancy between the actual emotional state and the optimal zones indicates a high probability of less-than-successful performance. At the same time, optimal emotional state usually strongly deviates from the dysfunctional intensity zones on the selected emotions.

In predicting emotion-performance relationships, one should consider interactive as well as separate effects of emotions on sport activity. As figure 3.4 shows, maximum enhancing and minimum impairing effects indicate a high probability of individually successful performance. Other combinations indicate high probabilities of average or poor performance.

FUNCTIONAL INTERPRETATION OF EMOTION-PERFORMANCE RELATIONSHIPS

Interpretation of emotion-performance relationships in the IZOF model is based on the idea that emotion is functionally significant for behavior and performance (Oatley & Jenkins, 1992; Rubinstein, 1946; Simonov, 1970); psychosocial and psychobiological perspectives are emphasized. However, since a detailed description of the performance process is lacking, only tentative explanations are suggested here.

Appraisal Patterns as Determinants of Emotion Process

The psychosocial perspective is central to the IZOF model (Hanin, 1980, 1985, 1989, 1991, 1992). Emotion is conceptualized as an unfolding process (Folkman & Lazarus, 1985) reflecting person-environment interactions. The individual appraises these interactions, and the appraisal influences the content and intensity of performance-related emotional experiences. Further, changes in performance process during task execution trigger functional reversals in emotion content: these occur as a "response to the relational meaning of an encounter in terms of a person's perception of the harms and benefits" (Lazarus, 1993, p. 13). Anecdotal data and preliminary findings accord with

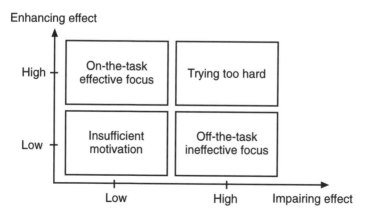

Figure 3.4 Interactive effects of emotion and performance prediction.

this conceptualization (Hanin, 1994, 1995; Hanin & Syrjä, 1995b, 1996, 1997; Pesonen, 1995; Saarnio, 1995; Tarvonen, 1995). Specifically, optimal emotions (P+N+) before and during activity are usually anticipatory and are triggered by appraisals of challenge and threat. In contrast, situationally dysfunctional emotions (P–N–) are usually triggered by premature perception of achieved outcomes (appraisals of gain and loss) before task completion. Since athletes continually reappraise their performance process, they tend to shift from the anticipatory, active mind-set to the outcome emotion—a relatively passive "I did it" response. Prematurely experiencing an outcome emotion (P–N–) may result in impaired energy mobilization, utilization, or both, and a sudden drop in performance. More research is needed to test the validity of the psychosocial interpretation of emotion-performance dynamics.

Effort (Energy) and Skill Facilitating/Inhibitory Functions

The psychobiological perspective in interpretation of emotion-performance relationships has been detailed and substantiated elsewhere (Hanin, 1997a, 1997b); therefore the following sections outline only the main features.

Two constructs related to energizing and organizing aspects of emotion may account for the impact of emotions upon performance process (Hanin, 1993, 1994, 1995): energy mobilization (demobilization) and energy utilization (misuse). Energy here resembles Martens's notion of psychic energy as "vigor, vitality, and intensity with which mind functions" (1987, p. 92), but also more generally signifies an active force, vigor, vitality, intensity of effort (see *Collins English Dictionary*, 1991), persistence, and decisiveness. Thus, the major focus is on the functional meaning of emotions, both positive and negative. In contrast to other views (Martens, 1987; Loehr, 1982a), the IZOF model makes no distinction between physical and psychic energy or between positive and negative energy.

The constructs of energy mobilization and energy utilization were derived from anecdotal evidence in applied work with top athletes (Hanin, 1978), as well as from content analysis of the functional interpretation of emotion patterns by athletes (see chapter 7; Hanin, 1993, 1994, 1995; Hanin & Syrjä, 1995a, 1995b).

Interestingly, these two aspects of emotion's effect on behavior were implicit in several conceptualizations of emotion and arousal or activation functions in mainstream psychology (Duffy, 1951, 1962; Neiss, 1988; Oatley & Jenkins, 1992; Thayer, 1978). Many researchers in European sport psychology used "mobilization" in describing psychological readiness for competition (Puni, 1969; Genov, 1976). Researchers and practitioners occasionally referred to energizing aspects of arousal and energizing intervention techniques (Aleksejev, 1969; Annesi, 1998; Blumenstein, Bar-Eli, & Tenenbaum, 1997; Burton, 1990; Gissen, 1973; Il'in, 1980; Klavora, 1979; Landers & Boutcher, 1986; Loehr, 1982a, 1994; Machac, 1976; Mahoney & Avener, 1977; Martens, 1987;

Sonstroem, 1986; Weinberg & Hunt, 1976; Zaichkowski & Takenaka, 1993). However, neither energy mobilization nor energy utilization was used as an explanatory principle.

In the IZOF model, *functioning* emphasizes the role of optimal functions of emotions in performance quality (Hanin, 1993, 1994, 1995). One such function is optimal task involvement as manifested in one's readiness to perform up to one's potential through active and sustained efforts. This becomes possible through

- ▶ generating enough energy to initiate and maintain the task with an adequate effort level and
- ▶ efficient use of available resources until successful task completion.

Dysfunctional emotions typically result in too much (or too little) energy generation in relation to the resources available and in inefficient, erroneous, or inappropriate use (e.g., task-irrelevant focus or faulty information processing). From these two factors, four relatively independent global emotion functions are derived:

1. An energizing or energy-mobilizing (M+) function
2. An energy-demobilizing (M−) function
3. An energy utilization or regulation (U+) function
4. An energy misuse or deregulation (U−) function

These functions allow us to interpret separate and interactive effects of emotions upon performance. Depending on the interactions, the total impact of emotions can be optimal (in both effort and skill), para-optimal (only effort or skill is optimal), or dysfunctional (in both effort and skill) (figure 3.5).

Several exploratory unpublished studies reported by Hanin (Hanin, 1992, 1997a; Hanin & Syrjä, 1995a; Syrjä, 1993) showed that positive optimal emotions usually serve mobilizing and organizing functions, whereas negative optimal emotions are typically more instrumental in energy production than in energy utilization. The dysfunctional effect of positive emotions (for instance, complacency) may cause a reversal in energy generation—an athlete prematurely stops working or fails to invest even minimum effort (energy demobilization effect). Positive dysfunctional emotions also disturb utilization of available resources due to a low alertness level or inefficient information processing; negative dysfunctional emotions trigger erroneous or inappropriate use of energy by distracting resources to task-irrelevant (performance damaging) aspects of the situation. Additionally, sometimes the motivational effect of negative emotions triggering increased energy and effort (Eysenck & Calvo, 1992; Mahoney & Avener, 1977) results in overload of the cue utilization or control function (Easterbrook, 1959).

From the functional effect perspective, the constructs of energy mobilization and utilization help explain why in some athletes optimal emotions are

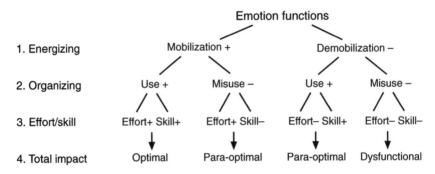

Figure 3.5 IZOF-based conceptualization of emotion function.

predominantly positive and in others negative. For instance, low-anxious athletes are typically "smart users" of energy and less distracted by task-irrelevant concerns. High-anxious athletes typically generate more energy because they often use energy less efficiently due to narrow attention focus and information-processing overload. Thus negative emotions such as anxiety are functionally useful in helping these athletes generate the additional compensatory energy. Since the quality of performance relates to both the amount and the use of energy, different athletes can achieve the same level of performance either through increasing total effort or skillfully utilizing available resources (efficiency).

This interpretation seems consistent with anecdotal data and empirical findings indicating that high-anxious subjects used "more energy than necessary" and expended it over a longer duration (Weinberg, 1978; Weinberg & Hunt, 1976). They were also less efficient in energy expenditure than their low-anxious counterparts. However, since resources and their control or utilization are limited-capacity functions (Kahneman, 1973), their interaction is the critical factor for successful performance. For instance, excessive or uncontrolled energy production can overload or disturb processing efficiency (Eysenck & Calvo, 1992; Humphreys & Revelle, 1984; Lang, 1984; Simonov, 1970), resulting in impaired performance. It is argued, therefore, that one can better predict the total emotion impact upon performance on the basis of interactive rather than separate effects of energy mobilization and energy utilization functions.

CONTRASTING THE IZOF MODEL WITH OTHER APPROACHES

As mentioned earlier, the IZOF model is consistent with several existing orientations within psychology. The IZOF model differs mainly in its emphasis on intraindividual dynamics in emotion-performance relationships. Furthermore, the aim is motivational—to present individually oriented, task-relevant, and restructured information about an athlete's subjective performance-related experiences and thus to influence a person's awareness, acceptance, and intention to systematically and actually use his or her subjective experiences. But the intent here is not to show that the IZOF model is better than others. Moreover, if "all models are wrong [in some respect . . . then] our task is to try to find the most useful models to help [describe, predict, and] interpret our data" (Schutz, 1998, p. 406). Interested readers may consult recent reviews addressing, for instance, anxiety-performance relationships (Gill, 1994; Gould & Krane, 1992; Gould & Tuffey, 1996; Hardy, 1996; Jones, 1995a; Landers, 1994; Morgan, 1997b; Raglin, 1992; Weinberg, 1990). Additionally, several chapters in this book outline approaches to primary emotions such as anxiety (chapter 4), anger (chapter 5), and joy (chapter 6) and to repeated emotion patterns (chapters 8-11).

The remaining sections here outline major differences between the IZOF model and other approaches to studying emotion-performance relationships in high-achievement settings.

Conceptual Distinctions Between the IZOF Model and Other Approaches

The IZOF model differs conceptually from other orientations to emotion-performance relationships in several ways.

1. **The IZOF framework recognizes that emotion is a major component of the performance-related psychobiosocial state.** The model not only emphasizes the importance of systemic multidimensional description of psychobiosocial states, but also uses a penta-basis to identify components and markers within each dimension. Furthermore, although the model emphasizes the intraindividual level, it does not exclude other levels. Other models and nomothetic orientations focus mainly on selected form (usually cognitive-somatic) and intensity (high-low) dimensions of emotion outside the context of performance-related psychobiosocial states.

2. **The IZOF model conceptualizes emotion content within four global emotion categories (P+N+P–N–) derived from two factors: hedonic tone and predominant functional impact upon performance process.** To provide a tentative structure to help identify performance-induced emotions really experienced by athletes in a wide range of situations, this emotion content is individually relevant and also functionally meaningful for subsequent content analysis within the existing conceptualizations of emotion content (basic emotions, global affect, or performance-related functions). In contrast, nomothetic orientations using psychometric scales depend on available instruments with "fixed" emotion content based on unquestioned researcher-generated items. Thus, a functional interpretation of emotion-performance relationships is often unrelated to the content of actually experienced emotions or to specifics of the performance process.

3. **The IZOF model proposes empirically established criteria (zones) to evaluate individually optimal intensity of emotion, and the in-out of the zone principle predicts either individually optimal or poor performance.** Unlike nomothetic orientations, this model is motivational and user oriented. Descriptions of emotion-performance relationships at the group or interindividual level usually do not specify individually optimal intensity of specific emotions. Moreover, claims about the shapes (inverted-U, linear) of unidirectional emotion-performance relationships have never been empirically scrutinized. Two to three cross-sectional measures of anxiety at the group level cannot describe the dynamics of emotion-performance relationships within the whole working range of intensity (see chapter 7; Hanin, 1997c).

4. **The IZOF model considers the interactive effects of optimal and dysfunctional emotions.** Prediction of individually excellent, average, and poor performance is based on the interaction of optimal and impairing effects of various emotions. Until recently, nomothetic models typically considered multiple dimensions separately (Gill, 1994); several investigators from these orientations have now examined interaction effects (Gould et al., 1993; Hardy, 1990, 1996; Kerr, 1997; Krane, 1993; Morgan, 1985, 1997a, 1997b).

5. **The IZOF model attempts to provide tentative functional explanations of emotion-performance relationships from the psychosocial and psychobiological perspectives.** These perspectives are based on empirical data and realities of sport activity. Other approaches emphasize group-level descriptions of emotion-performance relationships and testing of hypotheses and models developed in non-sport settings (test-anxiety approach, cusp catastrophe model, reversal theory).

Methodological Distinctions Between the IZOF Model and Other Approaches

Methodologically, several features distinguish the IZOF model from other systems.

▶ The IZOF framework is conceptually broad and therefore not limited to specific instruments. Individually optimal zones can be assessed using standardized instruments such as STAI, POMS, CSAI-2, PANAS, and BAS (body awareness scale). The in-out of the zone notion and assumptions about athletes' awareness of and ability to accurately report their subjective emotional experiences (Hanin, 1980, 1989, 1992, 1997a, 1997b, 1997c; Hanin & Syrjä, 1996) allow assessment of emotion intensities even within the nomothetic framework.

▶ The IZOF model provides a structure, as well as step-wise procedures, for developing and validating individualized scales with individually relevant emotion content. Additionally, IZOF-based assessment takes into account the dynamics of individual subjective experiences (enhanced awareness, development of emotion patterns for new and more demanding tasks).

▶ The IZOF-based methodology developed for emotions may be used in assessing other components of the psychobiosocial state such as cognitive, motivational, bodily-somatic, motor-behavioral, performance, and communicative (see appendixes).

SUMMARY

This chapter overviewed the theoretical underpinnings of the IZOF approach based on concepts from educational, social, personality, and performance enhancement psychology. The IZOF model, an integrative framework for studying emotions in sport, examines the multidimensionality of subjective performance-related experiences. A systems description of psychobiosocial states offers a comprehensive approach to characterizing and conceptualizing subjective emotional experiences. Emotion represents an important component of psychobiosocial state that is closely related to the other modalities (domains) of total human functioning. The content of emotions in sport is described through a two-factor categorization including hedonic tone and the impact of emotions upon performance. These four categories provide a framework for identifying prototypes of individually optimal and dysfunctional positive and negative emotions. The in-out of the zone concept is proposed as a principle for predicting and accounting for separate and interaction effects in emotion-performance relationships for individuals and groups.

Basic Emotions
and Athletic Performance

CHAPTER 4

Competitive Anxiety

John S. Raglin and Yuri L. Hanin
United States/Finland

Of all the psychological factors thought to influence sport performance, anxiety is often considered the most important. Sport psychologists have produced scores of articles, manuals, and tapes to help athletes deal with anxiety. Yet considerable disagreement remains about the most useful theory of anxiety and sport performance, as well as the most appropriate instrument for measuring anxiety in athletes (Ostrow, 1996). There is also growing acknowledgment that traditional theories of anxiety and performance have fared poorly in the case of sport. Moreover, the importance of individual differences in athletes' responses to anxiety is now recognized, and several theories of sport performance have been developed to account for this heterogeneity (Fazey & Hardy, 1988; Hanin, 1978; Kerr, 1989).

This chapter will focus on one such explanation, the Zones of Optimal Functioning (ZOF) model—on its development as applied to anxiety and on findings from research involving ZOF procedures. The successor of the ZOF model—the Individual Zones of Optimal Functioning (IZOF) model (described in greater detail in chapters 3 and 7)—is also outlined.

DEFINITION AND MEASUREMENT OF ANXIETY

Spielberger (1972) defined anxiety as an emotional reaction to a stimulus perceived as dangerous. This stimulus, or "stressor," results in dysphoric thoughts and feelings, unpleasant sensations, and physical changes. If a person does not find a stimulus threatening, then changes in anxiety should not result: the same stimulus may be perceived as a beneficial challenge to one individual, threatening to another, and neutral to a third.

Means of assessing anxiety include observation of overt behavior, physiological indicators (e.g., heart rate, galvanic skin activity, stress hormones), and self-report (Hackfort & Schwenkmezger, 1989). Each approach has limitations. Assessments of behaviors indicating anxiety can be time consuming or even misleading: the behavior (e.g., pacing) may be unrelated to anxiety or may be a coping strategy that reduces anxiety. Commonly used physiological assessments of anxiety (e.g., heart rate) are sometimes unrelated to anxiety state and often invasive. Thus, anxiety is most commonly assessed through self-report.

Self-report measures have been developed to assess both transitory and stable aspects of anxiety (Spielberger, 1972). Because psychological states can change dramatically in intensity from moment to moment, it is important to measure *state anxiety*, or anxiety intensity at a given time (Spielberger, Gorsuch, Lushene, Vagg, & Jacobs, 1983). *Trait anxiety* refers to an individual's general tendency to experience elevations in state anxiety when exposed to stressors. Persons high in trait anxiety should experience greater increases in state anxiety when exposed to a stressor than those low in trait anxiety. In fact, athletes with higher levels of trait anxiety do exhibit greater increases in state anxiety before competition than low-trait-anxious athletes (Raglin & Turner, 1993; Hanin, 1978, 1986).

Although self-report measures provide advantages over most physiological assessments of anxiety, they also have limitations. The validity and reliability of self-report measures can be affected by verbal ability and the level of self-awareness (Hackfort & Schwenkmezger, 1989). Responses may be distorted by social desirability, demand characteristics, and expectations (both social and experimental), any of which may invalidate self-reports. Repeated assessments of state anxiety, especially over a short time span, can result in habituation, or stereotypical responses. Finally, assessing anxiety prior to competition may be distracting or may actually alter responses by directing attention to emotional states (Hackfort & Schwenkmezger, 1993). Despite these problems, most researchers agree that appropriately used, validated self-report measures provide accurate assessments of anxiety. There is some disagreement as to whether measures specific to context (e.g., sport) or subtypes of anxiety components (e.g., somatic) are more accurate than general measures.

TRADITIONAL THEORETICAL PERSPECTIVES

Sport psychologists have long believed that high levels of anxiety during competition are harmful, worsening performance and even leading to dropout (LeUnes & Nation, 1996; Martens, Vealey, & Burton, 1990). Another widely accepted assumption is that all positive emotions facilitate sport performance. Consequently, sport psychology interventions have almost exclusively involved techniques to control or reduce anxiety (Taylor, 1996) and enhance positive affect. Typical methods include hypnosis, progressive relaxation, visualization, biofeedback, autogenic training, meditation, negative thought stopping, and confidence enhancement (Martens et al., 1990; Taylor, 1996).

Drive Theory

Despite the common belief that anxiety is detrimental, it has been proposed that anxiety may sometimes facilitate performance. Drive, or Hullian, theory holds that performance is a function of drive (i.e., physiological arousal or anxiety) and habit strength (Hull, 1943). For well-learned skills, high anxiety levels will increase the likelihood of correct behavior. Hence, in a highly skilled athlete, stressful interventions such as emotional pep talks should enhance performance. Evidence for drive theory in sport settings, however, is absent and methodological problems in drive theory research are common (Martens, 1971; Raglin, 1992). Currently the theory has little support in sport psychology.

The Inverted-U Hypothesis

In contrast, theoretical explanations indicating that high anxiety harms performance have had high standing in sport psychology—perhaps none more so than the Yerkes-Dodson law, or inverted-U hypothesis. In a classic study, Yerkes and Dodson (1908) examined the influence of stimulus intensity on habit formation in mice using a maze discrimination task. Electrical shocks of varying intensities served as the stimulation and illumination was manipulated to alter discrimination difficulty. An interaction between stimulus intensity and discrimination difficulty was observed, and in some trials habit formation was hastened by shocks. The highest-intensity shocks tended to slow learning under the most difficult maze trial, suggesting that moderate stimulation was best for such conditions.

Whereas Yerkes and Dodson examined the influence of the intensity of a single aversive stimulus (i.e., electrical shock), their results have been generalized to a variety of constructs. These include drive, motivation, and learning; but the hypothesis is most commonly associated with arousal (Teigen, 1994; Winton, 1987). The construct of global arousal, which came into use in the 1940s, is defined as a generalized state of physiological activation that may range from very low (i.e., sleep) to extremely high. Because the physiological responses associated with arousal are generalized and systemic, physiological measures should be highly intercorrelated (Gould & Krane, 1992). Consequently, one physiological variable, most commonly heart rate, is usually considered a valid measure of arousal. Similarly, because arousal has been widely implicated in dysphoric emotional states, particularly anxiety (Duffy, 1957), self-report measures of psychological state have also been assumed to accurately indicate arousal. Consequently, the Yerkes-Dodson results were generalized to humans as optimal arousal theory (Malmo, 1959; Hebb, 1976).

Inverted-U Modifications Considering Motor Task Requirements and Skill

The inverted-U hypothesis has been modified to account for variations in motor requirements and differences in skill levels. Some suggest that sport tasks requiring precise motor control and minimum physical effort (e.g., putting in golf) benefit when anxiety or physiological arousal is relatively low (Oxendine, 1970). Higher anxiety levels should facilitate sport tasks requiring greater physical effort and less motor control (e.g., shot putting). Accordingly, one can locate sport tasks on a continuum of low to high anxiety depending on their motor requirements. This modification stems largely from Yerkes and Dodson's finding that as the maze task became more difficult, the optimal level of stimulation (i.e., electrical shock) decreased. However, Neiss (1988) has reported a lack of evidence for the inverted-U hypothesis in electrical shock studies, stating, "There is no basis for the assumption that all stressors are equivalent producers of undifferentiated arousal" (p. 349).

As adapted further for sport, the inverted-U hypothesis considers skill level and sport experience. Just as increased anxiety should benefit performance in sport tasks requiring substantial physical effort, it has generally been assumed that a skilled athlete should be able to harness higher anxiety than a less skilled individual, whatever the task (LeUnes & Nation, 1996). Hence, in any sport, optimal anxiety should be highest in the most skilled performers. With adequate information about sport and skill level, one should be able to establish an inverted-U for any athlete (Landers & Boutcher, 1986).

Surprisingly, few have attempted to empirically test either of these modifications to the inverted-U hypothesis (Raglin, 1992). Research does not support the contention that optimal anxiety levels are a function of the motor skills (i.e., fine or gross) required for a sporting event (Imlay, Carda, Stanbrough, & O'Connor, 1995; Krane & Williams, 1994). Nor is there evidence that comparably skilled athletes in the same sport benefit from similar anxiety levels (Sonstroem & Bernardo, 1982; Morgan, O'Connor, Ellickson, & Bradley, 1988; Morgan, O'Connor, Sparling, & Pate, 1987). In part because of the problems mentioned previously, two other sport-specific perspectives have been derived from traditional explanations, test anxiety studies, and other research: the multidimensional theory of Martens et al. (1990) and the cusp catastrophe model (Fazey & Hardy, 1988). Each further develops the arousal/ anxiety-performance relationship by questioning the unidimensional conceptualization and assessment of anxiety. Brief accounts of these theories follow; readers may also consult more detailed reviews (Landers & Boutcher, 1998; Raglin, 1999).

Multidimensional Inverted-U Modifications

Sport psychologists increasingly view unidimensional conceptualizations to the arousal/anxiety-performance relationship as ineffective and simplistic (Fazey & Hardy, 1988; Gould & Krane, 1992; Hardy, 1990; Jones, 1995b; Landers, 1994; Weinberg, 1989, 1990). Several investigators have proposed more complex theories involving multiple anxiety components that exert independent or interactive effects on athletic performance (Burton, 1990; Fazey & Hardy, 1988; Gould, Tuffey, Hardy, & Lochbaum, 1993; Hardy, 1990; Martens et al., 1990; Smith, Smoll, & Schultz, 1990).

Martens et al. (1990) proposed a multidimensional theory of sport anxiety involving three components—cognitive anxiety, self-confidence, and somatic anxiety. Their 27-item Competitive State Anxiety Inventory (CSAI-2) assesses these dimensions. Multidimensional theory predicts separate effects of each anxiety component upon athletic performance: thus optimal intensity levels should be moderate and in the form of a quadratic function (i.e., inverted-U) for somatic anxiety; high and in the form of positive linear function (i.e., drive theory) for self-confidence; and low and in the form of a negative linear function for cognitive anxiety. Multidimensional theory assumes implicitly that cognitive and somatic anxiety have additive rather than interactive effects on performance (Hardy, 1990, 1996). However, other researchers contend that the influence of different aspects of anxiety is even more complex. An alternative cusp catastrophe model of anxiety and performance has been proposed to describe how cognitive anxiety, self-confidence, and somatic anxiety interact to influence performance (Gould & Krane, 1992; Fazey & Hardy, 1988; Hardy, 1990). These factors are assumed to form a three-dimensional function in the shape referred to as a butterfly cusp. However, much of the research on this model has been limited to cognitive and somatic anxiety.

While some evidence supports the catastrophe model, its practicality has been questioned because of the complexity of testing its basic assumptions. As Gill (1994) states, "Catastrophe theory . . . is incredibly limiting in comparison to the broader implications of Lazarus's model" (p. 24). Therefore it is unknown whether the proposed interaction effects of anxiety components upon performance generally hold, or whether they apply to a wider range of positive and negative emotions (see chapters 3 and 7).

In addition, Gould and Tuffey (1996) have identified a serious concern regarding multidimensional anxiety that has implications for the catastrophe model. These reviews cite evidence that the traditional worry-emotionality dichotomy may be too simplistic, even more specific components of anxiety may actually exist. If so, this would indicate the need to examine a wider range of negative and positive emotions than traditionally studied in sport (Hanin, 1995, 1997a; Kerr, 1989; Morgan, 1985; Prapavessis & Grove, 1991).

Criticisms of the Inverted-U Hypothesis

While most sport psychologists have uncritically accepted the inverted-U hypothesis, the general literature shows that empirical support is surprisingly weak (Näätänen, 1973), if not altogether absent (Neiss, 1988).

A general assumption has been that anxiety influences performance through its effects on cognitive (Humphreys & Revelle, 1984) and attentional resources (Easterbrook, 1959). Elevations in anxiety or arousal have been hypothesized to result in a reduction in the span of attentional awareness, with the degree of narrowing in the span corresponding to the increase in anxiety. With increased anxiety, the reduced attentional capacity should eventually lead to a decline in performance as crucial information is not perceived (Easterbrook, 1959). Related explanations propose that high levels of arousal or anxiety interfere with cognitive memory retrieval (Eysenck & Calvo, 1992; Humphreys & Revelle, 1984) or result in non-task-oriented cognition. However, the research is not entirely consistent with these contentions (Allard, Brawley, Deakin, & Elliot, 1989), and some evidence suggests that elevated anxiety may selectively restrict central rather than peripheral vision (Shapiro & Lim, 1989). Negative mood has also been found to be associated with enhanced information processing in some tasks (Schwarz, 1990).

Another common assumption is that physiological changes associated with high anxiety interfere with performance. However, Landers and Boutcher (1998) cite evidence that elite pistol shooters benefited from increased physiological activity during competition. Some performed well with heart rates over 50 beats per minute above resting; those whose heart rates did not increase by at least 5 beats per minute performed poorly. This example counters the inverted-U hypothesis that high physiological activation is particularly harmful to performance in fine-motor tasks. Another proposal is that excessive muscle tension compromises performance and may increase the risk of injury (Williams & Roepke, 1993). Again, however, empirical evidence is lacking: elevated muscle tension is common in chronic anxiety disorders (Hoehn-Saric, McLeod, & Zimmerli, 1989) but less consistently observed in the acute anxiety responses of nonclinical populations. Because of the lack of support regarding excessive muscle tension or other biological changes, Eysenck and Calvo (1992) conclude that physiological factors "make no more than a minor contribution to the anxiety-performance relationship" (p. 413).

Yerkes and Dodson (1908) examined the influence of stimulus intensity on learning and did not assess physiological responses later associated with arousal (Teigen, 1994; Winton, 1987). Another criticism concerns the definition of arousal. Arousal was initially defined as a generalized and undifferentiated response to a stressor (Duffy, 1957), but subsequent research has consistently suggested otherwise. Physiological responses to stressors are complex and often poorly intercorrelated. Moreover, such responses vary across individuals and situations (Lacey, 1967). This variability has also been found in central nervous system measures. Neurotransmitters commonly associated with activation (e.g., dopamine, noradrenaline) exhibit "rather different, sometimes context dependent, functions in arousal-like processes" (Robbins, 1997, p. 67). Yet despite this evidence, sport psychologists continue to conceptualize arousal as an undifferentiated physiological response (Gould & Krane, 1992).

Critics also maintain that inverted-U research uses arbitrary and inconsistent definitions of moderate arousal (Neiss, 1988). Moreover, physiological measures of arousal are often unrelated to anxiety. For example, classic indicators of arousal such as elevations in heart rate have been found to be absent during episodes of intense anxiety, including panic attacks (Aronson, Carasiti, McBane, & Whitaker-Axmitia, 1989).

Additionally, the sport literature shows a lack of empirical support for the inverted-U hypothesis (Fazey & Hardy, 1988; Krane, 1992; Morgan & Ellickson, 1989; Raglin, 1992). In a meta-analysis of the sport anxiety literature, Kleine

(1990) concluded that "evidence for the inverted-U relationship is still rather scarce" (p. 125). According to critics, inverted-U studies have problems such as use of unrealistic laboratory settings and novel motor tasks (ecological validity), use of nonathlete samples (external validity), and failure to distinguish between subjects at different stages of skill acquisition (Morgan & Ellickson, 1989). Experimental evidence for the assumed interaction between sport task or skill on optimal anxiety level as posited in the inverted-U relationship also is lacking (Raglin, 1992).

Perhaps most importantly, reviewers conclude that the inverted-U hypothesis cannot account for differences in the way athletes respond to anxiety (Fazey & Hardy, 1988; Kleine, 1990; Morgan & Ellickson, 1989; Raglin, 1992). Neiss (1988) argues, "The inverted-U hypothesis has primarily served thus far to obscure these important individual differences" (p. 355). Even reviewers sympathetic to the inverted-U hypothesis acknowledge that supportive evidence comes primarily from cognitive and not motor tasks, and that the "arousal-performance relationship may differ across these two domains of functioning" (Anderson, 1990, p. 99).

A SPORT-BASED THEORY OF ANXIETY AND PERFORMANCE: ZOF

The inadequacy of traditional theories such as the inverted-U hypothesis in sport settings has spurred development of alternative explanations specific to athletics. Among these, the theory of Zones of Optimal Functioning, now referred to as the Individual Zones of Optimal Functioning model, may have the strongest empirical basis (Landers & Boutcher, 1998).

Development of the ZOF Model

The ZOF model, developed by Hanin (1978, 1986, 1989, 1995, 1997a), originated in research assessing anxiety in several thousand athletes before competition. Athletes from many sports and competitive settings completed the Russian language version of the State-Trait Anxiety Inventory (STAI), a general measure of anxiety. Although the findings identified anxiety as a significant factor in sport performance, they did not support an association between anxiety and performance at the group level. Rather, the relationship existed at the level of the individual athlete, arguing for an idiographic explanation. Thus Hanin (1978) proposed that each athlete possesses an optimal zone or range of anxiety most beneficial for performance. This zone may be anywhere on a continuum of anxiety from low to high. Importantly, neither the type of event nor the athlete's skill level systematically alters optimal anxiety. This assumption distinguishes the ZOF model from the inverted-U hypothesis.

The range of the optimal zone was initially chosen on the basis of group results (Hanin, 1978), and an upper and lower span of one-half standard deviation (4 units for the STAI) was found to work best in group-oriented research. However, later studies established that just as the optimal zone of anxiety may differ across athletes, so too can the width of the optimal range (Hanin, 1995, 1997a; Salminen, Liukkonen, Hanin, & Hyvönen, 1995). Some individuals can tolerate a wide range of anxiety intensity before experiencing a decline in performance, whereas others perform best only when anxiety lies within a very narrow range.

Establishing Optimal Anxiety Zones

Hanin has developed two methods to establish an athlete's optimal anxiety range. In the direct method, precompetition anxiety is assessed until an athlete has a personal best performance. The upper and lower limits of the optimal zone are established by adding and subtracting four anxiety units (i.e., one-half standard deviation) from the anxiety score obtained prior to best performance. A potentially serious concern with this approach is that anxiety data must be collected until the athlete has an outstanding or personal best performance, perhaps over weeks or months. Other limitations of actual assessments have been well documented (Hanin, 1986, 1995; Hanin & Syrjä, 1995b). For instance, actual self-ratings may be too invasive immediately before important competitions, distracting athletes or disturbing their preparation strategies (Harger & Raglin, 1994; McCann, Murphy, & Raedeke, 1992); and they are often not feasible during performance. Furthermore, repeated actual assessments are usually time consuming and cost ineffective.

Therefore an indirect method based on retrospection was developed. Athletes complete the STAI with instructions to respond according to how they recall feeling before their best past performances or, more generally, when performance is optimal or near optimal. As with the direct method, the optimal anxiety range is established by adding and subtracting one-half standard deviation from the recalled best score. Accuracy can be determined by correlating recalled anxiety scores with precompetition anxiety values actually obtained for the recalled performance, and coefficients of correlation ranging from .60 to .80 have been reported by Hanin (1978). More recent studies on recall ability have yielded similar or even higher coefficients (r = .70 to .96) in recall durations ranging from two days (Harger & Raglin, 1994) to 22 months (Turner & Raglin, 1996). Figure 4.1 presents the results of studies examining recall accuracy with the STAI.

Some have challenged the accuracy of the recall method (Gould et al., 1993; Krane, 1993). For example, Gould et al. (1993) argued that performance outcome could bias recall. However, the research has shown that recall accuracy at the group level provides results comparable to those obtained with the direct method for establishing optimal anxiety (Jokela & Hanin, 1997; Randle & Weinberg, 1997), and also that recall accuracy is comparable in athletes who performed either better or worse than expected (Harger & Raglin, 1994).

A more fundamental issue is whether people can make accurate attributions regarding past events. On the basis of a review by Nisbett and Wilson (1977), it has been argued that athletes may not be accurate in reporting

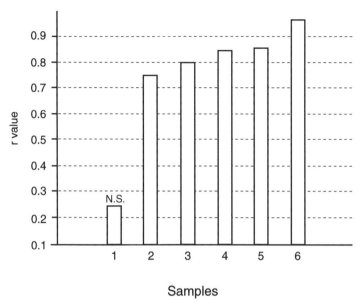

Samples

1. 7 months
   16 college track athletes (Imlay et al., 1995)
2. 3 months
   8 college women volleyballers (Raglin & Morris, 1994)
3. 3 months
   16 college track and field athletes (Imlay et al., 1995)
4. 4 months
   11 college track and field athletes (Raglin & Turner, 1993)
5. 22 months
   16 college track and field athletes (Turner & Raglin, 1996)
6. 2 days
   34 college track and field athletes (Harger & Raglin, 1994)

Figure 4.1   Correlations between actual and recalled precompetition anxiety (STAI) for different samples.

psychological states associated with past performance, especially for novel tasks or tasks with little personal relevance (Brewer, Van Raalte, Linder, & Van Raalte, 1991). Nisbett and Wilson (1977) summarized experimental evidence indicating that people often lack awareness of higher-order cognitive processes involved in decision making and the formation of attitudes. Applied to emotions, this would suggest that people may have little insight as to why they are experiencing an emotional state or what consequences a particular emotional state has for behavior (e.g., sport performance). In testing this possibility, Brewer et al. (1991) found differences in attributions of focus and greater confidence when performance outcome information was biased toward success in a motor skill task (rotary pursuit). These results, while limited to nonathletes performing in a laboratory setting, do suggest that higher-order attributions about athletic success may be subject to distorting biases. However, their relevance to the possibility of biasing recall accuracy of precompetition anxiety is questionable. Research consistently indicates that athletes are capable of accurately recalling anxiety levels associated with past competitions because of their high personal involvement in the activity, irrespective of performance level.

While athletes usually can accurately recall their emotional state for past performances, they may have little insight about the contributing factors (e.g., stressors). Athletes may be misled about which emotional or cognitive states facilitate or harm their performance, particularly with novel tasks. Blumberg and Wasserman (1995) cite an example from a study in a non-sport setting, in which stuttering was induced by exposing a subject to a continuous electrical shock and then withdrawing it whenever the subject stuttered. The subject did not correctly attribute the stuttering to the shock being withdrawn (i.e., negative reinforcement) when stuttering occurred, but instead to anxiety—mistakenly ascribing poor performance to an emotional state rather than to the causal stressor. The example of this phenomenon (which has been replicated elsewhere) is relevant because a recent revision of the most widely used sport-specific anxiety measure, the CSAI-2, establishes optimal anxiety by having athletes indicate whether anxiety items are beneficial or harmful to their performance (Jones, 1995b). Instead of simply recalling emotional state before a best performance as with the ZOF method, athletes must determine the consequences of specific anxiety factors on performance, the very type of higher-order attributions, it has been argued, that athletes can be biased in making (Brewer et al., 1991).

In summary, despite contentions that the recall method is flawed, the research consistently indicates that this approach for assessing optimal precompetition anxiety is sufficiently accurate for the majority of competitive and skilled athletes. However, some cases of inaccurate recall have been reported (Imlay et al., 1995; Raglin & Morris, 1994). In such instances, the direct method should be used.

Variability in Optimal Anxiety

The ZOF model also assumes that there should be considerable interindividual differences in the level of optimal anxiety associated with outstanding athletic performance. According to Hanin (1978, 1986) significant numbers of athletes indicate that high levels of anxiety are optimal for performance, and research with North American athletes has replicated this finding using recall. According to Morgan et al. (1987), 30% of a sample of elite U.S. women distance runners reported performing best when anxiety was significantly elevated. The percentage was even greater in a study of college track and field athletes, also using recall (Raglin & Turner, 1993): 51% of men and 48% of women reported best performances with high levels of anxiety (i.e., > one-half standard deviation above the published norm). Using a considerably higher cutoff of approximately two standard deviations above the norm, Imlay et al. (1995)

found that 19% of a sample of college track and field athletes had high optimal precompetition anxiety. Among players on a women's college volleyball team, 33.3% reported high optimal anxiety levels (Raglin & Morris, 1994). The percentage of younger athletes who report benefiting from high anxiety does not appear to differ from that for adults. In a study by Wilson and Raglin (1997), 26% of track and field athletes, aged from 9 to 12, indicated that they performed best with high anxiety.

Variability in optimal anxiety also does not appear to be related to average or typical levels of anxiety before competition. Turner and Raglin (1996) found that median precompetition anxiety, a measure that has been used to determine optimal anxiety according to the inverted-U hypothesis (Sonstroem & Bernardo, 1982), fell within the optimal zone in only 27.8% of cases.

Prediction of Precompetition Anxiety

Studies by Hanin (1978, 1986) indicate that athletes can also predict how anxious they will feel before upcoming competitions. In this research, athletes complete anxiety questionnaires several days before the competition with instructions to respond according to how they anticipate feeling immediately before the event. They again complete the questionnaire immediately before the competition under standard (i.e., "right now") instructions. (In some studies this has occurred at a prescribed interval before competition, such as 60 min, in an effort to minimize intrusiveness.)

Hanin (1978, 1986) reported that correlations between predicted and actual precompetition anxiety values generally ranged from .60 to .80, with higher coefficients for more difficult meets. While correlations of this magnitude are similar to the test-retest reliability of the STAI (Spielberger et al., 1983) and would be expected in within-subject assessments, importantly the mean values of predicted and actual precompetition anxiety assessments are quite similar.

When used in concert with optimal anxiety scores, predicted values are useful in identifying athletes likely to need some form of anxiety intervention at the time of competition. The discrepancy between predicted and optimal anxiety scores can indicate whether an athlete is likely to be too relaxed or too anxious, as well as how far from optimal the anxiety is likely to deviate. Identifying optimal or nonoptimal anxiety in athletes is crucial not only because anxiety responses are highly variable, but also because group-based interventions (i.e., either increasing or decreasing anxiety), as indicated by ZOF research, will often be unsuccessful.

Research with North American athletes has corroborated Hanin's (1978, 1986) reports. Studies of athletes in track and field, swimming, and volleyball have yielded correlations between predicted and actual anxiety generally within the range reported by Hanin. A recent meta-analysis of the IZOF anxiety studies (Jokela & Hanin, 1997) also supports the accuracy of precompetition anxiety predictions. In most studies, predicted anxiety is assessed from one to five days before actual competition; accuracy seems to be lower with longer intervals (e.g., 5 weeks) (Raglin & Morris, 1994). Figure 4.2 summarizes the results from a number of anxiety-prediction studies using the STAI.

Athletes' predictions of precompetition anxiety are not always accurate. Several studies involving adolescent female athletes showed nonsignificant correlations for easy or unimportant competitions; predicted values typically exceeded actual precompetition anxiety (Raglin, Morgan, & Wise, 1990; Raglin & Turner, 1992). But correlations for more difficult meets were comparable to those observed with adult athletes. The reasons for the results for easy meets are not clear, but one hypothesis concerns role orientation. Wilson and Raglin (1997) found that 9- and 10-year-old female track and field athletes accurately predicted precompetition anxiety for both easy and more difficult meets, whereas 11- and 12-year-old female athletes were inaccurate in the case of the

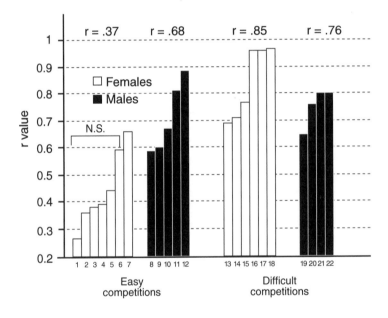

Samples

1. High school swimmers (N = 15)
2. 12-15-year-old track and field athletes (N = 17)
3. 9-10-year-old track and field athletes (N = 8)
4. High school swimmers (N = 17)
5. 16-18-year-old track and field athletes (N = 17)
6. College volleyballers (N = 9)
7. 11-12-year-old track and field athletes (N = 12)

8. 12-15-year-old track and field athletes (N = 10)
9. College swimmers (N = 16)
10. 16-18-year-old track and field athletes (N = 30)
11. 11-12-year-old track and field athletes (N = 14)
12. 9-10-year-old track and field athletes (N = 6)

13. College volleyballers (N = 9)
14. College track and field athletes (N = 26)
15. High school swimmers (N = 15)
16. High school swimmers (N = 17)
17. 9-10-year-old track and field athletes (N = 8)
18. 11-12-year-old track and field athletes (N = 12

19. 11-12-year-old track and field athletes (N = 14
20. College swimmers (N = 16)
21. College track and field athletes (N = 29)
22. 9-10-year-old track and field athletes (N = 6)

Figure 4.2 Correlations between predicted and actual precompetition anxiety (STAI) for different samples of female and male athletes.

easy meets. The authors suggested that sport participation may result in greater role conflict for the older girls, perhaps systematically biasing anxiety predictions. Further research is needed to explore this possibility. There is also some evidence that unsuccessful performers predict precompetition anxiety less accurately than their more successful counterparts (Raglin & Morgan, 1988; Raglin, Morgan, and O'Connor, 1991). However, one must recognize that predictions are more difficult than recall because they are based not only on awareness of past experiences but also on perception of the upcoming precompetition situation and factors that can alter it (Hanin, 1978).

The Influence of Optimal Anxiety on Sport Performance

Researchers have also used the ZOF model to examine the net effect of precompetition anxiety on sport performance. These studies used various methods to quantify performance, including subjective ratings by coaches or athletes and more objective interindividual or intraindividual criteria allowing standardization of results. Unfortunately, the use of such divergent performance criteria limits generalizability and direct comparisons across studies.

One such study examined the influence of anxiety on performance in a team of adolescent female swimmers (Raglin, Morgan, & Wise, 1990). Precompetition anxiety was assessed 1 hr before an easy and a difficult competition, and recalled optimal anxiety values were also obtained. The coach's performance ratings were used to categorize the swimmers as either successful or unsuccessful in each meet. In the case of the difficult meet, precompetition anxiety levels were closer to optimal for the successful swimmers than for those who performed poorly. Differences were not observed for the easy meet; the authors suggested that optimal anxiety may be less important for success in this situation. Other research (Salminen et al., 1995) has shown similar associations.

Imlay et al. (1995) studied 16 collegiate track and field athletes to determine whether above-average performances were related to optimal anxiety zones, assessing precompetition anxiety before seven competitions. The anxiety value for the best performance of each athlete during these competitions, in each case a personal best, was used to establish IZOF. Analysis of performances using national collegiate standards for different events showed that a greater percentage of the athletes who achieved good or outstanding performances had individually optimal anxiety values as compared to the percentage who had poor performances (63% vs. 31%, respectively, $p < .05$).

Another study addressed the net impact of anxiety on collegiate track and field athletes' performances according to the IZOF model and the inverted-U hypothesis (Raglin & Turner, 1993). Optimal anxiety was assessed via recall, and actual precompetition anxiety was assessed before three competitions. Individual performances, recorded for each meet, were transformed using four methods: (1) International Amateur Athletic Federation (IAAF) points; (2) a percentage based upon qualifying standards for national competition for the same event; (3) a percentage based on the athlete's personal best performance; and (4) a percentage based on the athlete's recent average performance. These transformations allowed analysis of performance results irrespective of event or sex. The authors also compared groups that possessed optimal and nonoptimal anxiety based on the inverted-U hypothesis using published optimal anxiety ranges for various sporting events (Landers & Boutcher, 1986). Performance based on national qualifying standards was significantly ($p < .05$) better for athletes whose precompetition anxiety values fell within their own optimal range. There was a similar but nonsignificant ($p = .06$) trend for contrasts based on IAAF standards; no tests of the inverted-U variants yielded significant differences.

Later, Turner and Raglin (1996) examined more closely the influence of optimal anxiety on sport performance. Precompetition anxiety was assessed in collegiate athletes before four meets, and optimal precompetition anxiety was determined via recall. Performances were recorded for each meet and transformed using three of the four methods just described. The results conformed to the IZOF model for each standard. Performance averaged approximately 2.0% higher ($p < .05$) in cases in which precompetition anxiety was inside the optimal range for IZOF. The inverted-U hypothesis was tested using published optimal anxiety tables for various sporting events and the median anxiety method for determining optimal anxiety (Sonstroem & Bernardo, 1982). For this method, the median level of anxiety an athlete experiences before a series of competitions is deemed optimal. To allow equitable contrasts, an optimal anxiety range equivalent to that with the ZOF method was formed around the median anxiety value.

The results for the median-based method were in the hypothesized direction but did not reach significance. For the sport task test of the inverted-U hypothesis, significant results were either nonsignificant or contrary to expectations. Additional contrasts were made for the ZOF results, and the mean performances for cases in which anxiety levels fell below or exceeded optimal anxiety were compared. Figure 4.3 summarizes these results. Performance decrements were largest when anxiety was within a one standard deviation range from optimal. Greater deviations from optimal anxiety were also associated with worsened performance—but surprisingly, the magnitude of the decrements was smaller than when the deviations from optimal were smaller. If the relationship between anxiety and performance described an inverted-U function, greater decrements would be expected. While the usual assumption is that too much anxiety is more common than too little (Taylor, 1996), precompetition anxiety was equally likely to be either above or below optimal. In addition, the decrement in performance was similar for the below- and above-optimal anxiety cases. The results reinforce Hanin's (1986) contention that athletes' anxiety responses are highly individual, again indicating that group-based anxiety interventions are likely to be counterproductive.

Salminen et al. (1995) used the IZOF model to study Finnish athletes in several sports. All athletes, via the Finnish language version of the STAI,

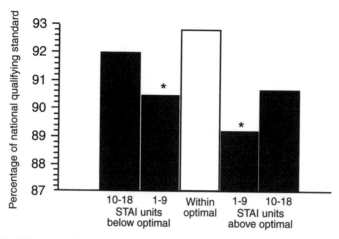

Figure 4.3 Mean performance in college track and field athletes with optimal precompetition anxiety or anxiety values at selected ranges above and below optimal (* < .05 from optimal).

Adapted, with permission, from P.E. Turner & J.S. Raglin, 1996, "Variability in precompetition anxiety and performance in college track and field athletes," *Medicine and Science in Sports and Exercise, 28,* 378-385.

completed retrospective recalls of best performance and assessments of anxiety within 2 hr of several competitions. Performance was self-rated following each competition using a 10-point scale. In the case of difficult competitions, performance ratings were higher ($p < .05$) for athletes whose precompetition anxiety fell within their own IZOF. A similar trend was observed for easier competitions but did not achieve significance.

ZOF Research With the Competitive State Anxiety Inventory-2

The studies thus far reviewed used versions of the STAI, a measure developed for general situations. However, some have proposed that multidimensional anxiety measures developed specifically for athletes will provide additional efficacy (Gould & Krane, 1992; Martens et al., 1990). The CSAI-2, which has been used in several ZOF studies, assesses self-confidence and somatic and cognitive anxiety. Gould et al. (1993) examined the efficacy of ZOF in college track athletes using the CSAI-2. Optimal anxiety was obtained via the retrospective method and compared with subjective performance ratings for each meet. The results were supportive of ZOF but, importantly, the authors diverged from previous ZOF research in their definition of optimal anxiety; there was no lower limit to the optimal range for cognitive anxiety. This resulted in a significant correlation of .30 with performance, whereas a standard definition of the optimal anxiety range according to ZOF procedures yielded a nonsignificant correlation of .24. The conclusion was that the multidimensional anxiety approach was more efficacious, despite a difference in explained variance of only 3.6% between the methods. The authors did not report what each anxiety component contributed to the overall correlation coefficient.

Krane (1993) examined the efficacy of ZOF in 16 members of a college women's soccer team using the CSAI-2. Optimal anxiety was defined as the best performance for the meets assessed, and the optimal anxiety ranges were determined using the procedure of Gould et al. (1993) rather than according to Hanin (1978, 1986). Performance in each meet was a composite score derived from various offensive and defensive statistics. General support for the ZOF model was obtained (although it should be noted that optimal anxiety ranges were based on one standard deviation cutoffs versus the one-half standard deviation used in most ZOF research). When either cognitive or somatic anxiety exceeded the optimal range, performance worsened. Performance was not adversely affected when anxiety fell below the optimal range, in contrast to findings from other ZOF studies based on the STAI (Turner & Raglin, 1996). However, statistical power was probably insufficient to test this possibility, as cases of below-optimal anxiety were few.

Randle and Weinberg (1997) examined the efficacy of ZOF in 13 female softball players. Cognitive, somatic, and combined cognitive/somatic anxiety zones were established for each athlete under three conditions (retrospective-best, immediate retrospective-postcompetition, and actual precompetition) and in the final analysis were aggregated based on similarity of group scores. Performance was established using subjective ratings; however, total scores were not specified. Although optimal cognitive and somatic anxiety showed large interindividual variability even in this small sample, the results did not support the ZOF-based predictions of performance. In fact, performances were better (close to the average level) when anxiety was outside the optimal aggregated combined cognitive/somatic range. Easy and difficult competitions were not differentiated, and, as already mentioned, there is evidence (Raglin, Morgan, & Wise, 1990; Salminen et al., 1995) that effects of optimal anxiety may be limited to difficult competitions. In team sports particularly, athletes are more influenced by intragroup and interpersonal communication both before and during the game; thus they are less preoccupied with their own concerns, and their emotional states can change more often. Researchers therefore need not only to identify optimal patterns of anxiety but also to determine how dynamic anxiety is across pregame and during-game situations. Additionally, the differences between pregame and during-game anxiety could be very large across athletes.

Woodman, Albinson, and Hardy (1997) used ZOF procedures to assess precompetition anxiety responses in 25 adult amateur bowlers via the cognitive and somatic subscales of the CSAI-2. Anxiety was assessed 20 min before the first game of 6 to 18 matches consisting of four games each. Optimal bowling performance of each subject was the score for the first game of all matches assessed; the subsequent three games were not considered. Again there was considerable interindividual variability in optimal anxiety. For cognitive anxiety, optimal scores ranged from 12 to 27; for somatic anxiety, the range was 9 to 23. Both cognitive and somatic anxiety were considered within a bowler's ZOF if the CSAI-2 score was within one-half standard deviation from optimal. For each subscale, anxiety was divided into three levels—below zone, in zone, and above zone. Performance means were plotted against these categories and, consistent with the ZOF model, performances tended to be better when anxiety levels fell within the optimal zone. However, interaction effects were found for anxiety type. Performances tended to be poorer when somatic anxiety was above the optimal zone, whether or not cognitive anxiety was optimal. According to the authors, these findings were contrary to the multidimensional theory underlying the CSAI-2; they concluded that the theory is "incomplete and overly simplistic" (p. 137). However, in other ZOF research using the CSAI-2, wider optimal anxiety ranges were used for cognitive anxiety as compared to somatic anxiety. Thus it is unclear whether these theoretical approaches are as divergent as Woodman and colleagues propose. The authors also found only partial support for the cusp catastrophe model.

To summarize, ZOF research involving STAI and CSAI-2 has generally been supportive of the model. Some contend that use of a multidimensional anxiety inventory specific to athletes, as compared to general measures such as the STAI, should provide additional efficacy. However, available evidence does not indicate that the efficacy of the ZOF model is improved by use of the CSAI-2 or adaptation of other theoretical approaches such as multidimensional anxiety theory or the catastrophe model. Somewhat surprisingly, no CSAI-2 study reviewed here used the self-confidence subscale of the instrument, even though self-confidence is a basic feature of both the multidimensional anxiety theory and the cusp catastrophe model. This research trend calls into question the importance of the self-confidence construct in multidimensional anxiety research.

Critiques of the ZOF Model

Despite the evidence supporting various aspects of the ZOF model, there has been criticism. Some reviewers fault the model for failing to explain individual differences in anxiety responses between athletes or to explain why anxiety may harm or help performance (Gould & Tuffey, 1996; Jones, 1995b). In fact, most published ZOF research has emphasized testing of the major tenets rather than providing explanations for interindividual variability in optimal anxiety. However, theoretical speculation would be inappropriate given the status of ZOF as a model. Moreover, a criticism of sport psychology has been its application of theory in the absence of an adequate database (Kane, 1970; Landers, 1994; Morgan, 1980b). Kane (1970) has argued that this may result in "the facile shifting of theoretical perspectives to accommodate all the contemporary moods and 'mini-theories' in psychology" (p. 236). Kane's concerns remain relevant. For example, the multidimensional anxiety theory of sport performance underlying the CSAI-2 has undergone significant revision since first presented by Martens et al. (1990), having recently been reconceptualized within the framework of the ZOF model (Krane, 1993).

Critics have also argued that ZOF research relies on a general measure of state anxiety rather than a sport-specific measure assessing multiple aspects of anxiety (Gould & Tuffey, 1996; Jones, 1995b), particularly the CSAI-2. Yet evidence suggests the CSAI-2 is less sensitive in assessing recalled and predicted precompetition anxiety (Annesi, 1997; Raglin & Turner, 1993), and the results of CSAI-2 research with the ZOF model have been mixed (e.g., Randle & Weinberg, 1997). In addition, not all agree that the CSAI-2 is an advance in sport anxiety research (Raglin, 1992). For example, Landers (1994) has concluded that the scale does not represent an improvement over more general measures; Landers and Boutcher (1998) argue that CSAI-2 research "does not yet constitute impressive or even promising evidence" (p. 209). Finally, recent factor-analytical research indicates that the CSAI-2 possesses four factors rather than three as originally conceptualized (Lane & Terry, in press), and other work (Lane, Terry, & Karageorghis, 1995) has failed to find unique antecedents to cognitive and somatic anxiety as hypothesized by the instrument's authors.

The question of what specific factors are most important to incorporate in a sport anxiety scale is crucial if such measures are to provide improvements over validated general anxiety scales now in use. For example, Endler and Parker (1990) found that an anxiety subscale for physical danger provides explanatory power not obtained with other traditional anxiety factors, and this subscale would seem relevant for many sporting contexts. Yet, of the more than 30 published anxiety scales developed for sport, none contain items pertaining to the risk of physical harm (Ostrow, 1996). Finally, in the development of measures, sport specificity was until quite recently limited to context specificity, whereas the relevancy of individual items describing emotional experiences of athletes was ignored (Syrjä & Hanin, 1997a, 1997b).

Although the idea of psychological instruments specific to sport is inherently appealing and may lead to greater explanatory power, one must acknowledge that sport itself is far from homogeneous. Any sport-specific anxiety measure is unlikely to adequately encompass the variability in conditions and athletics. Moreover, the very specificity of sport anxiety scales may make them overly restrictive. By focusing entirely on stressors directly linked with sport competition and performance, these scales may be insensitive to the impact of stress from sources not directly related to sport.

THE IZOF MODEL

Recently, Hanin (1995, 1997a) has extended the ZOF model into the IZOF model. The following sections outline the major features of the model; chapters 3 and 7 provide a fuller explanation.

Most significantly, the broader IZOF model includes not just the single emotional state of anxiety, but negative and positive affect. Several lines of evidence support this development. Increasingly, studies support conceptualizing affect as positive and negative states (Watson, Clark, & Tellegen, 1985). Moreover, positive and negative affect are not merely extremes on a single continuum but are orthogonal (Diener & Emmons, 1984). Some have contended that the negatively scored items on the STAI (the so-called anxiety-absent items such as "I feel relaxed") do not indicate simply the absence of anxiety but rather positive affect such as complacency (Hanin, 1993, 1995, 1996; Mook, Van der Ploeg, & Kleijn, 1992). Increasing evidence suggests that positive and negative affect can each enhance or harm performance (Schwarz, 1990). Several hypotheses have been proposed to explain these findings, and in each it is acknowledged that positive affect is not uniformly beneficial or negative affect always harmful.

Validated measures of positive-negative affect are available, but Hanin has instead employed idiographic methods. Athletes select items that are personally relevant or create their own items. This approach diverges from the trend in sport psychology to develop sport-specific psychology scales for use by all athletes. Supporting the contention that both positive and negative affect are crucial to performance, several studies have indicated considerable variability of positive and negative affect as experienced by athletes before both optimal and nonoptimal performances (Hanin, 1997a). The IZOF model has also been extended to include emotions during performance in order to determine whether emotional states during long sporting events interact with performance. However, the most important development is the notion that psychobiosocial states include both positive and negative emotions; the interactive effects of optimal and dysfunctional emotions should provide a better basis for predicting performance.

SUMMARY

Traditional theories of anxiety and performance have fared poorly when applied to sport. Although intervention techniques aimed at reducing or controlling an athlete's level of anxiety remain popular, ZOF research argues against indiscriminate use of this approach, instead suggesting that many athletes benefit from elevated or even very high levels of anxiety. Hanin's (1978, 1986) ZOF model—now the IZOF model—incorporates the perspective that athletes respond differently to anxiety and that interventions should take place at an individual level (chapter 7). Importantly, research has provided support for the ZOF model. Along with the finding of considerable interindividual variability in anxiety responses, studies indicate that performance tends to be better when anxiety is within the individually established optimal zone. Finally, recent developments have extended the model beyond anxiety to incorporate both positive and negative affect and to examine the influences of affect during, as well as before, performance.

CHAPTER 5

Anger, Aggressive Behavior, and Athletic Performance

Leif Isberg
Sweden

Anger is one of many emotions a human being can experience. In sport, it is often evoked by stress and associated with arousal in competitions. Anger may affect performance, disturbing precision and concentration or leading an athlete to injure another player. This chapter considers conceptual, definitional, methodological, and applied issues related to anger and aggressive behavior. It also addresses how context and personality factors may provoke and facilitate anger and aggressive behavior.

CONCEPTUAL AND DEFINITIONAL ISSUES

The relationships among "anger," "hostility," "aggression," cause confusion. Although hostility and aggression refer to different but related phenomena, the terms are often used interchangeably (Berkowitz, 1962). This section introduces these three terms and their interrelationships.

Anger and Hostility

For Kaufmann (1970), anger is "an emotion that involves a physiological arousal state coexisting with fantasised or intended act culminating in harmful effects on another person" (p. 12). Spielberger, Krasner, and Solomon (1988) see anger as an emotional state, hostility as a trait, and aggression as a behavioral manifestation of both. However, it is not clear whether they consider aggression and aggressive behavior synonymous or whether they include the "expression/ suppression" dimension (or anger-out/anger-in). Jenkins, Zyanski, and Rosenman (1978) suggest that Type A individuals deal with anger either through frequent expression (insufficient control) or unrealistic denial (too much control); on this view, both anger-in and anger-out are types of expression.

Others conceptualize aggression as the behavioral expression of anger and hostility, with the latter two distinguished by the seriousness of the act. Matthews, Glass, Rosenman, and Bortner (1977), investigating Type A behavior and coronary heart disease, found that the potential for hostility, anger directed outward, and getting angry more than once a week constituted a major coronary-prone component. Here again, hostility seems to be more serious than anger.

In an effort to integrate these concepts, Spielberger and coworkers (Spielberger, Gorsuch, Lushene, Vagg, & Jacobs, 1983; Spielberger, Jacobs, Russell, & Crane, 1983; Spielberger et al., 1985) brought anger, hostility, and aggression together into the AHA syndrome. Spielberger (1988) proposed distinguishing between anger as an emotional state (S-anger) and anger-proneness as a personality trait (T-anger). People high in T-anger and people low in T-anger experience S-anger in varying degrees of intensity. Highly intense anger tends to take expression as aggressive behavior or hostility depending on the attitudes involved. Aggression, hostility, and the attitudes involved need to be more clearly distinguished.

Aggression and Aggressive Behavior

Mainstream psychology places aggression and aggressive behavior along a continuum from aggression as an inherited trait to aggressive behavior as the result of learning. Freud (quoted in Carlström, 1983) defines aggression as an inherited trait, saying that the aggressive individual acts according to character. For Lorenz (1969), aggression is an expression of inner tension—the external situation is irrelevant. Dollard, Doob, Miller, Mowrer, and Sears (1939) suggest that all aggression, which results from frustration produced by the environment, is "a sequence of behaviour, the goal response to which is the injury of the person toward whom it is directed" (p. 9). For Berkowitz (1964), frustration creates a readiness for aggressive behavior. Environmental cues stimulate and release the behavior if the individual is prepared in this way. Berkowitz emphasizes the completion tendency: once an act [is] begun, it [has] a tendency to be continued until it [is] completed. In my opinion, *readiness* and *preparation* for aggressive action are Berkowitz's two most important concepts. Bandura and Walters (1963) suggest that the individual's experience of acting in a particular context determines which stimulating variable will lead to aggressive behavior.

Silva (1978) and Bredemeier (1983) propose similar definitions. Silva suggests that an aggressive act in sport (a) is intentional and observable, (b) is committed with the intent to injure, and (c) is personal (i.e., the person committing the act is responsible for the consequences); hostile aggressive behavior is not acceptable in sport even if the rules of a given sport justify aggressive behavior. Silva's conceptualization is similar to that of Fromm

(1976), who suggests that positive behavior includes pseudoaggressive behavior (acts causing unintentional injury) and defensive aggression (e.g., instrumental aggression not committed to achieve a personal end). Negative behavior is destructive and takes the form of "revenge," "ecstasy," or "adoration of destructiveness." A positive way of handling aggression is goal-focused reinforced physical behavior—for instance, a legal tackle in ice hockey that may nevertheless accidentally lead to an injury.

The difference between hostile and instrumental aggressive behavior is false, according to Smith (1983a), because all goal-oriented acts are instrumental and the only difference is in the goal itself. Understanding the context is important in judging the goal of an act. Smith (1971) therefore discusses moral aspects of sport behaviors as well as the importance of significant others as reference groups for interpreting the rules, norms, and value judgments in a sport. Significant others include normative others (parents, teammates, and coaches), who regulate norms and value judgments; individual others, who influence an athlete's perceptions of significant others' attitudes regarding aggressive behavior; and comparative others (often players, coaches, and referees), who are role models and legitimators, deciding what is acceptable. Numerous experiments have shown that subjects exposed to a filmed or televised model displaying aggressive behavior tend to exhibit similar behavior when subsequently given the opportunity (Smith, 1983a).

Isberg (1985) argues that aggression arises through an interaction between one's personality and the specific situation. Different individuals might react in different ways in the same situation, and the same individual might react differently in the same situation within a different context. The experiences people acquire, directly and vicariously, are stored in the brain as a "frame of reference." When a situation recurs, the individual interprets it after comparing the situational factors and the frame of reference, and acts on this basis. Thus far Isberg sees aggression as does Bredemeier (1983)—as an unobservable starting point for potentially aggressive behavior. An individual's personality, as well as earlier experiences, the stimuli, and the person's present physical and psychological state, determines whether the end result is aggressive behavior or withdrawal.

One can conclude from Spielberger et al. (1985) that anger-out is the same as aggressive behavior. The type of aggressive behavior one chooses depends on previously experienced positive consequences. Therefore, Isberg (1985) argues the importance of finding out how significant others evaluate the consequences of an aggressive behavior. To define an aggressive act, Isberg (1985) states, "A player commits an aggressive act if he or she takes the initiative to and commits an irregular act, which he or she is aware will injure or risk injuring an opposing player" (p. 98).

Instead of the frequently used concept of intent to injure, Isberg (1985) proposed the concept of *awareness* that an act will or could injure someone. If a player has this awareness and still commits the act, the act should be judged as aggressive whether or not it leads to an injury. To determine whether an athlete is aware that an act may injure, one needs to observe the act and then talk with the athlete.

Isberg (1985) argues that provocation is not acceptable as a reason to act aggressively (with risk of causing injury) but may be considered when one is examining an act's consequences. Silva (1978, 1979) found that those who preferred hostile aggressive behavior in sport showed less guilt in non-sport contexts and did not seem aware of the risk of injuring, suggesting that hostile aggressive behavior is somewhat legitimized within socialization to sport. Gill (1985) writes of the "grey zone of sport violence" in which violent acts forbidden by the rules are more or less accepted by significant others. One boundary of the grey zone is defined by the rules of the sport or the interpretation of those rules, and the other is defined by the society's laws and norms. Gill concluded from interviews that players were well aware of these meanings of the grey zone. Gill agreed with Berkowitz (1964), Bandura (1973), and Isberg (1987) that if an athlete found aggressive behavior effective in a specific situation, the same behavior would be manifested again when a similar situation occurred.

We can conclude that aggression is an antecedent of aggressive behavior and in the AHA syndrome is the same as aggressive behavior. The difference between hostile behavior and anger becomes evident after the act is committed. Environmental cues, together with earlier experiences around aggressive behavior in a setting, determine whether one expresses or suppresses aggression. In sport, this means that one must know the rules and their official interpretation in the actual context, as well as significant others' attitudes. It is also important to know the aim and motive of an act (instrumental or hostile) and to pay attention to events in the "grey zone." To evaluate whether an act is aggressive or not, or why athletes commit such acts, one needs to measure the important elements.

MEASURING ANGER: BASIC DIMENSIONS

The Individual Zones of Optimal Functioning (IZOF) model (chapter 3; Hanin, 1997a) includes seven components that make up a person's psychobiosocial state and describe the form of an emotion. Three components (cognitive, affective, motivational) represent the mental aspects of the state. Bodily-somatic and motor-behavioral components represent biological aspects. Performance and communication components reflect observable interactions with the environment, as well as the social aspects of one's state. We will consider the dimensions of anger using this approach.

Anger Form Manifestations

Anger has a major affective component (at the core of the AHA system; Spielberger et al., 1983), closely related to the behavioral manifestation (Feshbach, 1964) component. The motor-behavioral and bodily-somatic components of anger have been well substantiated in mainstream psychology outside sport.

▶ **Affective component.** The distinction between "angry temperament" (no particular provocation required) and "angry reaction" (provocation required) in anger-proneness (Spielberger & London, 1990) indicates that a person may let all anger out in one situation but keep a tight lid on it in another; this clearly implies the context dimension of anger.

▶ **Cognitive and motivational components.** These components of anger, though not often mentioned in mainstream psychology research, are clearly relevant in sport. Strong anger can either enhance or impair focus, information processing, and decision making. Anger, tension, and dissatisfaction may also affect achievement motivation (chapter 1; Hanin & Syrjä, 1995a). These two components become important especially in relation to the motivational role of the context in reinforcing and inhibiting aggressive behavior in sport (see discussion later in this chapter).

▶ **Bodily-somatic component.** Of the great volume of research on this component we consider only a few highlights.

1. Funkenstein, King, and Drolette (1954) found that subjects suppressing anger (anger-in group) had a pulse rate three times greater than subjects expressing their anger (anger-out group). In anger-provoking situations, the anger-in subjects had also significantly higher blood pressure (Harburg et al., 1973; Johnson, 1984).

2. In another study (Johnson, 1984), those high in both anger-in and anger-out scores had elevated blood pressure; that is, expressing angry feelings does not help if one continues to "boil inside." Moreover, suppressing anger may result in elevated blood pressure even in healthy and well educated subjects.

3. Lai and Linden (1992) showed that the opportunity to release anger facilitated heart recovery in men but not in women; inhibiting anger appeared to raise cardiovascular disease risk. On the basis of other research, Spielberger and London (1990) concluded that anger and hostility are among the most health-threatening components of Type A behavior. The findings that a hostile, competitive, hurried pattern of living is an important risk factor for heart disease reflect the importance of considering psychobiological measurements of anger.

▶ **Behavioral component.** The behavioral component reflects an individual's observable interactions with the environment and is manifested in expression (or suppression) of anger. The expression of anger (anger-out) usually results in an aggressive, perhaps harmful behavior. The behavioral aspect clearly distinguishes anger from other emotional experiences such as anxiety, fear, and frustration. However, we are not sure of the extent to which the behavioral component and angry feelings interrelate, and what the relationships are. For instance, suppression of anger indicates the intention not to manifest anger; and strong feelings of anger do not always accompany expression of anger (see chapter 1; Hanin, 1980, 1992).

Anger Intensity

Intensity, a quantitative characteristic of emotional experiences, is closely related to the effort invested in a sporting activity. Intensity can be expressed in either objective or subjective metrics and is typically measured on a selected parameter using self-report scales, for example. Such measures have been taken on only very few single-emotion clusters (e.g., anxiety, depression, joy; Hanin, 1997a). Other chapters deal with assessment of emotion intensity using the IZOF model (chapter 3), optimal and dysfunctional anxiety (chapter 4; Hanin, 1978, 1986, 1989), and positive and negative idiosyncratic emotions (chapter 3 and 7; Hanin, 1993, 1997a; see also Hanin & Syrjä, 1995b). However, research has not systematically addressed optimal and dysfunctional intensity of anger in sport. It would appear worthwhile to extend the IZOF conceptualization of optimal anxiety to the study of anger-performance relationships using existing normative and individualized scales. Additionally, according to Spielberger and Sydeman (1994), intensity would appear to be important for distinguishing between anger and feelings of hostility.

The Content of Anger

There are two major approaches to the content dimension of anger: the single-emotion approach, and the global affect approach that conceptualizes content in terms of hedonic tone (Hanin, 1997a). Facilitating/debilitating effects upon athletic performance have also been used to conceptualize emotion content. Additionally, the content of the anger dimension includes feelings of different intensities, from mild irritation to rage, for example. Therefore, it would seem useful to reexamine the content of the existing anger scale to identify what is consistent across settings and people. On the other hand, content analysis of athlete-generated general affect items might be useful in restructuring aggregated emotional experiences and contrasting them with those obtained from group-oriented instruments (see "Concluding Remarks"; Hanin, Jokela, and Syrjä, 1998; Hanin, 1997a).

Temporal Patterns in Anger

The time dimension reflects the dynamics of emotional experiences. For example, an athlete might feel anger, then commit an aggressive act, and then have other feelings upon seeing the consequences of the act. We need to examine the dynamics of situational anger before, during, and after performance as well as during specific game episodes.

The Context Dimension in Anger

The context is an environmental characteristic (situational, interpersonal, or intragroup) that determines the intensity and content of anger. This dimension identifies subjective experiences triggered by the environment—appraisals of performance, relations between athletes and significant others, and so on. An example identified in soccer (Hanin, 1976, cited in Hanin, 1980, p. 74) was status-role dyadic relationships (between high- and low-status groups on the same team). In 115 conflicts between partners, aggressive behavior was almost always initiated by players of higher (60.8% of cases) or equal (33.3%) dyadic status. Most of these acts were unidirectional; lower-status players usually did not express their feelings. This suggests an important direction for future research, as context-related data in both individual and team sports, especially in field studies, are virtually nonexistent (Hanin 1978, 1989, 1997a; Isberg, 1985, 1987, 1989). A later section in this chapter will address the role of context.

MEASURING ANGER, HOSTILITY, AND AGGRESSIVE BEHAVIOR

The first three components of the form dimension (cognitive, affective, and motivational) have been measured mostly by self-report scales. The bodily-somatic dimension can be examined both by physiological assessments and by self-ratings, which are usually combined. Other form components, such as motor-behavioral, performance-operational, and communicative-interactional, require an observational technique that can be combined with inventories measuring subjective and perceptional aspects of psychobiosocial states. All seven form components can be assessed by self-report measures reflecting various aspects of subjective experiences. The following sections present some general and sport-specific inventories that measure anger.

Nonspecific anger inventories developed in mainstream psychology usually distinguish between verbal and nonverbal expression of anger, anger and hostility, state and trait anger, and anger-in and anger-out. Sport psychology uses both general and sport-specific inventories (mainly measures of hostile or instrumental aggressive behavior).

Non-Sport-Specific Inventories

Several nonspecific measures of hostility, anger, and aggressive behavior have been developed outside the sport setting (table 5.1).

Early Anger Measurement Scales

Three anger scales from the 1970s (Reaction Inventory [RI; Evans & Stangeland, 1971], Anger Inventory [AI; Novaco, 1975], and Anger Self-Report [ASR; Zelin,

Table 5.1 Summary of Anger, Hostility, and Aggression Measures Commonly Used Outside Sport

Instrument	Reference	Measure	Comments
BDHI (Buss-Durkee Hostility Inventory)	Buss & Durkee (1957)	75-item scale assessing: indirect assault irritability negativism resentment suspicion verbal guilt	True-false format 7 dimensions
BPAQ (Buss-Perry Aggression Questionnaire)	Buss & Perry (1992)	29-item scale assessing: physical verbal anger hostility	5-point scale 4 dimensions
RI (Reaction Inventory)	Evans & Stangeland (1971)	76-item scale assessing: anger hostility	5-point scale 2 dimensions
AI (Anger Inventory)	Novaco (1975)	90-item scale assessing: anger hostility	5-point scale 2 dimensions
ASR (Anger Self-Report)	Zelin et al. (1972)	Scale assessing: anger hostility	
STAS (State-Trait Anger)	Spielberger et al. (1983)	Scale assessing: state anger trait anger	4-point scale 2 dimensions
AX scale (Anger Expression-Suppression scale)	Spielberger (1988)	20-item scale assessing: anger-expression anger-suppression	4-point scale 2 dimensions
STAXI (State-Trait Anger Expression Inventory)	Spielberger (1989)	44-item scale assessing: T-anger reaction T-anger temperament	5 primary subscales 2 dimensions
POMS (Profile of Mood States)	McNair et al. (1971, 1992)	65-item scale assessing: tension fatigue confusion vigor depression anger	5-point scale 12 anger items

Adler, & Myerson, 1972]) clearly indicated the need to distinguish between anger and hostility (Spielberger, 1988). These instruments were intended to describe anger-provoking incidents (AI), "awareness of anger," and various modes of anger expression (ASR).

However, these scales failed to distinguish clearly between anger as an emotional state and anger-proneness as a personality trait. Additionally, the experience and expression of anger were confounded with situational determinants of anger reactions (Spielberger, 1988). Furthermore, all three scales had problems with construct validity (Spielberger & Sydeman, 1994). Spielberger, Reheiser, & Sydeman (1995) concluded that although the Buss-Perry Aggression Questionnaire (BPAQ; classified as a trait measure of individual differences in the disposition to engage in various forms of aggressive behavior) had a high test-retest reliability, the construct validities of the Buss-Durkee Hostility Inventory (BDHI), RI, AI, and ASR were not yet established.

Spielberger et al. (1985) emphasized the need to assess the intensity of angry feelings at a particular time, the frequency of experiencing anger, and the way anger is handled (i.e., expressed or suppressed). The importance of evaluating attempts to control anger has also been emphasized, as has the role of context and personality. These conceptualizations imply the multidimensional nature of anger as a component of the psychobiosocial state (see chapter 3; Hanin, 1997a).

State-Trait Anger Scale and Anger Expression Scale

Extensive research using the State-Trait Anxiety Inventory (STAI; see chapter 4) suggests that the State-Trait Anger Scale (STAS; Spielberger, Jacobs, Russell, & Crane, 1983) could be useful for future research on optimal and dysfunctional impact of anger intensity upon athletic performance.

Similar to the STAI, the STAS includes two subscales, one assessing intensity of S-anger and the other assessing frequency of T-anger. S-anger items (e.g., "I am furious," "I feel irritated") are rated on a 4-point intensity scale to yield the total intensity score of angry feelings experienced "right now" or at some other given time. T-anger subscale items (e.g., "I have a fiery temper, "It makes me furious when I am criticized in front of others") are rated on a 4-point frequency scale based on how one generally feels. Persons high in T-anger perceive a wider range of situations as anger provoking, tend to experience more intense S-anger (angry feelings) in annoying or frustrating conditions, and respond to such situations with elevations in S-anger. Factor analyses of S-anger identified one underlying factor, Anger Feelings, that varied in intensity for both males and females. Factor analysis of T-anger items showed two related factors, Temperament and Angry Reaction.

An important addition to these two subscales was a dimension related to patterns of expression or suppression of anger, proposed by Spielberger (1988). Spielberger found that when anger was expressed (anger-out) as aggressive behavior it was externally directed as a result of an increase in S-anger. However, when anger was suppressed (anger-in), the feelings were directed inward. Anger-in was defined based on "how often an individual experiences but does not express angry feelings"; anger-out was defined in terms of "the frequency that an individual engages in aggressive behavior when motivated by angry feelings" (Spielberger, 1988, p. 95). The Anger Expression (AX) scale was developed to measure the intensity of S-anger as well as the frequency of its expression or suppression. In experimental tests of a preliminary version of the AX scale (30 items), two independent dimensions, Anger-in and Anger-out, emerged (Johnson, 1984). The final AX scale has 20 items, 8 with high loadings for Anger-in and 8 for Anger-out; the other 4 items were intended to measure the middle region of the anger-in/anger-out continuum. Three of the four items intended to measure the middle region ("Control my temper," "Keep my cool," and "Calm down faster") were also found to form a nucleus of an anger-control (AX/con) factor. Complemented with five other items, the AX/con subscale on eight items was constructed.

Recently Spielberger, Reheiser, & Sydeman (1995) proposed combining the STAS and the AX scale into the State-Trait Anger Expression Inventory (STAXI), consisting of 44 items in five primary scales (State Anger, Trait Anger, Anger-in, Anger-out, and Anger-control) and two subscales (T-anger temperament and T-anger reaction). Spielberger also recognized the importance of distinguishing between "keeping cool" to control outward expression of anger and calming down to reduce the intensity of suppressed anger. This distinction was influenced by Lakoff's (1987) psycholinguistic analysis of English anger-related metaphors pertaining to "the heat of hot liquid" (e.g., "keeping it bottled up").

The Buss-Perry Aggression Questionnaire

Russell (1981) found three factors in hostility: neuroticism, general hostility, and expression of anger. The BPAQ, often used as a trait measure of the disposition to behave aggressively, focused on four components of aggression—physical, verbal, anger, and hostility.

Anger Subscale in the Profile of Mood States

The anger subscale in the Profile of Mood States (POMS; McNair, Lorr, & Droppleman, 1971, 1992) includes 12 adjectives such as "angry," "spiteful," and "bad-tempered." In almost all POMS-based studies in sport, the anger subscale has been used as a component of the iceberg profile or of the total mood disturbance score. An exception is a study of male karate players using the Competitive State Anxiety Inventory-2 and the POMS 40 min before a competition; 91.96% of participants could be correctly classified as winners or losers based on pre-performance mood scores, and high anger was one of many mood factors in winners (Terry & Slade, 1995).

Validity and Reliability of Non-Sport-Specific Inventories

Spielberger, Reheiser, and Sydeman (1995) emphasized the importance of construct validity, the distinction between state and trait anger measures, and the need for large testing samples.

State-Trait Anger Scale and the Anger Expression Scale

Validation studies have focused mainly on psychobiological correlates of anger-out and anger-in using blood pressure and pulse rate measures (Funkenstein et al., 1954) and significantly elevated blood pressure (Harburg et al., 1973). Similarly, hypertensive patients scored higher on T-anger/reaction than persons with normal blood pressure (Crane, 1981). Spielberger, Krasner, & Solomon (1988) point out the limitation in classifying anger-ins and anger-outs based on answers to a few hypothetical questions and suggest measuring the intensity of real experiences of S-anger and the frequency of S-anger expressed as anger-out or anger-in. Deffenbacher (1992) found that individuals high in T-anger experienced greater intensity and frequency of day-to-day anger than persons low in T-anger, and also reported more anger-related physiological symptoms across many provocative situations. Additionally, persons high in T-anger showed stronger general tendencies to express and suppress anger, and failure seemed to have a more catastrophizing impact on them (Story & Deffenbacher, 1985). Validation studies of the STAXI and the anger-control items are discussed in greater detail elsewhere (Spielberger, Reheiser, & Sydeman, 1995).

In other replication studies (Fuqua et al., 1991) testing the STAXI with a large sample of college students, seven factors were extracted. Six were consistent with Spielberger's results, and the seventh had salient loading for 3 of the 10 STAXI S-anger items.

The Profile of Mood States Scale

The validity of the POMS was examined in studies (Lorr, McNair, Weinstein, Michaux, & Raskin, 1961) comparing psychotherapy with four other treatments over eight weeks. The total sample, 180 outpatients, showed highly significant improvement in tension, depression, anger, and fatigue; the control group showed no significant changes on any of the mood subscale scores. McNair, Lorr, and Droppleman (1992) provide more examples of criterion studies. The POMS is recommended primarily as a measure of mood state changes for certain categories of subjects, but for research purposes only (McNair et al., 1992, p. 2; see also chapter 12).

Sport-Specific Measures of Aggressive Behavior

As mentioned earlier, almost all sport-specific measures concern aggressive behavior rather than anger emotion. Various inventories focus on behaviors in a specific sport and others on specific age groups or behaviors. Table 5.2 summarizes aggression scales currently used in sport (see Ostrow, 1996, for more details).

The predominance of aggressive-behavior inventories indicates the persistence of this behavior, especially in team sports allowing bodily contact. The inventories also measure hostile, instrumental, physical, and verbal aggressive behavior, as well as perceptions of the legitimacy of aggressive behavior. But there is no sport-specific measure of situational anger.

Table 5.2 Summary of Anger, Hostility, and Aggression Measures Commonly Used in Sport

Instrument	Reference	Measure	Reliability
ATBQ (Aggressive Tendencies in Basketball Questionnaire)	Duda et al. (1991)	6 scenarios of aggressive acts for assessing: physical intimidation nonphysical intimidation	Not reported
BAAGI (Bredemeier Athletic Aggression Inventory)	Bredemeier (1975)	30-item scale assessing: reactive aggression instrumental aggression	Alphas: .90 .86
CSAG (Collis Scale of Athletic Aggression)	Collis (1972)	50-item scale assessing: legal aggression extra legal aggression	Not reported
RRAMB (Rice Reactive Aggression Measure for Baseball)	Rice et al. (1989)	32-item scale assessing: four types of situations evoking aggression in baseball	Alphas: .54 to .94 .83 overall
SCATS (Scale of Children's Action Tendencies)	Bredemeier (1994)	10-story scale assessing: aggression submission assertion	Alpha (KR-20): .85 .66 .68
SMAI (Spectator Misbehaviour Attitudinal Inquiry)	Cavanaugh & Silva (1980)	28-item scale assessing: spectators' perceptions of 14 factors facilitating fan misbehavior	Intraclass correlation (N = 27): .79
SAQ (Sport Aggression Questionnaire)	Thompson (1989)	Scale for assessing: 5 primary motivators of aggression in sport	Test-retest: .84 (N = 32)

The Bredemeier Athletic Aggression Inventory

The Bredemeier Athletic Aggression Inventory (BAAGI) assesses reactive (hostile) aggression, instrumental athletic aggression, and overall athletic aggression (Bredemeier, 1983). Scales consist of 30 statements (14 for reactive, 14 for instrumental, and 2 for overall aggression) describing people in specific sport situations. In my opinion, the overall athletic aggression category would be strengthened by additional items. We need better measures to determine whether aggressive behavior is encouraged in sport in general or only in particular sports.

The Sport Aggression Questionnaire

The Sport Aggression Questionnaire assesses acts of aggression occurring in specified sport situations. It focuses on five primary motivators of aggression:

injustice to self, injustice to teammate, frustration, aiding the team, and unprovoked aggression (Ostrow, 1996).

The Scale of Children's Action Tendencies

The Scale of Children's Action Tendencies (SCATS) assesses children's behavioral responses to conflict situations in sport. Ten stories are followed by three response alternatives—aggressive, assertive, and submissive—in a paired-comparison format (Ostrow, 1996).

Validity and Reliability of the Sport-Specific Inventories

The question of validity and reliability is crucial for the applicability of the inventories.

The Bredemeier Athletic Aggression Inventory

Wall and Gruber (1994) questioned the validity of the BAAGI for sport situations because it does not consider game importance and game outcome. Others have found the BAAGI to be valid (Bredemeier & Shields, 1985; Isberg, 1989). Isberg's study included world championship, elite, and youth games and compared test scores with results from video observations combined with stimulation-of-recall interviews. The hostile and instrumental categories showed high validity; the overall level showed validity but, as mentioned earlier, could be strengthened by additional questions.

As already noted, the rules and norms of a sport, together with earlier experiences of the consequences of acts, determine athlete behavior. Therefore inventories should be more context specific; most of those listed in table 5.2 are not. Spielberger, Krasner, & Solomon's (1988) distinction between state and trait anger could be instrumental in reinterpreting, for example, overall athletic aggression in the sport-specific BAAGI. Spielberger, Reheiser, & Sydeman's (1995) scales of anger-out and anger-in control would seem relevant for developing sport-specific measures for this dimension.

The Profile of Mood States

Cockerill, Nevill, and Lyons (1991) found the POMS valid as a predictor of cross-country performance among experienced male athletes. The accuracy of prediction of performance in a second race was acceptable ($r = 0.74, p < .01$). Renger (1993) found that the results of several POMS-based studies had limited value for differentiating successful from unsuccessful athletes, suggesting as a reason the failure to identify personality characteristics of athletes versus nonathletes and athletes of different ability levels. Two studies, a meta-analysis of 33 POMS-based studies (Rowley, Landers, Kyllo, & Etnier, 1995) and an investigation on prediction of team performance (Hassmén & Blomstrand, 1995), aimed at reexamining Renger's findings. Because of several methodological concerns, the findings are still contradictory.

CONTEXT AND PERSONALITY AS INHIBITORS OR FACILITATORS OF AGGRESSIVE BEHAVIOR

Aggressive behavior in sport occurs in a specific context with its own rules, norms, and traditions. An athlete's personality (including value judgments about how to act toward others) interacts with these norms and traditions, and the outcome of the interaction influences behavior and performance. Assessment of this interaction requires an observational technique in combination with interviews and inventories (Hanin, 1980, 1992; Isberg, 1985; Smith, Smoll, & Hunt, 1977; Spielberger, Reheiser, & Sydeman, 1995). Observation provides information about triggers in a situation and about the athlete-environment interaction process. What is important is the athlete's ability (or inability) to actively resist aggressive behavior prompted by environmental cues, although it is also important to know how aware athletes are of their own behavior.

Coach-Related Factors

Various types of controlled observations have been used to measure the athlete-context interaction; one example is the Coaching Behavior Assessment System (CBAS; Smith et al., 1977). The CBAS comprises 12 behavioral categories divided into reactive and spontaneous behaviors. Reactive behaviors include positive reinforcement, failure to respond to good performance, and responses to mistakes and misbehavior. Spontaneous behaviors are either game related (general technical instruction, general encouragement and organization) or game irrelevant (general communication).

According to Smoll and Smith (1984), distributions in the CBAS categories indicated that nearly two-thirds of coaches' behaviors fell within the instructional and supportive categories of general technical instruction, general encouragement, and reinforcement. Coaches responded to about 20% of the observed mistakes with either negative reinforcement or technical instruction. Correlations between coaches' ratings of their own behaviors and CBAS observed behaviors were generally low and nonsignificant, as were those between players' perceptions of coaches' behavior and the coaches' self-ratings. The only significant correlation was found for the punishment category.

Communication Factors Influencing Aggressive Behavior

In studies of the communication in top-performance teams, Hanin (1980, 1992) used controlled observation to assess the content, frequency, direction, and temporal patterns of contacts between athletes and between coach and athletes. Categories for content analysis of interactions included orientation/planning and coordination; stimulation to maintain or increase activity level; evaluation of players' actions or behavior; task-irrelevant messages; and performance actions and interactions (Hanin, 1980). The first four categories related to the content of interpersonal contacts of athletes and reflected the specifics of their perceptions of the game situation. Top teams in different sports had different communication profiles, but within the particular sport the typical communication profile was highly stable. Thus the content of communication can be described on three different levels as sport activity profile, team profile, and individual profile (Hanin, 1992). The number of players on the team and the available working space affected the communication pattern. On the basis of applied work and systematic studies, Hanin (1980, 1992) identified three major practical problems a coach and team members must deal with:

▶ Coping with major conflicts and aggressive behavior of leaders toward lower-status players

▶ Providing support for inexperienced and emotionally unstable players

▶ Dealing with insufficient communication between low- and high-status players or with inappropriate behavior that provokes interpersonal conflicts (primary and secondary)

Elsewhere Hanin (1992) presents proposals for solving those problems.

Sport-Related Factors

Isberg (1985, 1986, 1987, 1989) investigated the context-personality relationship by examining how ice hockey players of various skill levels (from novice to European elite) interpreted the rules. The main purpose was to find out how players interpreted and acted with reference to the rules and if the acting was influenced by the context-personality relationship. Athletes were interviewed about their knowledge of the rules, tested by BAAGI; their hostile and instrumental aggressive behaviors were observed and recorded. Data on the "context part" were gathered by video-recording referees' behavior and tape-recording coaches' communication with players during the game. Players later were asked to comment on their aggressive behaviors and on whether the coaches' communications (representing the context in the relationship context-personality) stimulated them to act aggressively. Coaches and players were then asked to comment on how interrupted video-recorded situations would develop, with emphasis on their experience of what is or is not acceptable in the context; their opinions and the actual behaviors were then compared. Coaches' and players' experiences of various aggressive behaviors were then tested with video-recorded situations (with one mild and one serious alternative) and analyzed within the framework of attribution theory. The players were asked to describe what happened, label the fault, predict the expected penalty, and evaluate whether the act involved the risk of injuring the opposing player. The aim was to examine players', referees', and coaches' perceptions of the seriousness of the fault and the players' capacity to act differently and according to the rules. Additional questions elicited players' knowledge of possible consequences of aggressive acts and the reasons behind this behavior.

Results showed that serious violations of the rules occurred every third minute of the game and very few resulted in a penalty (Isberg, 1985). Coaches encouraged players to commit aggressive acts to win the game. Such acts were often rewarded by the coach and teammates. The author concluded that because of the power of the context on elite level, players with a different orientation would be forced to either accept the traditions of the context or leave. Stephens and Light-Bredemeier (1996) observed similar tendencies in elite-level athletes, 12-year-old boys, and 12- and 14-year-old female soccer players.

Smith (1977) examined the effects of minor hockey competition on aggression in boys using level of competition (competitive vs. house league) and test period (pregame, postgame) as independent variables. Ninety-six 13- and 14-year-old players completed the BDHI. The competitive group scored significantly higher on the behavioral components whereas the house league group reflected significantly more of the attitudinal component. The competitive players displayed more aggressive behavior during hockey contests. Apparently, the competition itself is an important factor in aggressive behavior.

In another study, using the BAAGI, Isberg (1989) found that 12-year-old ice hockey players were familiar with the use of hostile and instrumental aggressive behavior. These findings indicate the importance of the context and the need to use instruments focused on sport-specific problems that would tap athlete-environment interactions. Environmental acceptance of more and more irregular and aggressive acts is what has created the "grey zone" (Gill, 1985). Because of the power of the context, significant others reward irregular aggressive acts, perhaps forcing players to act this way in order to stay on the team (Isberg, 1987). Significant others also offer excuses for more aggressive acts. The upper limit in the grey zone is sometimes reached when players refuse to follow these unwritten norms and to injure an opponent in order to win. These data accord with Smith's (1971) conclusions about the importance of significant others as a reference group in sport. Players who perceived that their coach strongly emphasized winning showed significantly higher levels of reactive aggression, were more willing to use illegal tactics, and had a more highly professional attitude toward competition than players whose coaches did not emphasize winning (Smith, 1977).

In ice hockey, players and coaches do not think about injuring opposing players when they plan game strategies, and their main motive is to win the game (Isberg, 1987). This indicates the need to discuss not only the athlete-context interaction but also issues of moral judgment that influence aggression. In research by Bredemeier (1983, 1985), morally mature athletes generally felt that sport aggression was legitimate as long as the intention was not to inflict a postgame injury. Young athletes also reflect this sense of an upper limit in the "grey zone."

Kemler (1988), focusing on the relationship between aggressive behavior and competition in several sports, determined the level of reactive, instrumental, and unacceptable athletic aggression among 520 male and female high school athletes. Athletes completed the BAAGI 1 hr before and 15 min after three closely spaced events. Male athletes and contact athletes expressed lower instrumental aggression and higher athletic and reactive aggression than female and noncontact athletes; precompetitive scores for instrumental aggression were higher and those for reactive aggression were lower than the postcompetitive scores. The results indicated that noncontact and female athletes were more likely to express aggression in an acceptable way and that competition increased undesirable aggressive behavior in all subjects. The difference between precompetitive and postcompetitive results is interesting; perhaps something that happens during a game is responsible for this change.

The Aggression-Winning Relationship

Worrell and Harris (1986) studied the relationship between self-perceived aggression and observed aggressive behavior using the BAAGI and a modification of Russell's (1981) aggression formula in 19 male ice hockey players over a season. Players were more aggressive at home than away and in games they won than in games lost or tied. Players' perceived aggression was not consistent with observed and recorded aggression.

Bredemeier (1995) used four hypothetical dilemmas featuring parallel moral issues in sport and daily life contexts in a study of 110 girls and boys aged 11 to 15 years. A sport and a life moral reasoning score for each child was based on Haan's (1977) interaction model of morality. The sport reasoning of children in grades 6-7 was significantly lower and more egocentric than their life reasoning; this discrepancy was significantly greater in older children. Only the older children showed context-specific reasoning; age and sporting experiences of baseball or softball correlated positively with expectations of peer cheating, aggression, and the belief that the coach would sanction it if these acts were necessary to win (Bredemeier, 1995). Other important context factors included team's moral atmosphere, team norms regulating aggressive acts, players' perception of these norms, coach characteristics, and players' motives for aggressive behaviors (Stephens & Light-Bredemeier, 1996).

No significant differences in anger feelings were found by Mace and Baines (1989) in a comparison of personality characteristics between nonparticipants and sport participants (in competitive and noncompetitive sports) (N = 34 female student teachers) using the EPQ (Eysenck Personality Questionnaire), POMS, and a questionnaire on sport participation preferences. McCarthy and Kelly (1978) found a significant relationship between aggression and successful performance. This relationship can be rewarding and can positively reinforce aggressive behaviors both in a player and in the team.

Do such results mean that winning teams commit more aggressive acts? Scholtz and Willemse (1991) examined this question in a content analysis of 300 episodes of sport aggression. Participants from both winning and losing teams committed aggressive acts; losers were more prone to do so, especially in high-intensity contests. High-intensity competition, especially in highly combative sports, also evoked more cases and variations of aggressive behavior. Aggression in sport settings seems to be a multiple-factor phenomenon triggered by motive blocking, attack, frustration, anger, combativeness, and environmental cues operating interactively (Scholtz & Willemse, 1991).

Other Factors and Conclusions

Among several other factors, task complexity and anger intensity may also influence aggressive behavior. McGowan and Schultz (1989) found that athletes performing relatively simple tasks appeared to utilize anger as a pre-event motivating strategy. Hasegawa (1994) asked 612 rugby football players to recall a recent episode involving intense anger and to rate it with respect to instigations, motives, and responses. Anger intensity was affected by evaluations of the instigation, the causal attribution, and perception of the opposing player's hostile intent: aggressive behaviors and nonaggressive behaviors were differentiated (and induced) according to the type of motives (e.g., winning at any price).

Gender differences also seem to be important, since socialization in sport appears to legitimize aggressive behavior for males but not for females (Rainey, 1986). As noted earlier, Kemler (1988) found that male athletes in contact sports expressed lower instrumental aggression and higher athletic and reactive aggression than female athletes in noncontact sports, and that female athletes in all cases were more likely to express aggression in a more socially acceptable way (Kemler, 1988).

Bond and Nideffer (1992) examined the role of gender and age in 1798 elite Australian athletes using the Test of Attention and Interpersonal Style (Nideffer 1978). They found that self-esteem scores progressively declined with age in female athletes, while the opposite occurred in male athletes. Expression of anger showed a progressive decline with age for both sexes; however, the male athletes scored consistently higher.

Finally, the use of anabolic steroids appears to be relevant to aggression in sport. Lefavi, Reeve, and Newland (1990) compared nonusers and current users of anabolic steroids in male body builders via the Multi-Dimensional Anger Inventory. Taken together, the findings suggest that steroid use may be associated with more frequent episodes of anger of greater intensity and duration, as well as with more hostile attitudes toward others.

In conclusion, the role of context in inhibiting or facilitating aggressive behavior appears to depend on several factors. First, in some sports there seems to be a positive relationship between aggressive behavior, anger management, and successful performance (Striegel, 1993). Second, the data on aggressive behavior in team sports indicate that context may be more important in determining and reinforcing certain behaviors than personality characteristics of a single player. Third, a team's moral atmosphere appears to indirectly reflect context pressures on athletes to commit irregular aggressive acts or to behave according to the rules. A fourth influence consists of athletes' experiences in sport settings regarding hostile and instrumental aggressive behavior, as well as potential risks of injuring an opponent. Therefore, athletes' insights into their own behavior, especially in combative and contact sports or at times when winning is unusually important, become critical. Fifth, the communication between coach and athletes and between athletes seems to have a major role.

ANGER MANAGEMENT

Aggressive behavior is more or less common in sports. What measures have been taken to help people cope with their anger?

Anger-Management Programs in Non-Sport Settings

Mainstream psychology suggests various strategies to cope with expression of anger. For instance, Gibbs (1996) found that youth were especially effective as peer helpers in training antisocial adolescents in moral judgment and anger management. Banks (1997) reported that culturally specific "Social Skills Training" programs could produce significant gains in anger management for inner-city African-American adolescents.

Programs have often addressed the lack of ability to control anger as a cause of violence. Keidler (1996) presents programs focusing on anger cues, triggers, and reducers and communication skills. Marion (1994) encourages anger management in children through increasing their understanding of anger and their communication expectations. Freeman (1992) presents the CALMER strategy (learning to Check if there is a problem, Assess the problem, List possible solutions, Make a choice, Evaluate, and Repeat if necessary). Activities include brainstorming, group discussions, and role-playing; positive outcomes have been reported.

In testing interventions to treat maladaptive anger, Andersen (1985) found that any direct intervention to treat maladaptive anger expression was better than none at all. A multifaceted training program consisted of desensitization, relaxation training, stress inoculation, cognitive preparation, skill acquisition, rehearsal, and practice including social skills and problem solving.

Anger Management in Sport Settings

Since very little research has been done on anger management in sport settings, it is not surprising that interventions from non-sport settings have been used in sport settings. Anger-management interventions in non-sport settings usually emphasize life skills training (correction of social and communication skills, attitudes, values) rather than performance enhancement. Sport psychologists have tried to utilize techniques with more focus on enhancing athletic performance in competition. Greenspan and Feltz (1989), after reviewing 19 published studies describing 23 interventions, concluded that in general, educational relaxation-based interventions and cognitive restructuring interventions with individual athletes were effective for handling anger problems in competitive situations. Since very little research has been done on anger management in sport, selection of these interventions has not always been based on adequate empirical findings.

Similar to earlier research and interventions in competitive anxiety, most efforts in anger management have stressed reduction of anger. Therefore, additional research is needed to empirically test Hanin's hypothesis on the individual variability of optimal and dysfunctional anger intensity (chapters 3 and 7; Hanin & Syrjä, 1995a). If optimal anger can be high, moderate, and low, and if it varies among athletes, then strategies for reducing and increasing situational anger should be developed. At this point, controlling excessive anger intensity seems to remain a problem. Although systematic research on anger intensity in sport is still sparse, observational and anecdotal data related to behavioral manifestations of anger are available (Hanin, 1980, 1992; Smith et al., 1977).

Hanin's (1980, 1989, 1992) summary of research and applications with elite athletes in team sports, focused on optimizing communication between interacting partners, provides insight into indirect strategies of anger control during competition. Hanin suggests that player contacts be optimized when teammates are not communicating or are communicating poorly owing to inadequate emotional control. Three basic strategies have been effective: changing group/team composition; redesigning group tasks; and directly managing players' communicative behaviors with regard to the content, form, direction, or frequency of messages. Changing aggressive behaviors into focused support and encouragement is usually accompanied by dramatic changes in anger intensity and even complete extinction. Other cognitive-behavioral techniques such as assertiveness training, communication skills training, and team building could also be useful indirect strategies for preventing and controlling excessive anger and aggression in sport.

CONCLUSION

Measurement of anger feelings should employ multimodal markers including psychological, physiological, and social (context-related) parameters. Therefore inventories, tests, interviews, and observational techniques including video recordings appear to be useful when context specific. It will be important in future research to use both nomothetic (group-oriented) and individualized approaches in assessments (Hanin, 1997a; Hanin, Jokela, & Syrjä, 1998; Hanin & Syrjä, 1996; Syrjä & Hanin, 1997a). Such a strategy must also focus the effects that different situational cues have both on the group and on each individual.

In a competition or practice, athletes may experience a number of performance-induced emotions. Future research should examine these idiosyncratic constellations of emotions that may enhance or impair performance, as well as their interaction effects on performance (chapters 3 and 7; Hanin, 1997a). There is need for more research into situational and performance-related anger and its manifestations and functional meaning in the performance process. Research should test several interaction effects of positive and negative emotions on athletic performance as predicted by the IZOF model. Of special relevance would be the study of emotions in athletes before, during, and after performance. Video recordings and stimulated recall could be used to identify the cues, as well as the intensity of the feelings and their effect on performance. The IZOF model appears to offer a promising multidimensional perspective for further study of anger in sport and exercise settings.

SUMMARY

An athlete's proneness (T-anger) to react with anger is a factor determining how often he/she experiences situations as threatening. The intensity of anger (S-anger), together with environmental cues and moral reasoning in the context of what is acceptable and unacceptable, determines an athlete's behavior. Consequences of the chosen behavior create experiences that are stored as an athlete's frame of reference regarding how to act in the future. An athlete's anger, suppressed or expressed, may have positive or negative consequences on performance. Aggressive behavior as an expression of anger seems to be relatively more common in sport than in daily life situations, in team sports than in individual sports, in high-level and high-intensity competition, and in combative and contact sports. Socialization to some sports seems to legitimize aggressive behavior, especially for males. Teams whose coaches strongly emphasize winning seem to be more willing to use aggressive behavior and illegal tactics. The patterns of anger control differ between skillful and less skillful athletes, and different sports provide different opportunities for handling these feelings in a competition situation.

CHAPTER 6

Joy, Fun, and Flow State in Sport

Susan A. Jackson

Australia

The topic of this chapter—the positive experiences that sport offers participants—is important for several reasons. As a context in which people experience positive affect, sport provides a useful setting for examining such psychological concepts as joy, fun, and flow. Sport is usually freely chosen, is widely participated in, and occurs in many different forms, allowing for investigation of factors that might impact the quality of participants' experiences. Emotions not only are often visible, but may be more pronounced than in daily life settings. This is so because sport is a public activity and a microcosm of life, maximizing the effects of interactions based on structured rules and uncertain outcomes. Although sport begins as an activity viewed as fun, it can yield a mix of positive and negative emotions. Understanding the factors that contribute to a positive sport experience is important for those interested in explaining and enhancing these aspects of sport.

POSITIVE EMOTIONS IN PSYCHOLOGY

Emotions are difficult to describe and define. Emotion may best be viewed as an integrative concept (Lazarus, 1991b) comprising several components and functions. For Lazarus (1991b), emotions are "complex, patterned, organismic reactions to how we think we are doing in our lifelong efforts to survive and flourish and to achieve what we wish for ourselves" (p. 6). There seems to be general agreement that evaluation of events related to a person's needs or goals elicits emotions (Oatley & Jenkins, 1992). Hanin (chapter 3) discusses Vygotsky's (1926) person-environment interaction model as an early representation of how the perception of balance between resources and environmental demands helps to explain emotional experiences. In his cognitive-relational-motivational theory, Lazarus (1991b; chapter 2) has developed the idea that emotions are triggered by appraisal into a detailed, integrative account of the interplay between cognitions and emotions.

Determining what qualifies as an emotion is as difficult as defining one. In broad terms, many hold that emotions have either a positive or a negative dimension: that is, hedonic tone (Hanin, chapter 3) seems to be a basic dimension. Using factor analyses of many studies of self-reported mood, Watson and Tellegen (1985) classified emotions into two major factors: positive affect and negative affect.

Despite recognition of both negative and positive sides to emotion, psychological research has focused overwhelmingly on the former. Perhaps negative emotions and their consequences appear more important for understanding behavior, and their impact more significant. Historically, the health disciplines have focused on problems and pathology rather than wellness and prevention. Because the clinical disciplines have influenced other areas, a negative bias also predominates in educational and sport settings. Because of a recent movement toward understanding and promoting a preventive and positive approach to health and an acceptance of the importance of psychological factors in health outcomes, we may see a resurgence of interest in concepts such as joy and happiness as researchers explore keys to wellness. This trend in psychology was the theme of the 1998 American Psychological Association's annual convention: positive psychology. The millennial issue of *American Psychologist* was devoted to this topic. Martin Seligman (1998), president of the American Psychological Association for 1998, explained, "As psychology at the millennium begins to take the building of the best things in life as seriously as it has taken the healing of the worst, we need more of a science than presently exists. A focus of the convention in San Francisco and a central mission of my presidency is to nurture a science and a practice of positive psychology."

POSITIVE PSYCHOLOGICAL EXPERIENCES IN SPORT

Sport psychology, like general psychology, has tended to emphasize negative experiences, with plentiful research on anxiety and associated topics. But sport psychology has also included a positive perspective (especially in youth and children's sports), and performance enhancement is still a predominant focus. However, the growing trend toward clinical approaches within sport psychology may reinforce a focus on problems and difficulties rather than optimization.

This chapter addresses aspects of positive sport experiences studied in sport psychology to date; considers the scope for further research; and points out the need for balance in the study of emotional aspects of sport participation. The focus is on competitive sport rather than leisure or exercise activities.

Rationale for Studying Positive Sport Experiences

Sport almost always begins as a free-choice activity. Most people have experienced sport in some form, and many view it as a highly positive aspect of life. Sport gives participants of all ages opportunities for self-expression, personal achievement, competitive strivings, and fun. One could argue that sport exists to make us feel good and therefore that the more we know about this process, the better—both for participants and for sport as an institution.

The Concepts of Joy, Fun, and Flow

When global positive affect is categorized into specific emotion clusters, joy generally appears as a primary positive emotion (e.g., Derogatis, 1975; Lazarus, 1991b; Shaver, Schwartz, Kirson, & O'Connor, 1987). Other primary positive emotions include love and pride, and possibly relief (Lazarus, 1991b). This chapter concerns joy as an emotion salient in sport. What place, then, do the concepts of fun and flow have in a book on emotions in sport? First, although few sport psychology studies specifically address joy, a number deal with fun and flow. Second, these concepts relate to the experience of positive affect; they help to describe, and, I will argue in the case of flow, to explain positive sport experiences.

Before writing this chapter, I knew that definitional aspects would prove a major challenge. What are joy, fun, and flow? How do they relate to each other and to other constructs such as enjoyment and peak experiences? It is not easy to obtain definitive answers based on current knowledge of positive psychological experiences in sport. I will offer working definitions of these constructs and suggest a framework for understanding their possible interrelationships. I do so acknowledging the various ways one can look at these constructs and their interrelationships to each other and to performance, and emphasize that this chapter reflects one working approach.

Izard, Kagan, and Zajonc (1984) make a point about definitions of constructs such as emotion that is significant here. They argue that although definition is important, there are advantages to refraining from strict formal demands on definitions at particular stages of development of a discipline:

> The more specific the definition, the sharper the boundary it draws among phenomena. And at some stages of knowledge it isn't always clear where these boundaries should be. Therefore, when knowledge is lacking, formal definitions may sometimes do more harm than good. They may, for example, eliminate from analysis some aspects of phenomena that may eventually turn out to be essential to the understanding of the entire process. (p. 4)

Joy

Joy is a concept that brings to mind high levels of positive experiencing—and a special type of experience, involving feelings of intense happiness and possibly spiritual qualities.

Many regard joy as a core positive emotion, uniting terms that have a positive connotation (see Shaver et al., 1987). Shaver et al. view joy and sadness as opposites: joyful situations involve a desired outcome, whereas sadness results from loss or failure. Lazarus (1991b), characterizing joy and happiness as interchangeable terms (as have others, e.g., Shaver et al., 1987), holds that for happiness, the core relational theme—the central underlying relational harm or benefit—is making reasonable progress toward realization of a goal. Although he views happiness and joy as essentially synonymous, Lazarus distinguishes the terms by their intensity: while happiness brings contentment, joy can lead to ecstasy. Support for this distinction comes from *The Oxford English Reference Dictionary* (1996), which defines joy as a vivid emotion of pleasure, or extreme gladness, and happiness as a state in which one feels or shows pleasure or contentment.

Although joy is a central positive emotion in psychology, little sport psychology research has focused directly on joy. A few researchers have investigated peak experiences in sport, notably Ravizza (1977, 1984). Because peak experience is defined as a moment of highest happiness, or intense joy (Maslow, 1968; Privette & Bundrick, 1991), peak experience research covers the concept of joy, albeit indirectly. Peak experience will be reviewed later in this chapter.

To date, most sport psychology literature on positive experiences has focused on fun and enjoyment, which we consider next.

Fun

Fun seems at first a more straightforward concept than joy, especially in sport, where the term is used so often. Everyone knows what fun is, right? But getting beyond "sport is fun" is not easy. Fun is often linked with enjoyment, but it is not clear whether or not the terms are indeed synonymous. Sport psychology has tended to consider them as one and the same, but consistent definitions and lines of demarcation (or correspondence) have been lacking. Here, the two terms are considered similar enough to be used interchangeably.

While sport psychology often classifies enjoyment as an emotion, some have raised questions about the best way to view the concept (e.g., Kimiecik & Harris, 1996; Wankel, 1997). Wankel and colleagues (e.g., Wankel & Kreisel, 1985; Wankel & Sefton, 1989), in their fruitful research on enjoyment of youth sports, demonstrated an intuitively accepted understanding: that sport is fun (defined as a positive affective response), and that a major reason for participation in sport is the enjoyment it provides. Wankel and colleagues have attempted to delineate the nature of fun in sport. Wankel and Sefton (1989) found that fun was consistently related to positive affect in ratings of semantic differential scales; terms connected with fun were "happy," "friendly," and "cheerful." This hints at a social component in fun—as Podilchak (1991) emphasizes in saying that fun is a social process requiring interaction with others.

Scanlan and colleagues (e.g., Scanlan, Carpenter, Lobel, & Simons, 1993; Scanlan & Simons, 1992; Scanlan, Stein, & Ravizza, 1989) have contributed substantially to knowledge about enjoyment in sport. They define enjoyment as "a positive affective response to the sport experience that reflects generalized feelings such as pleasure, liking, and fun" (Scanlan & Simons, 1992, pp. 202-203). Scanlan et al. (1993) view enjoyment as more differentiated than global positive affect, but not as specific as an emotion such as pride. Wankel and Sefton (1989) similarly concluded from their study with youth sport participants, on the basis of high correlations between fun and positive mood states, that fun is a positive emotional state. In this study, fun was also related to challenge and perceptions of personal achievement, and the authors drew links with both the flow model of Csikszentmihalyi (1975) and achievement motivation theory (Nicholls, 1984).

Csikszentmihalyi (1975, 1990, 1997) approaches enjoyment rather differently, linking it with the positive psychological experience of flow rather than emphasizing an affective dimension. Csikszentmihalyi (1990) distinguishes enjoyment from pleasure. Pleasure here—"a feeling of contentment that one achieves whenever information in consciousness says that expectations set by biological programs or by social conditioning have been met" (p. 45)—recalls the earlier definitions of happiness/joy as a state of having achieved a goal. Enjoyment, according to Csikszentmihalyi (1990), occurs

> when a person has not only met some prior expectation or satisfied a need or a desire but also gone beyond what he or she has been programmed to do and achieved something unexpected, perhaps something even unimagined before. (p. 46)

Csikszentmihalyi (1990) argues that enjoyment, but not pleasure, leads to psychological growth or complexity. Therefore, to experience enjoyment one must have invested effort and attention. Pleasure does not require any effort.

What makes experience enjoyable? The elements of flow provide the keys to enjoyment in the work of Csikszentmihalyi (e.g., 1990, 1997). Indeed, Csikszentmihalyi uses the terms *flow* and *enjoyment* interchangeably, along with a third term, *optimal experience*. Defining enjoyment in *Creativity* (1996), Csikszentmihalyi writes, "This optimal experience is what I have called flow, because many of the respondents described the feeling when things were going well as an almost automatic, effortless, yet highly focused state of consciousness" (p. 110). Enjoyment as optimal experience is different from enjoyment as a positive affective state. The growth-producing perception of enjoyment described by Csikszentmihalyi seems more exclusive and less readily achieved than good feelings during a "fun" activity.

Dictionary definitions of the terms fun and enjoyment hint at subtle differences between these two concepts and may also clarify the link between fun/enjoyment and emotions, although such definitions will not solve the definitional problem in the psychological literature. The *Collins English Dictionary* (1991) defines fun as (1) a source of enjoyment, amusement, diversion, etc. or (2) pleasure, gaiety, or merriment. One has fun, makes fun, but does not feel or experience fun. Enjoyment is defined as the act or condition of receiving pleasure from something. Joy, on the other hand, is defined as a deep feeling or condition of happiness or contentment. It may be more appropriate to regard enjoyment as a process of experiencing an emotion such as joy, rather than as an emotion in itself (Hanin, personal communication, October 14, 1997). And, as I will argue, flow is central to this process of experiencing positive emotions.

Nonetheless, substantial research in sport and exercise psychology presents fun and enjoyment as positive affective states (e.g., Scanlan, Stein, & Ravizza, 1989; Scanlan & Simons, 1992; Wankel, 1997; Wankel & Kreisel, 1985; Wankel & Sefton, 1989); this line of thinking has provided rich data on what enjoyment and fun appear to mean to participants. Wankel (1997) argued that flow is but one part of the enjoyment experience and that sport and exercise enjoyment experiences include a range of positive factors. To summarize up to this point, then, the central issue appears to be whether to view enjoyment in a broad, inclusive, positive-affect sense (e.g., Wankel, 1997; Scanlan et al., 1993) or as a more exclusive concept, tied to flow (e.g., Csikszentmihalyi, 1990; Kimiecik & Harris, 1996). The aim of this chapter is not to provide a thorough or definitive delineation of these concepts. Concentrating on terminology differences may not advance understanding of the underlying concepts; sport psychology may benefit from remaining open to differing perspectives regarding definitional problems until demarcation issues are more firmly resolved.

This chapter focuses on flow as a central and unifying construct in relation to positive experiences in sport. It is one way of addressing the positive experiential aspects of sport, based on Csikszentmihalyi's sound and eloquent analyses of flow.

Flow

Flow has been defined and described in some detail, notably by Csikszentmihalyi over a period of 30 years to date. Nine defining characteristics will be detailed later. More generically, flow is an optimal psychological state in which complete absorption in the task at hand leads to a number of positive experiential qualities. Csikszentmihalyi defines flow as "the state in which people are so involved in an activity that nothing else seems to matter; the experience itself is so enjoyable that people will do it even at great cost, for the sheer sake of doing it" (1990, p. 4). Flow metaphorically suggests the sense of effortless action felt when experiencing the best moments in one's life (Csikszentmihalyi, 1997, p. 29).

Not happiness, but flow, is the key to an excellent life, according to Csikszentmihalyi. Interestingly, being in flow and feeling happy are not coincidental in this view:

> When we are in flow, we are not happy, because to experience happiness we must focus on our inner states, and that would take away attention from the task at hand. . . . Only after the task is completed do we have the leisure to look back on what has

happened, and then we are flooded with gratitude for the excellence of that experience—then, in retrospect, we are happy. (Csikszentmihalyi, 1997, p. 32)

Flow is a unified construct defining positive or optimal experiences in sport. As an optimal psychological state, flow is a precursor to joy and is associated with other experiences such as fun/enjoyment. Maddux (1997), citing other research (Diener, Sandvik, & Pavot, 1990), supports this in stating that the most important factor in predicting happiness is the frequency of positive affect. And what leads to experiencing positive affect? In Maddux's words:

Curiously, and consistent with the assumptions of Eastern philosophies, it is this ability to become absorbed in whatever activity one is engaged in at the present moment. In other words, it is the capacity for experiencing flow. (p. 344)

This line of argument suggests a series of events: the experience of flow leads to positive affect, which in turn predicts happiness. When referring to happiness, Maddux (1997) seems to be suggesting a concept akin to subjective well-being: "The kind of happiness I am concerned with involves having a sense of meaning and purpose throughout the course of one's day-to-day life" (p. 338).

Not that flow is the only path to joy or happiness: rather, flow is an important, yet understudied, pathway to positive sport experiences.

FLOW AS AN OPTIMAL PSYCHOLOGICAL STATE

In flow, everything is optimal. Mind and body are in harmony, negative thinking and self-doubts are absent, and functioning is enhanced. Flow is not easy to attain; however, once it is attained, the experiencer feels clear that this is an optimal psychological state. Several qualities make flow optimal.

Qualities of the Flow Experience

Csikszentmihalyi (e.g., 1990, 1996) describes nine dimensions of the total state of flow: a balance between perceived challenges and skills; a merging of action and awareness; having clear goals; receiving unambiguous feedback; being totally concentrated on the task; having a sense of control over what one is doing; not being self-conscious; losing track of time; and experiencing high levels of intrinsic satisfaction from the activity. Research in sport has confirmed these nine dimensions, although support for the time transformation dimension appears equivocal (e.g., Jackson, 1996; Jackson & Marsh, 1996). Future research should be able to more precisely describe flow experience in sport and to uncover any unique aspects of flow across physical activities.

Challenge-Skill Balance

First, flow is a balance between challenges and skills: when these are evenly matched, the situation is ripe for flow to occur. But both challenges and skills must be at personally high levels, according to the operational definition as revised by Csikszentmihalyi (Csikszentmihalyi & Csikszentmihalyi, 1988) on the basis of other research (Massimini and Carli, 1988). If challenges and skills are in balance but at low individual levels, the result will be apathy.

The model predicts that anxiety will occur when challenges are perceived to outweigh skills. The concept of confidence becomes critical to moving from anxiety to flow, as what is important is the subjective perception of challenges and skills rather than any objective notion. However, the balance between perceived skills and challenges is delicate, as too much confidence (in relation to challenges) might topple the person from flow into relaxation or boredom. The title of Csikszentmihalyi's first full exploration of flow, *Beyond Boredom and Anxiety* (1975), captures this balance.

Merging of Action and Awareness

The second flow dimension signifies a melding of action and actor. Because of the total focus that is another characteristic of flow, the actor (athlete) ceases to be aware of herself as separate from her action and experiences a feeling of oneness with the activity. For athletes, the feeling is often one of automaticity and unity with the environment. Movement often is perceived as effortless—which is one of the reasons for the term *flow*.

Clear Goals and Unambiguous Feedback

Csikszentmihalyi often (e.g., 1990) discusses the third and fourth flow dimensions together, and I consider them together here. Clear goals, the third dimension, make possible the fourth dimension of unambiguous feedback. First, goals. In flow, there is a clarity about what one is to do, experienced as a moment-by-moment awareness of the right actions. Hand in hand with this is unambiguous feedback (i.e., ongoing appraisal and reappraisal of the performance process) about the successfulness of one's actions. The feedback in turn provides a clear idea of the next action, and the cycle of specific goals and clear feedback continues.

Total Concentration on the Task at Hand

Total concentration, the fifth dimension, has already been alluded to. A complete focus on the task is the clearest indication of the flow state. Often during activities, our minds constantly shuffle between isolated pieces of information. This creates frustration and of course is not conducive to effective performance. In flow, moments of total absorption allow freedom from our usual worries and lead us toward optimal performance. Athletes must be able to sustain concentration throughout an event to attain peak performance levels. Often this is a struggle, but in flow, the concentration seems to occur effortlessly.

Sense of Control

A sense of control is the sixth dimension. Athletes report a feeling of total control of their performance when in flow. In actuality, people in flow are not in total control; if they were, skills would outweigh challenges and thus one would be out of the flow channel. What seems to prevail is a clear sense of the ability to exercise control in difficult situations. Athletes are often in situations of perceived if not real threat; but when in flow, they feel able to perform without fear of failure and regardless of its potential consequences. Rock climbers ascend difficult routes fearlessly, divers execute precisely within inches of the board, and surfers ride waves that could pummel them to pieces—feeling certain that there is no prospect of failure.

Loss of Self-Consciousness

The seventh dimension is a loss of self-consciousness. Often we are caught in the hold of our negative consciousness, questioning our adequacy and concerned about others' opinions. Flow provides release from this weight. Because the person in flow is so totally absorbed in the activity, there is no room for worries about the self or evaluation by others. Loss of self-consciousness does not imply a lack of awareness: what recedes is the evaluative and questioning ego.

Transformation of Time

As well as transcendence of the ego, a transcendence of time can occur when one is deeply absorbed in an activity. Described as transformation of time, this eighth flow dimension involves a loss of sense of the ordinary passage of time. Usually in flow, time seems to speed up: an event is over before one knows it. But the opposite can also occur, so that the feeling is that one has "all the time in the world." In research with athletes, I have not found universal endorsement of this dimension. It is generally the least mentioned flow dimension in qualitative research (Jackson, 1996), and psychometric scale work (e.g., Jackson & Marsh, 1996) has not shown that time transformation relates strongly to other flow dimensions. Csikszentmihalyi (1990) acknowledges that time transformation may not always occur in flow: for a surgeon, for example, "The ability to keep track of time becomes one of the skills necessary to do well in the activity, and thus it contributes to, rather than detracts from, the enjoyment of the experience" (p. 66). Further research is needed for a better understanding of the time transformation dimension in physical activity.

Autotelic Experience

Enjoyment, central to flow, is captured in the ninth flow dimension, termed autotelic experience. As Csikszentmihalyi (1990) notes, the word "autotelic" is derived from two Greek words, *auto* ("self") and *telos* ("goal"). An autotelic activity is one done for its own sake because it provides its own reward: enjoyment. This flow dimension is the end product of the others (Csikszentmihalyi, 1990). When the other positive qualities converge, the resulting experience is highly enjoyable, or intrinsically rewarding. The auto-telic dimension is similar to a paratelic state in reversal theory (Apter, 1989).

The foregoing analysis demonstrates that flow is an optimal and multidi-mensional state. Using Hanin's Individual Zones of Optimal Functioning (IZOF) model (chapter 3) describing the basic dimensions of performance-related states, one can say that the flow dimensions encompass Hanin's seven form dimensions (cognitive, affective, motivational, bodily-somatic, motor-behavioral, performance-operational, and communicative), as well as having links with the time, intensity, content, and context dimensions that Hanin uses to describe optimality. For example, the challenge-skill balance is linked to the form dimensions (cognitive, motivational, and performance); merging of action and awareness is linked to cognitive, motor-behavioral, and perfor-mance dimensions; sense of control is linked to cognitive, affective, bodily-somatic, performance, and motor-behavior dimensions. Analyzing flow characteristics in terms of the IZOF model underscores the multidimensional nature of the experience.

This chapter concerns flow as a specific state experienced during perfor-mance of an activity like sport. Flow can also be viewed more globally, as the process of total involvement with life (Csikszentmihalyi, 1990, p. xi). Interested readers may wish to explore Csikszentmihalyi's rich writings on flow as a way of living (e.g., Csikszentmihalyi, 1990, 1996, 1997).

MEASUREMENT ISSUES

A great challenge in flow research, as with any research involving subjective experiences, is finding ways to accurately and reliably assess the constructs of interest. Flow is an optimal experience, an optimal state of consciousness. Like all experiential phenomena, it cannot easily be pinned down by objective psychometric tools. Qualitative approaches have provided rich descriptions of flow, and investigative interviewing has uncovered associated factors. How-ever, neither quantitative nor qualitative methods, nor physiological assess-ments (could they be reliably made), will be able to provide trouble-free assessments of the flow experience. This leaves two options: ignore flow as a concept and do not attempt to measure it, or use whatever imperfect measures are available. Believing that flow is too important to ignore, I have attempted to develop ways to research flow in sport that may help to define the experience and make it more accessible to both researcher and practitioner. The following sections review these approaches, and also outline how others who have studied optimal experience have assessed their constructs of interest.

Qualitative Approaches

Qualitative methods, the means used first by Csikszentmihalyi (1975) to understand flow, provide rich accounts of the phenomenon. In studying flow in athletes, I first used a primarily quantitative, questionnaire-based approach

(Jackson & Roberts, 1992). In that initial study, I also interviewed a small sample of athletes on an ad hoc basis about their flow experiences and was so impressed with the quality of the information that I undertook two larger-scale interview-based studies of flow with elite athletes (Jackson, 1992; Jackson, 1995, 1996). These studies showed that elite athletes have a good grasp of flow experientially, if not theoretically. Athletes' descriptions of being in flow were content analyzed for similarity with Csikszentmihalyi's nine dimensions (e.g., 1990), and almost all of the athletes' themes could be categorized in this way (Jackson, 1996).

Qualitative approaches have become popular for obtaining information about how athletes experience their sport, and much rich information has come from qualitative studies of optimal moments in sport. For example, Loehr (1982b), Garfield and Bennett (1984), and Unestål (1986) have compiled information about optimal performance states through interviewing elite athletes. Some of these findings will be reviewed later.

Limitations of qualitative approaches include the retrospective element of interviews, the small samples appropriate for this type of research, and the interpretive biases of the researchers—all of which may influence the results. However, that positive sport experiences are amenable to understanding through qualitative means justifies the continued use of these approaches.

Experience Sampling Method

The Experience Sampling Method (ESM; Csikszentmihalyi & Larson, 1987) is the primary means of assessing flow in the work of Csikszentmihalyi and colleagues (e.g., Bidwell, Csikszentmihalyi, Hedges, & Schneider, in press; Carli, Delle Fave, & Massimini, 1988; Csikszentmihalyi, Rathunde, & Whalen, 1993). Via a beeper, programmed to go off usually eight random times a day for one week, ESM allows assessments of subjective states as they occur. Although both quantitative and qualitative data can be collected, the majority of the data are coded into quantitative terms. Measurements of flow characteristics, as well as other factors such as motivation regarding the activity under way at the time of the beep, are recorded in self-report booklets carried by ESM partici-pants. Using an operational definition of flow based on equivalence of chal-lenges and skills, quality of experience in and out of flow is assessed.

Although Csikszentmihalyi and colleagues (e.g., Csikszentmihalyi & Csikszentmihalyi, 1988) have included ESM in assessments of sport and recreational activities, this approach has not been used extensively with athletes. Stein, Kimiecik, Daniels, and Jackson (1995), using a combination of questionnaire and modified ESM procedures, showed that basketball stu-dents, tennis players, and golfers enjoyed better quality of experiences when in flow than when in other states assessed by the ESM: apathy, boredom, and anxiety. The results did not support predicted relationships between flow and other psychological factors such as goals and competence.

Assessments in this study were not based on a true ESM approach, but instead on preplanned and structured incidents such as particular holes in a round of golf. The idea of random beeping of athletes during performance is understandably greeted with skepticism, since it would involve disruption of attention and of the performance. However, the research by Csikszentmihalyi and colleagues suggests that ESM should not be bypassed as an approach to assessing flow in sport; creative applications may be productive. In a recent study by Massimini, Delle Fave, and Bassi (1997), mountaineers completed ESM assessments over a continuous period of 39 days while on a climbing expedition. If it is possible to get mountaineers to complete ESM assessments, it should be possible (and logistically easier!) to have other athletes wear ESM watches over selected periods of time and thus to have access to their experience as it occurs. One could compare experiences during sport with those during other activities, as well as across sport situations (e.g., competition, practice, performing alone vs. with others, etc.). As with any empirical measure, one needs to consider limitations of the ESM. The disruption of performance presents potential problems in the competitive sport environment. And scoring the ESM, particularly determining whether or not someone was in flow on the basis of ESM data, is complicated. These issues are beyond the scope of this chapter; however, a recent methodological paper by Moneta and Csikszentmihalyi (1996) addresses questions regarding assessment via the ESM.

Flow Scales

Another means of assessing flow in sport is via questionnaires such as the Flow State Scale (FSS; Jackson & Marsh, 1996). To facilitate examination of associations between flow and other psychological constructs, I developed the FSS and a corresponding trait version of the instrument, the Trait Flow Scale (TFS; see Jackson, Kimiecik, Ford, & Marsh, 1998). These instruments have undergone psychometric analyses under the direction of Professor Herbert Marsh and have acceptable factor structure and reliability (Jackson & Marsh, 1996; Marsh & Jackson, in press).

The nine subscales of the FSS/TFS have demonstrated adequate internal reliability, with alphas ranging from .80 to .86 in an initial retrospective study using the FSS (Jackson & Marsh, 1996), and from .72 to .91 in a study using the FSS with masters athletes (alphas for the TFS in this study ranged from .70 to .88) (Jackson et al., 1998). Similar reliability estimates for the TFS and FSS were obtained in a recent study of younger competitive athletes (Jackson, Thomas, Marsh, & Smethurst, 1999). There are four items for each of the nine flow factors, and respondents rate their extent of agreement ("Strongly Disagree" to "Strongly Agree") with the experience of each dimension in a selected activity for the FSS. The TFS assesses the frequency of the flow experience during their activity, in a "Never" to "Always" format.

Nine factors corresponding to the nine flow dimensions have been validated through confirmatory factor analyses of the instruments. There has been some support for a higher-order global flow factor through these analyses, but the fit of this model is not as strong as that for the nine first-order factor model. The scales are still under development, and item modifications are currently being assessed. The time transformation factor has shown little relation to the global flow factor, perhaps in part because of the items used to assess the factor but also possibly because time transformation is not central to athletes' flow experiences. Further research is needed to determine the best item fits and the relative usefulness of the various subscales assessing flow. As with any measurement approach, there are limitations to the usefulness of the flow scales. Because the FSS and TFS are designed to assess all nine dimensions of flow, independent factors were formed to tap into each dimension. In scoring the scales, one can use single-factor scores or a global measure combining all the scales. Psychometrically, the single-factor approach has received stronger initial support. However, the single-factor approach involves reducing flow to its various components, providing specific but incomplete information about the total flow experience. Other issues associated with the scales are the fallibility of self-report instruments, the retrospective nature of the assessments, and the reduction of a subjective experience to quantifiable terms.

For understanding positive experiential states in sport, a multimethod approach to measurement will yield the greatest amount and variety of information, and will help to minimize the limitations of any one approach. As the tools of measurement are refined and new approaches developed, the possibilities for gathering more detailed information about such experiences should increase significantly.

RELATIONSHIPS BETWEEN FLOW, PERFORMANCE, AND EXPERIENCE

Many sport psychologists, as well as competitive athletes and coaches, have great interest in understanding the factors related to peak performance. This has been a common thread in research from several perspectives in sport psychology. Another focus has been the quality of experiences gained through sport. A brief overview of the peak performance/peak experience research will illustrate the connection between these phenomena and the optimal psychological state of flow.

Qualities of Peak Performance

Researchers have examined ideal, or peak, performance both in and outside of sport. Taking a generalist position, Privette (1981) defined peak performance as optimal functioning—full use of one's potential—in any activity. Full focus and sense of self in clear process were the two distinguishing characteristics of peak performance in a study by Privette and Bundrick (1991).

Research with athletes has uncovered physical and mental factors as characteristic of feelings at moments of peak performance. In an interview study with elite athletes, Garfield and Bennett (1984) identified a number of factors critical to peak performance: physical and mental relaxation, confidence, a present-centered focus, being highly energized, extraordinary awareness, feeling in control, and "in the cocoon" (detached from the external environment and its distractions). From analysis of several hundred reports of athletes, Loehr (1982b) identified several categories reflecting an ideal performance state: physically relaxed, mentally calm, low anxiety, energized, optimistic, effortless, automatic, alert, mentally focused, self-confident, and in control. In another qualitatively based study of competitive golfers, Cohn (1991) found a set of factors closely resembling those of the other two studies. A narrow focus of attention, being immersed in the present, feelings of control, being confident, having no fear, and feeling physically and mentally relaxed surfaced as key characteristics of peak performance.

It is evident that definable mental characteristics are associated with optimal performance in sport, and there are parallels between these characteristics and those of flow. For comparative purposes, table 6.1 compares peak performance characteristics identified by a number of researchers with the dimensions of flow.

Table 6.1 Comparison of Attributes of Peak Performance and Flow

Peak performance			Flow
Garfield & Bennett (1984)	Loehr (1982b)	Cohn (1991)	Csikszentmihalyi (1990)
• Confidence	• Confident	• Confident	• Challenge-skill balance
• Physical and mental relaxation	• Low anxiety/ physically relaxed	• Physically and mentally relaxed	
• Highly energized	• Energized		
• Extraordinary awareness	• Automatic	• Immersed in present	• Action-awareness merging
	• Effortless		• Clear goals and unambiguous feedback
• Present-centered focus	• Focused/alert	• Narrow focus of attention	• Concentration on task at hand
• In control	• In control • Mentally calm	• Feelings of control • No fear	• Sense of control
• Detached from external environment			• Loss of self-consciousness
			• Transformation of time
			• Autotelic experience

Qualities of Peak Experience

A related but independent concept is peak experience. Maslow (1968) first systematically examined peak experience, described as moments of highest happiness that lead to growth, or actualization. Maslow developed a long list of factors characterizing peak experience, such as total attention, rich perceptions, time-space disorientation, perceptions of unity, and feelings of wonder and awe. Ravizza (1984) examined Maslow's concept in sport by asking athletes to describe their one most joyful, blissful moment in sport. Three common characteristics emerged: focused awareness, leading to total absorption in the task; feelings of complete control of self and environment; and a sense of self-transcendence.

In *In the Zone*, Murphy and White (1995) described the transcendent potential of sport. The authors compiled over a thousand references to "metanormal" experiences in sport, defined as human functioning that in some respect radically surpasses what is typical for most people (p. ix). They describe mystical sensations that can accompany sport moments, such as peace and stillness, freedom, and feelings of immortality, and also discuss altered perceptions and extraordinary athletic feats. Uneståhl (1981, 1986), in research on altered states of consciousness in sport, describes a state he calls the Ideal Performing State (IPS) as an alternative state of consciousness (ASC) akin to hypnosis. It is during an ASC, according to Uneståhl's model, that peak performance will occur. Characteristics of the IPS include amnesia related to the performance, concentration-dissociation, pain detachment, perceptual changes, and feelings of power and control.

The peak experience approach differs from that of peak performance in its more immediate focus on actual experience. Highest happiness is how Maslow (1968) described peak experience. Privette and Bundrick (1991)—specifically interested in delineating peak performance, peak experience, and flow—defined peak experience as intense joy or highest happiness. For Privette and Bundrick, the distinguishing characteristics of peak experience were fulfillment, significance, and spirituality. One can view peak experience as more closely aligned with a positive-emotions focus, whereas for peak performance the focus seems to be on the behavioral outcomes. To distinguish peak experience and peak performance, Privette and Bundrick used gradients of feeling and performance as identifying markers and then placed peak experience at the positive extreme of feeling, and peak performance at the positive extreme of performance. They found support for the independence of peak experience, peak performance, and flow. Their definition of flow, as the last time one played a sport or game, calls into question their findings in relation to flow, since flow is not guaranteed in each such undertaking. Nonetheless, their research has demonstrated that one can distinguish between the two types of positive experiential events. For example, peak experiences may occur after struggling to break through a problem, or in feeling a oneness with teammates. A peak experience may not involve optimal performance, and conversely, peak performance may occur without the presence of heightened emotions.

Peak experience and peak performance seem to share an underlying thread. When in flow, one experiences many of the characteristics associated with peak performance and peak experience. Although not a necessary precondition to peak experience or peak performance, flow may operate as a process underlying these events.

Links Between Flow and Quality of Performance

Achieving optimal performance is the goal of many elite athletes, coaches, and sport psychologists. Flow is all about optimal mental functioning, and it is often when athletes are in flow that they produce outstanding performances. In a study with collegiate athletes, Jackson and Roberts (1992) found correlational support for a link between flow and peak performance, operationally defined as one's best-ever performance. Qualitative analyses also supported a flow-peak performance link, with best performances being associated with flow state characteristics.

A recent study using Jackson's flow scales (TFS and FSS) (Jackson et al., 1999) showed some support for relationships between flow and performance. In a sample of competitive athletes in surf lifesaving, orienteering, and cycling, the TFS and FSS predicted small amounts of variance in an objective performance measure, finishing position. In addition, the FSS accounted for substantial variation in a subjective performance measure. These findings were based on retrospective self-report data, and predictive studies are needed to allow any firm conclusions about the relationship between flow and performance.

The link between flow and peak performance can also be demonstrated in the similarity between the characteristics used to describe the two concepts. Descriptions of the peak performance process by various researchers closely resemble flow descriptors, as shown in table 6.1.

Although more research on the flow-peak performance link is needed, the empirical findings to date—plus an intuitive relatedness between the two factors—suggest that one important consequence of experiencing flow in sport is performing optimally. However, one can produce outstanding results when not in flow, and flow can occur outside of high-performance contexts. Nevertheless, when the context is one of high performance, the optimal functioning that is flow seems likely to be associated with positive performance outcomes.

Links Between Flow and Quality of Experience

Flow experiences remain etched in people's memories because they are so positive. Athletes use a variety of terms to describe them: "in the zone," "on auto," and "in the groove" are examples of phrases that denote what happens when everything clicks and nothing matters but the experience itself.

Flow experiences are autotelic, or intrinsically motivating. While at the time of being in flow one may not be aware of positive affect as part of the experience, the feelings can be very intense afterward; the person may be "on a high" for hours. Flow experiences take place on a continuum of intensity, from relatively minor occurrences during daily tasks to the peak experiences of amazing human accomplishments.

In addition to the associated positive affective qualities, the potential for psychological growth through flow experiences as described by Csikszentmihalyi (1990) demonstrates important life consequences. After a flow experience, according to Csikszentmihalyi, the organization of the self becomes more complex through the opposing processes of differentiation and integration:

> Differentiation implies a movement toward uniqueness, toward separating oneself from others. Integration refers to its opposite: a union with other people, with ideas and entities beyond the self. A complex self is one that succeeds in combining these opposite tendencies. (p. 41)

According to Csikszentmihalyi (1990), differentiation occurs after flow because of the increase in skill one perceives after successfully meeting a challenge. Integration follows from the ordering of consciousness that occurs in flow, leaving one feeling more in tune with oneself and with the world.

FLOW AS A UNIFYING POSITIVE PSYCHOLOGICAL CONSTRUCT

The constellation of positive experiences considered here includes joy, happiness, fun, enjoyment, optimal experience, peak performance, peak experience, and flow. While each might be seen as independent, the terms overlap to some extent, and the experiences have common threads. I have suggested that flow is key to understanding the joy, happiness, fun, and enjoyment in sport and also that it underlies peak performance and peak experience. Not that flow is the only path to these experiences, but that it is a sure way to enjoy the positive qualities of sport. When challenges and skills are balanced and are at the same time extending the individual, the potential for surpassing previous limits and experiencing total task absorption can lead to a spiral of events involving outstanding levels of performance as well as highly positive experiences.

FACTORS INFLUENCING FLOW IN SPORT

If flow is a key positive psychological state, the question of how one achieves flow becomes most significant, presenting a challenge to researchers and practitioners alike. Many athletes and coaches, as well as sport psychologists, regard flow as rather elusive. The individual who has experienced it feels fortunate, but frequently is left wondering whether and when it will occur again.

Is Flow Controllable?

In an interview-based study, I asked elite athletes whether they thought flow was controllable (Jackson, 1995). Predictably, responses ranged from assertions that it was totally controllable to exactly the opposite. Of the 28 athletes, 71% said that flow was controllable; for this sample, then, flow appeared less ephemeral than might have been expected, as illustrated by the response of a triathlete:

> I think you can set it up. You can set the scene for it, maybe with all that preparation. It should be something that you can ask of yourself and get into, I think. Through your training and through your discipline.

For this sample, whether flow could be controlled depended on the controllability of factors that made flow more or less likely to occur. Of the many factors participants mentioned as helping them get into flow, 82% were perceived as controllable. On the other hand, the factors seen to disrupt flow were largely (72%) seen as uncontrollable. So the athletes perceived that in the presence of the largely controllable factors (e.g., physical and mental preparation) that helped them get into flow, they would be likely to stay in flow until or unless a largely uncontrollable event (e.g., changes in weather, getting a flat tire) intervened.

Although some of these athletes perceived it possible to improve the chances that flow would occur, it was "a little bit of magic" and could not be guaranteed. Others perceived that flow just happened independent of their input. For athletes on teams where there was a sense of interdependence, the experience of flow depended on the successful integration of team members. In another study with elite figure skaters (Jackson, 1992), several of the pairs skaters perceived partner unity as critical to flow.

Factors Influencing Flow

Jackson (1992, 1995) interviewed elite athletes about factors that in their perception favored the occurrence of flow, and developed categories of themes from analysis of athlete transcripts.

Confidence came through strongly as an important flow facilitator. This fits with the concept in the theory that flow occurs only when a person perceives his skills as matching the challenge. Another important factor was how well the athlete had prepared for the event and planned for her performance. The importance of mental plans to optimal performance is well recognized in the performance enhancement literature (e.g., Orlick, 1986); thorough planning permits a complete task focus, and this ability to tune in to the event would greatly facilitate the occurrence of flow. Other factors that these athletes identified included optimal arousal levels, high motivation, feeling good during the performance, maintaining an appropriate focus, having optimal environmental and situational conditions, and positive team play and interaction (Jackson, 1992, 1995).

Jackson (1992, 1995) also obtained data on factors that athletes felt prevented or disrupted flow. Prominent in this regard were nonoptimal environmental or situational conditions such as undesirable weather, uncontrollable event influences, and distracting interactions with others. Lack of physical preparation or readiness, and physical problems such as injury or fatigue, also stood in the way. Other factors were lack of confidence or a negative mental attitude (as would be expected from the challenge-skill balance equation); lack of motivation for the event; and inappropriate focus—thinking too much, not focusing enough, or worrying. Problems with performance during the event, including problems in team play, were other obstacles.

The scenarios for facilitative or debilitative flow conditions resemble the individual zones of optimal functioning for various components of psychobiosocial states. This qualitative research provided interesting information about how athletes perceived influences on flow. Another source of such information is recent quantitative research in which responses on Jackson's flow scales (TFS and FSS) were compared to those on other self-report instruments. A study assessing intrinsic/extrinsic motivation, perceived ability, and anxiety in relation to flow (Jackson et al., 1998) showed correlational support for a relationship in each case. In particular, perceived ability, cognitive components of anxiety, and an intrinsic motivation dimension were significantly associated with flow dimensions. One can draw parallels between these quantitatively based correlates of flow and qualitative dimensions such as confidence, optimal arousal, appropriate focus, and high motivation reported by elite athletes (Jackson, 1995).

Kowal and Fortier (1999) recently examined the relationship between flow, as assessed by the FSS, and motivation. Using Deci and Ryan's (1985) self-determination theory to examine motivation, the authors found positive relationships between flow and situational self-determined forms of motivation, specifically intrinsic motivation and self-determined extrinsic motivation. Flow and the situational motivational determinants, autonomy, competence, and relatedness, were also positively associated.

Self-concept and psychological skills are still other factors associated with flow, as assessed by the TFS and FSS. Jackson and colleagues (Jackson et al., 1999) reported that positive perceptions of one's physical and mental abilities, as well as mental skills such as controlling thoughts and feelings during performance, were related to flow in a sample of competitive athletes.

FUTURE RESEARCH DIRECTIONS

The potential for research in the area of positive sport experiences, and flow in particular, is limitless. Understanding the factors that make sport positive is a critical first step in helping to make sport enjoyable for all. Further study of joy, fun, and flow and the related factors in various sport contexts is warranted. Qualitative as well as quantitative methods yield information about such concepts, and we need to be eclectic in our approaches in order to maximize opportunities for progress.

Definitional aspects require thoughtful analysis and conceptualization, and attempts to integrate past knowledge with more unified understandings of terms will help provide a clearer picture of positive sport experiences. Measurement depends on specific definitions, and development of assessment instruments will require careful operational definitions. However, remaining fluid in developing and evaluating definitions and associations between constructs will help to ensure that the doors to discoveries remain open.

In addition to using available psychological assessment tools and keeping an open perspective toward positive sport experiences, an interdisciplinary stance will help us uncover more information than reliance on psychological approaches alone. Psychophysiological and social psychological assessments in particular may provide new information about factors related to positive experiences in sport.

ENHANCING POSITIVE SPORT EXPERIENCES

For some, sport offers more fun and excitement than any other activity. For others, sport is threatening or boring. What makes the difference? Flow theory holds that the challenge-skill balance is crucial to the quality of the experience. Applying this concept means paying attention to the challenges in the specific environment and the objective level of participants' skills. However, it is crucial to understand the challenge-skill balance as perceived by the individual. Presuming that a talented athlete will perform well is as precarious as believing that a learner will always continue to develop and be motivated if environments are progressively more challenging. The individual challenge-skill equation is what makes flow both a personal and a universal experience. Flow occurs when the balance is optimal for the individual, and this theoretically can occur for any person; thus flow is an experience accessible by all performers.

In addition, providing clarity of goals and unambiguous feedback regarding performance will enhance the quality of experience. Choice and freedom from evaluation allow a sense of control and loss of self-consciousness—other flow characteristics.

Finally, emphasis on the intrinsically rewarding aspects of sport will make it a positive experience and provide participants with many joyous, fun, and flowlike episodes. Currently in elite sport this is a real challenge in that the external environment (media, sponsors, sport politicians, spectators) emphasizes successful outcomes, often at any cost.

SUMMARY

The aim of this chapter has been to address the positive side of sport experiences, to spotlight the fact that sport potentially fosters such experiences, and to suggest how much there is to learn about the factors in sport that lead to positive emotions such as joy. Concepts related to positive sport experiences have been reviewed, including joy, happiness, fun, enjoyment, flow, peak performance, and peak experience. Questions concerning use of various terms to describe aspects of the sport experience and the ways these terms relate to one another, as well as to positive aspects of sport, have been raised. The concept of flow has been highlighted as a central and unifying phenomenon that can help explain what makes sport positive.

CHAPTER 7

Successful and Poor Performance and Emotions

Yuri L. Hanin
Finland

This chapter examines research testing the basic assumptions of the Individual Zones of Optimal Functioning (IZOF) model (see chapter 3; Hanin, 1997a, 1997b, 1997c; Bortoli, Robazza, & Nougier, 1997). It addresses IZOF-based assessment procedures for identifying performance and individually optimal and dysfunctional emotions; patterns of emotions related to individually successful and poor performances in athletes; emotion-performance relationships as predicted by the in-out of the zone principle; and seven IZOF-based principles to guide interventions to regulate emotion.

IZOF-BASED ASSESSMENT OF PERFORMANCE-RELATED EMOTIONS

The IZOF model focuses on emotions of individual athletes prior to, during, and after performances. It assumes that the major role of emotions is to reflect person-environment interactions and provide conditions for performing. Thus a key construct is athletic performance conceptualized as a task-execution process resulting in a specific outcome (Hanin, 1993, 1994). In the past, most researchers focused on the end result of movement or skill quantified in some performance outcome measure (Weinberg, 1989, 1990).

Successful and Poor Performance Measures

Because developing performance measures, especially in team sports, remains a challenge (Courneya & Chelladurai, 1991), the following sections introduce problems related to assessing the performance process; elaborate on performance outcomes; and discuss criteria for establishing an individual success-failure range.

Performance Process Measures

Process-oriented performance measures should focus on "how individuals organize and integrate their energies in the execution of motor skills" (Weinberg, 1989). Since everyone exhibits particular patterns of task execution, understanding emotion-performance relationships requires identification of movement patterns and their underlying processes. Biomechanical analysis of movement data may be especially helpful (Yeadon & Challis, 1992)—for example, identifying elements of technique in best performances (Ferrario, Sforza, Michielon, Mauro, & Miani, 1995). However, few researchers have combined psychological and biomechanical performance aspects. One study examined the impact of arousal on motor behavior using kinematic characteristics of a stepping motion in two anxiety states (Beuter & Duda, 1985); another, assessing movement quality using electromyogram markers, showed that neuromuscular energy patterns are important in performance (Weinberg, 1978; Weinberg & Hunt, 1976).

Performance profiling, based on Personal Construct Theory (Kelly, 1955) and work with elite athletes (Butler & Hardy, 1992; Doyle & Parfitt, 1996; Jones, 1993; Vanden Auweele, Cuyper, Mele, & Rzewnicki, 1993), holds promise. Performance profiling maps the performer's personal construct system onto a performance profile (Butler, 1989), extending traditional methodologies to uncover what athletes consider important and to enhance awareness about the best approaches to training and preparation. In comparing current and ideal conditions of an athlete on personally relevant dimensions, profiling is developmental, athlete oriented, and idiographic. It is limited in that it typically focuses more on the factors related to ideal performance than on the process itself.

In contrast, the aim of the IZOF model is to identify an athlete's emotional state (in terms of individually relevant descriptors) and performance characteristics (in terms of specific strengths and limitations). The model assumes that during performance each athlete has different resources he or she can use in different ways. Therefore a ratio between realized strengths and nondelivery of expected performance represents an athlete's total contribution to the task. The ratio takes visual form as an individualized performance profile.

Hanin and Syrjä (1997) tested these assumptions in an unpublished study with the Finnish Olympic soccer team. A head coach identified each player's greatest strengths and weaknesses; the authors compiled these into a single list; and players then selected from the list the four or five qualities that characterized their own performances. These were then arranged into individualized performance profiles reflecting the interaction of strengths and weaknesses. Figure 7.1 shows one such profile.

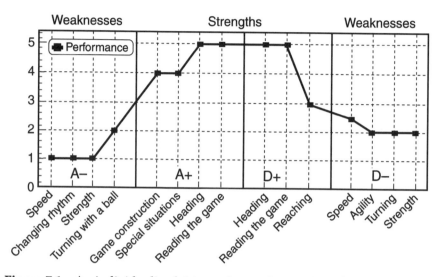

Figure 7.1 An individualized "strengths-weaknesses" performance profile of a soccer player.

Note that this player's strengths appear in the middle of the profile and his limitations at the sides. This player's strengths in attack include ability to contribute to the game constructively, skills in playing in special situations, playing with the head, and reading game situations. In defense, he was skillful in reading the game, using his head, and reaching. Weaknesses or limitations in performance of this player included insufficient speed (both in attack and defense), strength, turning with the ball, and changing the rhythm of the game in the attack. In his best games, when this player realized most of his strengths and kept weaknesses minimal, his total performance profile was shaped like an iceberg; for poor games it would be shaped like a cavity. The iceberg and cavity profiles represent different interaction effects of emotion on performance in terms of a player's strengths/weaknesses ratio. These profiles can be used to monitor the dynamics of individual performance during a game or across several games, as a goal-setting tool, and as an aid in post-performance analysis (Hanin, 1999b).

Performance Outcome Measures

As mentioned earlier, sport psychology research and practice have typically used only outcome measures to evaluate athletic performance. These evaluations typically involve three groups of criteria:

▶ Task- or activity-oriented criteria including a range of results achieved on a particular sport task

▶ Normative criteria based on seasonal (or sport career) statistics, typically for a specific group of performers (e.g., top 10 in the world, qualification norms)

▶ Self-referenced criteria based on repeated observations and including a particular athlete's results during a specified period of time (e.g., season, Olympic cycle)

All three types of criteria can be used in evaluating performance outcomes at the group, interindividual, or intraindividual levels. Current outcomes of performance can be expressed as a percentage of achievement specified by the selected criterion (Raglin, 1992; Turner & Raglin, 1996; Imlay, Carda, Stanbrough, & O'Connor, 1995) or as z-score transformations (Males & Kerr, 1996; Yarnold, 1988). However, in the field setting of elite sports it is important not to limit analysis to a cross section of actual outcome measures. One should also consider customary and within-individual performance variability (Klavora, 1979; Sonstroem & Bernardo, 1982), including sudden peaks (Uneståhl, 1986; Orlick, 1990; Kreiner-Philips & Orlick, 1993) and troughs (Bar-Eli, 1985, 1997; Bar-Eli, Taoz, Levy-Kolker, & Tennebaum, 1992; Hardy, 1990, 1996), and examine this variability from both short- and long-term perspectives.

In a recent meta-analysis, Jokela and Hanin (1999, in press) demonstrated, for instance, that criterion-referenced and self-referenced (% best) performance measures quantified performance better than self-referenced (% average) measures. For the "% personal best" measures, the effect size (ES) was .45 ($k = 6$, $N = 480$), whereas for the "% personal average" the ES was $-.27$ ($k = 2$, $N = 119$). This finding calls into question the recommendation to use customary (Klavora, 1979) and median (Sonstroem & Bernardo, 1982) intraindividual performance measures as direct criteria for individually optimal performance (Raglin, 1992). However, the deviations from the customary to the best (and worst) performance, if established beforehand, might be a useful indirect measure.

Individual Success-Failure Performance Range

A description of performance usually implies two extreme categories—two poles of one continuum. Successful performance is at least equal to that realistically expected relative to one's resources and readiness for a contest, and poor performance is defined accordingly. However, in other areas, such as management and small business research, different empirical indicators have been used to describe success and failure (Kelmar, 1990). Therefore it has been argued that success (and nonsuccess) and failure (and nonfailure) should be considered two relatively independent continua (Kelmar, 1990; Hanin, 1992, 1993, 1995).

This conceptual distinction suggests that one should establish the total functional impact of various emotions on athletic performance through their interaction effects. Functionally optimal emotions critical for success are termed success-related or S-emotions, whereas dysfunctional emotions detrimental to performance are termed failure-related or F-emotions. Since an athlete can experience S-emotions and F-emotions at the same time, one can predict the total impact based on their interaction effects; for example, successful performance usually results from the interaction of S-emotions with a minimum of F-emotions (see chapter 3).

Individually successful, average, or poor performances can be identified according to either the quality of performance process (movement patterns, actions) or the achievement level (a range of outcomes). However, since multiple factors determine performance, an excellent performance process does not always produce exceptional outcomes, and an average performance process can produce outstanding results. Therefore, additional and individual-oriented criteria reflecting a better- or worse-than-usual level of an athlete's readiness and the external conditions (weather, opponents, etc.) might also be appropriate (Gould & Krane, 1992; Martens, Vealey, & Burton, 1990; Rushall, 1978). In all cases, however, it is best to consider success-failure range on the basis of an individual's performance quality and/or achievement level.

Measuring Subjective Emotional Experiences

Analysis of emotion patterns in the IZOF model is based on the notion that skilled athletes are aware of and able to report their subjective emotional experiences related to performance. Therefore, assessments use a wide range of self-report scales, both standardized (normative, group oriented, nomothetic) and individualized (person oriented, idiographic) (Zevon & Tellegen, 1982).

Idiographic Assessments Using Psychometric Normative Mood Scales

Most standardized psychometric scales measuring emotion focus either on global affect or on single, primary emotions. Examples of the former are the Positive and Negative Affect Schedule (PANAS; Watson & Tellegen, 1985) and the Affect Balance Scale (Derogatis, 1975); examples of the latter are measures of anxiety (chapter 4) and anger (chapter 5), and the Profile of Mood States (POMS) scales. Psychometric scales emphasize between-individual differences conceptualized within the framework of fixed emotion content assessed by researcher-generated items. In contrast, educational testing measures used to reflect within-individual growth and change contain a so-called edumetric dimension (Carver, 1974). Edumetric measures are mainly used for within-individual self-referenced descriptions and as a motivational tool. For instance, measuring productivity and feeding the data back to personnel in an organization will produce change leading to increased productivity (Pritchard, 1990; Pritchard, Jones, Roth, Stuebing, & Ekeberg, 1989). Examples in sport include descriptions of idiosyncratic emotion (Hanin, 1978, 1993, 1994, 1995, 1997a) and performance profiling (Butler & Hardy, 1992; Jones, 1993).

Although normative psychometric scales provide a basis for interindividual comparisons, the researcher-generated fixed item content is a limitation. The relevance of item contents to an athlete's history and emotional experiences is usually not known. An individualized technique of recall, actual, and anticipatory self-report was developed to overcome some of these problems (see chapter 4; Hanin, 1978, 1986, 1989, 1993).

Individualized Emotion Profiling

Individualized emotion profiling incorporates four important features: individually relevant (a) emotion content, (b) emotion intensity, (c) context, and (d) interaction effects of optimal and dysfunctional emotions. A comprehensive IZOF-based assessment program examines the individual's performance history, generates individually relevant emotion content, and then identifies optimal (and dysfunctional) intensities for each emotion. Finally the emotion profile (with intensity zones for each item) is validated and refined in a series of repeated self-ratings in specific performance situations (practice or competitions) (see appendixes).

Generating Individually Relevant Emotion Content

The first step in individualized emotion profiling is to identify the content of functionally optimal and dysfunctional emotion patterns. Athletes generate items using the positive-negative affect (PNA) stimulus list (PNA-77) of 40 positive and 37 negative emotions. The PNA-77 was compiled through selection and revision of items from the 10 global PNA scales described by Watson and Tellegen (1985). Some positive affect items are "active," "calm," and "determined"; representative negative affect items are "nervous," "angry," and "uncertain."

Syrjä & Hanin (1997a) have conducted interscale comparisons and shown that the PNA-77 stimulus list includes items similar in content to 17 (85%) State-Trait Anxiety Inventory (STAI) items, 12 (60%) PANAS items, and 16 (37.2%) POMS items; this is a moderate amount of overlap (.43 for STAI, .33 for POMS, and .31 for PANAS). However, content overlap scores were significantly lower between the PNA-10 aggregated scale (with 10 most-selected items) and the STAI (.15), POMS (.19), and PANAS (.10) (figure 7.2).

To develop individualized emotion scales, athletes select 4 or 5 positive and 4 or 5 negative items that best describe their emotions related to past successful performances; they then do the same for poor performances. Emphasis is on repeated experiences. Athletes use the PNA-77 stimulus list or can add their own emotion words. A profile has 16 to 20 individual items and two subscales, each with 8 to 10 descriptors: the optimal emotion scale (P+N+) and dysfunctional emotion scale (P–N–). For repeated assessments in a field setting, the total emotion profile can be condensed to the 12 most important markers (Hanin, 1997c; Hanin & Syrjä, 1997; Robazza, Bortoli, Zadro, & Nougier, 1998).

Interscale content overlap

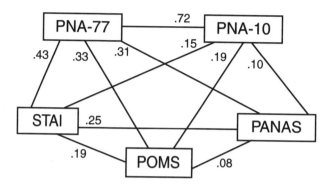

Figure 7.2 Content overlap in general and sport-specific mood scales.

Assessing Individual Intensity Zones

Intensity levels (and zones) for each emotion are established using a separate scale. Athletes indicate a level or range of intensity ("How much of this feeling or emotion is usually helpful [or harmful] for your performances in competition [or in practices]?"). Intensity level/range (a minimum and maximum amount of emotion that was helpful or harmful) is measured using Borg's Category Ratio (CR-10) scale (Borg, 1982, 1998), which allows ratio comparisons of intensities as well as determinations of direct intensity levels. A standard format of the CR-10 scale as applied to emotion intensity (Hanin, 1994; Hanin & Syrjä, 1995a, 1995b, 1996) is shown in appendix B.

The intensity zones become individualized criteria for estimating the expected functional impact of actual (or anticipated) emotions. The emotion profiles are then used as individualized emotion scales for self-ratings with either actual, retrospective, or anticipated instruction sets to identify an athlete's emotions.

There are two complementary methods of establishing optimal intensity zones: a recall (indirect) and an actual or empirical (direct) assessment method.

▶ The **recall method** consists of retrospectively rating optimal intensity levels based on the *best ever* performance in one particular competition (as in step 4, p. 306) or several successive competitions. For each emotion, these intensity levels are considered to be midpoints, and an arbitrary range of ±2 points (established for the CR-10 scale) is then added to derive roughly defined optimal zones. The other option is to focus directly on the optimal range by asking an athlete to establish a minimum and a maximum amount of intensity for each emotion that is helpful for performance. Thus a zone is established at the outset rather than a particular level, or midpoint, of intensity. The advantage of the second option is that it is based on past performance history and identifies patterns rather than an emotional state coming about due to one specific situation. The limitation of this approach is that it relies heavily on an athlete's awareness of his or her subjective experiences. Therefore, initial zones identified by recall should be considered as tentative; repeated assessments are required for further validation and refinement.

▶ The **empirical method** consists of repeating actual assessments in several successful and unsuccessful competitions, plotting emotion intensity levels, and evaluating the distribution of optimal intensity scores. The optimal intensity level zones are based upon either the mean ±1/2 the standard deviation range or upon the interquartile range (IQR), which includes the range of scores from the 25th percentile to the 75th percentile. IQR is one of the several interpercentile measures of variability that tells how the middle 50% of the distribution is scattered. The clear disadvantages of this assessment method are that it requires many data points, it ignores an athlete's past performance history, and it is limited to pre- and post-performance assessments (see chapter 4).

Validity, Reliability, and Content Relevancy of the Individualized Mood Scales

To get a developmental perspective in highly skilled athletes, it is usually important to examine performance history. Recalls provide important preliminary information about an athlete's awareness and performance-related experiences. Since actual assessments are often intrusive, cost ineffective, and impractical (Hanin, 1989, 1997a; Hanin & Syrjä, 1996; Harger & Raglin, 1994), emotion profiles obtained through recall are important; but they are still tentative. Given that recalled experiences are critical for both research and interventions, one should consider two factors in examining reliability. First, the accuracy of such recalls can vary with the level of analytical skills, self-awareness, and experience of the athlete. Second, there are large differences in recent performance history across athletes in terms of the success/failure ratio and consistency. These can influence the content, quality, and accuracy of recall; for example, recent success may result in more accurate reports of optimal than of dysfunctional experiences.

Tentative emotion profiles are validated either by recalls or by assessment of actual emotional states in practices or in several competitions. Three to five actual or recalled assessments usually enable athletes to learn the procedure and gain awareness of their emotions. Repeated assessments also help in refining item emotion content and intensity ranges as a check of the content validity of the emotion scales. Regular post-performance recalls following big successes and unexpected failures are also recommended for processing new experiences, and predictions and recalls can be used to develop emotion profiles for new and more challenging tasks.

Reliability of individualized emotion scales is established intraindividually by calculating Cronbach alpha coefficients for each athlete based on repeated assessments across several performance situations. In a sample of 17 Olympic-level soccer players (Hanin & Syrjä, 1996), mean intraindividual alphas ranged from .76 to .90 for various subscales, with the highest internal consistency (alpha = .90, SD = .04) observed in positive and negative optimal (P+N+) items. Additionally, the accuracy of one-day predictions and immediate post-performance recalls of pregame affect in international matches using individualized emotion scales was established. Specifically, intraindividual contrasts of emotion profiles in each player via a systemic modification of sign test (SMST) revealed that highly skilled soccer players were accurate in both recalls and predictions ($p < .01$).

Another important feature of the individualized mood scales is the content relevancy of athlete-generated emotions. Athletes select emotion descriptors within the framework of four global affect categories, but this selection is based primarily on their awareness of their idiosyncratic emotional experiences related to performance. Therefore, Syrjä and Hanin (1997a, 1997b) have conducted two studies to compare the content similarity of emotion descriptors in individualized PNA scales with those in the selected normative (standardized) mood scale.

The first study (Syrjä & Hanin, 1997a), involving 50 Finnish Olympic-level soccer players (mean age = 19.62, SD = 1.09), compared three standardized non-sport-specific scales: STAI (Spielberger, Gorsuch, & Lushene, 1970), POMS (McNair, Lorr, & Droppleman, 1971), and PANAS (Watson, Clark, & Tellegen, 1988). The PNA-77 stimulus list and the PNA-10, an aggregated mood scale with 10 most frequently selected items (N = 138 athletes, 7 sports), were also included. The content similarity was established by calculating the amount of overlap (Krahé, 1986), or shared items (worded exactly the same way), between each athlete's individualized scale and the normative scales (Hanin, 1997a; Syrjä & Hanin, 1997a, 1997b). Individual overlap scores varied from 0 (all items were different) to 1.0 (all items were similar). As expected, the content of items across the normative nonspecific scales measuring different emotions varied greatly: total overlap values were .08 (between POMS and PANAS), .19 (between POMS and STAI), and .25 (between STAI and PANAS). There was also a relatively low overlap between the PNA-10 and the STAI (.15), POMS (.19), and PANAS (.10). Mean intraindividual scores of overlap between individualized PNA scales and the three normative scales were quite low, ranging from .11 (PANAS) to .16 (POMS) and .17 (STAI). In other words, at the group level, these psychometrically acceptable group-oriented scales did not include 83% to 89% of items most often selected by athletes. In contrast, about 45% of idiosyncratic items in individualized scales were similar in content to emotion items in the sport-specific aggregated PNA-10 scale.

The authors replicated and extended these findings in a study (Syrjä & Hanin, 1997b) involving 46 junior male ice hockey players. Players' mean age was 16.3 years (SD = 0.6), and sport experience ranged from 5 to 10 years

(M = 6.9, SD = 1.4). As in the soccer study (Syrjä & Hanin, 1997a), three standardized non-sport-specific scales (STAI, POMS, and PANAS) were compared. Also included were the sport-specific Competitive State Anxiety Inventory (CSAI-2; Martens et al., 1990) and the PNA-10 scale based on aggregation of individually relevant items. As predicted, mean content overlap scores were low for the non-sport setting scales, ranging from .10 (PANAS) to .16 (POMS) and .17 (STAI). A surprisingly low overlap was found for the CSAI-2 (.15) but not for the PNA-10 aggregated scale (.41). Effect sizes for overlap difference between the PNA-10 scale and other normative scales were 2.7 (with STAI), 2.9 (with POMS and CSAI-2), and 3.4 (with PANAS).

These data strongly support Hanin's (1997a) notion that emotion content is individually specific in its functional significance. This is consistent with the widely held assumption (Arnold, 1960; Frijda, 1988; Higgins, 1987; Ortony, Clore, & Collins, 1988; Schwarz, 1990; Schwarz & Bohner, 1996) that different affective states are closely linked to different psychological situations. Specifically, "Emotions arise in response to the meaning structures of given situations" (Frijda, 1988, p. 349). Another assumption is that the relationship between emotions and the meaning structures constituting a psychological situation is bi-directional: whereas different psychological situations result in different emotions, the presence of a given emotion also informs the individual about the current psychological situation (Schwarz, 1990; Schwarz & Bohner, 1996).

These findings might have important theoretical and practical implications. For instance, high-achievement settings emphasize how emotions enhance or impair performance, whereas clinical and educational settings focus on assessing well-being or mental health. Therefore, group-oriented normative emotion scales from non-sport settings with acceptable psychometric characteristics may not be appropriate for assessing individual emotional experiences in elite sports. On the other hand, such scales simply overlook certain meaning structures and the functional significance of individually relevant emotions for elite athletes. Thus, low content overlap between individualized and group-oriented emotion scales from non-sport settings reflects apparent functional differences between performance-induced and general well-being emotions.

The surprisingly low content overlap (from .07 to .19) between individualized PNA scales and the CSAI-2 calls into question the content specificity of this group-oriented sport-specific scale. Moreover, the content of the CSAI-2 items differed from that in all other mood scales: overlap scores were .02, .12, and .30 with PANAS, POMS, and STAI, respectively. These results seem to suggest that the cognitive anxiety (self-doubts) and self-confidence subscales in the CSAI-2 assess antecedents of emotions (negative and positive expectations) rather than the emotion itself. An implication for applied research and consultancy is that sport-specific mood scales should be not only setting- or situation-specific but also content-specific. This argues for the construction of sport content-specific mood scales through the aggregation of athlete-generated items. However, the use of individualized PNA scales is clearly indicated in applied research and consultancy with individual athletes (Hanin, 1997a, 1997b; Hanin & Syrjä, 1996; Syrjä & Hanin, 1997a, 1997b). Additionally, individualized mood scales are a direct method of assessing psychologically meaningful responses of athletes to the functional meaning of different performance situations.

Finally, a word of caution about the effect of language on athlete-chosen emotion descriptors. In the development of equivalent forms of psychometric scales in different languages, several validation procedures (blind back-translations, use of bilingual subjects, etc.) are usually recommended. However, literal translations, although accurate and technically valid, are often perceived by native speakers as strange, inappropriate, or psychologically meaningless. Researchers should avoid this by making sure that emotion lists are appropriate for the athletes involved. For instance, as mentioned earlier, the initial PNA stimulus list was compiled from items from 10 global PNA English language scales described by Watson & Tellegen (1985). However, for the Finnish language version, items were selected more on the basis of appropriateness for the performance context than on literal equivalences of emotion words translated from English. Furthermore, athletes could add their own words to make sure that emotion content was psychologically meaningful for them. There are still validity problems to be addressed. For instance, the emotion words in tables 7.1 and 7.2 are translations from Finnish. "Excited" is listed as both a strong emotion and a complacency emotion. The problem is that in Finnish the word *jännitynyt* has both positive and negative connotations—excited and tense. Charles Spielberger encountered a similar problem in developing the state anxiety measure: he had to eliminate the best item—*anxious*—because its positive and negative connotations caused confusion. In our case it is the intensity of emotion that determines either its strength or weakness. Additionally, an English- or an Italian-speaking sample might select somewhat different emotions or synonyms. However, in "core" or most often selected emotions (Hanin & Syrjä, 1995a, 1995b; Hanin, 1997a; Robazza, Bortoli, & Nougier, 1998; Robazza, Bortoli, Zadro, et al., 1998), one would still expect the emotion content at the group level to be similar. Additional research is needed on cross-cultural aspects of emotion scales; meanwhile researchers and practitioners should avoid slavishly following literally translated lists.

PATTERNS OF OPTIMAL AND DYSFUNCTIONAL EMOTIONS

A prototype analysis of emotion patterns (content and intensity) across athletes, sports, settings (practices and competitions), and tasks can use one of two types of scales: the existing standardized, psychometric mood scales (global affect or single primary emotion) with researcher-generated items; or individualized scales with athlete-generated items. Non-sport-specific standardized and sport-specific but group-oriented (psychometric) scales describe fixed emotion content and intensity across athletes, tasks, and settings; but the emotion content has relatively low relevance. Idiosyncratic markers relevant and meaningful to individual athletes might be preferable for understanding the functional meaning of real emotions in a sport setting. Therefore, the IZOF model suggests the use of individualized PNA scales with athlete-generated items. This idiographic approach focuses more on the dynamics of individually relevant (edumetric) content, context, and intensity of emotions than on interindividual differences. On the other hand, items from the individualized PNA scales can be aggregated across athletes, tasks, and settings. These aggregated items can be recategorized in terms of the existing emotion classifications (global affect or single primary emotions) or on the basis of their functional impact on athletic performance.

Optimal and Dysfunctional Emotion Content in Sport

Three consistent findings have emerged from IZOF-based studies in various sports (Hamill, 1996; Hanin, 1993, 1994, 1995, 1997a, 1997b; Hanin & Syrjä, 1995a, 1995b, 1996, 1997; Johnson, Anderson, AhYee, & Makua, 1995; Liukkonen, 1995; Robazza, Bortoli, Zadro, et al., 1998; Saarnio, 1995; Syrjä, 1993, 1997; Syrjä, Hanin, & Pesonen, 1995; Syrjä, Hanin, & Tarvonen, 1995; Tarvonen, 1995; Zaichkowski, Hamill, & Dallis, 1994).

1. Athletes used a wide range of individually relevant words to describe their optimal (P+N+) and dysfunctional (P–N–) emotions. Moreover, these descriptors usually included all four global affect content categories. Differences in the selection of emotions within these categories were usually at the interindividual and group levels.

2. Some emotions within each major content category were selected more often than others. Three types of emotion descriptors were identified (Hanin, 1993; Hanin & Syrjä, 1995a, 1995b): core or sport-specific items reflecting task demands and individual preferences; idiosyncratic items used by one or two athletes; and items not selected (nonspecific, irrelevant). To illustrate, tables 7.1 and 7.2 present selection frequencies for positive and negative emotions that athletes perceived as optimal or dysfunctional. The sample included 138 skilled athletes representing seven sports: badminton, ice hockey, orienteering, cross-country skiing, swimming, squash, and soccer. For both positive (table 7.1) and negative (table 7.2) emotions, the same descriptors were selected as optimal by some athletes and as dysfunctional by others. The predominant function of each emotion is seen in the selection percentage; however, the positive emotion "energetic," for example, was selected as enhancing performance by 39.9% of the sample and as impairing performance by only 5.8%. "Easygoing," topping the list of positive dysfunctional emotions, was selected as impairing performance by 30.4% and as enhancing performance by 6.5%.

Table 7.1 Top 15 Positive Emotion Markers Selected as Optimal or Dysfunctional (N = 138 Athletes, 7 Sports)

Predominantly optimal (P+) emotions (%)			Predominantly dysfunctional (P–) emotions (%)		
	P+	**P–**		**P–**	**P+**
Energetic	39.9	5.8	Easygoing	30.4	6.5
Charged	39.9	3.6	Excited	22.5	18.8
Motivated	37.7	—	Tranquil	18.1	2.9
Certain	30.4	13.8	Relaxed	16.7	10.3
Confident	29.0	2.2	Animated	16.7	0.7
Purposeful	29.0	—	Overjoyed	15.2	0.7
Willing	22.5	2.2	Fearless	15.2	8.7
Resolute	21.7	—	Satisfied	14.5	3.6
Alert	21.0	1.4	Exalted	13.8	6.5
Excited	18.8	22.5	Certain	13.8	30.4
Rested	18.1	7.2	Pleasant	13.0	1.4
Brisk	18.1	2.2	Comfortable	13.0	1.4
Cheerful	14.5	5.1	Nice	10.9	—
Enthusiastic	14.5	3.6	Daring	10.1	3.6
Brave	13.8	0.7	Calm	9.4	9.4

Note: P+ = emotion descriptors selected as positive and optimal (enhancing) for performance; P– = emotion descriptors selected as positive but dysfunctional (impairing) for performance.

Table 7.2 Top 15 Negative Emotion Markers Selected as Optimal or Dysfunctional (N = 138 Athletes, 7 Sports)

Predominantly optimal (N+) emotions (%)			Predominantly dysfunctional (N–) emotions (%)		
	N+	**N–**		**N–**	**N+**
Tense	49.3	10.1	Tired	44.2	2.9
Dissatisfied	49.3	5.8	Unwilling	39.9	1.4
Attacking	34.5	—	Uncertain	37.0	5.1
Vehement	24.6	—	Sluggish	29.0	0.7
Intense	21.7	2.9	Depressed	26.8	—
Nervous	20.3	10.1	Lazy	23.2	0.7
Irritated	19.6	4.3	Distressed	20.3	5.8
Provoked	13.0	4.3	Sorrowful	17.4	—
Angry	12.3	4.3	Afraid	15.9	3.6
Furious	10.9	2.2	Exhausted	14.5	—
Uneasy	10.1	2.2	Dejected	11.6	—
Tight	8.7	8.7	Sad	11.6	—
Restless	8.0	5.1	Concerned	10.9	6.5
Concerned	6.5	10.9	Unhappy	10.9	—
Distressed	5.8	20.3	Nervous	10.1	20.3

Note: N+ = emotion descriptors selected as negative but optimal (enhancing) for performance; N– = emotion descriptors selected as negative but dysfunctional (impairing) for performance.

3. Evidence about the relationships between hedonic tone and perceived consequences (functional impact) of emotions on athletic performance was compelling. Specifically, both positive and negative emotions can produce optimal, dysfunctional, or optimal *and* dysfunctional effects. Moreover, hedonic tone and functional impact in selected emotions are often reversed: positive emotions are perceived as dysfunctional, whereas negative emotions are rated as functionally optimal (Hanin, 1993, 1994, 1995; Hanin & Syrjä, 1995a, 1995b). In view of extant literature on optimal anxiety (see chapter 4; and Gould & Tuffey, 1996; Hanin, 1978; Hardy, 1990; Jokela & Hanin, 1997; Jones, 1993; Mahoney & Avener, 1977; Morgan, 1985, 1997b), the fact that negative (unpleasant) emotions can sometimes be optimal for some athletes is not surprising. However, less obvious is the finding that not all pleasant emotions are always beneficial for individual performance, especially in extremely demanding sport tasks. In fact, such positive emotions as calm, relaxed, satisfied, content, or too self-confident can be detrimental. Thus, hedonic tone and the functional impact of emotion are closely related, but independent. These data also support the assumption that emotions in high-level sport differ functionally from those in educational or clinical settings (Hanin, 1997a, 1997b; Syrjä & Hanin, 1997a, 1997b).

At the group level across seven sports, positive emotions experienced in competitions were perceived by athletes as optimal in 25.3% of all 275 cases (total number of selected words), as dysfunctional in 35.3% of cases, and as optimal by some athletes but dysfunctional by others in 39.6% of cases. Negative emotions were perceived as optimal in 22.1% of all 238 cases, as clearly dysfunctional in 43.7% of cases, and as optimal by some athletes but dysfunctional by others in 35.2% of cases.

Similar findings were combined for skilled swimmers (N = 18) and elite cross-country skiers (N = 12) for practices. Here, 23.6% of positive emotions (of 68 cases) were perceived as dysfunctional, 38.2% as optimal, and 38.2% as optimal by some athletes and dysfunctional by others. For negative affect, 19.1% of the selected emotions (of 63 cases) were perceived as optimal, 33.3% as clearly dysfunctional, and 47.6% as optimal by some and dysfunctional by others. Several replication studies have consistently shown a reversal effect of positive and negative emotions (Hanin, 1993, 1994; Hanin & Syrjä, 1995a, 1995b, 1996; Pesonen, 1995; Saarnio, 1995; Syrjä, 1993, 1997; Tarvonen, 1995) summarized in Hanin (1997a).

Another important aspect in research on emotion patterns is the notion that the content of the most frequently selected emotions reflects typical action tendencies in a given setting (Frijda, 1988; Hanin, 1993; Hanin & Syrjä, 1995a, 1995b; Schwarz, 1990; Schwarz & Bohner, 1996). Regarding positive affect, the top 10 functionally optimal emotions were *energetic, charged, motivated, certain, confident, purposeful, willing, resolute, alert,* and *excited* (table 7.1). These "strong" action-oriented emotions reflect availability of resources for starting and maintaining performance at a relatively high level. In contrast, *easygoing, excited* (if low in intensity), *quiet, relaxed, animated, overjoyed, fearless, satisfied, exalted*, and *pleasant* (complacency emotions), perceived by athletes as dysfunctional, are "weak," reflecting no need for further action. ("Excited" appears on both lists because in Finnish this word has both positive and negative connotations—"excited" or "tense.") Therefore, they are usually more relevant in post-performance success situations as an "achieved gain" response. For negative affect, the top 10 functionally optimal emotions were *tense, dissatisfied, attacking, vehement, intense, nervous, irritated, provoked, angry,* and *furious* (table 7.2); again, "strong" emotions reflecting the need to continue activity despite a possible resource deficit. The top 10 negative dysfunctional emotions, *tired, unwilling, uncertain, sluggish, depressed, lazy, distressed, sorrowful, afraid,* and *exhausted,* reflect a deficit in available resources and/or a relative inability to cope actively with the situation.

Interestingly, at the group level the top positive emotions conceptualized as optimal were selected as helpful in 94.1% of cases; positive emotions conceptualized as dysfunctional were selected as harmful in 77.5% of cases. For negative affect, optimal emotions were perceived as helpful in 85.3% of cases, and negative dysfunctional emotions as harmful in 93% of cases. Taken together, these findings support the validity of the four global affect categories in the IZOF model. That the content of the most frequently selected emotions did not overlap even at the group level indicates that these emotions represent two relatively independent factors. Thus, the orthogonality of the positive-negative and optimal-dysfunctional dimensions has been confirmed, at least descriptively and intuitively. Although more research is needed to test this hypothesis, it appears that athletes' success and failure are influenced by the interaction of functionally optimal and dysfunctional emotions.

Emotion Intensity: Optimal and Dysfunctional Zones

The IZOF model assumes that the impact of emotions varying in content is determined by their intensity. Several studies have assessed individually optimal and dysfunctional intensity of various emotions. The following sections briefly review these findings.

Optimal Intensity Levels

Empirical findings have indicated that optimal and dysfunctional intensity is individual and that it differs across athletes and sports. At the most general level, however, several regularities have been observed. For positive optimal emotions (P+), mean optimal intensity levels were 7.2 ("very much" on the CR-10 scale); negative optimal emotion intensity was 4.2 or in the range of "somewhat much" (4) and "much" (5); positive dysfunctional intensity was 6.2 (between "much" [5] and "very much" [7]). Finally, negative dysfunctional intensity was 6.8 or close to "very much" (7). Table 7.3 summarizes studies examining optimal and dysfunctional intensity of emotions in various sports.

Optimal performance-enhancing effect is usually related to intensive positive emotions and to negative emotions of moderate intensity. A dysfunctional effect was observed in athletes who reported experiencing much or very much

Table 7.3 Mean Intensity of Optimal and Dysfunctional Emotions in Various Sports

Author/year	N	Gender	Sport	Mean emotion intensity			
				P+	N+	P–	N–
Hanin & Syrjä (1995a)	46	M	Ice hockey	7.0	4.9	6.7	6.5
Hanin & Syrjä (1995b)	25	M	Soccer	6.5	4.1	4.3	6.0
Hanin & Syrjä (1997)	12	M/F	Cross-country skiing	8.4	5.1	5.6	7.7
Pesonen (1995)	25	M	Soccer	6.5	4.5	7.4	7.5
Syrjä (1993)	18	M	Ice hockey	7.6	5.9	7.3	7.1
Tarvonen (1995)	21	M/F	Squash	7.2	4.1	5.1	6.2
Tarvonen (1995)	16	M/F	Badminton	7.0	4.9	6.7	6.5
Robazza, Bortoli, Zadro, & Nougier (1998)	34	M/F	Track and field	6.0	3.9	5.3	5.7

Note: P+ = functionally optimal positive emotions; N+ = functionally optimal negative emotions; P– = dysfunctional positive emotions; N– = dysfunctional negative motions. Emotion intensity was measured on the CR-10 scale with scores ranging from 0 (nothing at all) to 10 and • maximal possible.

intensity in the selected performance-impairing emotions. Moreover, significant differences were consistently found for both optimal and dysfunctional emotions when individual intensity ranges were examined in athletes within and across sports (Hanin & Syrjä, 1995a, 1995b, 1997).

Optimal Intensity Zones

Several studies have been efforts to identify individually optimal and dysfunctional intensity zones. In Hanin and Syrjä's (1995a) study of 46 ice hockey players (ages 15-17 years), 78.8% of all subjective estimations of the intensity zones were in the range of 0-4 points on Borg's CR-10 scale. There were significant differences at the group level in the zone ranges for positive (P+ as compared to P–, $t = -2.8$, $p < .01$), negative (N+ as compared to N–, $t = -7.64$, $p < .01$), and ineffective (P– as compared to N–, $t = -4.35$, $p < .01$) emotions. In contrast, differences between intensity zones for optimal positive and dysfunctional negative emotions were not significant ($t = 1.05$, $p = .3$). Another study with skilled players (Hanin & Syrjä, 1995b) yielded similar findings. However, in initial assessments, 81% to 92% of these players indicated optimal and nonoptimal intensity levels but not the zone ranges (for P+ = 86.5%; for P– = 91.2%; for N+ = 91.9%; for N– = 80.8%). Initial difficulty in identifying the individual intensity zones appears to reflect a lack of awareness, more characteristic of younger than of elite athletes.

Emotion Patterns in Practices and Competitions

Although idiographic analysis of emotion content and intensity initially focused on sport activity in competitions, there have also been studies across settings (e.g., competitions and practices) (Hanin & Syrjä, 1997; Pesonen, 1995; Tarvonen, 1995). For instance, Hanin and Syrjä (1997) investigated, via recall, emotions in 12 elite Finnish cross-country skiers during racing, highly intensive training, and technical skills training. The athletes perceived over 50% of all positive emotions as facilitating in competitions and technical skills training; they perceived only 14.2% of negative emotions as facilitating in skills training. From 20% to 45.7% of positive and negative emotions in different settings had either facilitating or debilitating effects. Moreover, intraindividual scores of mean content overlap between optimal and dysfunctional emotions were quite low for both positive (M = .08, R = .00-.28) and negative (M = .20, R = .7-.36) affect. That is, to describe optimal and dysfunctional emotions in different settings, each athlete selected items differing in content for both positive and negative emotions.

For the skiers, on the other hand, the mean overlap for emotion words for competitions and hard training was moderate (M = .41, SD = .28, ranging from 0 to 1.00). The mean overlap for skills training as compared to hard training ranged from 0 to .87 (M = .31, SD = .22). As expected, for competitions as compared to skills training the overlap was even lower (M = .27, SD = .23, ranging from 0 to .71). Friedman Two-Way ANOVA revealed significant differences among these three pairs of contrasts (p = .05). Specifically, similarity between words chosen for competition and hard training was relatively greater than between those for competition and skills training. Words for the two types of training showed the least content overlap. Friedman Two-Way ANOVA also revealed significant differences in intensity for similar positive facilitating (p < .02) and negative debilitating emotions (p < .03). Additionally, the Wilcoxon test showed that optimal positive emotions for competitions were significantly (p < .02) more intensive than those for hard training. As expected, positive optimal emotions for competition were significantly more intense (p < .03) than those for technical skills training. In within-individual comparisons, independent t-tests revealed significant differences (t = 3.92, p < .01) in intensity between positive optimal and positive dysfunctional emotions. In the case of negative affect, the intensity of optimal emotions was significantly (t = 4.5, p < .01) lower than that of dysfunctional emotions.

These findings provide clear support for the multidimensional concept of affect in sports from which the content, intensity, and context (setting) dimensions were derived (chapter 3; Hanin, 1993, 1994, 1995, 1997a, 1997b, 1997c). The data from this exploratory study are consistent with earlier suggestions (Ebbeck & Weiss, 1988; Hanin, 1978; Neiss, 1988) and with previous empirical IZOF research (Hanin, 1994; Hanin & Syrjä, 1995a, 1995b; Syrjä, Hanin, & Pesonen, 1995) showing individual patterns of optimal and dysfunctional emotions within and across sports. Elite skiers were able to identify emotions that were helpful and harmful in three different settings; and optimal and dysfunctional emotions in these athletes were not only individual but also different across the performance settings. Studies contrasting emotion content and intensity in practices and games in other sports (skilled squash and badminton, Tarvonen, 1995; soccer, Pesonen, 1995) have confirmed these findings.

The data clearly contradict the hypothesis that "the optimal level of arousal for a typical performer for a given activity" (Oxendine, 1970) exists. Hanin's multi-setting hypothesis has received initial empirical support and seems to be instrumental for describing intraindividual emotion patterns across settings within the same sport. Future studies should examine emotion content and intensity at three different levels: the sport activity, the setting, and the task or situation (see chapter 1; Vallerand, 1997). This multiple-level perspective can provide a more differentiated approach to the study of performance affect in such multitask sports as Nordic combined, biathlon, triathlon, gymnastics, and decathlon.

EMOTION-PERFORMANCE RELATIONSHIPS IN SPORT

The IZOF model suggests that emotion-performance relationships in sport are bi-directional (chapters 2 and 3; Hanin, 1997a). Emotions influence performance process, and the ongoing performance process strongly impacts emotion content and intensity. Additionally, emotion-performance relationships are dynamic, differing prior to the performance (preparatory stage), during performance (task-execution stage), and post-performance (evaluation stage). Because most of the IZOF research reported here addresses emotion impact on performance, this chapter will not examine how athletic performance influences emotion states. The following sections examine the validity of performance predictions based on the in-out of the zone concept as extended to individually experienced emotions; address the possibility of moving beyond the zones and developing individual emotion-performance contingencies; and, on this basis, suggest an estimation of total impact of emotions on individual performance.

Prediction of Individual Performance: The In-Out of Zone Principle

Studies have tested the validity and practical utility of the in-out of the zone principle in predicting athletic performance in soccer (Syrjä, Hanin, & Pesonen, 1995; Pesonen, 1995), badminton and squash (Syrjä, Hanin, & Tarvonen, 1995; Tarvonen, 1995), and track and field (Robazza, Bortoli, Zadro, et al., 1998).

In 1995, Syrjä, Hanin, and Pesonen examined emotion-performance relationships in 27 junior soccer players aged 15-17 years. Recall and current idiographic scaling were used to identify the PNA patterns (content and intensities) of players' emotional experiences in successful and unsuccessful performances in practices and games. Intensities (level and zones) for emotions and performances were estimated on the CR-10 scale. Individualized PNA scales were used in three games to assess each player's emotional states 30 min prior to performance and 5 min post-performance, and a recall of emotion and performance during the game was also elicited. Each player's current and recalled PNA measures were contrasted with his PNA profile in five practices and three games separately. Then deviations from individually optimal and dysfunctional zones for each emotion were calculated across all players who were within the successful (7-10), average (4-6), or poor (0-3) performance ranges in games and practices. Differences in PNA deviations before and during game performance were significant and in the predicted direction (in 81.0% of all 21 cases). As expected, successful players were closer to their optimal zones and were outside dysfunctional zones. In practices, significant differences in the predicted direction were observed during but not before performance. Regression analysis indicated that the joint impact of the negative harmful (N–) and positive helpful (P+) emotions accounted for 41.8% of variance (F = 23.0, $p < .01$), whereas negative harmful emotions alone accounted for 34.0% of variance in game performance (F = 33.5, $p < .01$). In practices, 31.6% of variance in performance was explained by the joint impact of positive helpful (P+) and negative harmful (N–) emotions (F = 20.3, $p < .01$), while positive helpful emotions alone explained 26.7% of variance (F = 32.5, $p < .01$).

The Friedman Two-Way ANOVA revealed that emotion intensity changed over time, but differently in successful and unsuccessful players. In 88.2% of the poor performance group, players' emotions were already outside optimal zones before the game and athletes failed to enter their optimal emotion zones during performance. In the successful performance group before the game, players were closer to their optimal zones on facilitating emotions and outside of their dysfunctional zones on debilitating emotions; they also maintained their optimal emotion states until task completion. Consequently, during performance, emotions in successful players changed less often (37.5%). However, these findings should be interpreted with caution, since the causality in this study was not specifically tested. Whereas successful performance might facilitate maintaining optimal emotion states, poor performance might do the opposite, perhaps causing changes in the emotional state and producing a more pronounced dysfunctional impact on emotions.

Syrjä, Hanin, and Tarvonen (1995) replicated the soccer study in national- and international-level Finnish squash (N = 17) and badminton (N = 13) players. Current pre-performance and recalled (during and after performance) PNA measures in five game practices were contrasted with previously established individualized optimal and dysfunctional zones. In the squash players, all differences in emotion deviations from the zones were significant and in the predicted direction, except for the negative optimal and positive dysfunctional emotions. As expected, emotion intensity scores in successful players were closer to their optimal zones and outside of their dysfunctional zones. However, before practices, significant differences were found only for positive optimal and negative dysfunctional emotions. After practices, the significant differences were for positive optimal, negative dysfunctional, positive and negative dysfunctional, and total deviation scores.

In the squash group, predicted relationships were observed in 52.4% of all 21 cases. There were significant correlations between performance and deviations in dysfunctional (P–N–), optimal (P+N+), and total PNA scores. In the badminton group, there were significant correlations between performance and PNA deviations post-performance only for positive optimal ($p < .01$) and positive and negative optimal emotions ($p = .01$), but not before practices. Significant relationships between PNA deviations and performance level before practices were observed only in 14.4% of all cases. During performance these relationships were significant for deviations in positive optimal emotions, and combined positive and negative optimal emotions ($p < .01$), as well as for the total deviation score ($p < .05$). The interactive effect of positive and negative optimal emotions during performance in the squash players accounted for 51.2% of the variance (F = 38.9, $p < .01$), whereas positive optimal emotions alone accounted for 40.4% of the variance (F = 50.8, $p < .01$). In badminton players, 27.2% of the variance in performance was explained by the interactive effect of positive (optimal and dysfunctional) emotions (F = 10.1, $p < .01$), whereas positive optimal emotions alone explained 21.1% of variance (F = 14.7, $p < .01$). Thus, the PNA deviations from optimal and dysfunctional zones during the activity were in the predicted direction in both successful and poor performance groups.

In all cases, emotion intensity changed significantly over time. Additionally, in general, players were better aware of the effect of positive optimal and negative dysfunctional emotions on their performance; some were less aware of the effect of negative optimal and positive dysfunctional emotions. Taken together, the findings indicated that the best predictors of performance before and during practices were positive optimal and negative dysfunctional emotions. During practices, emotion-performance relationships were in the predicted direction and were more significant than either before or after performance. The study supports the utility of the in-out of the zone concept to examine interactive effects of emotions. It also demonstrates the need to identify emotion patterns during performance, as well as the ways emotions change during task execution.

What Is Beyond the Zones?

In describing emotion-performance relationships, two aspects have special interest: the optimal emotion intensity level, and the form of the relationship along the whole working range intensity. Until recently, research on emotion-performance relationships in sport was limited to a single (or repeated) cross-sectional (nomothetic) interindividual investigation of the unidirectional impact of, for instance, precompetition anxiety on athletic performance (see chapter 4). Moreover, the laboratory-based strategy of manipulating anxiety or performance levels seems neither practical nor feasible in sport field settings (Martens, 1974; Landers & Boutcher, 1986), nor even in animal studies (Yerkes & Dodson, 1908).

The idiographic approach provides conceptual, methodological, and practical solutions. For instance, we can now establish optimal levels and zones of anxiety and other emotions for each athlete. We can also identify the content and intensity of individually performance-enhancing and -impairing emotions. The IZOF model has so far emphasized optimal and dysfunctional intensity zones and their separate and interaction effects. However, we still do not know what is beyond the optimal and dysfunctional zones or what the form of the emotion-performance relationship is.

Previous research (Hanin, 1997a, 1997b; Hanin & Syrjä, 1997; Harger & Raglin, 1994; Jokela & Hanin, 1997, in press) led to the hypothesis that elite athletes would be able not only to identify the intensity zones relevant to their performances but also to establish the whole working range of intensity of their emotions. It was also expected that emotion-performance relationships would have similar shapes for similar emotions. In an exploratory study (Hanin, 1997c; Hanin & Syrjä, 1997) involving 12 top Finnish cross-country skiers (8 male and 4 female), aged 23-38 years (mean = 27.8), individualized PNA profiles with intensity ranges on the CR-10 scale were developed for each athlete according to the procedures described earlier and through recall. After athletes were interviewed to evaluate the importance of each emotion for their performance using the CR-10 scale, three emotions in each category (P+ N+, P–, N–) were retained for further evaluation. The mini-max. range of working intensity and a typical (customary) intensity of each emotion in races were then identified. The impact of each positive and negative emotion was then rated using the CR-10 scale for each intensity level within the individually established working range. Table 7.4 presents the descriptive statistics for intensity levels for each of the four major emotion content categories.

Table 7.4 Mean and Standard Deviations of Intensity in Optimal and Dysfunctional Emotions (N = 12 Finnish Elite Cross-Country Skiers)

Emotion intensity	Emotion categories			
	P+ M ± SD	N+ M ± SD	P– M ± SD	N– M ± SD
Optimal	7.0 ± 1.4	4.9 ± 2.2	6.7 ± 2.6	6.5 ± 3.5
Typical	6.6 ± 2.1	3.8 ± 1.5	4.2 ± 2.1	1.9 ± 1.2
Mean	6.2 ± 1.3	3.9 ± 1.4	4.3 ± 1.7	2.6 ± 1.2
Maximum	9.4 ± 1.0	6.7 ± 1.8	6.9 ± 2.2	4.9 ± 2.1
Minimum	3.1 ± 2.0	1.2 ± 1.2	1.7 ± 1.5	0.3 ± 0.4
Range	6.3 ± 1.8	5.6 ± 1.5	5.2 ± 1.5	4.6 ± 2.0

Note: P+ = functionally optimal positive emotions; N+ = functionally optimal negative emotions; P– = dysfunctional positive emotions; N– = dysfunctional negative emotions. Emotion intensity was measured on the CR-10 scale with scores ranging from 0 (nothing at all) to 10 and • maximal possible.

Mean working intensity ranges of emotions varied from M = 6.3 (SD = 1.8) for positive optimal emotions to M = 4.6 (SD = 2.0) for negative dysfunctional emotions. The highest optimal intensity (largest enhancing effect) was in positive optimal emotions, whereas the lowest intensity was in positive dysfunctional emotions (least impairing effect). Wilcoxon test revealed that average intensity levels for functionally optimal positive (P+) and negative (N+) emotions were significantly higher than either mean (z = −5.16, p < .001) or typical (z = −4.78, p < .001) intensity levels. As expected, typical intensity of emotions during athletic activity was often equal to mean scores and outside both optimal and dysfunctional zones. Also noteworthy was the finding that mini-max. ranges of working intensity for optimal (6.3 and 5.6) and nonoptimal (5.2 and 4.6) emotions did not cover the whole intensity range on the CR-10 scale (from 0 to 10 and • maximum possible). Thus, even at the minimum intensity, emotions in competitions were often close to the average intensity (ranging from moderate to high levels) on the CR-10 scale. Optimal intensity was higher than typical intensity levels experienced in athletic activity in positive optimal (P+), negative optimal (N+), and negative dysfunctional (N−), but not in positive dysfunctional (P−) emotions. Figure 7.3 shows the impact of emotions varying in intensity on athletic performance in the form

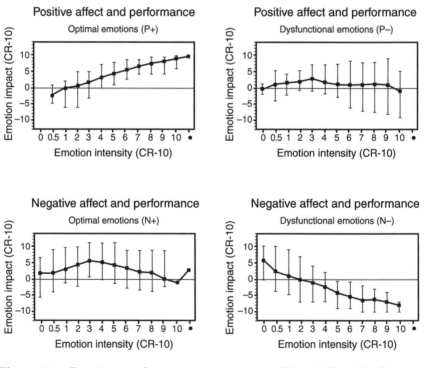

Figure 7.3   Emotion-performance contingencies (N = 12 Finnish elite cross-country skiers).

of curves aggregated separately for positive optimal, positive dysfunctional, negative optimal, and negative dysfunctional emotions.

At the group level, the enhancing impact of optimal positive emotions steadily increased with increased emotion intensity. Mean impact of negative optimal emotion was more pronounced at a moderate level, whereas detrimental effects of both positive and negative emotions were the largest at high intensity. Furthermore, the influence of emotions on performance at each intensity level was characterized by an "impact range." As expected, the effect of emotions across all four global PNA categories was more pronounced, and in the predicted direction, if emotions subjectively rated as "most important" were contrasted with "least important" emotions (figure 7.4).

Both positive optimal and dysfunctional emotions showed the "scissors" effect for most intensity ranges. The difference in impact was somewhat less pronounced for the negative optimal (high intensities only) and negative dysfunctional emotions (low and high intensities). The impacts of emotions of different content were then contrasted (figure 7.5).

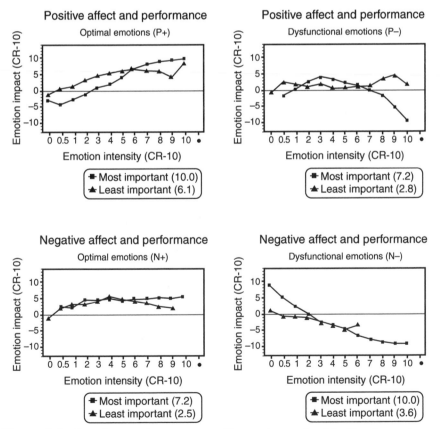

Figure 7.4 Emotion-performance contingencies and subjective importance of emotions (N = 12 Finnish elite cross-country skiers).

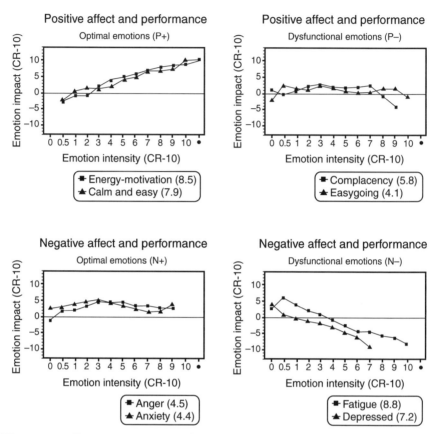

Figure 7.5   Emotion content and perceived impact on athletic performance (N = 12 Finnish elite cross-country skiers).

The low and high intensity ranges showed a significant difference only for the fatigued-depressed (N–) group. There were no significant differences in the impact of the three other emotion categories—energetic/motivated versus calm/relaxed (P+), content and easygoing (P–), and experiencing anger versus anxiety (N+)—at the group level. In most cases emotion-performance relationships, as perceived by athletes for separate emotions, were neither linear nor curvilinear—contradicting predictions from most nomothetic models.

This study, besides suggesting that skilled athletes can describe how emotions impact their performance along the whole intensity range, also demonstrated the feasibility of procedures previously used only in organizational settings (Pritchard, 1990). As applied to emotion-performance relationships, the intensity-impact contingencies might be especially useful for analyzing the dynamics of emotion processes. The findings also argue for application of the individualized recall method in assessing emotion impact along the whole intensity range in field conditions. Future research is warranted to examine the stability and dynamics of such self-ratings and the contingencies resulting from increased self-awareness in elite athletes; the findings might have an important implication for improving quality of training, as well as consistency of excellence in competitions. Finally, this approach provides new tools for an individualized self-analysis of performance-related emotional experiences and possibly other modalities of psychobiosocial state (Hanin, 1997a).

Estimating the Total Interaction Effects of Emotion On Performance

In earlier IZOF formulations, the total impact of emotion on athletic performance was predicted by the in-out of the zone dichotomy implying an interaction of the enhancing and inhibiting effects of various emotions (see chapter 3; Hanin, 1995, 1997a, 1997b). The ski study (Hanin, 1997c) provided initial empirical data for a more detailed estimation of the total interactive (additive) effect of different emotions. Being outside the optimal zones may produce a less enhancing effect on individual performance and sometimes can be detrimental (e.g., absence of motivation or energy). Similarly, being out of the dysfunctional zone on performance-inhibiting emotions can be less detrimental and sometimes even enhance the individual performance effect (e.g., an absence of fatigue or depression). Therefore, individualized emotion-performance contingencies allow more accurate estimation of the total emotion impact on performance. Figures 7.6 and 7.7 illustrate how the contingencies generated by two top cross-country skiers were used to estimate their best, typical, and poor performance profiles based on the whole working range of intensities for each emotion.

To be successful, the first skier needs to be in the optimal zones on his performance-enhancing emotions. Even keeping his dysfunctional emotions minimal, does not seem to directly contribute much to successful performance, but it does help him stay focused. In contrast, the second skier needs to keep his dysfunctional emotions as low as possible, since this contributes directly to successful performance. Thus it is critical that this athlete's dysfunctional emotions not distract his motivation and energy. Figure 7.8 shows how individual emotion impacts differ for these athletes.

Data describing what is beyond the zones allow development of emotion profiles that visually represent interaction effects. In previous publications (Hanin, 1997a), emphasis was on optimal zones in performance-enhancing emotions and dysfunctional zones in performance-inhibiting emotions. Predicting successful performance was based on the "in the optimal zone, out of the dysfunctional zone" principle. Now we can identify optimal zones in both optimal (high intensity in P+N+) and dysfunctional content emotions (low intensity in P–N–). Figure 7.9 illustrates IZOF emotion profiles based only on optimal intensity zones identified for both performance-enhancing and -impairing emotions; the emotions include the five most often selected by athletes in cross-country skiing and ice hockey in each category.

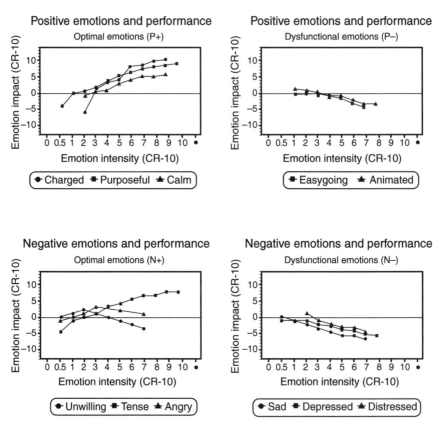

Figure 7.6 Individualized emotion-performance contingencies (top Finnish cross-country skier K.).

These profiles (aggregated for sport events or individualized) are similar in shape to the POMS iceberg profiles proposed by Morgan (1985), but different in their meaning. The POMS iceberg profile implies an interaction of positive affect (vigor) and negative affect (tension, anger, confusion, fatigue, depression), a point often missed in POMS-based studies examining emotion subscales separately: positive and negative affects are measured by the same set of descriptors. Since the IZOF iceberg profile emphasizes how positive and negative emotions impact performance, the contrast is between functionally optimal emotions and dysfunctional emotions. However, both optimal and dysfunctional emotions include positive (P+ P–) and negative (N+ N–) affect athlete-generated items. Therefore, the IZOF profile does not contrast positive and negative emotions representing different modalities of hedonic tone as in general well-being studies. Instead, it emphasizes interaction effects and the functional significance of enhancing and impairing emotions (positive and negative) (see chapter 3).

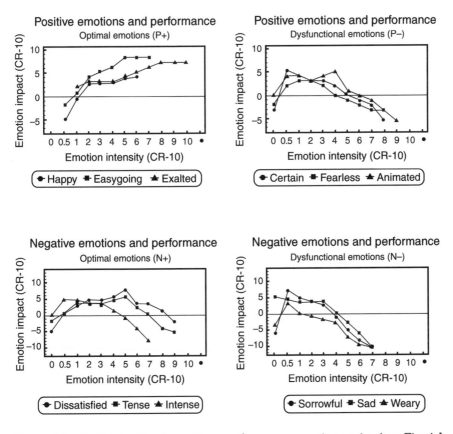

Figure 7.7 Individualized emotion-performance contingencies (top Finnish cross-country skier M.).

The IZOF emotion profiles can take three different shapes: the iceberg profile indicating a success-related predominance (interaction) of functionally optimal emotions over dysfunctional emotions; a flattened profile indicating typical emotion states related to average performance; and a cavity-shaped profile indicating a predominance of dysfunctional emotions (either negative or positive) over functionally optimal emotions and consequently a high probability of less-than-successful performance.

IZOF-BASED PRINCIPLES TO GUIDE EMOTION REGULATION IN SPORT

Any model and intervention program implies specific principles guiding procedures for self-regulation. Since the IZOF framework describes, predicts, and explains emotion-performance relationships, the supporting evidence

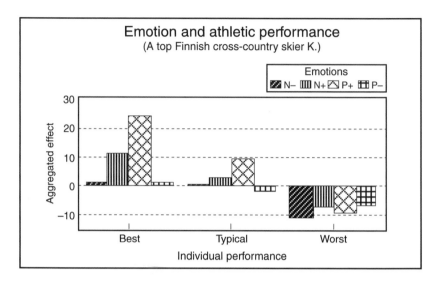

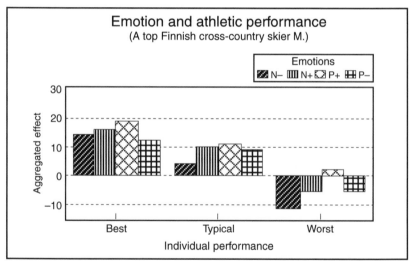

Figure 7.8　Aggregated effect of emotion on performance (top cross-country skiers K. and M.).

may provide a database for individualized regulation of performance-related emotions. The aim of the following sections is to translate IZOF concepts and data into action-oriented notions that might enhance future sport psychology research and practice. The IZOF database provides resources for formulating the working principles to guide self-regulation strategies.

▶ **The multimodality principle.** Multimodal interventions (Annesi, 1998; Burton, 1990; Davis & West, 1991) and assessments of emotions typically include

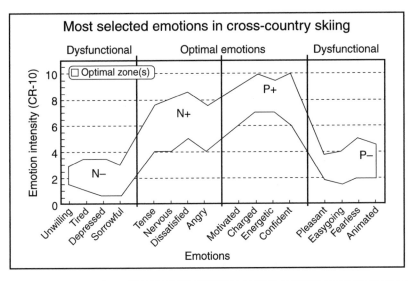

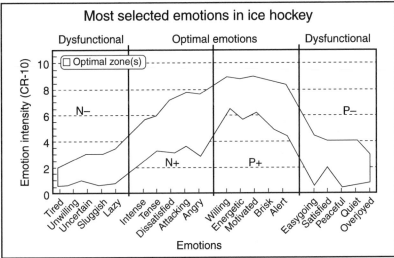

Figure 7.9 IZOF-based emotion iceberg profiles in cross-country skiing and ice hockey.

three modalities, such as cognitive, affective, and somatic components of precompetition anxiety. The IZOF-based multimodality principle regarding self-regulation comes from conceptualization of different forms of the psychobiosocial state related to performance (see chapter 3). It states that the psychobiosocial state can be manifested in at least seven basic interrelated forms (modes). Therefore, before attempting any regulation program it may be useful to select one or more target modalities: affective, cognitive, motivational, bodily-somatic, motor-behavioral, performance, or communication. It is also important to identify the idiosyncratic markers of the target modality and to consider how it interacts with other components of the psychobiosocial state (Hamill, 1996; Zaichkowski et al., 1994). For interventions to be effective, it is critical to identify the individual-relevant and task-relevant content of the markers. For each modality, individualized self-report scales can then be developed according to procedures used in scaling emotion profiles (see appendixes).

▶ **The multi-zone principle.** The multi-zone principle follows from findings demonstrating that any emotion varies greatly in intensity across athletes. Therefore, before any intervention one should establish individually optimal and dysfunctional intensity zones for performance-enhancing and -impairing emotions (Annesi, 1998; Hanin, 1993, 1997a). Another recommendation based on recent findings is to identify the whole working range of intensity in each emotion as well as typical, best, and poor performance intensity ranges (Hanin, 1997c). Individualized zones for both optimal and dysfunctional emotions are established from an analysis of performance history followed by refinement and validation of these data in a series of self-ratings of performance-related psychobiosocial states.

▶ **The multidirection principle.** According to the multidirection principle, the direction of regulation (intended impact) is based on comparison between previously established individual zones and actual intensity scores. Deviations from the optimal intensity zones in the selected modality indicate tentative directions for regulation (increase or decrease). The multidirection principle is also based on the interaction effects of optimal and dysfunctional emotions. An aim of self-regulation or intervention is to help an athlete enter or reenter the optimal zones, as well as to stay out of the dysfunctional zones by keeping the intensity of performance-impairing emotions low.

▶ **The multifunction principle.** According to the multifunction principle, the total intervention effect should not be evaluated by change in intensity of the selected targets. The total emotion impact on athletic performance is manifested in an increase or decrease in effort (energy) and/or skill level (an application of energy). Thus, although one monitors the effectiveness of regulation by change in intensity, one should evaluate its major impact by efficiency of recruitment and utilization of resources or their short- and long-term recovery.

▶ **The multistage principle.** The multistage principle refers to the temporal patterns, or dynamics, in emotion-performance relationships. It suggests that content and intensity of optimal and nonoptimal emotions will change over time—not only with regard to fixed patterns of emotions before, during, and after performance but also with regard to patterns of transitions between stages. These stages may differ in some athletes more than in others. Additionally, one should expect emotions to change during the task-execution process, especially in long-duration tasks (lasting hours or days). Therefore, predictions should take into account not only precompetition affect but also its dynamics during task execution.

▶ **The multitask principle.** The multitask principle derives from the notion of sport activity as a long-term repeated sequence of tasks varying in complexity. Tasks may vary across settings, conditions, degrees of importance, and skill levels (Ebbeck & Weiss, 1988); for example, tasks across an athlete's sport career may include season, world and European championships, and Olympic cycles (Stambulova, 1994). Athletes in self-regulation programs should compare patterns of emotions across tasks; there are large interindividual differences in patterns of preparation, execution, and recovery among various tasks. The multitask principle also emphasizes the need to examine an athlete's performance history and present performance with future performances in mind.

▶ **The multimethod principle.** The multimethod principle reflects two important concepts that could enhance individualized interventions or self-regulation programs. First, sport psychology offers several equally effective methods, and an intervention that fits the target modality and direction should be optimal for the athlete and the situation. That is, the method should be based on previously established individual patterns of emotion-performance relationships and thus should be individual- and task-specific. Second, the intervention program should include not one but a combination of methods of self-regulation that fit other principles described earlier.

SUMMARY

This chapter reviewed empirical evidence supporting the IZOF model as extended to positive and negative emotions related to successful and poor performance situations. The emphasis was on individualized assessment methods, patterns of positive and negative affect prior to and during athletic performance, and emotion-performance relationships. Finally, several IZOF-based principles were proposed to guide interventions and self-regulation procedures used in sport psychology.

Three Approaches to Training
and Emotional Exhaustion

CHAPTER 8

Overtraining in Athletes

John S. Raglin and Gregory S. Wilson
United States

Over 40 years ago, Roger Bannister broke the 4-min mile, an achievement many did not think possible. Although such records have continued to fall, most people assume that the human ability to continue improvement is gradually diminishing and will eventually plateau. Accordingly, some have tried to predict the decrease in the rate of progression in world records (Peronnet & Tribault, 1989). Yet in many track and field events, world record performances have already exceeded these estimates. For instance, in the men's 10,000 m running event, the world record has been broken seven times since 1993 by six different runners. The increment of this improvement during this 5-year period was 2.5% as compared to only 1.9% in the previous 28 years. Other events show similar trends.

Coaches and athletes alike constantly seek strategies to sustain such improvement. Methods include nutritional practices such as carbohydrate loading (Fox, Bowers, & Foss, 1989) and creatine supplementation (Spriet, 1997), as well as training techniques such as altitude work (Faulkner, Daniels, & Balke, 1967; Beidleman et al., 1997) and plyometrics (Radcliffe & Farentinos, 1985). Yet most coaches and athletes regard training as the single most important factor in performance improvement (Bompa, 1983). As exercise physiologist David Martin wrote, "Athletes instinctively realize the records are accessible. They tell themselves 'All I've got to do is train harder'" (Bloom, 1997, p. 2).

Bompa (1983) estimated that for many sports the average training load increased by approximately 10% to 22% between 1975 and 1980. In some sports the increase has been even greater. For example, Mark Spitz, winner of seven gold medals in the 1972 Olympics, reportedly trained up to 9000 m a day. But within 20 years, the average college swimmer exceeded this training load (Counsilman & Counsilman, 1990); some Olympic swimmers exceed twice this volume. There are more recent reports of swimmers training in excess of 36,000 m (DeHart, 1995).

Although this intensified training is often beneficial, it can sometimes worsen performance (Griffith, 1926; Parmenter, 1923). Approximately 10% of those undergoing intensive training experience the staleness or overtraining syndrome. Unfortunately, there is no generally accepted method to determine the appropriate level of training to optimize overload (Fry, Morton, & Keast, 1991) while minimizing potentially detrimental effects.

This chapter introduces the concepts of overtraining and staleness. Other aims are to discuss problems of terminology; to describe the condition known as the staleness syndrome and its major physiological and psychological markers; and to review research on the use of psychometric measures to monitor mood states as a means of assessing athletes' responses to overtraining.

TERMINOLOGY

Considerable debate surrounds the definition of phenomena associated with overtraining. A variety of terms have been used to describe these phenomena. The problem of defining them is further compounded by the wide variation in performance capabilities of athletes in response to intense training.

▶ **Overtraining.** Unfortunately, use of terminology in the overtraining literature is inconsistent. Researchers have defined overtraining both negatively and positively, and as a stimulus, response, or process. For European coaches and sport scientists, "overtraining" denotes the detrimental consequences of excessive training (Harre, 1982). For others, it means a prescribed period of intense training that is generally beneficial, which may sometimes result in decreased performance (Morgan, Brown, Raglin, O'Connor, & Ellickson, 1987). We will accept the definition of Morgan and colleagues (1987): overtraining is part of a purposeful phase of a training cycle, specifically the most intense phase or peak training load. The goal is to present a maximal training stress in order to maximize training adaptations in the athlete. Typically, a relatively brief training phase of lower volume (training distance), known as a taper, follows.

▶ **Staleness.** We will use the term "staleness syndrome" to refer to the undesirable outcome of overtraining. Staleness results from the athlete's inability to adapt to the prescribed training regimen. Other terms that refer to this phenomenon are overwork, overstress, overreaching, and overuse (O'Connor, 1997).

▶ **Burnout.** Although many view "burnout" and "staleness" as synonymous (Henschen, 1990; Mahoney, 1989; Rowland, 1986), Raglin (1993) has suggested that these are separate conditions requiring distinct medical interventions. Here, burnout denotes a negative emotional reaction to sport participation, while staleness denotes a disorder combining affective and physiological maladaptive responses to intense training. The following sections present further distinctions between overtraining, staleness, and burnout.

OVERTRAINING IN ATHLETES: TRAINING VOLUMES AND REGIMENS

Most recognize that success in endurance sports depends largely on progressive increments in training load above the amount required for maintaining physical fitness (Bompa, 1983; Harre, 1982): the so-called overload principle. Effective training regimens involve working the muscular and cardiorespiratory systems at a rate "higher than normal" in order to produce training adaptations (Getchell, 1992). The athlete performs acute bouts of intense exercise at very high intensities approaching maximal aerobic capacity ($\dot{V}O_2$max) over a few days to several weeks.

Traditionally, overtraining has been viewed as a means of stressing the athlete to the point where incomplete recovery occurs between training sessions (Harre, 1982); this is considered necessary for eliciting the compensatory effect of "physiological superadaptation" (Bompa, 1983; Harre, 1982). Because the workout session is so intense, overtraining typically consists of short cycles (microcycles) of prescribed training loads that are near the athlete's maximal capacity (O'Connor, 1997). Additionally, advances in conditioning programs, including a greater emphasis on weight training (Eksten, 1995) and plyometrics (Radcliffe & Farentinos, 1985), have led to increasingly greater training volume for both aerobic and anaerobic sports relying on both aerobic and anaerobic energy demands. Consequently, the average weekly training time for many athletes has increased dramatically over the past decade. It is no longer accepted that either endurance or nonendurance athletes can achieve high levels of performance without these supplemental forms of training.

Overtraining appears to improve athletic performance through the interaction of biochemical, neurological, cardiovascular, and muscular adaptations (O'Connor, 1997; Morgan, Brown, et al., 1987; Bompa, 1983). For example, the principal cardiovascular adaptation to endurance training is increased cardiac output (Neufer, 1989), while muscular adaptions include increases in mitochondrial content through training-induced elevations in enzyme levels (Baldwin, Klinderfuss, Terjung, Mole, & Holloszy, 1972). Some have questioned the necessity of high training volumes for these performance gains (Costill, King, Thomas, & Hargreaves, 1985), as evidence suggests that reduced training volumes performed at high intensity can yield comparable results (Costill, 1985). However, these findings have been challenged because the evidence is limited to nonelite athletes (Counsilman & Counsilman, 1990), and further research is needed.

Typically, overtraining is followed by a significant reduction in training volume referred to as a taper, or tapering-off period (Houmard, 1991; Costill, et al., 1985). In the taper phase, athletes often maintain or even increase training intensity but systematically reduce the volume; as an example, in one study, male collegiate swimmers attained a training peak of 12,000 yards per day during the overtraining phase but only 4500 per day during the taper in preparation for a championship meet (O'Connor, Morgan, Raglin, Barksdale, & Kalin, 1989). Tapers may last anywhere from a few days to several weeks (Houmard, 1994). $\dot{V}O_2$max does not significantly change following a 20-day taper (Van Handel, Katz, & Troup, 1988), whereas significant improvements in anaerobic power (Costill et al., 1985) and performance generally result (Costill et al., 1988; Raglin, Koceja, Stager, & Harms, 1996). Although the specific adaptations responsible for enhanced performance following tapers remain poorly understood, they appear to involve physiological, neurological, and psychological changes (Costill et al., 1985). It is difficult to accurately quantify overtraining loads versus normal and taper volumes because of wide variations in training practices across sports and individual differences in response to training adaptations (O'Toole, 1998).

THE STALENESS SYNDROME

Staleness, also referred to as the overtraining syndrome, represents the detrimental responses to overtraining. This condition is characterized by a chronic decrease in performance that does not improve with either reduced training or brief rest. Athletes who experience an intermediate condition—referred to as overreaching (Hooper & MacKinnon, 1995; Kuipers, 1996)—usually respond favorably to brief rests of one to two days or to temporary reductions in training, whereas stale athletes may require complete rest for several weeks to months.

Staleness fits the definition of a syndrome because of its multiple symptoms. These include psychological depression and other mood disturbances, loss of sleep and appetite accompanied by weight loss, reduced libido, muscle soreness, and fatigue. Illnesses, particularly upper respiratory tract infections, are also common (Barron, Noakes, Levy, Smith, & Millar, 1985; Davis & Colbert, 1997; Fry et al., 1991; Kuipers & Keizer, 1988). Psychological consequences typically include clinical depression, similar in appearance to melancholia (Morgan, Brown, et al., 1987; King, Taylor, Haskell, & DeBusk, 1989). Because staleness has both biological and psychological symptoms, and because the psychological changes closely correspond to various physiological variables including neuroendocrine hormone levels (Barron et al., 1985; O'Connor et al., 1989) and neuromuscular measures (Raglin et al., 1996), it appears most accurate to conceptualize staleness as a psychobiological phenomenon.

Athletes differ significantly in their ability to tolerate and adapt to intense training. Comparably skilled athletes may respond quite differently to standard training loads (Costill et al., 1988; Morgan, Costill, Flynn, Raglin, & O'Connor, 1988). Hence, physiological markers can be highly idiosyncratic: a training schedule that improves one athlete's performance may be inadequate for another and even worsen performance in a third. Although the reasons for this variability are not clear, factors such as genetic capacity, current fitness level, motivation, and general health appear to be important (Fox et al., 1989).

Researchers have additionally classified staleness into sympathetic and parasympathetic types based on the apparent consequences on metabolism (Kereszty, 1971; Kuipers & Keizer, 1988). Lehmann, Foster, and Keul (1993) suggested that sympathetic overtraining is more prevalent in anaerobic athletes, and parasympathetic in endurance athletes. However, it is unclear whether these categories actually represent discrete subtypes or instead reflect extraneous factors such as individual differences in training response, stages of staleness, or types of training (Raglin, 1993).

Distinguishing Staleness From Burnout

Symptoms unique to staleness include hypercortisolism and decreased immune functioning (Fry, Morton, Garcia-Webb, Crawford, & Keast, 1992) accompanied by premature fatigue during exercise, loss of performance capacity and muscular strength, and alterations in perceived physical effort (Stone et al., 1991; Callister, Callister, Fleck, & Dudley, 1990). Stale athletes also show decreases in muscular strength. None of these symptoms has been explicitly associated with burnout. Although athletes experiencing both staleness and burnout may exhibit depression, the mood alterations associated with staleness are directly linked to increases in training load (Morgan, Brown, et al. 1987) as opposed to the cognitive stressors implicated in burnout. Moreover, the Maslach Burnout Inventory (Maslach & Jackson, 1981a) includes a measure of depersonalization, a symptom not reported in staleness. These lines of evidence suggest that staleness and burnout are discrete conditions that may sometimes co-occur (chapters 9 and 10).

Can Staleness Be Detected Early?

Because it is seldom if ever practical to prevent staleness by not overtraining, researchers have sought to identify reliable physiological markers for use in preventing onset through detection of early warning signs. Variables have primarily involved biological factors including cardiovascular, metabolic, and hormonal changes. However, research examining the predictive utility of these physiological markers has been largely inconclusive (Fry et al., 1992; Hanne-Paparo, 1983; Kuipers & Keizer, 1988). For example, increased resting morning heart rate may be the most commonly cited indicator of excessive training (Burke, 1990; Dressendorfer, Wade, & Scaff, 1985; Ryan, 1983). Yet some researchers have failed to show significant differences in this parameter for some athletes undergoing intense training (Callister et al., 1990; Kirwan et al., 1988), whereas others have shown reductions (Kuipers & Keizer, 1988). Blood lactate levels, another commonly accepted indicator, appear to decrease with overtraining because of reduced muscle glycogen stores (Jeukendrup &

Hesselinnk, 1994). However, recent studies have shown that factors unrelated to training, such as diet, may influence maximal lactate levels (Hooper, Mackinnon, Howard, Gordon, & Bachmann, 1995). Such discrepancies suggest that most physiological variables do not display consistent changes that can be reasonably discriminated from the consequences of less intense training (Fry et al., 1991; Hanne-Paparo, 1983; Hooper & Mackinnon, 1995; Kuipers & Keizer, 1988). Hence these physiological factors may have little predictive value. Moreover, hormonal monitoring is problematic because of the difficulty of obtaining individual comparative data under standardized conditions (Urhausen, Gabriel, & Kindermann, 1998).

Some physiological variables appear to be more reliably associated with overtraining. Athletes performing intensified training have elevated serum creatine kinase (CK), an indicator of muscle trauma. For instance, Burke, Falsetti, Feld, Patton, and Kennedy (1982) reported that CK values changed according to alterations in the training of distance swimmers. But CK responses do not appear to distinguish healthy athletes from those at risk for staleness. Kirwan et al. (1988) found that swimmers undergoing 10 days of intense training also exhibited significant elevations in CK, but the degree of increase was similar between athletes adapting successfully and those having difficulty completing the training. Finally, while CK may increase with increased training, the precise location of actual muscle damage cannot be identified (Fry et al., 1991).

However, some physiological markers seem specific to staleness. Depletions of muscle glycogen (Costill et al., 1988) and neuroendocrine variations, including altered testosterone/cortisol ratios (Aldercreutz et al., 1986), depressed hypothalamic function (Barron et al., 1985), and elevations in cortisol (O'Connor et al., 1989), have each been found in athletes displaying signs of staleness. However, it is not clear whether these are casual factors or are outcomes of the disorder (Raglin, 1993). More importantly, the cost, technological requirements, and invasiveness associated with physiological markers often preclude their use in field settings (Hooper & Mackinnon, 1995).

Prevalence and Frequency of Staleness

Staleness is an inherent problem in training for all types of endurance activities (Fry et al., 1991; Ryan, 1983), yet we know little about its prevalence. Studies examining this issue have often used intensive training lasting only a few days or weeks (Hooper & Mackinnon, 1995), which may produce fatigue or overreaching but not necessarily staleness. Furthermore, the training schedule, as well as coaching strategies designed to prevent staleness, can significantly affect the rate of staleness for a specific sport (Raglin, 1993). Finally, ethical concerns should generally preclude intentional excessive overtraining of subjects in an attempt to induce staleness.

In studies of collegiate swimmers and other endurance athletes undergoing competitive training, the reported yearly incidence of staleness averaged approximately 10%, ranging from a low of 7% (Raglin & Morgan, 1994) to a high of 21% (Hooper, Mackinnon, & Hanrahan, 1997; O'Connor et al., 1989). In perhaps the only studies addressing the long-term risk in athletes, by Morgan and colleagues (1987, 1988), 60% of female and 64% of male elite long-distance runners reported experiencing at least one episode of staleness during their running career. The percentage for nonelite runners was 33%. The weekly training mileage of the elite athletes was significantly greater, suggesting that the likelihood of staleness increases with exposure to overtraining. Status as an elite athlete does not confer resistance to staleness—rather, elite athletes' capacity to endure intense training likely places them at greater risk. Moreover, while one study suggested that female athletes experience staleness to a greater extent than males (Ryan, 1983), most of the extant research indicates that the risk is equal. Additionally, age also does not appear to be a factor in staleness. Wilson, Raglin, & Harger (1999) found that 31% of adolescent distance runners reported experiencing staleness with the average episode persisting an average of three weeks. This finding is similar to previous reports of staleness among adult nonelite distance runners.

Information concerning susceptibility to staleness is equally sparse. Raglin (1993) reported that 91% of college swimmers who developed staleness in their first year became stale again at some point in their collegiate career. In contrast, of swimmers who were free of staleness during their freshman year, only 30% experienced staleness later. Additional longitudinal work on the prevalence of staleness is needed in order to develop effective means of identifying athletes at particular risk. Also, researchers need to replicate previous findings with larger samples, utilizing athletes from a variety of sports, to establish frequency and prevalence rates across sports.

The factors influencing the risk of staleness are not known, although both genetic and developmental variables may play a role. External factors such as nutritional deficiencies (Costill et al., 1988; Wheeler, 1989), dehydration (Costill, 1988), and physical illness (Mellerowicz & Barron, 1971) may increase susceptibility. Psychological traits may also play a role: Goss (1994) reported that high psychological hardiness alleviated mood disturbances in collegiate swimmers during overtraining. However, the mood disturbance scores (Profile of Mood States, POMS) of the low-hardy group were already significantly elevated above the published norm in an assessment made during easy training (M = 167.3), and the increase in total mood disturbance during overtraining was minimal (7.2 units). Hence it remains unclear whether hardiness is associated with mood state responses to overtraining. Knapp, Guttmann, Foster, and Pollock (1984) reported that speed skaters with lower levels of self-motivation were more prone to mood disturbances than skaters with higher levels. However, Raglin, Morgan, and Luchsinger (1990) found that the same measure of self-motivation did not distinguish female collegiate rowers who experienced excessive mood disturbances during training from those who did not. Thus far research has not identified physiological or psychological factors that reliably alter the risk of developing staleness.

Psychometric Monitoring

Compared to physiological factors, psychological responses to overtraining are more consistent across athletes. After reviewing research on identifying markers of staleness, Davis and Colbert (1997) concluded that self-report measures are probably the most accurate. This consistency, along with the limitations of physiological markers, suggests psychological assessments as a useful means of monitoring athletes who overtrain. Verde, Thomas, and Shepard (1992) found that mood state assessment as measured by the POMS (McNair, Lorr, & Droppleman, 1971) was more sensitive in identifying athletes at potential risk than were widely advocated physiological measures.

Initial work with swimmers and other endurance athletes indicated that changes in training volume are predictably related to mood state (Morgan, Brown, et al., 1987; Raglin, Morgan, & O'Connor, 1991). Increases in training distance result in corresponding elevations in mood disturbance, with the peaks in training and mood disturbance typically coinciding. With reduced training, mood disturbance usually falls; and as tapering ends, mood scores generally return to baseline values (Morgan, Brown, et al., 1987; Morgan, Costill, et al., 1988; Wittig, Houmard, & Costill, 1989; O'Connor et al., 1989; O'Connor, Morgan, & Raglin, 1991; Raglin & Morgan, 1994; Raglin, Eksten, & Garl, 1995; Raglin et al., 1996). In contrast, mood disturbances in stale athletes are typically more chronic, with associated elevations in negative mood states such as depression failing to return to baseline. Hence, while mood state profiles of endurance athletes are generally healthier than those of nonathletes (Morgan, 1985), the stress of routine physical training results in shifts in negative mood state scores such that the values may equal or exceed population norms. This observation is consistent with Morgan's (1985) mental health model of sport performance, which posits that from a long-term perspective, psychopathology is inversely related with performance. Unfortunately, some reviewers of the mental health model have failed to consider the consequences of physical training on most mood states in athletes, leading to rejection of the model on false grounds (Renger, 1993; Rowley, Landers, Kyllo, & Etneir, 1994; Terry, 1993).

The mood state responses of men and women athletes undergoing comparable training are remarkably similar (Raglin, Morgan, & O'Connor, 1991). Both male and female swimmers undergoing comparable training schedules displayed similar mood state responses (Morgan, Brown, et al., 1987; O'Connor et al., 1991; Raglin et al., 1991). These results indicate an absence of gender differences in psychological responses to comparably intense training.

The majority of this research has used the POMS (Morgan, Brown, et al., 1987; O'Connor, 1997), a questionnaire that assesses the stable mood states of tension, depression, anger, vigor, fatigue, and confusion (McNair, Lorr, & Droppleman, 1971, 1992). These specific mood factors can be combined to yield a higher-order measure of global or total mood disturbance. The total measure of mood state is determined by adding the five negative mood states and subtracting the positive factor of vigor. A constant of 100 is added to this value to prevent the occurrence of negative scores. The POMS has four instructional sets but is typically completed under instructions to respond according to how one has been feeling "the last week including today." This set is also most commonly used in overtraining research. These instructions yield test-retest reliabilities ranging from .65 to .74, lower than values associated with personality measures (r = .80-.90). This lower reliability range is intentional, resulting in assessments of "typical and persistent mood reactions" (McNair et al., 1992, p. 2) that are sensitive to various stressors or beneficial interventions. The moderate test-retest responsiveness to both positive and negative stimuli makes the POMS useful in athletic monitoring research.

Dose-response relationships between training and mood state are seen in other endurance sports including distance running (Raglin & Morgan, 1994; Wittig et al., 1989), rowing (Cogan, Highlen, Petrie, Sherman, & Simonsen, 1991; Raglin, Morgan, & Luchsinger, 1990), and race canoeing (Berglund & Säfström, 1994). Changes in specific POMS factors also exhibit dose-response patterns, with the possible exception of tension. Raglin et al. (1991) found that POMS tension did not decrease during tapers in college swimmers and speculated that this reflected the stress of upcoming conference championships. In contrast, other POMS factors responded positively to the training load reduction (figure 8.1). The failure of tension to fall during the taper may not be undesirable, as other research indicates that between 30% and 45% of athletes benefit from elevated anxiety (chapters 3 and 4; Hanin, 1997a). Importantly, the degree of mood disturbance is higher in stale athletes (Morgan, O'Connor, Ellickson, & Bradley, 1988; Morgan, Costill, et al., 1988; Raglin & Morgan, 1994). According to research with college swimmers, POMS vigor and fatigue scores exhibit the largest shift for most athletes, whereas depression is relatively unaffected (Raglin et al., 1991). In contrast, depression increases more than any other POMS factor in athletes who develop staleness.

Acute Overtraining Research

Not all physical conditioning regimens involve gradual adjustments to the training load; in some sports the training increases quite rapidly. Mood state monitoring can be used in these circumstances also. Typically athletes complete the POMS according to how they feel "today" or "right now." O'Connor and colleagues (1991) observed the responses of collegiate men and women swimmers during a three-day period of increased training, from a previous average 6800 meters a day to an average 12,075 meters a day for the three-day period. Mood state was determined each morning using the "today" version of the POMS; also, muscle soreness, perceived exertion, exercise heart rate to a paced swim, and salivary cortisol were assessed daily. Significant ($p < .05$) elevations in mood disturbance were observed by day 2 of increased training; responses for the men and women were similar. Perceived exertion (total and local) and muscle soreness were significantly elevated, but salivary cortisol was unchanged.

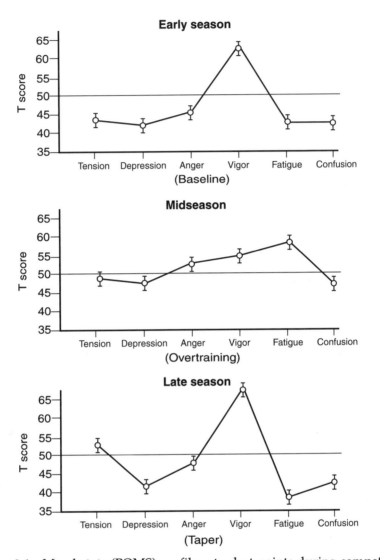

Figure 8.1 Mood state (POMS) profiles at select points during competitive training in (N = 35) male and female varsity collegiate swimmers.

Reprinted with permission of Macmillan Library Reference USA, from HANDBOOK OF RESEARCH ON SPORT PSYCHOL-OGY, by Robert N. Singer, Milledge Murphey, & L. Keith Tennant. Copyright © 1993 by The International Society of Sport Psychology.

Fry et al. (1994) examined the influence of 10 days of intense interval training followed by 5 days of active rest on mood state, self-esteem, and selected physiological variables in five adult males. The dependent variables were assessed at five-day intervals. Several physiological variables, particularly immunological markers, showed significant changes. These occurred prior to significant mood disturbances, leading the authors to suggest that "physiological mechanisms may mediate some of the mood changes associated with overtraining" (p. 245). Unfortunately, the sensitivity of the mood state assessment was constrained because a shortened version of the POMS was used. The POMS tension scores decreased from baseline to overtraining— a paradoxical change the authors did not comment on. Finally, while there was evidence of a performance decrement due to training, it is unclear whether this is indicative of overreaching or is a normal consequence of the training regimen.

In a study that is atypical because both training volume and intensity were controlled, Morgan, Costill, et al. (1988) examined responses of male collegiate swimmers to 10 days of intensified training. Swimmers performed a daily training load averaging 8900 m at a pace equaling 94% $\dot{V}O_2$max. Mood state, muscle soreness, and perceived exertion were assessed daily, as were selected physiological variables (Costill et al., 1988). It was anticipated that some swimmers would have difficulty completing the training regimen (i.e., over-reaching), and an attempt was made to identify such cases using the psycho-logical and physiological results. Predictions were made in a blind fashion. The training was supervised by a coach who had no access to the experimental data, and the researchers did not observe the swimmers during training. Three swimmers were unable to complete the regimen, and their daily training loads were reduced. Total mood disturbance scores for the total sample increased linearly during the initial 5 days of training before leveling off, and results were similar for perceived exertion and muscle soreness; the POMS results pre-sented in figure 8.2 typify this general trend. However, the responses were not consistent for all swimmers: four swimmers showed pronounced elevations in their total mood scores. On the basis of their mood responses, it was predicted that these individuals would have difficulty completing the training regimen

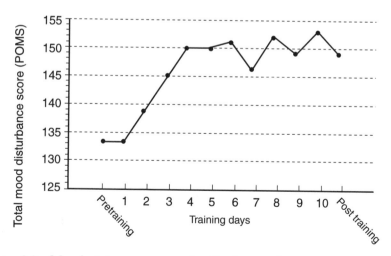

Figure 8.2 Mood state responses of collegiate male swimmers to 10-day period of intense training.

Adapted, by permission, from W.P. Morgan, D.L. Costill et al., 1988, "Mood disturbances following increased training in swimmers," *Medicine and Science in Sports and Medicine* 23: 408-414.

(i.e., overreaching). Performance results indicated that three of the four swimmers who actually could not complete the training regimen were in this group of psychological "responders." Physiological information also indicated that these three swimmers were responders: they had lower levels of muscle glycogen than the rest of the sample (Costill et al., 1988), and this depletion was mirrored by a deficit in daily caloric intake during training averaging 1036 kcal. The psychological and physiological predictions corresponded closely, and overall agreement between the approaches was 89%. These results support the efficacy of examining staleness from a multidisciplinary perspective, and also underscore individual differences in athletes' ability to tolerate intensive physical training.

Mood Disturbances in Nonendurance Sports

Most mood disturbance studies have focused on endurance sport training. However, intensive training has become common in many nonendurance sports, and some research has examined the potential effect on mood of intensive anaerobic training. In a review of psychological monitoring studies, Morgan, Brown, et al. (1987) reported that collegiate wrestlers, presumably performing significant amounts of anaerobic conditioning, showed elevations in mood disturbance during a training season. Judo athletes also showed alterations in some POMS factors during progressively increased training (Murphy, Fleck, Dudley, & Callister, 1990). Raglin et al. (1995) observed mood disturbances in collegiate basketball players in an off-season conditioning program. The athletes underwent between 3 and 4 hr of weight training and sprint running, four days a week for five weeks; and training intensity increased throughout the five-week period. Total mood state scores, obtained weekly by means of 30-item set POMS (McNair et al., 1992), increased in a linear fashion during the five weeks. Two days after the end of the training, the mood disturbance score returned to the pretraining baseline. However, two athletes still exhibited significantly elevated total mood disturbance scores, and the authors speculated that these athletes might be at increased risk of staleness. Other research (Fry et al., 1994) also showed increases in some POMS factors following 10 days of intense sprint training.

Moger and Raglin (1998) examined mood state in a collegiate women's varsity volleyball team throughout a season of training and competition. Elevations in total mood disturbance during training were similar in magnitude to those commonly found in endurance athletes. In contrast to the typical trend, however, mood state remained elevated at the end of the season after training had been reduced to maintenance levels. The authors speculated that the mood changes reflected not only the athletes' current training load but also nontraining factors such as competition and interpersonal conflicts. This is consistent with other overtraining research (Raglin et al., 1991) indicating that some POMS components of mood state and tension may be influenced by both training load and competition. These results suggest the benefit of quantifying the influence of stressors other than training in research on monitoring.

Mood Response Between Stale Athletes and Non-Stale Athletes

As noted earlier, mood state responses to standardized training differ between stale and non-stale athletes. In studies of collegiate swimmers (Costill et al., 1988; Morgan, Costill, et al., 1988), athletes who experienced the most difficulty completing the prescribed training load also displayed the largest increase in mood disturbance. In a study of female collegiate rowers undergoing training (Raglin, Morgan, & Luchsinger, 1990), athletes who were unsuccessful (i.e., not selected to the starting team) were more likely to exhibit excessive increases in mood disturbances during intense training than were rowers who were eventually selected to compete regionally. The unsuccessful athletes also did not show favorable mood responses to a training taper. In a study of psychological and hormonal responses of collegiate female swimmers across a season of competitive training (O'Connor et al., 1989), athletes identified by the coach as stale showed significantly greater levels of depression during overtraining (POMS) than swimmers who did not become stale. Depression remained elevated in the stale athletes even following a taper, whereas mood state returned to baseline levels in the others. The stale swimmers also had significantly greater elevations in salivary cortisol, a hormone that has been linked to depression.

Importantly, in all these studies, athletes who were stale as a result of overtraining had displayed the iceberg profile at the outset of training. This indicates that mood state assessments prior to intense training cannot distinguish athletes who eventually become stale from those who do not. Only after exposure to increased training did significant differences in mood state become evident (see figure 8.3 for symptoms of staleness).

Problems in Monitoring Staleness in Athletes

As measured by the POMS, mood changes appear to be more specific and sensitive to staleness than do most physiological indicators. However, one should note that the detection of staleness using these measures has been post hoc: psychometric evaluations were done only after significant performance deficits identified athletes as stale. Other limitations to psychometric monitoring of staleness relate to use of the POMS. Raglin et al. (1991), assessing changes in specific POMS variables (i.e., tension, depression, anger, vigor, fatigue, confusion) during training in both female and male collegiate swimmers, found that each mood factor, except for tension, consistently displayed a dose-response relationship with training distance. Tension either remained elevated throughout the taper or continued to increase. This nonspecific effect could be problematic for use of global mood to identify athletes at risk for staleness (Raglin, 1993).

Additionally, non-stale swimmers in response to overtraining consistently display the largest changes for fatigue and vigor (measured by the POMS) as compared to the other mood factors, whereas depression changes less (Raglin et al., 1991; Morgan, Brown, et al., 1987). This contrasts with the profile of stale athletes, where depression is far more pronounced (Morgan, Brown, et al., 1987; O'Connor et al., 1989). Consequently, large increases in total POMS

Psychological	Immunological
Affective components	Increased susceptibility to illness/colds
Decrease in vigor	Possible glandular fever
Increase in fatigue	Flulike illness
Increase in anger	One-day colds
Increase in tension	Minor cuts and scratches heal slowly
Increase in depression	Swelling of lymph glands
Decrease in self-esteem	Decreased functional activity of neutrophils
	Bacterial infections
Cognitive components	Reduced response to mitogens
Increase in confusion	
Decrease in ability to concentrate	**Performance**
	Decreased athletic performance
Motor-behavioral	Inability to meet previous performance
Loss of coordination	levels
Decrease in muscular strength	Prolonged recovery from workouts
	Reduced ability to handle training loads
	Decrease in maximum work capacity

Physiological/biological

Depressed muscle glycogen concentration	Abnormal T-wave pattern in electrocardiogram
Decreased bone mineral content	Changes in blood pressure
Delayed menarche	Increase in resting heart rate
Decreased hemoglobin	Decrease in body fat
Decreased serum iron	Chronic fatigue
Decreased serum ferritin	Possible eating disorders
Hypothalamic dysfunction	Headaches
Mineral depletion	Nausea
Elevated cortisol levels	Muscle soreness/tenderness
Elevated ketosteroids in urine	Loss of appetite
Low free testosterone	
Increase uric acid production	

Figure 8.3   Commonly reported symptoms of staleness.
Adapted, from R.W. Fry et al., 1991, "Overtraining in athletes," *Sports Medicine* 12: 32-65.

scores could reflect either a "normal" overtraining-induced disturbance consisting primarily of somatically related changes (i.e., vigor and fatigue), or distress related to staleness in which depression is more pronounced.

Prevention and Treatment of Staleness

The only reliable means of treating stale athletes is prolonged rest (Griffith, 1926; Karpovich, 1941). Most studies cite a minimum of two weeks rest, but more severe cases may require up to several months. Some athletes still exhibit disturbed neuroendocrine function after as much as six months rest (Barron et al., 1985). Hence cases of staleness must be addressed on an individual basis. Mood disturbances associated with staleness may not fully diminish following reduced training in the stale athlete (O'Connor et al., 1989; Raglin, Morgan, & Luchsinger, 1990)—reinforcing the need for complete rest. Supplemental forms of treatment have included the use of steroids, sedatives, and vitamins (Kereszty, 1971; Mellerowicz & Barron, 1971), but there are no reports of controlled trials utilizing such therapies. Kuipers and Keizer (1988) have further suggested that a high-carbohydrate diet may aid recovery. Often the most difficult aspect of treatment is convincing the athlete of the need for rest, as athletes and coaches typically respond to poor performance by increasing training.

Some have suggested cognitive tools such as mental imagery and relaxation to treat staleness (Henschen, 1998). However, such methods are unlikely to affect either the medical complications or the clinical depression common in stale athletes. Standard sport psychology interventions may be harmful if essential psychotherapy or medical treatment is delayed. It is imperative that sport psychology practitioners understand the potential for underlying pathology in terms of both physical and mental distress before initiating treatment. Until we have empirical support for the effectiveness of cognitive sport psychology techniques, stale athletes should receive more conventional psychological treatment such as counseling or psychotherapy.

Because of the evidence for the reliable association between mood state changes and training load, researchers have examined the feasibility of mood state monitoring to prevent staleness. Morgan and colleagues (reported by Raglin, 1993) assessed mood state daily in a collegiate men's and women's swimming team during overtraining. The total mood disturbance scores of each swimmer were contrasted with the mean of the entire team, and the training load was reduced for swimmers with significantly elevated mood state profiles until mood state responded. An assumption was that swimmers showing mood state scores lower than those of other team members were understressed; for these athletes, training was increased. At the end of the season the swimmers were evaluated by the coach, and no cases of staleness were reported. The absence of staleness was unlikely to be a chance occurrence, because in none of the previous 10 seasons had the entire team been free of the disorder.

Berglund and Säfström (1994) employed a similar intervention strategy with men and women race canoeists training for Olympic competition. Mood state (POMS) was assessed weekly throughout the training season using the Swedish language version of the POMS, and training load was adjusted on the basis of total mood scores. Training was reduced for athletes whose total mood disturbance scores exceeded their own baseline scores by at least 50%. As in the previous example, the intervention operated in both directions. Training loads were increased when mood scores dropped to within 10% of a preseason baseline score. Of the total sample, 64% had training reduced at some point and 57% had training increased, indicating that some athletes required both interventions. While 50% of the athletes exhibited what the authors regarded as excessively high mood disturbances at some point, none developed staleness, and it was concluded that the monitoring paradigm was successful. Later interviews of the athletes indicated that the majority found the monitoring useful. While this does not constitute evidence, it is notable that the athletes favorably regarded a psychologically based intervention that often resulted in increased training and psychological stress—unlike the majority of psychological interventions, which involve alleviating stress and negative affect.

Appropriate control conditions were absent in the two examples just cited, so this approach still needs to be tested more rigorously and with larger samples. If these results can be replicated and generalized to other sports, then mood state monitoring, combined with selective physiological assessments, could be an effective means of preventing staleness in athletes who must overtrain. This same approach may also aid in optimizing the adaptive consequences of intense training on sport performance.

RECENT RESEARCH
AND FUTURE DIRECTIONS

There has been a recent effort, partly in response to the limitations of the POMS, to develop a mood measurement scale specific to overtraining-induced stress. Raglin and Morgan (1994) attempted to determine which POMS items were most sensitive in discriminating between non-stale and stale athletes, using data on more than 186 college swimmers collected over several years. The swimmers completed the POMS at regular intervals during training and were classified as healthy or stale based on information from the coaches. Discriminant function analysis was used to identify POMS items that best differentiated healthy athletes from those who developed staleness. A subset of POMS items emerged that identified stale swimmers at levels significantly greater than predictions based on elevations in POMS total or POMS depression scores. The authors are still validating this scale, and its use in applied settings is not recommended. The combination of these items may indicate the potential benefit of individually derived scales that might provide even greater accuracy in predicting staleness.

SUMMARY

Most believe that periods of intensive training, or overtraining, are necessary for optimal sport performance. Long used in endurance sports, this form of training is becoming increasingly common in nonendurance activities. Overtraining is necessary, but unfortunately is not without risk. Approximately 10% of athletes who overtrain develop staleness, a syndrome associated with chronically worsened performance and other undesirable responses. Overtraining influences mood state in a predictable fashion, resulting in significant mood disturbances in otherwise healthy athletes. Stale athletes also exhibit neuroendocrine disturbances and other biological changes.

The staleness syndrome can be effectively treated through complete rest or prevented through reduced training loads, but neither of these is desirable for competitive athletes. Consequently there is interest in identifying psychological and physiological variables that may signal impending staleness. Psychological responses have potential, and limited research suggests that mood state monitoring may be useful for preventing the development of staleness in athletes who must overtrain. Additionally, idiographic scales based on Hanin's Individual Zones of Optimal Functioning model (1997a) may indicate specific individual responses to training and may be an improvement over nomothetic scales. However, further research is needed before these strategies are used routinely. Because staleness is a psychobiological syndrome, the addition of relevant physiological markers has the potential to enhance the efficacy of this approach.

CHAPTER 9

Burnout in Athletes and Coaches

K. Wolfgang Kallus and Michael Kellmann
Austria/Germany

This chapter addresses burnout in athletes and coaches from a biopsychological perspective, explaining the complex relationships between mood, staleness, overtraining, stress, coping, recovery, and symptoms. This approach has much in common with Hanin's psychobiosocial model (see chapter 3). We begin with a stress model in which burnout results from accumulating stress without appropriate recovery (cf. Debus, Erdmann, & Kallus, 1995; Janke & Wolffgramm, 1995; Smith, 1986).

In this model, stress is an unspecific reaction syndrome characterized by deviation from the psychobiological homeostatic state of the organism. Stress is accompanied by emotional symptoms such as anxiety and anger as well as elevated autonomic and central activation, humoral responses, changes in immune function, and behavioral changes. Stress sends processes of adaptation and coping into action.

For recovery, which is less well defined, we use a definition complementary to the concept of stress in order to account for the most important aspects of recovery. Recovery includes goal-oriented regeneration, physiological and behavioral processes, social activities, and elements of coping responses (Kellmann & Kallus, 1999). Thus it includes intentional as well as biological and other aspects. Figure 9.1 presents a set of recovery characteristics (Kallus, 1995).

The stress-recovery approach reveals parallels between the overtraining syndrome or sport-specific staleness and the burnout syndrome in general. Both syndromes result from excessive stress without appropriate recovery. Thus, staleness is one potential source of burnout, and both reflect the consequences of long-term imbalance between stress and recovery.

> ▶ Recovery is a process in time.
> ▶ Recovery is dependent on the type of and duration of strain.
> ▶ Recovery depends on a reduction of, a change of, or a break from stress.
> ▶ Recovery is individually specific and depends on individual appraisal.
> ▶ Recovery ends when a psychophysical state of restored efficiency and homeostatic balance is reached.
> ▶ Recovery includes purposeful action (active recovery), as well as automated psychic and biological processes restoring the initial state (passive recovery).
> ▶ Recovery can be described on various levels (somatic level, psychic level, behavioral level, social level, sociocultural level, environmental level).
> ▶ Recovery processes involve various organismic subsystems.
> ▶ Various subprocesses of recovery can be dissociated.
> ▶ Recovery is closely tied to situational conditions (e.g., sleep, partner contact, etc.).

Figure 9.1   Characteristic features of recovery.

A biopsychological stress model (Janke & Wolffgramm, 1995) suggests that treatment of conditions such as burnout necessitates a multidimensional approach dealing with physiological, emotional, cognitive, behavioral/performance, and social aspects of the problem—both separately and together. Since the early 1970s a multidimensional strategy has proven useful within biopsychological stress research in health, work, clinical, and sport psychology (Burchfield, 1985; Goldberger & Breznitz, 1993; Stanford & Salmon, 1993; Weiner, Florin, Murrison, & Hellhammer, 1989). We now know that many systems participate in adapting to and coping with stress; and we better understand relationships between stress and the immune system, the autonomous nervous system, the central nervous system, the humoral system, the muscular system, and mood and behavior (e.g., Debus et al., 1995; Stanford & Salmon, 1993; Weiner et al., 1989). Recovery has received comparatively little attention, however.

The ideal multidimensional approach—directly measuring changes in systems—is hardly practical. The Recovery-Stress-Questionnaire (RESTQ; Kallus, 1995) examines various dimensions as perceived by the performer, considering stress and recovery processes simultaneously. Because biopsychosocial research on recovery is still sparse, this chapter focuses on preliminary results based on self-assessment, which show that at least some RESTQ data accurately reflect the physical and behavioral aspects of stress and recovery.

BURNOUT: CONCEPTUAL AND DEFINITIONAL ISSUES

The definition of burnout is not as simple as might first appear. Maslach (cf. Maslach & Leiter, 1997) defines burnout as an individual syndrome including emotions, attitudes, motives, and expectancies. Burnout is a negative individual experience encompassing problems, distress, negative mood states, dysfunction, and negative consequences. For Maslach, the central dimensions are emotional exhaustion, depersonalization (i.e., loss of social interest), reduced personal accomplishment, and involvement. The Maslach Burnout Inventory (MBI) operationalizes these dimensions (Maslach & Jackson, 1981a, 1981b, 1986; Maslach, Jackson, & Leiter, 1996).

Although Maslach's approach has been generally accepted, it gives rise to two concerns. First, the MBI emphasizes the cognitive components of burnout and underrepresents specific physiological, emotional, and behavioral components. Second, standardization is limited because of the occupation-specific formulation of items.

Freudenberger (1974), another pioneer in the area, proposed a multidimensional definition that considers the literal meaning of the word: to fail, to wear out, or to become exhausted through excessive demands on energy, strength, or resources. Freudenberger, writing from a psychoanalytic perspective, proposed the following symptoms:

▶ Biological and physical symptoms (e.g., exhaustion, fatigue, proneness to catching a cold, stomach complaints)

▶ Behavioral and emotional symptoms (e.g., irritability, depression, tendency to cry and shout, paranoid symptoms, enhanced risk behavior, cynicism)

▶ Cognitive, social, and performance deficits (inflexibility of thinking, ineffective prolonged working hours, social isolation)

A problem with such a broad definition concerns its theoretical and practical value: so defined, the syndrome can hardly be distinguished from other constructs such as depression, chronic fatigue syndrome, chronic stress syndrome, and post-traumatic stress disorder. Some authors emphasize specific aspects of burnout; e.g., according to Pines (1993), long-term striving for strong personal values is a necessary process component of burnout. The process aspect is also included in Maslach's conception. The major advantage of Maslach's approach is that it operationalizes burnout so as to distinguish it from other psychological constructs.

BURNOUT AND SPORT: A BRIEF OVERVIEW

In our view, burnout is closely related to stress, and a model of constant wear and tear without appropriate recovery ("unwinding"; Frankenhaeuser, 1978) might best explain how the burnout syndrome develops. Moreover, the stress model presents concepts that can help prevent burnout. The general stress model (Janke & Wolffgramm, 1995) encompasses the occupational stress model of burnout proposed by Cherniss (1980). Others have suggested process models to explain how burnout develops (Burisch, 1988; Maslach & Leiter, 1997)—all compatible with the stress model.

Burnout, Stress, Recovery, and the Individual Zones of Optimal Functioning Model

The burnout model that has gained widest acceptance within sport psychology, developed by Smith (1986), is in line with the stress-recovery approach. While not emphasizing recovery processes, Smith maintains that burnout results from repeated imbalance between demands and resources, accompanied by low social support. Social support includes social recreation and recovery activities. Thus, in using concepts of resources and social support, Smith's model corresponds well to the stress-recovery approach; the two also share the conception of stress. The cognitive transactional stress model of Lazarus (1966) is as central to Smith's model as to the biopsychological approach of Janke and Wolffgramm (1995).

Kellmann (1991, 1997) has proposed a model describing the interrelations of stress, strain, and recovery demands (figure 9.2). The basic assumption is that growing stress necessitates increasing recovery. Limited resources (e.g., time) initiate a vicious cycle: under increased stress and unable to meet

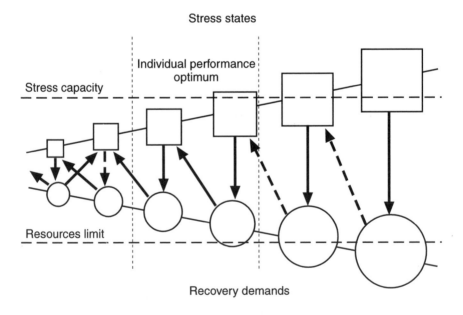

Figure 9.2 The "scissors model" of the interrelation between stress states and recovery demands.

increased recovery demands, the athlete incurs more stress. People may be stressed to the point that they fail to find or take time to recover adequately, or to consider better ways of coping with the situation.

In this model (figure 9.2), the simplest case is a symmetrical increase in stress and recovery demands: the two axes drift apart with elevated stress levels ("scissors" function). With intermediate levels of stress, one can find an area of optimal performance and thus an area of adequate recovery (continuous arrows in figure 9.2). Beyond this point, one cannot meet recovery demands without additional recovery activities. Stress will accumulate, and without intervention, burnout symptoms will likely develop. The state of balanced stress and recovery is related to optimal performance, and perhaps to the performance-related psychobiosocial states and their emotional correlates within the Individual Zones of Optimal Functioning (IZOF) model (chapter 3; Hanin, 1997a). In a state of adequate recovery, the individual can react appropriately and cope successfully with stress without additional recovery activities. Lack of recovery (Kellmann & Kallus, 1994) can trigger a process that brings on a state of elevated strain. As increasing stress limits recovery possibilities, the athlete must be given special opportunities for recovery to reestablish an optimal level of performance.

Burnout and Overtraining

Considering a stress-recovery imbalance in terms of physical training, we find parallels between the overtraining syndrome, staleness, and burnout. Lehmann, Foster, and Keul (1993) define overtraining/staleness as an imbalance between training and recovery, exercise and exercise capacity, and stress and stress tolerance. If stress tolerance depends on the efficiency of recovery, one recognizes the close relationship between burnout and staleness. Overtraining research shows that the linearly diverging branches in the "scissors" model (figure 9.2) may be too simple. To obtain the benefit of overreaching, the athlete must perform high doses of training. Thus, there is a fluid border between optimal adaptation and functional impairment due to overtraining. Consequently it is difficult to monitor training limits physiologically in any straightforward way. Lehmann et al. (1993) differentiate between overreaching (short-term overtraining) and long-term overtraining in the classical sense of the overtraining syndrome. In their definition, the overtraining syndrome is an agglomeration of exercise and nonexercise fatigue, disturbance of mood state, reduction or stagnation of performance capacity, and competitive incompetence; central fatigue and overtraining are associated with many changes in the peripheral stress systems.

Lehmann et al. (1998) associated overtraining with autonomic, sympathetic insufficiency. Reduced catecholamine levels are accompanied by reduced reactivity to sympathetic stimulation. The hypothalamus-pituitary-adrenal stress axis is disturbed and testosterone levels are decreased. The picture of staleness on the physiological level suggests hypotheses of comparable changes in burned-out athletes. Morgan and associates (e.g., Morgan, Brown, Raglin, O'Connor, & Ellickson, 1987; O'Connor, Morgan, & Raglin, 1991; Raglin, Morgan, & Luchsinger, 1990) showed that mood states assessed by the Profile of Mood States (POMS; McNair, Lorr, & Droppleman, 1971, 1992) indicated overtraining and staleness. During overtraining high scores in depression, anger, and fatigue occurred, which were associated with a drastically reduced score in vigor. Thus, the overtrained athlete's mood profile is comparable to the burned-out athlete's. From our perspective, overtraining is a possible source of burnout in athletes as well as a model for burnout. One should also note that enhanced stress levels due to nontraining and noncompetition situations are risk factors for developing an overtraining syndrome (Raglin, 1993).

Burnout in Athletes

Burnout in sport as discussed by Smith (1986) and Gould (1983) has stimulated much research (Dale & Weinberg, 1990). The burnout concept has contributed substantially to our understanding of dropout, sport injury, and sport commitment (Schmidt & Stein, 1991).

On the behavioral level, burned-out athletes have less input into training, fewer practice days, difficulties in motivation, poorer coping behavior, and a longer history within the sport (Gould, Tuffey, Udry, & Loehr, 1996; Gould, Udry, Tuffey, & Loehr, 1996). Gould and colleagues showed in tennis players that Smith's (1986) model well described the antecedents and consequences of burnout. Thus, one can view a model of chronic stress as a good basis for explaining burnout in athletes. Cohn (1990) identified too much practice or competition, lack of enjoyment, and too much pressure from self or others as the main sources of burnout. Furthermore, stress associated with injuries and resumption of training can drastically increase risks of dropout and burnout.

These models and the empirical evidence suggested that assessing an individual recovery-stress state might have value for monitoring training and preventing burnout. The Recovery-Stress-Questionnaire for Athletes (Kellmann & Kallus, in press) may provide early warnings of development of staleness and/or burnout. For high performance, athletes and coaches must recognize quickly that a decrement in performance has resulted from training and/or nontraining stressors. Thus they need information about an athlete's recovery-stress state before negative consequences become visible during phases of high demands. Adequate recovery, which does not sufficiently take place during resting periods, is needed to prevent overtraining (chapters 8, 10, 11; Henschen, 1993; Raglin, 1993) and burnout.

Burnout in Coaches

Researchers addressed burnout in coaches earlier than in athletes, and the issue is perhaps less complicated in coaches (Dale & Weinberg, 1990). The work environment of coaches involves long hours, demands much mental and emotional energy, and exerts considerable subjective pressure due to standards set by the coaches themselves or by fans and athletes.

A large survey by Vealey, Udry, Zimmermann, and Soliday (1992) demonstrated the importance of the coach's personality as a factor in development of burnout. This finding could be partly attributable to the survey method, as the questionnaire data for trait anxiety as compared to other predictors had the strongest relationships to burnout. Possibly method variance (burnout as well as trait anxiety was assessed by questionnaire) explains why anxiety contributed more to burnout than coaching time, leisure hours, or coaching experience. Interestingly, perceived overload seemed to be less important than trait anxiety. Results supported the contribution of reward factors as buffers against burnout, which can be derived from Smith's (1986) model. Perceived rewards and perceived value of the social role, together with engagement, are the most important anti-burnout buffers as evidenced in recent research in organizations (Maslach & Leiter, 1997).

In an unpublished study by Wilson and Bird (1984; cited by Dale & Weinberg [1990]), Canadian full-time university coaches who had had an unsuccessful season and a high number of contact hours with athletes showed a significantly increased risk of burnout. In a study of 332 coaches by Capel (1986), role conflict was an important predictor of burnout dimensions as measured by the MBI. However, these studies did not differentiate between full-time, part-time, and amateur status of coaches, which could be an important moderator between role strain, general stress factors, sport-specific stressors, and burnout (Kallus, Kellmann, Eberspächer, & Hermann, 1996).

ASSESSMENT OF BURNOUT

Although the early 1980s saw the development of several questionnaire measures to assess burnout (Maslach & Jackson, 1981a, 1981b, 1986; Pines, Aronson, & Kafry, 1981), assessments of burnout in coaches and athletes almost all used the MBI (Maslach & Jackson, 1986).

The Maslach Burnout Inventory

The MBI measures three dimensions of burnout reflecting increasing intensity:

1. **Emotional Exhaustion** is operationalized as feeling emotionally worn out.

2. **Depersonalization** refers to loss of interest in other people.

3. Decrement in **Personal Accomplishment** denotes a feeling that it is no longer worthwhile to pursue goals.

A basic problem with the MBI is that internal consistencies are not sufficiently high for all subscales. The original subscales as well as the German translations show acceptable coefficients only for Emotional Exhaustion and

Personal Accomplishment (Büssing & Perrar, 1992). Therefore, only these two scales of the MBI are included in our questionnaires.

Measuring Recovery-Stress State

If one views burnout as a syndrome resulting from prolonged stress without adequate recovery, it is reasonable to measure both stress and recovery and the relationship between them. Examining the stress dimension alone is inadequate, especially in high-performance contexts, as the management of high workload/high training intensity and volume is tightly linked to outstanding performance. The RESTQ (Kallus, 1995) is one of the few psychometric instruments addressing the recovery-stress state in order to prevent overtraining (Kenttä & Hassmen, 1998).

The Recovery-Stress-Questionnaire and Its Sport-Specific Versions

The RESTQ and the RESTQ-Sport are modular, with 12 subscales in the standard module and additional sport-specific subscales. Subscales 1-7 assess stress aspects; subscales 8 to 12 address recovery-related activities and states (cf. table 9.1). Subscales 1-12 were developed according to a multidimensional biopsychological stress model (Janke & Wolffgramm, 1995). Added to behavioral and performance-related items were items addressing emotional, physical, and social aspects of stress and recovery. Subjects rate the frequency of their stress- and recovery-related mood states, social activities, performance, and specific physical states. The standard version of the RESTQ assesses behavior or states during the past three days/nights on a 7-point frequency scale ranging from never (0) to always (6).

The sport-related subscales use the same response mode (cf. table 9.1); classical principles of test construction (Lord & Novick, 1968) were followed to develop area-specific subscales. Thus, the first subscales of the RESTQ allow comparisons of recovery-stress profiles across areas of application, and the sport-specific subscales allow one to relate this information to more sport-specific concepts.

Two sport-specific versions of the RESTQ were developed for athletes and coaches. The Recovery-Stress-Questionnaire for Athletes (RESTQ-Sport) measures sport-specific and general aspects of stress and recovery in athletes (Kellmann, 1991; Kellmann & Kallus, in press). Sport-specific subscales 13-19 are presented in table 9.1.

The second version was developed to assess aspects of stress and recovery of special interest to coaches in elite sports (RESTQ-Coach; Kallus & Kellmann, 1995). Table 9.2 presents the coach-specific subscales of this version. Both sport-specific versions of the RESTQ include burnout items adopted from the MBI using the frequency-scaled version.

To check the psychometric characteristics of the RESTQ, internal consistencies were calculated based on data obtained from samples of athletes and coaches. The RESTQ-Sport subscales showed sufficient internal consistency (table 9.1). Comparable results were obtained for the coach-specific subscales

Table 9.1 Scales of RESTQ-Sport, One Representative Item and Cronbach α

	Subcale	Example	α	Retest
1	General Stress	I felt down	.75	.71
2	Emotional Stress	I was in a bad mood	.73	.72
3	Social Stress	I was angry with someone	.87	.77
4	Conflicts/Pressure	I felt under pressure	.71	.73
5	Fatigue	I was overtired	.76	.81
6	Lack of Energy	I was unable to concentrate well	.70	.68
7	Somatic Complaints	I felt uncomfortable	.73	.76
8	Success	I finished important tasks	.67	.70
9	Social Relaxation	I had a good time with my friends	.84	.70
10	Somatic Relaxation	I felt at ease	.84	.74
11	General Recovery/Well-Being	I was in a good mood	.85	.79
12	Sleep Quality	I had a satisfying sleep	.84	.70
13	Being in Shape	I was in a good condition physically	.89	.71
14	Injury	My performance drained me physically	.80	.59
15	Emotional Exhaustion	I felt that I wanted to quit my sport	.69	.72
16	Personal Accomplishment	I dealt very effectively with my team-mates' problems	.79	.81
17	Self-Regulation	I prepared myself mentally for per-formance	.80	.77
18	Disturbed Breaks	My coach demanded too much of me during the breaks	.80	.64
19	Self-Efficacy	I was convinced that I had trained well	.88	.82

Notes: α = German rowers (N = 87); Retest = Test-retest reliability after three days; German rowers (N = 58).

Table 9.2 Unique Scales (13-19) of RESTQ-Coach, One Representative Item and Cronbach α

	Subcale	Example	α
13	Success as a Coach	I made the right decisions during competition	.78
14	Motivation as a Coach	I motivated my athletes well	.48
15	Fitness	I was physically relaxed	.82
16	Emotional Exhaustion	I felt burned out	.76
17	Personal Accomplishment	I dealt with emotional problems of my athletes very calmly	.75
18	Self-Efficacy of Coaches	I was convinced that I prepared my athletes as well as possible	.81
19	Conveyance of Self-Regulation Techniques	I spoke with my athletes about the advantages of mental training	.86

Notes: Sample: German male coaches (N = 148); Items on Motivation as a Coach were modified for the current version of the RESTQ-Coach.

(cf. table 9.2). The two burnout areas of the MBI (Personal Accomplishment, Emotional Exhaustion), which yielded consistently high internal reliability coefficients across studies, also showed high values after being adapted into the RESTQ.

Interrelation of Stress and Recovery Dimensions

Table 9.3 summarizes the results of intercorrelational analysis of RESTQ-Sport, based on a sample of 96 American swimmers and golfers.

High positive correlations (+, ++) cluster in the stress dimensions (subscales 1-7), within recovery dimensions (subscales 8-12), and in the sport-specific

Table 9.3   Subscale Intercorrelations of RESTQ-Sport

Subscale	1	2	3	4	5	6	7	8	9	10	11	12	13	14	15	16	17	18
1 General Stress																		
2 Emotional Stress	+++																	
3 Social Stress	+++	+++																
4 Conflicts/Pressure	++	+++	+															
5 Fatigue	+++	+	+															
6 Lack of Energy	++	++	+	++	++													
7 Somatic Complaints	+++	++	+		+++	++												
8 Success																		
9 Social Relaxation	−																	
10 Somatic Relaxation	−			−	−	−−		++										
11 General Recovery	−−	−−	−−			−−		++++	+++									
12 Sleep Quality	−−	−−	−	−−	−	−−			++	+								
13 Being in Shape				−		−−		+	++++	++								
14 Injury			+			+												
15 Emotional Exhaustion	+	+	+	+		+					−	−		++				
16 Personal Accomplishment										+			+++					
17 Self-Regulation						−			+				+++		+++			
18 Disturbed Breaks	+					+										+		
19 Self-Efficacy							−−	+	++++	+			++++			++	+++	

Notes: + = .40 ≤ r < .50; ++ = .50 ≤ r < .60; +++ = .60 ≤ r <.70; ++++ = r ≥ .70
− = −.40 ≥ r > −.50; −− = −.50 ≥ r > −.60. Sample: American athletes (swimmers and golfers; N = 96).

dimensions (subscales 13-19). The sport-specific subscales are related to recovery in a consistent pattern.

The burnout subscale Emotional Exhaustion is related to stress, and Personal Accomplishment is related to recovery, while the stress and recovery subscales show only moderate inverse correlations. Factor analyses of the RESTQ with different samples showed that frequency of stress and recovery are two independent factors (Kallus, 1995).

Recovery-Stress-Questionnaire and the Prediction of Athletic Performance

Studies on training monitoring (see following paragraph; Kellmann & Kallus, 1993) and performance prediction have strongly supported the validity of RESTQ-Sport. Data obtained at the German National Team Championships for swimming reflect its predictive value in elite athletes (table 9.4).

Athletes were divided into those with high, medium, and low overall scores in the RESTQ-Sport scale General Recovery/Well-Being, obtained one day before competition, and grouped according to performance (Kellmann, Kallus, & Kurz, 1996) into three terciles (top performance: 1; good: 2 to 4; low: lower than 4). Table 9.4 depicts the results. The chi-square test showed a highly significant relationship between recovery and performance (Chi^2 = 17.71, df = 4; $p < .001$). Low recovery levels were associated with low performance, and high recovery was related to good performance; the stress scores show corresponding relationships. As RESTQ-Sport data are stable up to 48 hr, performance can be predicted in advance, in time for intervention before important competitions. However, our work with the RESTQ in training monitoring (Kellmann & Günther, in press; Kellmann & Kallus, 1999; Kellmann, Kallus, Günther, Lormes, & Steinacker, 1997) revealed that the recovery-stress profile as a whole is an even more comprehensive database for intervention.

Table 9.4   Performance Prediction by the RESTQ-Sport (Scale: General Recovery/Well-Being)

		Rank			
		1	2, 3, 4	5, 6	Σ
RESTQ	Low	1	0	6	7
Recovery/	Medium	5	2	6	13
Well-Being	High	1	6	0	7
	Σ	7	8	12	27

Notes: Sample: German swimmers, National Team Championships (N = 27); Chi^2 value = 17.71; df = 4; $p < .001$.

Recovery-Stress-Questionnaire and Mood State

Because performance predictions in other areas (Morgan, O'Connor, Ellikson, & Bradley, 1988), as well as research with Hanin's IZOF model (1997a), have often used the POMS (McNair et al., 1971, 1992), the relationship between the RESTQ and POMS is of interest. Both provide an integrated score for a time period in the past, whereas other inventories assess emotional states at a specific moment or refer to concepts such as personality traits (e.g., State-Trait Anxiety Inventory; Spielberger, Gorsuch, & Lushene, 1970). The POMS and RESTQ seek to indicate an intermediate state of mood or recovery-stress state, respectively. Although these instruments apply different types of scales (frequency vs. intensity; cf. Diener & Emmons, 1984), analyses revealed close and theoretically expected correlational patterns (table 9.5).

The frequencies of General, Social, and Emotional Stress are related to the mood states of Tension, Depression, and Anger, whereas the frequencies of Conflicts/Pressure, Fatigue, Lack of Energy and of Somatic Complaints showed the highest correlations to POMS Fatigue and Confusion. Vigor on the POMS is closely related to recovery, Being in Shape, Self-Regulation, and Self-Efficacy. Fatigue in the POMS shows high correlations to frequency of Injury, Emotional Exhaustion, Personal Accomplishment, and the frequency of Disturbed Breaks. Emotional Exhaustion is positively related to Tension, Depression, and Fatigue and negatively to Vigor. Personal Accomplishment shows no substantial correlational pattern to athletes' mood state. Overall, the correlational pattern allows an interpretation of parallel results obtained via the POMS and RESTQ. However, some differences between POMS and RESTQ-Sport should be stressed.

The POMS assesses current mood state and therefore indicates no specific starting point for intervention: it is restricted to the affect level, not directly related to behavior. The RESTQ-Sport deals with mood-oriented activities and states and therefore provides a clear picture of occurrences over recent days in the athlete's life. Thus, starting points for individual work with the athlete can be found immediately (see case studies later in this chapter).

RECOVERY-STRESS STATE IN COACHES AND ATHLETES: EMPIRICAL EVIDENCE

Research with coaches, as well as studies of monitoring during training and during a competition season, support the close link between stress-recovery disbalance and burnout.

Recovery-Stress State in Coaches

The Federal Sports Association of Baden-Württemberg offers full-time professional and part-time semi-professional coaching positions. We assumed that the professional coaches' job stress is higher because of performance pressures,

Table 9.5 Correlation Matrix of RESTQ and POMS Scales

RESTQ	Total	Tension	Depression	Anger	Vigor	Fatigue	Confusion
	Profile of Mood States (POMS)						
1 General Stress	++++	+++	++++	++++	– –	+++	+++
2 Emotional Stress	++++	+++	++	++++	– –	++	++
3 Social Stress	+++	++	++	++++	–	+	++
4 Conflicts/ Pressure	++	+++	++	+		++	++
5 Fatigue	+	+	+			++++	+
6 Lack of Energy				+		+	++
7 Somatic Complaints	++	++	+	+	– –	++++	+
8 Success							
9 Social Relaxation					+++		
10 Somatic Relaxation	–	–		–	+++	–	–
11 General Recovery	– –	–	–	– –	+++		–
12 Sleep Quality	–	–	–	– –	+	–	– –
13 Being in Shape					+++		
14 Injury						+++	
15 Emotional Exhaustion	++	+	++		–	++	+
16 Personal Ac- complishment							
17 Self- Regulation			+		++		
18 Disturbed Breaks	+	+			– –	+++	+
19 Self-Efficacy	–				++		

Notes: + = .40 ≤ r < .50; ++ = .50 ≤ r < .60; +++ = .60 ≤ r < .70; ++++ = r ≥ .70
– = −.40 ≥ r > −.50; – – = −.50 ≥ r > −.60. Sample: U.S. athletes (N = 73).

but also that semi-professional coaches, who have a regular job as well, could experience high stress and low recovery because of time pressures (Kallus et al., 1996). We surveyed all 360 coaches in the organization; 195 coaches (20 females; age: M = 40.95, SD = 1.75; 175 males; age: M = 41.94, SD = 8.72) completed the RESTQ-Coach. The differences between full-time (n = 65) and semi-professional coaches (n = 130) were examined by T^2-Test and subsequent t-tests via MANOVA. We analyzed 144 coaches whose questionnaires were complete.

Results showed that full-time coaches experienced significantly higher strain and less recovery than their counterparts (F(36,125) = 1.72; $p < .043$) as reflected in General Stress (F(1,142) = 8.52; $p < .004$), Emotional Stress (F(1,142) = 13.3; $p < .000$), Social Stress (F(1,142) = 5.46; $p < .021$), and Fatigue (F(1,142) = 3.19; $p < .076$), as well as in the recovery-related subscales Social Relaxation (F(1,142) = 19.12; $p < .000$), Somatic Relaxation (F(1,142) = 10.11; $p < .002$), and General Recovery (F(1,142) = 19.23; $p < .000$). On the coach-specific stress and recovery subscales, scores for Fitness (F(1,142) = 3.43; $p < .013$) were lower, and Emotional Exhaustion (F(1,142) = 3.83; $p < .052$) were higher for the professional coaches.

A secondary analysis including age as a factor showed that on coach-specific subscales, issues such as job experience were more relevant than professional status. The use of Self-Regulation techniques increased significantly (F(2,138) = 7.14; $p < .001$) with age, while no effect of occupational status and no interaction (age $\times$ occupational status) emerged from MANOVA.

In summary, the full-time coaches were more burned out and highly stressed, were experiencing less recovery, and were less fit than the semi-professionals. Feedback workshops with the coaches supported the view that our findings reflect changes in lifestyle. Apparently, professional coaches have lost their hobby: they can no longer compensate for occupational stress by coaching during leisure time. Furthermore, they have less continuous contact with their athletes and spend more time driving. Burnout-relevant factors as described by Maslach and Leiter (1997)—work overload, lack of control, insufficient reward, breakdown of work-related social networks, absence of fairness, conflicting values—correspond closely to these results.

Coaches' recovery-stress state and coping strategies are important in terms of retention. The risk of burnout was higher for the professional than for the semi-professional coaches. The professional coaches also showed deficits in coping strategies as measured by the German Stress Coping Inventory (Streßverarbeitungsfragebogen; Janke, Erdmann, & Kallus, 1985) and therefore may possibly react less effectively in critical situations. Group differences in the general recovery-stress state were not influenced by variables such as age. The stability of our results supports the idea of optimizing the situation for professional coaches in large sport organizations. Our results could be summarized by the equation:

Stress + Recovery Deficit + Deficient Coping → High Risk of Burnout

Coping research suggests possible modes of intervention (Cameron & Meichenbaum, 1983). Additionally, the differences between the two groups indicate methods of reducing occupational stress and enhancing personal resources (Schönpflug, 1983). However, we cannot exclude the possibility that the results were influenced by selection and/or self-selection processes, as no comparable longitudinal data are available.

Recovery-Stress State in Elite Athletes

The RESTQ-Sport can be used to monitor subjective stress and recovery during training cycles before competitions and throughout the season (Ferger, 1998; Kellmann, Kallus, Günther, et al., 1997; Kellmann, Kallus, Steinacker, & Lormes, 1997). We present examples from rowing (training camps and competition) and a Mountain Biking World Cup season.

Recovery-Stress State in Training Camps: The German Junior National Rowing Team

To prevent negative consequences of training camps, an interdisciplinary approach helps coaches, physicians, and sport psychologists to share information and to draw mutual conclusions. One goal is to identify athletes whose recovery-stress states deviate from those expected based on individual or group profiles. A short feedback loop is useful for integrating the sport psychologist into the team. As athletes complete questionnaires, the various coaches and physicians get immediate feedback and so can react quickly.

A basic question in training monitoring by questionnaire concerns how subjective ratings relate to objective parameters. Kellmann, Kallus, Günther, et al. (1997) and Kellmann, Kallus, Steinacker, et al. (1997) used average daily rowed kilometers as an indicator of training volume and demonstrated a close relationship between RESTQ and training volume.

Participants

Forty-one German junior national rowing team athletes participated voluntarily in our study during preparation for the 1995 World Championships. Each athlete (or his/her parents) gave written informed consent prior to inclusion in the study. The study was approved by the ethical committee of the Medical Faculty of Ulm University. The 41 participants included 14 females, age 17.8 (16.4-18.4) years (mean and range), and 27 males, age 18.1 (17-18.4) years (mean and range).

Procedure and Statistical Analysis

All subjects completed the RESTQ-Sport, after lunch, five times during the training camp and before preliminaries. Changes during the preparation period were evaluated using trend parameters obtained by data transformation with orthogonal polynomials (Ferguson & Takane, 1989).

Results

Figure 9.3 shows scores on the subscale Emotional Exhaustion for the five measurements (T1: arrival at camp; T2-T4: during camp; T5: before preliminaries), and includes average daily rowed kilometers for the reference period of the RESTQ-Sport (past three days). Orthogonal polynomials revealed a significant overall test ($F(4,36) = 5.7$; $p < .01$) with a quadratic trend of the dependent variable Emotional Exhaustion ($F(1,39) = 17.01$; $p < .001$), with the highest value at the third measurement.

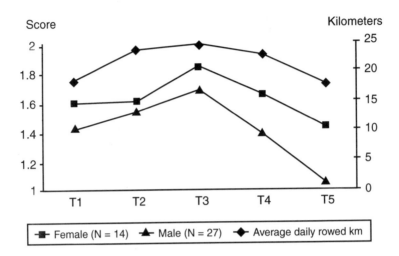

Figure 9.3 Means of the RESTQ-Sport subscale Emotional Exhaustion and average daily rowed kilometers throughout training camp.

This finding accords with other results (Guttmann, Pollock, Foster, & Schmidt, 1984; Morgan, Brown, Raglin, O'Connor, & Ellickson, 1987; O'Connor et al., 1991; Raglin, Morgan, & O'Connor, 1991; Raglin, Morgan, & Luchsinger, 1990; Wittig, Houmard, & Costill, 1989) indicating that increases in training parallel elevations in mood disturbance whereas mood improvements occur with reduced training.

Training Camp Case Studies

Individual recovery-stress states have been regularly assessed during preparation camps for the Junior Rowing World Championships since 1995. The following case studies, from the German junior national rowing team during preparation camp for the 1996 and 1997 World Championships, illustrate the value of the RESTQ-Sport for individual assessment. Usually an athlete's recovery-stress state is judged by (a) the individual profile with reference to the team at each measurement and (b) changes in individual scores over time. Since training volume changes during the camp, the reference norm—computed by the mean plus/minus standard deviation of the whole team—is calculated separately for each measurement occasion. If more than two RESTQ-Sport scores deviate from the reference norm, a qualitative interpretation of the patterns provides practical information. The following case studies illustrate how recovery-stress state scores were used to monitor athletes' individual training.

Case Study B
Description and Diagnosis. At the beginning of camp the recovery-stress state was assessed in all rowers. A 17-year-old female rower showed very low scores on Sleep Quality, resulting in a combined low value in Somatic Relaxation and an elevated score in Fatigue (see figure 9.4). The coach had no explanation for

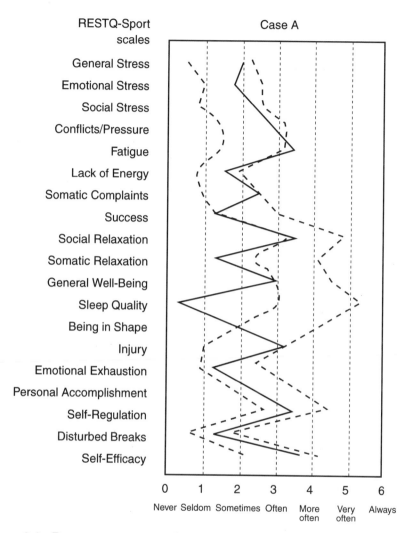

Figure 9.4 Recovery-stress state for rower in case A (solid line) and reference norm of the whole team (mean ± one standard deviation between dotted lines).

Reprinted, by permission, from M. Kellmann and K.W. Kallus, 1999, Mood, recovery-stress state, and regeneration. In *Overload, fatigue, performance incompetence, and regeneration in sport*, edited by M. Lehmann et al. (New York: Plenum).

the results but found a simple solution when he talked to the athlete: she was sleeping in a very uncomfortable bed.

Intervention. A new bed board was arranged, and scores in the RESTQ-Sport improved considerably by the next measurement. The solution is not always that simple, but often easier than expected.

Case Study B

Due to injury of the female four-coxed stroke one day before the preliminary heat of the 1997 World Championships, another rower had to take the critical stroke position. The coach made his decision based on the available information. As all four athletes had completed the RESTQ-Sport four times, their profiles could be compared across time. The coach's basic question was: Can I do any harm by putting rower B on the stroke position? In this case all information, especially for the sport-specific subscales (e.g., Self-Regulation, Self-Efficacy) supported his choice. The boat won the World Championships.

Conclusions
The case studies illustrate some ways of using the RESTQ-Sport in training camps:

▶ To identify athletes' problems

▶ To provide support for coaches' decisions

▶ To optimize interpersonal communication within the team

As the RESTQ-Sport is based on a recovery-stress approach and is closely related to the frequency of stress- and recovery-related behavior, direct conclusions are often evident.

In summary, although the POMS has been used successfully in most studies on overtraining and mood, one advantage of the RESTQ-Sport is simultaneous assessment of subjective stress and recovery. Both methods demonstrate that athletes' self-report data constitute a powerful, convenient, and low-cost monitoring tool. Henschen (1993) and Raglin (1993) stressed the importance of adequate recovery during training in order to prevent overtraining. During training, the balance between physical stress, psychological stress, and recovery should be monitored routinely to prevent overtraining, staleness, and burnout (Gould, Udry, Tuffey, & Loehr, 1996; Gould, Tuffey, Udry, & Loehr, 1996; Kallus et al., 1996; Kellmann, 1997; Kellmann & Kallus, 1999). The RESTQ-Sport estimates current levels of stress and recovery in only one 10 min step.

Recovery-Stress State in Mountain Biking Competitions

During the 1997 World Cup, 16 mountain bikers completed the RESTQ-Sport weekly throughout the season (Eweleit, 1998). Data were not used to give athletes and coaches immediate feedback. For analysis of the RESTQ, an index (difference of standardized scores) was developed to combine stress and recovery values. The complete data set (12 measurement occasions × 16 athletes) was used to obtain total means and standard deviations for the overall stress scale and overall recovery scale. Using these, scores were standardized according to the formula used for standard normal distribution. The standardized values allowed computation of individual differences showing periods of balance, overshooting stress, and increased recovery usually associated with an enhanced performance potential.

The profile for the European champion (figure 9.5) shows values for stress, recovery, and stress-recovery difference indicating predictable changes in an athlete who performed his best at the right moment (arrow marks the competition date). Note the strong tapering phase, reflected in the recovery-stress

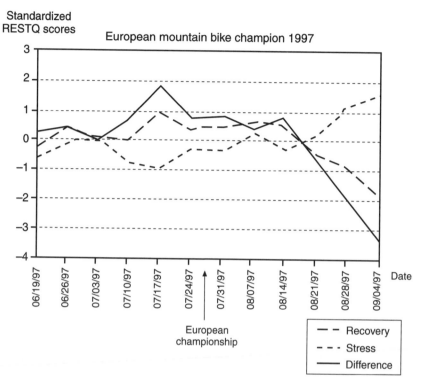

Figure 9.5 Standardized RESTQ-Sport scores of stress, recovery, and stress-recovery difference over a season with optimal preparation for a championship.

Reprinted, by permission, from M. Kellmann and K.W. Kallus, 1999, Mood, recovery-stress state, and regeneration. In *Overload, fatigue, performance incompetence, and regeneration in sport,* edited by M. Lehmann et al. (New York: Plenum).

state. Interestingly, at the end of the season this athlete seemed to be exhausted and exhibited widely deviating stress and recovery values.

During the season the athlete depicted in figure 9.6 was diagnosed as overtrained by the physician and had to take a break. This process is impressively reflected in the RESTQ scores.

The marked changes in stress and recovery over the season were also expressed in this athlete's burnout scores (figure 9.7), which show predictable peaks with overtraining.

Recovery-Stress State in Rowing Competitions

The next case study deals with events during the 1997 Junior World Championships in Hazewinkel (Belgium) from a different perspective. Again, athletes completed the RESTQ-Sport a total of five times during the camp and before and after the preliminary heat. The female coxed eight of the German junior national rowing team had won their preliminary heat by an outstanding 8 sec, immediately qualifying for the finals.

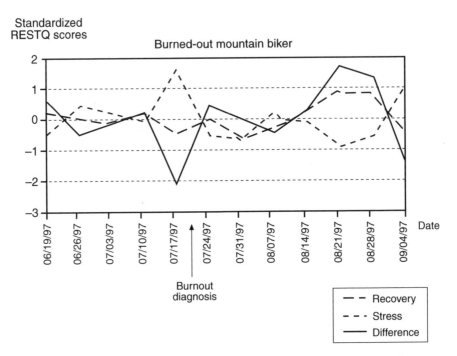

Figure 9.6 Standardized RESTQ-Sport scores of stress, recovery, and stress-recovery difference over a season for an overtrained athlete.

Reprinted, by permission, from M. Kellmann and K.W. Kallus, 1999, Mood, recovery-stress state, and regeneration. In *Overload, fatigue, performance incompetence, and regeneration in sport*, edited by M. Lehmann et al. (New York: Plenum).

Before the race, the opening of the World Championships and the first performance test in a real competition situation, some athletes came down with food poisoning and had to be replaced. Although the athletes and coaches were concerned about the practice program, the outcome of the preliminary race took some of the pressure off, telling them that they were well prepared.

But the victory was not obviously reflected in the individual recovery-stress profiles of the coxed eight. For key positions such as the stroke, scores for Self-Regulation and Self-Efficacy were relatively low. The coach was surprised, as all the athletes seemed self-confident and relaxed—but, experienced with the RESTQ-Sport, he used the information. He found out from the stroke that she was feeling additional pressure and anxiety because expectations for the final race were so high. Whereas most other team members seemed to feel decreased pressure after the win, she felt more. The coach held an informal meeting to review the victory and address the fact that it affected different rowers differently. The stroke tearfully communicated her feelings, her astonished teammates expressed their concern and support, and another rower divulged her insecurity. The meeting seemed to be another important step in a continuing team-building process. In the finals, the boat performed at the preliminary-heat level and won the World Championships.

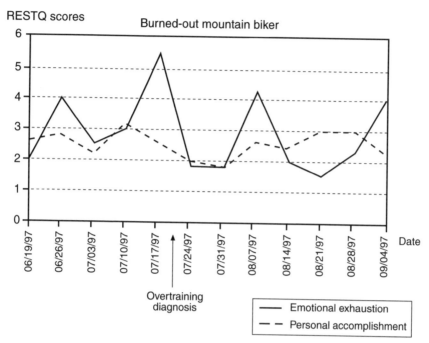

Figure 9.7 RESTQ-Sport scores for the subscales Emotional Exhaustion and Personal Accomplishment in the course of a season for an overtrained athlete.

What do we conclude? First, coaches must remember that their perspective and the athletes' may be different. Second, some athletes do not readily (openly) communicate their feelings to teammates. Third, coaches should use time during camps to initiate team-building processes so situations such as this can be buffered by team members—a good example of burnout prevention.

CONCLUSIONS

One can view burnout as the result of chronic or intermittent stress with inadequate recovery. Our recovery-stress state model emphasizes relationships between stress, recovery, and burnout as nonspecific states of the organism. Although the model is consistent with most burnout formulations, the concept of stress does not highlight specific stressors such as role ambiguity often discussed as a source of burnout in teachers and coaches (cf. Maslach & Leiter, 1997). Burnout signifies a state far beyond a zone of optimal functioning. Burnout and staleness or overtraining can be expressed by the formula:

Prolonged Stress + Insufficient Recovery + Deficient Coping → Burnout

What is the opposite of burnout? Hanin (chapter 3) defines the individual zone of optimal functioning (IZOF) as a multidimensional psychobiosocial state corresponding to optimal performance in elite athletes. We conceptualize burnout as a multidimensional psychobiosocial state similar to other states of stress and strain; thus, the opposite of burnout is the state of being in one's own IZOF. Hanin (see chapter 3) outlines assessment of a psychobiosocial state using seven components: cognitive, motivational, affective, bodily-somatic, motor-behavioral, performance-operational, and communicative aspects. Typically the IZOF is assessed by scales for mood and emotions; a major strength of the IZOF approach is that it systematically addresses the dynamics of subjective emotional states over time.

Our results indicate that the recovery-stress state is an alternative assessment approach. Short-term dynamics in time are aggregated, and the frequency of evaluated states and activities, rather than intensity, is measured. The multidimensional approach addresses emotional, social, motivational, performance-related, and physical aspects of stress and recovery supplemented by sport-specific states, which relate to the self-control dimension as well as outcomes like burnout.

The recovery-stress construct might contribute to the usefulness of the IZOF model. Sport-specific versions of the RESTQ reflect changes in coaches' and athletes' psychobiosocial states throughout training and competitions and even during different stages of a competition. Therefore, the questionnaire may help monitor how athletes enter, reenter, and exit their individual optimal working zones in relation to performance.

The most important practical aspect of recovery-stress assessment is the possibility of intervening without delay. Empirically tested methods to enhance coping with stress, change stress, and support optimal recovery are available. A second purpose of this chapter was to show that the recovery-stress approach advances understanding of psychobiosocial states such as optimal zones of functioning and the burnout syndrome. Future research will reveal more of the dynamics in stress-recovery sequences and ways to relate stress and recovery.

SUMMARY

In this chapter we suggested a stress-recovery approach to study burnout and overtraining in athletes and coaches, and outlined the advantages of a biopsychological concept including conceptual, methodological, and practical aspects. We also addressed problems of defining and operationalizing burnout and overviewed results on burnout in sport. The RESTQ for athletes and coaches is a tool for studying and preventing overtraining and burnout. Case studies in high-performance sports illustrate possible applications of the recovery-stress approach, which has parallels to the IZOF model.

CHAPTER 10

Maladaptive Fatigue Syndrome and Emotions in Sport

Keith Henschen
United States

From the publication of *The Expression of Emotions in Man and Animals* (Darwin, 1872/1965) to Izard's seminal *Human Emotions* (1977) to the present, thousands of scientific works on emotions have appeared. Developmental, personality, cognitive, and clinical psychology researchers have contributed to the field with its myriad theories and concepts, as have cognitive scientists, neuroscientists, and psychophysiologists. We now know that hormones and neurotransmitters serve emotions; that emotions influence relationships and social interactions; that there are emotion-cognition relations; and that there are relationships between psychological disorders and types of emotional experiences (Izard, 1991).

According to Izard (1991), there is wide agreement on five premises concerning the central issues in emotion theory:

1. Expression of emotions serves important communicative functions, especially apparent in early development.

2. Emotional experiences influence perception, thought, and action.

3. Emotions are central features of social bonds and integral to temperament and personality.

4. Knowledge of emotions is essential to the diagnosis and treatment of psychological disorders.

5. Positive emotions enhance a variety of constructive psychological and physiological phenomena while negative emotions frequently impair healthy functioning.

There is, then, little doubt that emotion figures prominently in all the human animal thinks, perceives, and does. Emotions are precursors to behavior as well as formulators and determinants of behavior, including one that plagues dedicated athletes and is the topic of this chapter—the Maladaptive Fatigue Syndrome (MFS). The chapter presents theory regarding MFS and addresses the role of emotion in prevention and rehabilitation.

CONCEPTS AND DEFINITIONS

What is MFS? How does it differ from overtraining, staleness, burnout, or chronic fatigue? The latter terms describe the same phenomenon or subsets of it—MFS. Exercise physiologists call it overtraining, psychologists refer to it as staleness or burnout (note that both are metaphors for a maladaptive state), and medical professionals identify it as chronic fatigue. But for all, the ingredients are the same. Let us examine some common definitions:

▶ **Burnout.** (1) A state of mental, emotional, and physical exhaustion brought on by persistent devotion to a goal whose achievement is dramatically opposed to reality (Freudenberger & Richelson, 1981; Maslach, 1982b; Pines, Aronson, & Kafry, 1981); or (2) an exhaustive psychophysiological response exhibited as a result of frequent, sometimes extreme but generally ineffective efforts to meet excessive training and competitive demands (Smith, 1986).

▶ **Chronic fatigue.** (1) "Chronic fatigue syndrome is a morass of ignorance. We don't know what it is, but patients are suffering from it" (Eichner, 1989); or (2) chronic fatigue syndrome, characterized by fatigue as the principal symptom, "is severe, disabling, and affects physical and mental functioning. The symptom of fatigue must be present for at least six months during which it occurs at least 50 percent of the time" (Smith & Jones, 1992, p. 263).

▶ **Overtraining.** (1) An abnormal extension of the training process culminating in a state of staleness (Morgan, Brown, Raglin, O'Connor, & Ellickson, 1987); or (2) a type of physical training performed primarily by highly motivated athletes (Morgan, 1997a).

▶ **Staleness.** (1) A symptom of ensuing burnout, or an early warning sign of the negative state to come (Fender, 1989); or (2) a state in which the athlete has difficulty maintaining standard training regimens and can no longer achieve previous performance results (Morgan, Brown, et al., 1987).

To further complicate matters, researchers in various countries have used terms such as "overreaching," "overload," and "overtraining" to denote staleness and overtraining. Thus confusion about markers of the overtraining syndrome results partly from "the lack of international agreement on terminology" (Hooper & Mackinnon, 1995). Terminology aside, the concepts are not new; researchers have studied them for over a century. Yet I am not sure we are any closer to understanding this issue than we were two decades ago.

Why does this concept remain so elusive? For one thing, it does not fit nicely into physiology, psychology, sociology, or medicine. For another, it is not conducive to solution through study of its components; real understanding requires a multidimensional approach (psychobiosocial; see chapter 3; Hanin, 1997a). So, getting beyond the nomenclature, I prefer to label this phenomenon the Maladaptive Fatigue Syndrome: first, because the term actually identifies the situation; second, because the other terms have a foundation in the fatigue syndrome that remains unaddressed; third, because the term indicates a more holistic psychobiosocial state than other labels; and finally, because this label allows for flexibility. Maladaptive Fatigue Syndrome is physical and/or mental fatigue caused by a combination of stressors from mental (psycho-), physical (bio-), and social sources. It is a multidimensional psychobiosocial state resulting in what Gould (1996) well described: a "psychological, physical, and emotional withdrawal from a formerly enjoyable and motivating activity" (p. 276) due to excessive fatigue.

PSYCHOBIOSOCIAL CHARACTERISTICS OF MALADAPTIVE FATIGUE SYNDROME

Many have identified the physical symptoms of maladaptive fatigue, which are the same as those characterizing overtraining, staleness, and burnout. The psychological characteristics are also clear. One interesting side note is that the signs of MFS are also commonly recognized signals of clinical depression. Also, many of the prevention strategies for clinical depression are very similar to those used for MFS (see figure 10.1).

While the social aspects of MFS are as important as the psychobiological characteristics, they are more difficult to identify because they vary greatly among individuals. Personal observation has shown several associated social behaviors: (a) athletes become less assertive and more lethargic in their interactions with others; (b) athletes generally become more withdrawn and less willing to communicate; (c) their usual communication network narrows; (d) conflict between athletes and significant others is heightened; and (e) the coach-athlete relationship becomes strained. These characteristics cause additional stress that can negatively impact relationships, traumatic life events, academic problems, performance issues, and other perceived pressures.

The Sandpile Paradigm and Maladaptive Fatigue Syndrome

People manifest the psychobiosocial symptoms of MFS differently. Some experience physical effects and exhibit them by going into a slump; others experience more emotional effects such as depression. Rather than labeling the condition overtraining because of physical fatigue, or burnout because of emotional

Physical symptoms	**Causes**
Severe fatigue	Length of total season
Chronic illness	Lack of positive reinforcement
Temperature swings	Feelings of helplessness
Lactic acid increases	Perceived low accomplishment
Excessive sweating	Monotony of training
Gastrointestinal disturbances	Perceived overload
Sleep disturbances	High levels of competitive stress
Increased resting heart rate	Boredom
Mild hypoglycemia	
Weight changes	**Prevention strategies**
Elevated resting blood pressure	Proper planning of training
Decline in performance	Scheduling time-outs
	Avoiding monotony in training
Psychological and emotional	Ample positive reinforcement
symptoms	Management of pre- and postcompetitive
Changeable moods	anxiety
Lowered tolerance of frustration	Utilizing mental practice (self-regulation)
Feelings of helplessness	Allowing athletes to make choices and
Negative self-concept	control outcomes
Feelings of worthlessness	
Increased irritability	
Apathy	
Depressed moods	
Excessive guilt	

Figure 10.1 MFS symptoms, causes, and preventive strategies.

problems, or overreaching because of performance decrements, it is more accurate to use a holistic descriptor. It is a syndrome with an idiosyncratic constellation of cognitive, affective, motivational, bodily-somatic, motor-behavioral, performance, and communicative components or symptoms (see chapter 3).

To illustrate how maladaptive fatigue develops, I borrow from physics the theory of self-organized criticality (Bak, 1996), which holds that an organism will sustain only so much pressure or stress before it needs to reorganize or readjust in order to handle additional stresses. With each added stress, the organism attempts to readjust according to its present state of homeostasis. The reorganization causes changes in the organism to facilitate accommodation of the new demands. These changes, major and minor, are analogous to small and large avalanches in a sandpile. The sandpile is the metaphor for self-organized criticality (figure 10.2).

With the addition of more and more grains of sand (stressors), the sandpile (human organism) keeps readjusting itself (small or large avalanches). For the athlete these stressors may be higher training loads; psychological pressures

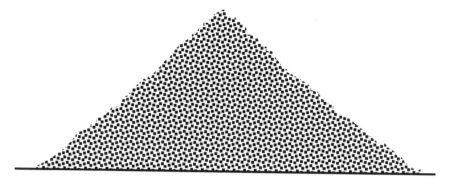

Figure 10.2   Sandpile paradigm as a metaphor model of MFS.

from competition; relationship issues with coaches, loved ones, or peers; or social problems (e.g., job, team dynamics). The athlete may readjust to each added stress but then run out of energy to accommodate or overcome them all, and the readjustment may manifest itself as MFS. Again: the syndrome reflects psychological, physical, and social problems occurring simultaneously. Why do many elite athletes train in isolation (away from family, friends, and the media) before important competitions? They are attempting to mitigate some of the energy-robbing stressors that could initiate MFS.

The Sandpile Paradigm and Adaptive Fatigue Syndrome

There is an optimal level of fatigue (Adaptive Fatigue Syndrome, AFS) that enhances performance physically, mentally, and emotionally. To become stronger, the human animal must face challenges and then have time to recover. Is this not the theory behind all training regimens? Train hard, rest, get stronger, and then repeat the cycle—as in periodization training, a prime example of the theory in practice. Optimal, adaptive fatigue is good. This is not a new concept. In the early 1970s, the great swimming coach Dr. James Counsilman advocated these very principles. His adaptive-superadaptation conditioning theories and practices produced a plethora of world-class swimming athletes. The trick, according to Dr. Counsilman, was to fatigue the body to near exhaustion—but not go so far as to cause complete exhaustion (MFS).

Optimal fatigue causes a small avalanche that both allows the athlete to recover relatively quickly and precipitates an increase in strength. Our bodies are sandpiles constantly readjusting to changeable demands. Fatigue to an individual level, facilitating this readjustment, is optimal. While to say so may sound like heresy, MFS may be beneficial in that it provides time for the body to readjust to additional demands. The in-out of the zone concept seems to fit nicely here—interindividual variability in fatigue tolerance is analogous to individually optimal levels and zones of functionally optimal (adaptive) and dysfunctional (maladaptive) fatigue (chapter 3).

CAUSES OF MALADAPTIVE FATIGUE SYNDROME

Investigators search for a single or simple cause for MFS but to date have been stymied. The reason is that there isn't one. Maladaptive Fatigue Syndrome can result from many factors, singly or in combination. Figure 10.1 lists some of the causes in athletes, which I characterize briefly here.

▶ **Maladaptive Fatigue Syndrome proneness.** Although accurate prediction is virtually impossible, certain types of individuals have a proneness to MFS. Athletes who are extremely dedicated, high achieving, success driven, highly responsible, other oriented, and perfectionistic seem to be likely candidates.

▶ **Length of season.** Contemporary athletes train year-round, and the competitive season in many sports is 8-10 months. During the "off-season," athletes attempt to catch up in other areas of their lives while staying in physical "shape"; thus the stresses never in fact subside. People tend to become fatigued particularly if they do not follow appropriate training principles. Constantly alternating between fatigue and recovery over too long a period can cause MFS.

▶ **Lack of positive reinforcement.** Prolonged periods of intensity with little positive reinforcement contribute greatly to a negative mental set. This in turn permits entry of adverse emotions that lead to fatiguing. Positive reinforcement, on the other hand, always seems to lift the emotions.

▶ **Feelings of helplessness.** Constantly struggling against perceived odds, with no light at the end of the tunnel, leads to feelings of helplessness. Whatever has caused the feeling, the athlete needs to expend much energy to get through the situation. This extra mental effort often contributes to MFS.

▶ **Perceived low accomplishment.** People may have unfulfilled or excessive expectations. Many high-level athletes are perfectionists, never satisfied with their efforts or results. Continual worrying about accomplishments, or lack thereof, will cause mental fatigue—and thus MFS.

▶ **Monotony of training.** Doing the same thing routinely contributes to a lack of stimulation, which is very tiring. Too many athletes participate in practice situations that resemble pure drudgery. Many embrace the philosophy of "the more the better." Motor learning research unequivocally refutes this concept and also offers insight for the design of creative and challenging practice sessions (Henschen, 1990). Variety is the spice of the training environment. Monotony leads to apathy, lack of focus, and fatigue.

▶ **Perceived overload.** Thinking that coming challenges are insurmountable will make them so. What you believe is what you will achieve.

▶ **High levels of competitive stress.** Consistent intense levels of competition bring on energy-draining competitive stress, which can exact a high price if not dealt with appropriately. Competitive stress unmitigated is a prime contributor to MFS, especially if left unchecked for too long.

▶ **Boredom.** Years ago, when I began a line of research on burnout and then MFS, I was unsure whether all the factors on this list contributed equally to the phenomenon. I now believe that there is one factor upon which the others continually load and is the main cause of maladaptive fatigue for athletes: boredom. Boredom is tiring. Being bored means that an athlete just goes through the motions, without involvement in the performance. Length of season, monotony of training, lack of positive reinforcement, and perceived overload exacerbate the boredom. Athletes are challenge-oriented people who need stimulation. Because of the hours they spend on the same activities (practice), they often feel helpless or trapped. The result is going through the motions and boredom.

EMOTIONS OF ADAPTIVE AND MALADAPTIVE FATIGUE

It is no secret that "virtually all of the neurophysiological systems and subsystems of the body are involved in greater or lesser degrees in emotion states" (Izard, 1991, p. 20). Emotional states affect perceptions, behaviors, and thoughts and may also contribute to mental health issues. Emotions (both positive and negative) can either activate the autonomic nervous system (as in adaptive fatigue) or shut it down dramatically (as in maladaptive fatigue) (Izard, 1991). The body reacts intensely to any emotional extreme, less intensely to more moderate emotions. Sometimes this bodily reaction is of short duration; but when emotions persist, they become moods. Emotions are activated by various processes—cognitive, neuromuscular, affective, and/or neurochemical.

Six emotions that commonly accompany MFS are anger-hostility, sadness, depression, anxiety, confusion, and lack of vigor or apathy.

▶ **Anger-hostility.** Frustrating situations often cause anger, as well as disgust and contempt. This combination is called the hostility triad (Izard, 1991). In MFS the athlete directs the hostility inwardly, so that it is hard to eliminate (chapter 5; Saul Rosenzweig's intrapunitive and extrapunitive reaction to frustration is appropriate to consider in this regard).

▶ **Anxiety.** Anxiety means different things to different people (chapter 4): feeling uneasy, apprehensive, shaky, fearful, shameful, or guilty. During MFS an athlete is probably experiencing a combination of these emotions rather than only one.

▶ **Confusion.** Athletes with MFS often do not think clearly and can experience short episodes of lack of focus. They seem incapable of sustained attention and/or quick comprehension. This confusion illustrates how emotions affect thoughts and perceptions.

▶ **Depression.** Depression is not a single emotion but rather "involves a complex combination of emotions, images, memories, and thoughts" (Izard, 1991, p. 209). It also involves physiological states. Depression often accompanies loss, and during MFS the athlete can easily identify the loss as one of excellence in performance. Not being able to deal with the loss magnifies the problem (chapter 2; Lazarus, 1993).

▶ **Sadness.** Fatigue often contributes to sadness, which is why sadness is a normal manifestation of MFS. Working hard and not being satisfied with one's progress naturally leads to sadness and discouragement. Sadness frequently interacts with other emotions that contribute to alterations of thoughts and behaviors.

▶ **Lack of vigor; apathy.** An athlete who is fatigued does not have much vigor or enthusiasm. More than likely, during MFS the athlete will display apathetic and/or lethargic behaviors and lack of interest.

When athletes experience these emotions for longer and longer periods of time (moods), chances are that they have MFS. Are the markers of adaptive and maladaptive fatigue different? Absolutely! Deterioration of emotions from positive to negative is a fairly accurate indication that MFS is developing. Whereas AFS is generally marked by a physical tiredness that dissipates with sufficient recovery time, the markers of MFS are psychological, physical, and emotional.

APPROACHES TO MEASUREMENT
OF MALADAPTIVE FATIGUE SYNDROME

Two methods have proven successful for assessing MFS. One is an objective psychological assessment, and the other is subjective self-profiling.

Psychological Assessment

The leaders in psychological assessment research have been William P. Morgan and colleagues at the University of Wisconsin, who have investigated mood states as markers of staleness as well as the relation between overtraining and psychological mood states. (Remember, moods are long-term emotions.) To measure mood, Morgan and colleagues have employed the Profile of Mood States (POMS; McNair, Lorr, & Droppleman, 1971), which measures six transitory emotional states (tension, depression, anger, vigor, fatigue, and confusion). Owing primarily to these investigators' efforts, extensive literature now documents the validity of psychometric monitoring of MFS. Since the POMS is a well-known psychological assessment instrument (discussed in detail in chapters 5 and 8), I will not elaborate on its scientific authenticity. The POMS-generated data show conclusively that the psychological mood profile of individuals who have MFS differs from that of people who do not. People experiencing MFS show increases in depression, anger, confusion, tension, and sadness, as well as decreased vigor. Because it measures nearly all the emotions (moods) that mark MFS, the POMS is the leading instrument for assessing the syndrome.

Self-Profiling

A more situation-specific and less psychometrically structured subjective method of assessing a perceived feeling or emotion is self-profiling, in which athletes report their emotional states every day. In this type of self-report rating, analogous to the Borg Scale of Perceived Exertion, athletes identify perceptions of emotional levels. Dr. William Sands at the University of Utah developed a self-profiling program for the women's gymnastic team. Each day before practice, the gymnasts use the computer to answer six to eight questions about their experience of emotions such as joy, sadness, depression, anger, and anxiety (item contents are similar to those on the POMS subscales), for example:

▶ Have you been angry in the last 24 hours? Yes-No

▶ To what degree was your anger? Low 1 2 3 4 5 High

▶ Have you experienced anxiety in the last 24 hours? Yes-No

▶ How anxious do you feel you were? Low 1 2 3 4 5 High

These questions resemble POMS questions, but the time frame is different—the last 24 hours instead of "the past week or month." Also, Sands's questions do not assess situational emotional responses; all athletes answer the same questions. Other questions concern sleep patterns, hours of sleep, and phase of the menstrual cycle. Finally, athletes answer questions about how they perceive their fatigue levels and whether they feel they need additional recovery time before the next phase of physical training. The self-profiling of emotions has received raves from the gymnastics coaching staff because it has allowed them to identify athletes who are candidates for MFS due to excessive training and lack of recovery time (see chapter 9).

The self-profiling also helps coaches determine when to reduce physical training to accommodate other stresses in the gymnasts' lives (e.g., exams). Each athlete seems to demonstrate a unique pattern of adaptation that coaches need to identify before a major avalanche sets in. Once coaches understand their athletes' idiosyncrasies, they can design physical training programs that encourage minor avalanches but avoid the major ones.

STRATEGIES FOR PREVENTION AND REVERSAL

Having identified MFS as a crucial issue confronting athletes, defined the concept, and outlined possible causes, I outline some strategies for prevention and reversal.

Prevention

I believe that a little fatigue (AFS) is not detrimental to an athlete and is probably even beneficial. Slight MFS or AFS will trigger small avalanches. These slight adaptations will lead to a stronger and more resilient athlete. The trick is to keep the maladaptive fatigue at a level the athlete can handle instead of causing extremely high maladaptive fatigue levels and major avalanches. In my opinion, MFS and AFS are qualitatively different modalities with different functional impacts upon the athlete. Adaptive Fatigue Syndrome has positive effects, such as (a) pleasure in or satisfaction with work completed, (b) enjoyment of exhaustion in the knowledge that the fatigue will result in adaptation and progress, (c) an overall ongoing sense of accomplishment, and (d) a sense of being in control despite the fatigue. Maladaptive Fatigue Syndrome causes dissatisfaction, a lack of joy, a sense of dread and loss, and a feeling of being out of control in all aspects of life. Having said all this, I want to caution that if AFS is prolonged or is too frequent, the likelihood of sliding into MFS is high.

Figure 10.1 lists prevention strategies, which I discuss briefly here.

▶ **Proper training.** Prevention of MFS starts with proper physical and mental training. Every coach and athlete should be an expert in periodization training. If more effective training techniques emerge, coaches and athletes must master them. Too many athletes do not fully understand the ramifications of proper physical training, let alone the relationship between emotions and training. Improper training is a major antecedent of maladaptive fatigue.

▶ **Time-outs.** Instead of training and competing year-round, athletes at certain stressful times should cease training and attend fully to other aspects of their lives. Taking a vacation, especially, will change the emotional atmosphere. A break from normal routines and stresses is rejuvenating and healthy.

▶ **Avoiding monotony.** When the human animal receives proper stimulation, fatigue is impossible. Lack of stimulation leads to boredom and poor concentration, resulting in physical and mental fatigue. Athletes, in particular, do not respond well to continual repetitive routines. Coaches should organize practices to avoid monotony by incorporating new challenges as frequently as possible.

▶ **Positive reinforcement.** People who feel good about themselves enjoy their activities and seldom experience fatigue. It is clear enough that most athletes respond better to positive reinforcement than to negativism; why are coaches negative so much of the time? Negativity fosters feelings of anger, helplessness, and anxiety—consuming energy and contributing to fatigue.

▶ **Management of pre- and postcompetitive anxiety.** Anxiety used inappropriately (focusing on irrelevant cues, worrying about past events or future possibilities, etc.) is a waste of energy. Some degree of precontest anxiety is almost always natural, is usually harmless, and typically dissipates as competition begins. Postcompetition anxiety is far more detrimental because it lasts longer, producing fatigue. After competition, athletes manifest one of three emotions: aggression (toward oneself or others), depression, or euphoria. The coach needs to recognize these strong emotional states and deal with them. If they persist, the athlete continues to experience high levels of stress that are likely to contribute to the onset of MFS (Henschen, 1993). Negative affect is noticed immediately, whereas euphoria usually is not perceived as a source of fatigue. Excessive and unrecognized euphoria usually masks fatigue and thus could be even more dangerous. Also, some athletes are prone to do more work than necessary following successful practices and do not notice the early signals of fatigue by ignoring the need for rest.

▶ **Mental practice.** Self-regulation skills such as relaxation, concentration, imagery, self-talk, and performance routines can help lessen much of the stress that leads to MFS. Even if the body is fatigued, the mind can continue to function almost indefinitely.

▶ **Choices.** Having athletes participate in decision making alleviates fatigue and leads to higher energy. Using athletes' suggestions helps to solidify their commitment and encourages them to regard the team as a primary rather than a secondary group. Athletes with primary commitment will do almost anything to garner success. Good team environment or cohesion increases motivation for more intensive work and thus results in adaptive fatigue instead of MFS.

Reversal

The issue of curing or reversing MFS is more delicate, especially since biological parameters are not always in evidence (Fry et al., 1993). The most effective cure, to date, has been rest. Historically the prescription has been for total rest, but recently many have questioned this approach. Current thinking favors an active recovery period involving regular light exercise. Another strategy is to change the athlete's routine and incorporate intellectual challenges at appropriate intervals. To offset boredom, psychological stimulation needs to accompany physical recovery. A multidimensional conception of the fatigue syndrome—both maladaptive and adaptive—as a specific constellation of psychobiosocial components could serve as a guide for describing and preventing MFS.

SUMMARY

Researchers have studied overtraining or MFS for well over a century. Gould (1996) probably said it best when he characterized MFS as a "psychological, physical, and emotional withdrawal from a formerly enjoyable and motivating activity" (p. 276) due to excessive (and also, perhaps, insufficient) fatigue. The emotional, physical, and social symptoms of this condition are clear. Interestingly, the emotional or psychological symptoms are virtually identical to the common indicators of clinical depression. Maladaptive Fatigue

Syndrome affects extremely dedicated, high-achieving, success-driven, highly responsible, other-oriented, perfectionistic people. The sandpile paradigm depicts MFS as an accumulation of stresses that the human body must readjust to in order to accommodate additional demands. Of multiple causes of the problem, excessive physical training and boredom are the most prominent. Since MFS is a psychobiosocial phenomenon, its causes originate in all systems affecting the human animal.

Six emotions symptomatic of MFS are anger, sadness, depression, anxiety, confusion, and a lack of vigor. In AFS, in contrast, the feelings are of complacency (sense of pleasure, contentment, satisfaction) and of still being in control. Two effective methods of assessment are the POMS psychometric test and self-profiling. The most effective preventive techniques are proper physical and mental training, time-outs, avoidance of monotony, positive reinforcement, management of pre- and postcompetitive tension, self-regulation techniques, and athlete involvement in decision making. There is no cure per se, but rest with light physical activity has produced promising results.

Sometimes what looks like maladaptive fatigue may be beneficial (i.e., adaptive) with proper identification, handling, and control so that it does not reach the exhaustion level—especially in sports. This condition will continue to plague the athletic community until we understand it better from a multidisciplinary perspective.

PART IV

Additional Issues in Emotion and Sport

CHAPTER 11

The Injured Athlete

John Heil
United States

Injury is an emotionally provocative experience for the athlete. It is also, unfortunately, common, especially in the highly competitive. Approximately 17 million sport injuries occur each year among American athletes alone (Booth, 1987). The ability to remain relatively injury free and recover quickly after injury is an essential athletic skill, linked to competitive success. Managing the emotions associated with injury, and dealing successfully with stress that might otherwise contribute to injury, are equally important to successful rehabilitation and injury prevention (Andersen & Williams, 1988; Smith, Smoll, & Ptacek, 1990).

The last 25 years have seen important developments in the applied sport sciences. Sports medicine has evolved, emphasizing active goal-oriented rehabilitation and quick recovery, and has had a significant impact on mainstream approaches to rehabilitation. Sport psychology has emerged as a discipline designed to enhance performance through mental skills training. The psychology of sport injury is a natural blending of sports medicine and sport psychology—athlete centered, skill based, team oriented. Recognizing the fundamental athleticism of rehabilitation, the psychology of sport injury emphasizes the transfer of psychological skills from training and competition to rehabilitation. Athletes bring unique assets to rehabilitation, including proclivity for physical conditioning, strong goal orientation, refined mental skills, and high motivation. But for the athlete, injury potentially carries greater emotional costs than for the general population. Thus the emotional aftereffects of injury can undermine the mental skills that should be an asset for rehabilitation. Hence, management of emotions is critical in the psychology of sport injury rehabilitation.

The perspective on emotion and injury presented here is a blending of applied practice, theory, and research in sport psychology and behavioral medicine. It reflects my personal bias and that of my associates. As would be expected for any standard of practice early in its evolution, there is considerable controversy. The goal of this chapter is to facilitate consensus building through constructive dialogue.

The following sections examine theory and research on the psychological course of injury; propose an affective cycle of injury that integrates stage theory and cognitively based appraisal models; review four psychological states that drive emotional response to injury; and present a conceptual strategy to engage coaches and sports medicine providers more fully in psychological management of the injured athlete.

THEORY AND RESEARCH

Initial attempts to understand the emotional response to athletic injury drew on the work of Dr. Elizabeth Kubler-Ross (1969). Kubler-Ross suggested that patients move through stages in struggling to cope with terminal illness: denial, anger, bargaining, depression, and acceptance. Her stage theory has been applied to many conditions, including athletic injury. Its strength is that it provides an intuitively sensible approach to understanding disruptive emotions without assuming underlying pathology. It also emphasizes the "work of recovery" as an active process—marked by a willingness to work through the negative emotional states attendant upon loss and a striving to energize positive affective states. The Individual Zones of Optional Functioning (IZOF) model (Hanin, 1997a) presents this process as awareness, acceptance, and action. A later section of this chapter elaborates on the work of recovery. However, research has failed to demonstrate that either terminally ill patients or injured athletes move predictably through stages (Brewer, 1994). Initial enthusiasm for this theory probably reflects not so much its clinical utility as the need practitioners feel for a model to explain the psychological sequelae of injury.

Much debate surrounds conceptualization of the psychological course of injury. A modified stage theory has received continued support. Pedersen (1986) suggests a three-stage process including shock, preoccupation, and reorganization. McDonald and Hardy (1990) describe a simpler two-stage model of shock followed by retrenchment and acknowledgement. But a two-stage theory, however well grounded empirically, has limited value in the applied setting.

A pragmatic resolution of the stage theory question shifts the focus from the psychological to the physical process. From this medically grounded perspective, injury and recovery are seen as a series of stages. One model, firmly rooted in the physical aspects of rehabilitation but also psychologically minded, is that of Steadman (1993), an orthopedic surgeon. Each stage presents interrelated physical and psychological demands:

1. Preinjury

2. Immediate postinjury

3. Treatment decision and implementation

4. Early postoperative/rehabilitation

5. Late postoperative/rehabilitation

6. Specificity

7. Return to play

Recently proposed cognitively based appraisal models (Brewer, Linder, & Phelps, 1995; Wagman & Khelifa, 1996; Wiese-Bjornstal, Smith, & LaMott, 1995; Udry, 1997) rest on the underlying assumption that athletes' emotional response to injury is influenced by their appraisal or interpretation of the injury as well as situational factors perceived to be either stressful or uplifting. Work that focuses on facilitating recovery supports this idea (Flint, 1993; Gordon, Milios, & Grove, 1991; Gould, Udry, Bridges, & Beck, 1996; Ievleva & Orlick, 1991; Wiese-Bjornstal et al., 1995).

THE AFFECTIVE CYCLE OF INJURY

The affective cycle of injury helps to assimilate the expanding injury literature into a unifying model that accounts for the disruptiveness of injury and recognizes the emotional ups and downs of rehabilitation. It reflects the assumption that the emotional reactions appear to be cyclical (rather than "stagelike") and to vary on the basis of individual differences and situational factors. The model includes three components:

▶ **Distress** reflects the effect of injury on emotional equilibrium. It includes symptoms, such as anxiety, depression, fear, anger, guilt, and bargaining, for which the athlete accepts ownership; it may also appear as more subtle, resistance-like behaviors such as redirected anger, complaining, and self-doubt. Key elements are the magnitude of distress and its appropriateness to the severity of injury.

▶ **Denial** is "unacknowledged" distress. The triggering events create a psychological tension that goes unrecognized while continuing to drive behavior. Ranging from mild to profound, denial includes avoidance, minimizing, feelings of shock and disbelief, and outright failure to accept the severity of injury (see later in this chapter).

▶ **Determined coping** involves moving beyond passive acceptance and proactively channeling knowledge, skill, and energy. It includes exploration (looking for possibilities, clarifying goals, seeking resources, exploring alternatives, learning new skills) and commitment (new focus, vision, teamwork, cooperation, balance) (Hanin, 1997a).

The affective cycle of injury assumes that emotional recovery is not linear, but cyclical: the balance between distress and coping varies over weeks, days, and even within a day (Yukelson & Heil, 1998). In the entire recovery process, or macrocycle, the athlete typically progresses from distress and denial to determined coping. In each stage of rehabilitation, or minicycle, the person must readjust to a new challenge, and the salience of distress at any stage reflects the person's sense of success in this regard. Shifts in emotional response among distress, denial, and determined coping can occur at any time, in microcycles. Even during a period dominated by determined coping, denial or distress may surface temporarily with varying degrees of impact. Simple things like a review of game films, or setbacks in treatment and pain flare-ups, are typical triggers. To the extent that these situations cause athletes to doubt their progress, they will tend to be a problem. The affective cycle facilitates awareness of and sensitivity to the challenge of rehabilitation and how the athlete is handling it day by day.

The dynamic quality of emotional response to injury unfolds as positive and negative affects seek a state of balance. Hanin (1997a) suggests that positive and negative affect are best understood not as poles of a single dimension, but as essentially independent dimensions that interrelate and co-vary. Sense of well-being (hedonic tone), in turn, reflects the relative balance of positive and negative affective states. Figure 11.1 portrays this two-dimensional model and integrates the elements of the affective cycle of injury.

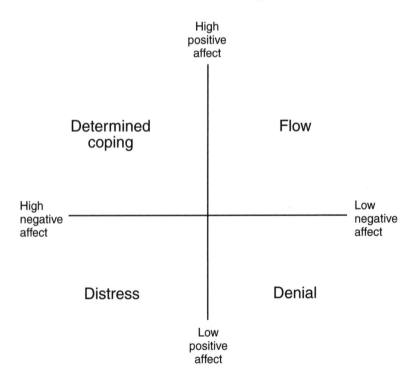

Figure 11.1   IZOF and the affective cycle.

Denial, the relative absence of both positive and negative emotions, gives way to such behaviors as minimization and numbing. Distress arises when negative affect predominates over positive affect. In determined coping, positive thoughts and feelings balance the negative aspects of injury, creating a sense of successful struggle. The fourth quadrant represents the IZOF or flow state, in which actions unfold unselfconsciously, effortlessly, and with confidence.

Athletes progress through rehabilitation with varying speed and levels of success. The differences underlying routine and problematic rehabilitation are fairly apparent; the differences between routine and remarkable recovery are much more elusive. Successful rehabilitation begins with adherence: "compliance + alliance" (Meichenbaum & Turk, 1987). Adherence encompasses positive effort and attitude, and a collective sense of ownership of the rehabilitation process (by athlete and treatment provider). A positive attitude, in turn, appears as a readiness to accept and address distress, adaptive use of denial, and commitment to determined coping. Collective ownership is built on a team approach: the athlete assumes responsibility, and the athlete and treatment provider collaborate in implementing the action tasks of successful rehabilitation—education, goal setting, social support, and mental training (Heil, 1993a).

The elements of remarkable recovery remain unclear. Steadman (1993) speculates that athletes who achieve higher levels of performance following severe injury have drawn significant knowledge from their injury experiences. Ievleva and Orlick (1991) found that an intense and resourceful psychological investment was positively linked to outcome. Consider rehabilitation as an ongoing athletic challenge, utilizing the same skills as competition (Heil, Wakefield, & Reed, 1998). Consider also Hanin's (1997a) characterization of positive and negative affect as relatively independent dimensions. By its nature, injury boosts the level of negative affect; the continuing quest for athletic excellence demands a corresponding increase in positive affect. In essence, the athlete's challenge is to raise the level of his or her game even as it shifts from competition to rehabilitation. As recovery progresses and negative affect diminishes, the athlete who has maintained elevated positive affect experiences an increasingly favorable positive-to-negative affective balance resulting in psychological momentum. This propels the athlete through return to play to a higher level of performance. What enables the athlete to first boost and then maintain a more effective zone of functioning is the critical question.

KEY ISSUES IN EMOTIONAL ADJUSTMENT TO INJURY

Injury is a broadly disruptive experience. It can take away a highly prized activity; it physically constrains an important mode of expression; raises uncertainty about return to competition; undermines the athlete's social structure; and threatens one's identity as an athlete. Thus it will give rise to a wide range of emotions. Four factors that bear heavily on emotional response to injury are denial, pain, fear, and culpability. In its multidimensionality, idiographic emphasis, and focus on performance-operational aspects of behavior, Hanin's IZOF model of emotion (1997a; chapters 3 and 7) is particularly useful for conceptualizing these key elements.

Denial

Practitioners and researchers appear divided on the utility of the concept of denial. Freud (1894) proposed that denial is an element of the foundation concept of defense mechanisms; Anna Freud and Fenichel (Seheult, 1997) in their reevaluation identified both maladaptive and adaptive applications—*in the case of the latter emphasizing the role of denial in stress tolerance.* Over time, the concept has separated from its psychodynamic roots and evolved as an eclectic mainstream concept in clinical psychology; it is often an issue in clinical case studies. Sport psychologist Linda Bunker was diagnosed with bone cancer and given one year to live. Five years later, she stated, "One of the things that happens to everyone facing this kind of illness is denial, anger, and frustration"; and, linking rehabilitation to sport, she added "like an athlete experiences if he or she loses a big match or suffers a career ending injury" (Wooten, 1997-1998, p. 16). It is not uncommon for clients in later stages of intervention to reflect on the denial of earlier stages.

Constraints on Assessment

Environmental (i.e., "the culture of sport") and methodological challenges appear to underlie the division over denial. Since the culture of sport emphasizes a positive attitude and discourages expression of vulnerability, athletes tend to underplay the severity of psychological distress. The competitive environment, where opponents may exploit vulnerability, reinforces this emphasis. Athletes often minimize psychological distress and even mask the severity of physical injury in order to remain in competition (Heil, 1993a; Gieck, 1990). This ultimately results in reporter bias, influencing the veracity of response to empirical approaches to assessment.

The manifestations of denial elude psychometric assessment. Clinical practitioners identify denial not simply on the basis of athletes' statements, but also according to how the statements diverge from what is otherwise observed or inferred about the athlete from multiple overlapping sources of information. One should judge denial on the basis of extensive personal contact with the athlete. Thus denial is particularly elusive in nomothetic research; the problem is exacerbated by the focus of some research on relatively minor injury, where denial is less prevalent. Denial is even difficult to detect in qualitative research where the interest in individual responses is balanced by a focus on trends across athletes. Consider the scenario in which an athlete, asked how his rehab is going, replies, "I let the doctor do surgery and now he has me on this ridiculous rehab schedule that is getting me nowhere. When I try to talk to him about it, all I get is a bad attitude from him. He obviously doesn't care a bit about me. It really makes me mad." What is the key theme here? Athlete distress, poor care, or denial? If the physician appears concerned about the athlete and indicates that the athlete has not been complying well, while insisting that something be done to speed the process, you might suspect that the athlete is in denial about what recovery entails.

As with most intuitively held eclectic concepts, there is considerable variability in the way people use the concept of denial. Gould, Udry, Bridges, & Beck (1996), studying severe injury in elite skiers, recast denial under the umbrella of information-processing problems. Gould, Udry, Bridges, et al. (1996) suggest that inaccurate comments or ill-advised actions result from the absence of information needed for appropriate assessment; or, if the information is present, from the athlete's failure to set realistic goals.

Clarifying the Concept

Following Gould's lead, we will consider denial a cognitive appraisal that has behavioral consequences (comments or actions) characterized by a failure to identify or accept realistic goals regardless of the evidence. Denial may be mild, moderate, or extreme, and may appear as distortion, minimization, avoidance, or blatant rejection of the obvious. Functionally, denial is often unacknowledged distress. Alternately, it is a failure to accept the severity of injury, which may be accompanied by an expressed distress attributed to causes unrelated to injury. Denial may be either functional or dysfunctional. The ability to remain positive and avoid distressing thoughts is functional when it protects the athlete from being overwhelmed by negative emotions. But denial is problematic, for example, when failure to recognize the severity of injury results in low motivation for rehabilitation or a disregard for prescribed limits.

Eddie, a cyclist racing in a world-class event, failed to negotiate a turn on a mountain course, went off the road, and crashed, fracturing his leg. A spectator captured on video the image of Eddie going down off the road and out of sight. That evening, I was with Eddie in his hospital room watching news coverage of the race when the video was shown, to his obvious surprise. I asked how he felt watching the video. His initial comment was "not too bad really." Then he explained that the poor quality of the video (he was unable to recognize his face or the colors of his uniform) helped him feel that it was not him, even though he knew, in reality, it was. He added that not actually seeing the crash landing made it easier for him to watch the video without feeling it on an emotional level. This appears to be adaptive denial, as Eddie used the visual vagueness of the image as a way of emotionally distancing himself. This enabled him to maintain a positive attitude and sustain hope as he awaited surgery the next day to repair a potentially career ending injury.

Eddie's use of denial was transparent and without defensiveness or strong affect—leaving me with the impression that Eddie was doing his best to deal with the situation, that he was emotionally resourceful, and that his prognosis was good. If his response to the video had been more emotionally charged ("I can't believe those idiots are showing that on TV"), or his demeanor more intensely defensive and his affect less appropriate to circumstances, I would have felt otherwise. In fact, Eddie returned to his preinjury status remarkably quickly.

One can argue that the difficulty in detecting denial relates to its relatively low frequency in injury rehabilitation. Though clinical frequency may (or may not) be low, denial is highly salient clinically. I base this assumption on the conventional wisdom that a problem unrecognized tends to go unsolved. Recent research supports the prevalence of denial in athlete response to injury (Shuer & Dietrich, 1997; Quinn, 1997; Newcomer, Roh, Perna, & Etzel, 1998). Shuer and Dietrich (1997) used the Impact of Events Scale (Horowitz, Wilner, & Alvarez, 1979) to assess the effect of chronic injury on 280 intercollegiate Division I athletes, 42% of whom met the self-report criteria for chronic injury. The Impact of Events Scale, sometimes used with victims of physical and emotional trauma, includes two contrasting subscales, Intrusion and Avoidance. Intrusion measures involuntary entry into awareness of thoughts and images, including dreams and intrusive daytime recollections. The Avoidance Scale (sometimes referenced as the Avoidance/Denial Scale) is limited to defensive maneuvers that the individual is aware of and includes ideational construction, diminished awareness, emotional numbing, blunted sensation, and behavioral inhibition. In total scores, the chronically injured athletes were comparable to victims of a natural disaster; on the Avoidance subscale they scored higher than the victims of a major earthquake and a large fire. Denial gradually decreased over the duration of injury.

One sees the most compelling manifestations of denial in the immediate postinjury period in response to the shock of injury, before other coping mechanisms can be activated. Denial may be directed to

- ▶ severity of injury,
- ▶ level of psychological distress,
- ▶ prognosis for recovery,
- ▶ need for surgery or complex rehabilitation, and/or
- ▶ impact on athletic career.

The Clinical Utility of Denial

Denial is clearly a social psychological phenomenon distinguished by an absence of cognitive awareness, or at least by a willing "suspension of belief." The response and its triggers are difficult to identify reliably. In general, any circumstance that calls forth the sense of loss or threat associated with injury may elicit denial; circumstances that demonstrate progress, foster hope, and instill confidence help to minimize it. Denial is challenged by situations that are performance-operational and communicative/interactive. Attempts to maintain positive hedonic tone through denial may be functional or dysfunctional depending on the context and level of intensity. For Eddie the cyclist, secure in his hospital bed, a low intensity of denial sufficed. Tim Hansel (1985), a climber who was severely injured in a fall, needed a more intense and sustained form of denial to help him maintain hope during his subsequent full-day walk out of the wilderness.

The previously described scenario of an injured athlete dissatisfied with his physician reflects a challenge to denial. It occurred as the physician mentioned the athlete's unwillingness to accept the severity of his injury and the difficulty of the rehabilitation. A performance challenge to denial occurs naturally as the athlete returns to play—as the ability to perform moves beyond speculation to the competitive test.

Pain

Pain in its many forms is ubiquitous in sport. How effectively the athlete manages pain influences not only performance, but also injury risk and rehabilitation—and ultimately athletic success. Conquering pain is a many-sided challenge to the rehabilitating athlete—one in which the coach, sports medicine specialist, and sport psychologist play important roles. According to leading pain physician and researcher, John Bonica (1991), many health providers lack an adequate understanding of pain, especially in relation to the involvement of emotion and other psychological factors. Unfortunately, many athletes, coaches, and treatment providers assume that their understanding of pain is much greater than it is. An adequate understanding of pain in sport requires knowledge of its biological and psychological substrates, the cultural context, and the pressures and expectations placed on an athlete.

The Biopsychology of Pain

The duality of pain as a biological and psychological phenomenon is reflected in the definition of the International Association for the Study of Pain (Merskey, 1986), which refers to pain as a "sensory and emotional experience." Pain begins as a stimulus that is transduced into a series of neuroelectric impulses proceeding along multiple pathways to the brain. Perception elicits further cortical activity that attempts to interpret pain in the context of everyday behavior. Action follows accordingly (figure 11.2).

The reception, transduction, and transmission of noxious pain-producing sensations are functions of the nociceptive system, a division of the nervous system. Pain stimuli are transmitted along peripheral nerves to the spinal cord. Here pain and other sensory stimuli (e.g., heat, cold, pressure) converge with information received via the spinal cord, and tracts descending from the brain, in a kind of neurosensory switching station. In 1965, Melzack and Wall proposed the Gate Control Theory of pain, which suggests that processing centers in the spinal cord may either decrease or increase the intensity of pain as a neuroelectric phenomenon, resulting in the perception of relatively lesser or greater pain. This theory has been used to explain the efficacy of various

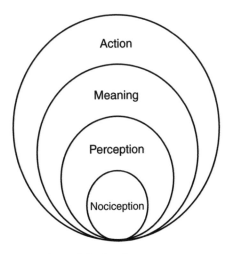

Figure 11.2   A conceptual model of pain.
Reprinted, by permission, from J. Heil, 1993, *Psychology of sport injury.* (Champaign, IL: Human Kinetics), 41.

therapeutic modalities including cryotherapy, massage, liniment, ultrasound, and acupuncture.

The perception of pain is a "whole-brain experience" derived from a summation of inputs from multiple brain centers including those that serve emotion and memory. Consequently, pain acquires some of its meaning from prior experience, present state of mind, and future expectations. Once perceived, pain sets off electrochemical impulses that move via feedback loops through the nociceptive and autonomic nervous systems. Phenomena ranging from postexercise mood enhancement to "runner's high," remarkable feats of pain tolerance, and the placebo response have been attributed to this feedback system. Why these phenomena are sometimes profound and sometimes relatively absent remains a mystery.

Clearly, naturally occurring opiate-like substances, such as endorphins, play an important role; but as the pain system is better understood, its complexity only becomes more apparent. For instance, endorphins represent only one of many types of neurotransmitters involved in pain modulation. Serotonin, also prominent in pain processing, has equally important influences on emotion and sleep. The endorphins and serotonin also influence many other brain functions.

Pain takes on meaning as a person evaluates initial perceptions in the light of physical limits, memory of other painful events, and assessment of how injury will influence activity. The single most important element of meaning is the status of pain as safe or as a sign of injury. This leads to responses ranging from relief (no problem! this is routine pain) to distress (oh no! I am really hurt!). Awareness of the meaning leads to a multilayered decision-making process. Is the pain routine and best ignored (e.g., in wrestling or cycling)?

Does it indicate a need to adjust pace (e.g., in swimming) or modify technique in order to avoid injury (e.g., in fencing)? If it does signal an impending injury, can the athlete hang on until the competition ends? What are the costs and benefits of these choices?

The Social and Cultural Context of Pain in Sport

Pain is essentially a private experience and can remain so, although it seldom does entirely. When communicated, pain takes on an added dimension. When and how pain is communicated are a function of the culture of sport. Athletes are reminded "no pain, no gain, no fame" and are trained to be mentally tough. They are implicitly encouraged to tolerate pain and to take risks. This influences not only athletes' behavior, but also the way they disclose pain. A critical aspect of the overall experience is how significant others (teammates, coaches, friends, health providers) react to the athlete's expression of pain.

Over time, pain and emotion become increasingly intertwined. Pain-related emotional responses vary, sometimes dramatically, across contexts. To those who wish to understand pain as simply biological, this variability is puzzling. However, it is well known that the nociceptive system responds to comparable pain stimuli differently over time. The truly remarkable biopsychosocial plasticity of the pain system provides the scientific context for understanding changes in pain and related behavior. Too often, coaches and care providers interpret pain-linked emotional displays as a lack of motivation, integrity, or toughness. It is more appropriate to attempt to understand displayed pain as a measure of distress that is a combination of nociceptive input and negative emotions. The athlete is communicating the need for understanding, support, and guidance in coping with pain and its emotional concomitants.

The context that gives rise to pain is important to its meaning. The cultures of various sports can create widely divergent norms for acceptable expression. For example, ice hockey, rugby, and Australian football are stoic sports that place a premium on toughness and an emphasis on minimizing public displays of pain. In contrast, the editor (Y.L. Hanin, personal communication, December 1998) has observed that displays of pain in soccer, in some countries, are acceptable as a badge of courage or as a measure of cunning (faking pain or injury to influence a referee).

An Eclectic Perspective

The conceptualization of multidimensionality of psychobiosocial states in the IZOF model is remarkably congruent with the prevailing perspective on pain as presented by Fordyce (1976, 1988). Common elements include the characterization of pain as a biopsychosocial phenomenon; an emphasis on precise measurement of pain intensity; attention to change in pain over time; and recognition of the context as a critical determinant of pain-driven behavior.

Since the IZOF model assumes that functional or dysfunctional behaviors can each be linked to either positive or negative hedonic tone, both positive and negative experiences—depending on their interpretation—can have either functionally optimal or dysfunctional consequences for performance or healing. Crossing hedonic tone with behavior yields four possibilities. *Positive* hedonic tone may lead to *functional* behavior when the athlete correctly interprets pain as a positive sign of effort (Peterson, Durtschi, & Murphy, 1990), reinforcing the athlete's behavior. *Positive* hedonic tone can be *dysfunctional* when the athlete fails to recognize pain that signals an injury in the making. Conversely, *negative* hedonic tone can be *functional* when it encourages the athlete to stop training or competing, thereby avoiding injury. *Negative* hedonic tone can be *dysfunctional* when the athlete misinterprets routine pain as reinjury (sometimes seen as a fear of reinjury). This perspective has much in common with Heil's (1993a) pain-sport attentional matrix.

Fear

Pain and fear have much in common as the body's danger warning systems. Whereas pain is often viewed as biologically driven, fear is usually characterized as psychological. But both are complex mind-body phenomena. Like pain, fear has adaptive value, but can cause problems. Fearful thoughts can intrude strongly into consciousness—but the athlete cannot and should not categorically ignore these. In high-risk activities (such as motor sports and extreme outdoor activities), fear can contribute to a respect for dangerous conditions and limit recklessness—or can undermine concentration and interfere with skill execution. For Olympic gold medal skier Kathy Kreiner-Phillips (1990), fear is an integral part of the sport that one must address routinely. In *Bone Games*, Rob Schultheis (1984) examines behavior in extreme wilderness sports and identifies a central role for fear as a doorway to self-discovery. Thus fear is a mental element of performance that one must assess, understand, and manage. As with pain, the critical task is to determine whether fear is simply a benign distraction or a harbinger of danger.

The injured athlete often has concerns about failed recovery or reinjury. Fear of reinjury can range from a routine concern to a subclinical syndrome to a diagnosable disorder. Research by Shuer and Dietrich (1997) suggests that coaches and treatment providers should pay careful attention to signs of fear and related traumatic response, even to relatively minor injury.

Effects on Rehabilitation and Sport Performance

Fear of reinjury may lead to interrelated psychological and physiological responses that can undermine rehabilitation, interfere with performance after return to play, and increase the likelihood of reinjury. Physiological factors (muscular or autonomic) may interact with psychological factors (either skill based or interpretive) and mutually reinforce one another. Resulting performance problems may exacerbate the initial physiological and psychological effects, undermining self-confidence and adding to a self-perpetuating cycle of negative effects (see figure 11.3).

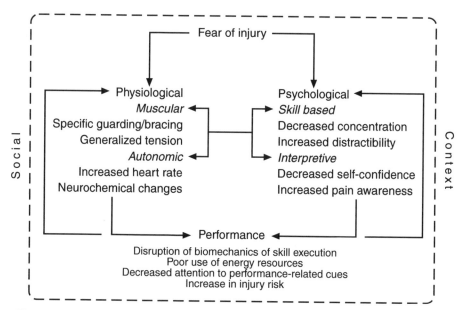

Figure 11.3 The mind-body connection: a social psychophysiological model of risk.

Adapted, by permission, from J. Heil, 1993, *Psychology of sport injury*. (Champaign, IL: Human Kinetics), 7.

For example, fear may diminish concentration and produce physiological changes, such as increased heart rate. Awareness of such autonomic changes may further undermine concentration. Simultaneously, the athlete may become preoccupied with physical sensations arising from the site of injury. Accelerated heart rate may intensify these sensations, so that the athlete misinterprets them as a sign of injury. Increased pain, perceived incorrectly as injury, may create self-doubt and further accelerate heart rate. Accelerated heart rate and diminished attention also undermine efficient use of energy and lead more quickly to fatigue.

Typically with fear comes increased muscle tension. Fundamental to successful performance is the body's ability to move freely, naturally, and efficiently. Fear undermines fluent movement by setting up a conflicting-action scenario: at one level the body intends and initiates action while at another, fear causes hesitance and inhibition of activity. As the muscles work in opposition, fluent, effective motion is lost. In summary, fear may undermine athletic performance through poor use of energy resources, decreased attention to performance-related factors, and decreased efficiency in skill execution.

In the injured athlete, pain and fear interact to elicit muscular guarding. Also called bracing or splinting, guarding is a natural protective response to injury that either isolates or decreases the mobility of the injured body part. This is usually an adaptive response during the initial phase of injury that facilitates natural healing; but it also results in increased muscle tension locally, and sometimes regionally, and tends to shift the dynamic balance of the body. Ingrained guarding can result in increased injury risk through improper body mechanics. Given its psychological roots, physical manifestations, and potential impact on performance, fear is best assessed collaboratively by the coach, sports medicine specialist, and psychologist.

Fear of injury unfolds within a social context that exerts subtle but important influences. These include sport culture-based norms and expectations about risk taking, mental toughness, and commitment; expressed and implied expectations of significant others; and the reactions of significant others to athlete behaviors that may display or deny fear.

An Eclectic Perspective

Fear is a broad-based experience spanning the seven forms proposed by the IZOF model. It is analogous to pain in its time line (typically, fear gradually decreases as the athlete succeeds in the competitive environment and gains confidence) and context (with hesitance, avoidance, or poor performance varying based on the fear the athlete attaches to the situation). When fear and its intensity are appropriate to context, fear is functional; otherwise, it is potentially dysfunctional. Fear can be motivating and mobilizing—or can be reason to rethink overly risky behaviors. While excessive fear is potentially immobilizing and dangerous in its own right, at times the absence of fear can be catastrophic.

Culpability

Often, injury just happens; athletes accept it as a part of sport and concentrate on rehabilitation. Preoccupation with culpability makes rehabilitation problems more likely. Though compelling from an applied perspective (Heil, 1993a; Ogilvie & Tutko, 1966), culpability and issues related to guilt and blame for injury appear infrequently in the behavioral medicine and sport psychology literatures. Research with general medical populations identifies culpability as a risk factor in treatment, linked to increased pain, greater emotional disturbance, and less successful outcomes (DeGood & Kiernan, 1997-1998; Williams, 1997). When injury occurs, it is reasonable to ask "why?"—but identifying the underlying cause is a thorny process. Injury risk is influenced by a multitude of factors endemic to sport. Ultimately, the responsibility for safety is shared broadly—by athletes and coaches, officials and sports governing bodies, equipment manufacturers, and even the media and fans. Preoccupation with blame can trigger emotions such as anger, guilt, mistrust, and hopelessness. It can arise as a direct consequence of injury; in conjunction with rehabilitation problems; or from underlying causes that are more diffuse and elusive or that trigger philosophic questions about sport.

Culpability as a Direct Consequence of Injury

Where culpability arises as a direct consequence of injury, it is most often directed toward another athlete or the coach—or perhaps inward. The athlete is far more likely to be disturbed when injury results from an intent to do harm, especially in conjunction with a rule violation, or from a situation seen as outside the bounds of fair play (Ford, 1983)—even more so when the behavior of the offender goes relatively unpunished.

Daniel, a minor league baseball player, sustained a career-ending injury from a blind-side blow to the head delivered by an opponent during a brawl. A video replay left it clear that the blow was intentional and without provocation. Daniel was never again able to engage comfortably in even casual recreational activities. He was traumatized not only by the injury, but also by the loss of his career and the physical limitations on starting a new one. Through a long, complicated course of rehabilitation Daniel stoically tolerated his injuries, but found it more difficult to tolerate thoughts of the circumstances and life consequences of the injury.

Coaches play an important decision-making role in athletes' lives and sometimes receive blame for injury. Coaches often work to protect athletes from their own desire to compete regardless of injury risk and are usually careful to encourage health-promoting behavior. But, both the popular press (e.g., Ryan, 1995; Fleming, 1997-1998) and the scientific literature suggest that there are exceptions. The greatest potential for problems arises if a coach returns an athlete to play too soon following injury. Coach-endorsed use of performance-enhancing drugs, and attitudes that foster disordered eating, are other examples of coaching practices that may lead to injury or more general health problems.

Ann was a track and field athlete whose versatility made her valuable to the team. In dual meets she would be placed in multiple events where she had the best chance of scoring points. Ann accepted this team role, but was disturbed when the coach made last-minute changes; she had been unsuccessful in communicating this concern to the coach. Then Ann experienced a season-ending (and potentially career-ending) injury when she fell in the hurdles after having been reassigned on such short notice that she could not warm up properly. Lying in the hospital bed after surgery, Ann was angry at her coach, feeling that it was a lack of respect that had led to her injury. Her recovery was likely to be complicated by the realization that after rehabilitation she would return to the same situation.

If injured athletes assume undue responsibility for the injury or interpret injury as a failure, they are likely to have feelings of guilt. In team sports, injured athletes may feel they have let the team down. Sometimes significant others (e.g., coaches, parents) with an investment in the athlete's competitive success inadvertently foster this response. Certain sports (e.g., tennis, gymnastics, figure skating) can require substantial financial sacrifice on the part of families; an athlete's injury is a potentially disrupting experience for them as well. When athletes turn blame against themselves, they are doubly victimized.

Culpability Secondary to Rehabilitation Problems

When rehabilitation or treatment does not proceed well, culpability may become an issue. In searching for a solution to rehabilitation problems, the provider may question the athlete's motivation and commitment. Athletes may question the adequacy of the treatment. A relationship of mutual respect and trust between athlete and physician is essential to an optimal outcome (Gieck, 1990; Petrie, 1993). Personality conflicts around responsibility for rehabilitation problems also undermine treatment. Fortunately, because sports medicine specialists and athletes share the same goal, such conflicts are more the exception than the rule. Nevertheless, the medical point of view is objective, reflecting a "normative standard" of recovery, and the athlete's perspective is subjective, perhaps influenced by the need to return to play quickly or by unresolved concerns regarding injury or pain. Such problems are far less common when the rehabilitation provider takes a psychologically minded approach to treatment. This includes identifying the provider's expectations of the athlete (e.g., compliance, procedures for resolving concerns) and clarifying the athlete's expectations (e.g., clear information, adequate pain control, participation in decisions).

Culpability as a Philosophic Question

Even when no one person is to blame for an injury, a sense of culpability may shape the athlete's psychological response. The question of "who?" is at fault is a compelling one. Responsibility may be diffused among many—athlete and coach, equipment manager and manufacturer, sports governing bodies. This happened with the football helmet, where litigation has dramatically influenced the helmet manufacturers. Sports governing bodies were also driven to enact and enforce rule changes, with the positive result of a reduction in the overall frequency and severity of those injuries most closely linked to use of the helmet.

Alternately, fault may be attributed to the prevailing "culture" of sport, which is in turn influenced by persons within the sport and in some cases by market forces. Culpability may be directed at the sport leadership, as in *Little Girls in Pretty Boxes*, Ryan's (1995) controversial journalistic account of female gymnasts and figure skaters.

Often with an especially severe illness or injury, the question is "why me?" The athlete who focuses on this question may experience an existential crisis. Some may question their sense of "how the world is supposed to work" or even their religious beliefs. From a psychological perspective, it would be a mistake to dismiss such ruminations. Those who share the athlete's sport experience are uniquely positioned to facilitate the person's "working through" this issue.

The question "why not me?" signals guilt on the part of a survivor, seen in sports in which safety as well as success hinges on teamwork. This is familiar as an issue among police and firefighters, and in the military. John Krakauer, a journalist and mountaineer, participated in an expedition to Mount Everest in 1996. This was a guided climb, with a group of elite mountaineers leading a group of relatively inexperienced and varyingly fit clients for a substantial fee—an approach markedly different from traditional climbing with its shared responsibility. On the day of the summit attempt, a sudden storm took the lives of eight climbers, including clients and guides. Krakauer survived. In *Into Thin Air* (1997), he harshly criticizes this style of climbing and examines the issue of culpability. He presents his writing as an act of responsibility to those who died, to future climbers, and to himself—and also as an attempt to purge himself of guilt. In an interview in *Outside* (Brewer, Linder, & Phelps, 1997, p. 61), he stated:

> I am doing better than I have right to. I mean, look at my role in the death of Andy Harris, the young New Zealand guide on our team. There is no way I should have ever headed down to camp and left him high on the mountain. I should have recognized that he was hypoxic and in trouble.

Survivor guilt can also arise in people who appear to have no shred of responsibility. Rod, a World War II paratrooper, was the sole survivor of a crash. Fifty years later, he continued to carry a gnawing sense of guilt into which he had insight, but which he was unable to resolve. He appears to have compensated as best he could by becoming a war history buff. He started treatment, ostensibly to work on this issue, but declined to continue. Perhaps denial prevailed as it had over the years, thinly veiled as an interest in war history.

Effects of Culpability

Culpability exerts a significant impact across social and psychological realms, diminishing performance. Although occasionally it may prompt constructive change, culpability is typically negative in hedonic tone and dysfunctional. It is typically triggered by the presence of culpable others. An intervention goal is to minimize intensity, often through refocusing techniques. As rehabilitation proceeds, culpability will ideally diminish via "working through" toward acceptance.

PSYCHOLOGICAL ASSESSMENT AND INTERVENTION

Management of emotions in injury demands a team-based approach to assessment and intervention. This in turn requires a structure for dialogue about the emotional impact of injury that should be meaningful to the athlete, coach, and sports medicine provider and clinically useful for the psychologist. Toward this end I propose a pragmatic model of emotion based on the assumption that much injury-associated distress can be understood as a combination of "loss" and "threat." Although user-friendly, the model has much in common (two-dimensional; depression-anxiety based) with the theoretically and empirically grounded model of Carver and Scheier (1998). *Loss*, a measure of the cost of injury to the athlete, may include physical functional limits, lost opportunities for training and competition, changes in team status, isolation from team members, and lost vitality (neurovegetative effects such as pain, sleep distur-bance, and diminished energy). *Threat* concerns uncertainty about the future—about recovery of physical ability, return to play, regaining performance skills, resumption of team role, and so forth.

Emotional response to loss and threat is on a continuum ranging from a normal reaction to a profound lifestyle disruption. When coping mechanisms balance the emotional impact of injury, the athlete will maintain psychological equilibrium and proceed on course through rehabilitation. Sometimes the intensity of emotional response will outstrip available coping mechanisms, most often when injury is severe or requires surgery or a long rehabilitation. In this case, loss and threat may emerge as depression and anxiety (respec-tively); a clinical diagnosis is warranted, and psychotherapeutic interventions should follow. Alternately, a subclinical syndrome may evolve, in which the level of distress is sufficient to impair performance and health but is not a clinical disorder as traditionally defined. An imbalance between distress and coping may cause a delay in mental readiness for return to play, ongoing psychological distress, and slow physical recovery. Those who have a subclini-cal syndrome should benefit significantly from sport psychology intervention that focuses on minimizing loss and threat by boosting the athlete's use of coping resources and transferring athletic skills to the challenge of rehabilita-tion. The subclinical syndrome thus defines a situation where intervention helps even though the need is not obvious.

The Coach's Injury Checklist (Heil, 1993a) (see figure 11.4) can guide coaches in assessing psychological adjustment to injury. (For a more detailed approach to assessment in complete injury, see "Sports Medicine Injury Checklist" [Heil, 1993a]). The "Look" section of the checklist directs the systematic assessment of situational (e.g., reinjury, mental errors) and personal (e.g., fear, withdrawal, pain) factors that signal difficulty in adaptation. The "Listen" section focuses on concerns not readily observable that may interfere with recovery (e.g., worry regarding recovery, inability to identify realistic goals).

Using the checklist as a guide to inquiry and discovery, the coach can identify problems with adjustment to injury. In general, the more risk factors, the greater the problem. Additionally, use of the checklist is an intervention that should function as an expression of concern for the athlete's well-being. Through a collaborative approach to assessment and intervention, the sport injury team (here broadly conceived) can optimize the athlete's use of coping resources and recovery.

INJURY PREVENTION

The ability to remain relatively injury free is clearly linked to athletic success. Michael Jordan's ability to avoid injury is among his least recognized skills. Factors that relate to injury include lifestyle (adequate rest, nutrition, sensible

---

Coach's Injury Checklist

<u>Look</u>

Situational:

____ Poor compliance with rehabilitation (exercise, medication, activity restrictions)

____ Rehabilitation setbacks

____ Reinjury following return to play

____ Mental errors following return to play

____ Failure to perform up to physical ability

Personal:

____ Loss (shows sadness or apathy; withdraws from team or coach; expresses guilt about letting team down)

____ Threat (often is nervous or uptight; shows outright fear at times; balks or is hesitant in key situations)

____ Overconfidence (acts unconcerned about injury; exaggerates past or future accomplishments)

____ Pain (complains or shows signs of physical discomfort)

<u>Listen</u>

____ Life problems? (sport, home, school, friends)

____ Physical problems? (headache, sleep, or stomach problems, or other worries about health)

____ Goals for performance? (unable to identify realistic goals)

____ Worry about injury? (uncertain regarding full recovery; concerned about making up for lost time; worried about teammates' or coach's reaction to injury)

Figure 11.4 Assessing adjustment to injury.
Reprinted, by permission, from J. Heil, 1993, *Psychology of Sport Injury.* (Champaign, IL: Human Kinetics), 258.

use of ergogenic aids), fitness, and conditioning; sport technical skills; pain/injury self-assessment, and risk-taking attitudes.

Research on the relationship between stress and injury is extensive. Stress is a significant risk factor, while coping skills and social support buffer its effects on sport injury (Smith, Smoll, & Ptacek, 1990; Williams & Roepke, 1992). Andersen and Williams (1988) proposed a model of stress-injury risk that has widespread appeal. However, neither this model nor current research offers clear direction about structuring or implementing psychological skills training to reduce injury risk.

An alternative model of psychological risk for injury (Heil, 1993b) (see figure 11.5), like that of Andersen and Williams (1988), maintains an emphasis on psychophysiological dynamics of the stress response and on the role of concentration/attention as the conduit by which stress influences performance. Heil's model examines more closely the relationship between cognitive appraisal and specific mechanisms of risk. It also identifies socially driven sport attitudes and behaviors that bear on injury risk (e.g., "no pain, no gain" mentality; pressures to use ergogenic drugs; pressures to achieve the ideal body for performance).

Generally, one can assume that the ideal psychological state for sport performance enables sensible risk taking and so is linked to injury prevention. Although every sport fan remembers heroic performances in which the athlete risked injury in pursuing a critical competitive goal (as did American gymnast, Kerri Strug, in the Atlanta Olympics), this is an unusual occurrence. For the vast majority of athletes, most of the time, successful performance and safety are

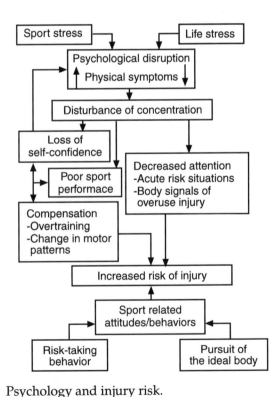

Figure 11.5 Psychology and injury risk.

Adapted, by permission, from J. Heil, 1993, "Sport injury risk: A psychological perspective," *Medical Proceedings/Lewis-Gale Clinic*, p. 8.

common goals. The IZOF (and the methods enabling the athlete to access the "zone") is akin to a universal standard of safety and performance. The sensible starting point for managing the stress-injury relationship is to provide psychological skills training, monitor athlete stresses, and offer intervention as needed.

More direct measures to train for injury prevention would target injury risk and related cognitive appraisals. This would focus on knowledge of injury risk factors in training and competition; skills in differentiating pain and injury; identification of triggers of risk-taking behaviors; and awareness of implicit and explicit decision-making strategies in the face of perceived risk. Injury risk management is a part of the fabric of sport. However, it is not typically addressed and trained for systematically as a mental skill—certainly not as a collaborative endeavor among athlete, coach, medical staff, and psychologist.

SUMMARY

Research on the psychology of sport injury, though relatively new, suggests several generalizations. Effective emotional management of injury is essential to efficient recovery. Emotional responses will cycle through distress, denial, and determined coping through the course of injury in response to the demands of rehabilitation. Pain, fear, and culpability will figure significantly in the challenges facing the injured athlete. Integration of coach, medical staff, and psychologist in a psychologically minded approach to intervention will optimize emotion management and treatment efficacy.

From an applied perspective, consensus is emerging on how to help guide the athlete through a relatively straightforward (though perhaps long and demanding) course of rehabilitation. It is less well understood why some who are successful as athletes fail at rehabilitation and others become virtual champions. This should be the focus of future qualitative study. Most desperately needed is a better understanding of the circumstances that lead to rehabilitation failure—what derails the process, and what prevents it from getting back on track. This type of study may teach providers as much about themselves and the treatment process as about the athlete. An expert-performer approach to the study of remarkable recovery can provide insight into how to supercharge the rehabilitation process, much as it already has into athletic performance. This type of research, complemented by the study of injury-resistant athletes, is needed to shed light on training athletes to avoid injury while preserving optimal performance under risky conditions. Whatever challenge rehabilitation presents, the athlete (relative to the general medical population) can be prepared to better manage. We could think of athletes as test pilots of rehabilitation, relying on the aptitude for physical training and the athlete mind-set to assess new methods or new applications of established procedures. The mark of a mature psychology of sport injury is its contribution to the field of general medical injury rehabilitation from which it has sprung.

CHAPTER 12

Exercise, Emotions, and Mental Health

Stuart Biddle
England

The case for exercise has never been stronger. Health professionals, agencies, and governments recognize that a physically active lifestyle is key to health enhancement and disease prevention.

▶ The World Health Organization (WHO) in *Targets for Health for All* aimed to "set out the fundamental requirements for people to be healthy, to define the improvements in health that can be achieved by the year 2000 for the peoples of the European Region of WHO, and to propose action to secure these improvements" (1986, p. 1). Physical activity features as part of the strategy.

▶ The *Health of the Nation* documents in Britain (Department of Health, 1991, 1992, 1993) marked a significant change in approach to health care and promotion in England, with overall aims of reducing premature mortality, improving life expectancy, and improving quality of life.

▶ The influential *Surgeon General's Report on Physical Activity and Health* (U.S. Department of Health and Human Services, 1996) recognizes the importance of physical activity for well-being as well as disease prevention.

This chapter reviews evidence for the well-recognized link between exercise and emotional well-being. I will discuss health-related quality of life and the interactions between exercise and emotion, mood, anxiety, and depression, focusing on structured, repetitive physical activity usually performed for fitness benefits. Preference has been given to papers published since 1987, particularly meta-analyses, epidemiological surveys, and controlled trials.

The research and writing on mood and affect in this chapter was supported by Somerset Health Authority.

HEALTH-RELATED QUALITY OF LIFE

Rejeski, Brawley, and Schumaker (1996) suggest that health-related quality of life (HRQL) is typically defined in terms of participants' perceptions of function. They outline six types of HRQL measures:

- ▶ **Global indexes of HRQL:** General life satisfaction or self-esteem
- ▶ **Physical function:** Perceptions of function; physical self-perceptions; health-related perceptions
- ▶ **Physical symptoms:** Fatigue; energy; sleep
- ▶ **Emotional function:** Depression; anxiety; mood; affect
- ▶ **Social function:** Social dependency; family/work roles
- ▶ **Cognitive function:** Memory; attention; problem solving

The U.S. National Institutes of Health mandates that researchers include measures of HRQL in most clinical trials (Rejeski et al., 1996). Although HRQL measures are usually viewed in terms of physical function (a narrow view), many include affect (see Bennett & Murphy, 1997). Muldoon, Barger, Flory, and Manuck (1998) suggest a simple classification for HRQL measures, into functional assessments and those addressing quality of life.

A key HRQL measure is the SF-36, a 36-item questionnaire assessing eight health dimensions covering functional status, well-being, and overall health (Dixon, Heaton, Long, & Warburton, 1994). Dixon et al. (1994) conclude that the SF-36 is not designed for specific patient groups, is not directly based on lay views, and does not reliably detect change. Indeed, health changes detected through interviews by Hill, Harries, and Popay (1996) went undetected by the SF-36 (see also Jenkinson, Layte, Coulter, & Wright, 1996). Therefore, reliance on the SF-36 in HRQL studies is not recommended. More specific measures are needed to assess mood, affect, and HRQL in physical activity interventions.

The Nottingham Health Profile (Hunt, McEwan, & McKenna, 1986) has been used since the 1970s and, along with the EuroQol (Buxton, O'Hanlon, & Rushby, 1990, 1992), assesses six dimensions of HRQL: energy, pain, physical mobility, emotional reactions, social isolation, and sleep. This needs further analysis (see Bowling, 1995, for a review of quality-of-life measures).

In a comprehensive review of HRQL and physical activity (PA), Rejeski et al. (1996) offer several conclusions:

- ▶ HRQL test batteries should include general and condition- or population-specific measures.

- ▶ The degree of change observed in HRQL through PA depends on baseline levels.

- ▶ The degree of impact of PA on HRQL depends on both the physiological stimulus and social and behavioral characteristics of the treatment or intervention.

► People vary in how highly they value certain health-related outcomes from PA; this will affect HRQL perceptions in intervention studies.

Therefore HRQL includes an affective dimension requiring further consideration.

EMOTION AND MOOD

If PA is a health behavior to be promoted, how people feel during and after activity may be critical in determining whether they continue. Hence, emotion and mood may be motivational; they are also important health outcomes in their own right. Morgan (1997c) believes that "prevention—not treatment— offers the best solution to the pandemic mental health problems that character- ize modern society . . . physical activity, a nonpharmacological strategy, can be effective in this regard" (p. xv).

Mood is the global set of affective states experienced on a day-to-day basis. Although one can conceptualize mood in terms of distinct mood states, such as vigor and depression, it differs from emotion, which normally refers to specific feeling states generated in reaction to certain events or appraisals. However, PA studies often leave the distinction unclear.

The nature of emotion is debated in psychology. Some define emotion in terms of discrete reactions such as pleasure, fear, and excitement (Clore, Ortony, & Foss, 1987; Lazarus, 1991b; Weiner, 1995), and others in terms of common properties, or dimensions, such as positive and negative affect (see chapter 2; Watson & Tellegen, 1985).

Measures of mood have typically involved the Profile of Mood States (POMS; McNair, Lorr, & Droppleman, 1971), although McDonald and Hodgdon (1991) also located exercise studies using the Multiple Affect Adjective Check List (MAACL; Zuckerman & Lubin, 1965). The MAACL, however, assesses only anxiety, depression, and hostility. The POMS comprises five negative mood scales and only one positive scale (vigor). The MAACL, therefore, does not measure psychological well-being (PWB) or mood; studies using the POMS are also limited. The POMS can be varied according to the instructions (e.g., to identify feelings "right now" or "over the past few weeks").

Abele and Brehm (1993) report studies conducted in Germany using the Befindlichkeitsskalen (BFS), which, like Russell's circumplex model (1980), places mood states along the continua of high-low activation and positive- negative mood. For example, one can contrast high-activation moods that differ in their positive or negative evaluation. A high activation-negative mood might be "anger" and a high activation-positive mood state "elation." Figure 12.1 illustrates the BFS model.

Most studies on exercise and PWB have assessed mood and affect using scales such as the POMS, MAACL, and the Positive and Negative Affect Schedule (PANAS; Watson, Clark, & Tellegen, 1988) (see table 12.1 for a summary of measures). Critics of the POMS, in particular, point to its inclusion of only one positive factor. Steptoe (1992), for example, argues that "measures

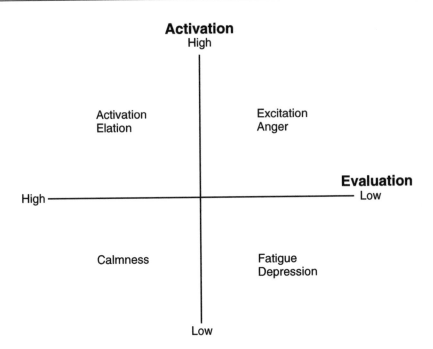

Figure 12.1   The BFS model.

like the POMS . . . fail to capture the positive feelings of well-being that are more than the mere absence of anxiety, depression or irritation" (pp. 208-209). The PANAS, although used increasingly in exercise research, is "restricted to the assessment of global affect" (Gauvin & Rejeski, 1993, p. 404).

Gauvin and Rejeski (1993) developed the Exercise-Induced Feeling Inventory (EFI) to capture four distinct feeling states in exercise: revitalization, tranquillity, positive engagement, and physical exhaustion. Psychometric support has been reported for adults (Gauvin & Rejeski, 1993) and children (Vlachopoulos, Biddle, & Fox, 1996). In adults, positive engagement, revitalization, and tranquillity scores all correlated highly with PANAS positive affect scores, thus demonstrating concurrent validity; EFI subscales were also sensitive to environmental cues (e.g., positive engagement scores were higher after exercise in a "real-world" as compared to laboratory setting; Gauvin & Rejeski, 1993).

Similarly, McAuley and Courneya (1994) developed the Subjective Exercise Experiences Scale (SEES) comprising positive well-being, psychological distress, and fatigue. Multisample analyses supported factorial invariance of the SEES with children across gender and two exercise modes, and for pre- and postexercise (Markland, Emberton, & Tallon, 1997). Both the SEES and EFI are easy to use in field assessments of exercise affect. Table 12.1 summarizes key measures (see also Gauvin & Spence, 1998).

Table 12.1 Summary of Mood and Affect Measures Commonly Used in Exercise Research

Instrument	Reference	Measures	Comments
POMS (Profile of Mood States)	McNair et al. (1971)	65-item scale assessing: tension depression anger vigor fatigue confusion	Only one positive subscale Used extensively in PA research Short and bipolar forms available Time instructions can be varied Can be a state or trait scale General scale not specific to PA
PANAS (Positive and Negative Affect Schedule)	Watson et al. (1988)	Two 10-item affect scales assessing: positive affect (e.g., excited, enthusiastic, inspired) negative affect (e.g., distressed, hostile, irritable)	Good psychometric properties Assesses only two general dimensions Time instructions can be varied Can be a state or trait scale General scale not specific to PA
BFS (Befind-lichkeitsskalen)	Abele & Brehm (1993)	40-item scale devised in German to assess two-dimensional model of mood: activation (high/low) and evaluation (positive/negative) 8 subscales: activation (high/positive) elation (high/positive) calmness (low/positive) contemplativeness (low/positive) excitation (high/negative) anger (high/negative) fatigue (low/negative) depression (low/negative)	Extensive German research supporting validity of scale in sport and exercise settings State scale

(continued)

Table 12.1 *(continued)*			
Instrument	**Reference**	**Measures**	**Comments**
MAACL (Multiple Affect Adjective Check List)	Zuckerman & Lubin (1965)	Scale comprises 132 adjectives, assesses anxiety, depression, and hostility	Time instructions can be varied Can be a state or trait scale General scale not specific to PA Some doubts expressed about psychometric properties (see McDonald & Hodgdon, 1991)
FS (Feeling Scale)	Hardy & Rejeski (1989)	Single-item scale assessing hedonic tone (pleasure-displeasure)	Developed for exercise research State scale 11-point scale ranging from –5 to +5

EFI (Exercise-Induced Feeling Inventory)	Gauvin & Rejeski (1993)	12-item adjective scale assessing four dimensions:
		    positive engagement
		    tranquillity
		    revitalization
		    physical exhaustion
			Developed for exercise research
			Sound psychometric properties
			State scale

SEES (Subjective Exercise Experiences Scale)	McAuley & Courneya (1994)	12-item adjective scale assessing three dimensions:
		    positive well-being
		    psychological distress
		    fatigue
			Developed for exercise research
			Sound psychometric properties
			State scale

EMOTION, MOOD, AND EXERCISE

Many studies address the relationship between exercise and affective states. I draw my conclusions from three types of studies (tables 12.2 and 12.3). Table 12.2 summarizes narrative and meta-analytic reviews on PA and mood/affect, excluding anxiety, depression, and self-esteem. The two published meta-analyses located (McDonald & Hodgdon, 1991; Schlicht, 1994a) were not in refereed journals. Table 12.3 summarizes large British population surveys on PA and PWB.

Narrative and Meta-Analytic Reviews

Twenty reviews (table 12.2) suggest cautious support for the association between exercise and enhanced affect and mood—cautious because of the relatively weak research designs. For example, Leith's (1994) review showed that experimental evidence is less convincing than that from pre- or quasi-experimental studies: the percentage of studies showing positive mood effects drops from pre-experimental studies (100%) to quasi-experimental (79.2%) to true experimental studies (62.5%). Similarly, Berger and colleagues (Berger & McInman, 1993; Wankel & Berger, 1990) conclude that although mood effects can be positive after exercise, causal links cannot be supported. They argue that certain conditions, such as noncompetitive aerobic exercise, might be needed to evoke such effects. Mediating variables will be discussed later in the chapter.

Nevertheless, these cautiously positive conclusions are enhanced by the diversity of the studies, which span several countries and several populations, such as persons in the workplace, women, and people with disabilities. Also, diverse methods and instruments have yielded similar findings, and almost no studies show negative mood effects.

In a meta-analysis on exercise and mood in aerobic fitness training studies only, McDonald and Hodgdon (1991) found that researchers used mainly the POMS (tension, depression, anger, fatigue, vigor, and confusion) or MAACL (anxiety, depression, and hostility). Results for mood (excluding anxiety and depression; table 12.2) suggest that exercise clearly relates to vigor and lack of negative mood; effect sizes (ESs) were small to moderate. McDonald and Hodgdon concluded that "aerobic fitness training produces some positive change in mood . . . at least on a short-term basis" (p. 98).

Interestingly, Schlicht (1994a) presented a brief meta-analytic review of 29 studies on exercise and mental health involving over 8000 participants that did not support the relationship between PA and PWB. The studies were not listed; additional information on study selection is needed before more can be concluded. Since the paper is in German, one wonders how many of the studies are in English and thus more likely to be included in the North American meta-analyses supporting a link between PA and other indexes of mental health (e.g., Petruzzello, Landers, Hatfield, Kubitz, & Salazar, 1991). Schlicht (1994a) reported an overall ES of only .15, but with a large range; the overall ES was not significantly different from zero (see table 12.2).

Population Surveys

Although population surveys often have methodological shortcomings, they usually have large samples representative of the population and thus allow good generalizability. Three such studies from Britain (table 12.3), including adolescents and adults, using clinical and nonclinical assessment tools, and covering a total sample of 15,577, show clear positive relationships between PA

Table 12.2 Summary of Findings From Meta-Analytic and Narrative Reviews Investigating the Relationship Between Physical Activity and Mood and Affect (Excluding Anxiety, Depression, and Self-Esteem)

Study	Review design and scope	Results and conclusions
Leith & Taylor (1990)	Narrative review of pre-, quasi-, and actual experimental studies of exercise and PWB, broadly defined	• Pre-experimental: 1 mood study reported. Effect of exercise was positive. • Quasi-experimental: 10 mood studies, all showing improvement with exercise; 1 affect study, no change detected. • Experimental: 4 mood studies; 1 showed positive change, 3 no change.
Wankel & Berger (1990)	Narrative review of the social psychological benefits of recreational sport; categories of benefit classified as personal enjoyment, personal growth, social harmony, and social change	• Enjoyment reported as a main reason for sport involvement; ". . . consistency of the accumulated results . . . is impressive" (p. 170). • Support for link between PA and PWB, but nature of this relationship remains unclear. • Sport has potential for developing positive values and social integration, but only if certain conditions are met.
Biddle & Mutrie (1991)	Narrative review of psychological effects of exercise in nonclinical populations	• Support for association of positive mood and exercise, but causal and and experimental links still to be established.
Jex (1991)	Narrative review of psychological benefits of exercise in work settings	• The small number of studies reported show a positive effect for exercise, but other factors accounting for this relationship cannot be ruled out.
McDonald & Hodgdon (1991)	Meta-analysis of the effects of aerobic fitness training on mood	• POMS ESs: anger ($-.182$), vigor ($.399$), fatigue ($-.271$), confusion ($-.402$).
Brown (1992)	Narrative review of the relationship between PA and PWB in elderly people	• Mood: 3 of 7 studies show positive effect. • Life satisfaction: none of 3 studies show effect.
Steptoe (1992)	Narrative review of PWB and PA	• Exercise has a positive long-term effect on mood and PWB. • This is not accounted for by selection, group socialization, expectations, or attentional factors. • Research indicates that high-intensity exercise may confer less benefit than exercise of a more moderate nature.

Study	Review design and scope	Results and conclusions
Abele & Brehm (1993)	Narrative review of psycho-logical effects of exercise and sport	• Mood effects of aerobic exercise: all 15 studies show positive effect. • Mood effects of sport competition: studies show increases in activation and excitation before a game and decreases after a game. • Evidence supports a "disequilibrium" model of sport mood (i.e., competitors compete to change their mood and seek excitement through sport) and an "equilibrium" model of exercise mood (i.e., to seek tension reduction and a "feel better" effect).
Berger & McInman (1993)	Narrative review of the assoc-iation between exercise and aspects of quality of life	• Mood: support for a relationship be-tween exercise and positive mood, but only if certain conditions are met.
Fillingim & Blumenthal (1993)	Narrative review of psycho-logical effects of exercise in elderly people	• Mood: aerobic exercise studies have yielded less consistent findings than for younger adults.
Hutzler & Bar-Eli (1993)	Narrative review of psycho-logical effects of sport for those with disabilities	• Mood: 4 of 5 studies showed similar mood profiles for athletes with disabil-ities and those without disabilities.
Tuson & Sinyor (1993)	Narrative review of the effects of acute exercise on affect/mood	• Anger: 6 of 12 studies showed im-proved scores after exercise. • Vigor: 6 of 15 showed improvement. • Fatigue: 3 of 13 showed improvement. • Confusion: 3 of 12 showed improve-ment.
Wykoff (1993)	Narrative review of the psycho-logical effects of exercise for adult women	• Nonclinical populations: support for mood-enhancing effect of exercise. • Clinical populations: no studies in-cluded mood.
Leith (1994)	Narrative review of exercise and mood	• Of 34 studies, 26 showed improve-ments in mood after exercise. • This includes 2 of 2 pre-experimental studies, 19 of 24 quasi-experimental studies, and 5 of 8 experimental studies.
Martinsen & Stephens (1994)	Narrative review of exercise and mental health in both clinical and "free-living" populations	• Good population surveys are rare. • Studies indicate mental health benefits. • Only limited support for the mental health benefits of exercise for those initially "well."

(continued)

Table 12.2	(continued)	
Study	**Review design and scope**	**Results and conclusions**
McAuley (1994)	Narrative review of PA and psychosocial outcomes	• Results of 23 published studies investigating PA and affect (excluding anxiety, depression, stress reactivity, and mood state scales primarily negative in nature) reviewed; 69% showed a positive relationship between PA and PWB.
Schlicht (1994a)	Meta-analysis of "sport" and PWB	• Overall ES (.15) was not significantly different from zero, but ranged from −.31 to .81. • Studies not listed, so quality and appropriateness of selection criteria could not be checked.
McAuley & Rudolph (1995)	Narrative review of PA and PWB in older adults	• Affect and mood: 25 studies reported; all but 2 showed positive effects. Positive mood changes generally more evident in men than women. • Life satisfaction/HRQL: limited evidence for a positive effect.
Mutrie & Biddle (1995)	Narrative review of exercise and mental health in non-clinical populations, with an emphasis on European research	• Mood: generally positive effects for exercise, but there is a limited amount of experimental research.
Berger (1996)	Narrative review of the psychological benefits of an active lifestyle	• Mood: support for a relationship between PA and positive mood, but causal links not established.

and PWB; however not all groups seemed to benefit from PA (Thirlaway & Benton, 1996). Additionally, one cannot conclude that these surveys show exercise-induced effects. Although the Allied Dunbar National Fitness Survey (ADNFS; Sports Council & Health Education Authority, 1992) demonstrates the same trend for persons in poor as well as good health, large-scale surveys offer few clues to the cause of PWB.

Nevertheless, these three studies are comparable to four North American surveys reflected in Stephens's secondary analysis (1988). Across several measures, and with over 55,000 adults, PA and PWB were clearly associated; for example, positive affect was associated with PA for both men and women in the two age groups under and over 40 years. Stephens (1988) offered this conclusion:

> The inescapable conclusion of this study is that the level of physical activity is positively associated with good mental health in the household populations of the United States and Canada, when

Table 12.3 Summary of Findings From British Population Surveys Investigating the Relationship Between Physical Activity and Psychological Well-Being

Study	Survey design and scope	Results and conclusions
Sports Council & Health Education Authority (1992)	Allied Dunbar National Fitness Survey (ADNFS) for England of 16–74-year-olds (N = 4316). One section of interview assessed perceived well-being.	• Small but consistent trend showing relationship between PA and well-being. Same trend evident for those in poorest health, reducing the chance that only those who are "well" choose to exercise. • Association between PA and well-being stronger for those 55 years and over. • Trends evident for all age groups and both sexes.
Thirlaway & Benton (1996)	National Health & Lifestyle Survey data. Representative British sample (N = 6200). Assessed on PA and General Health Questionnaire (unpublished survey data reported in book chapter).	• Higher PA associated with better mental health in women over 30 years and men over 50 years. • No relationship for those under 30 years of age.
Steptoe & Butler (1996)	Investigation of the association between emotional well-being and regular sport/vigorous PA in 16-year-olds (N = 5061). Data from 1986 follow-up to 1970 British Cohort Study.	• Greater sport/vigorous PA was positively associated with emotional well-being independent of gender or socioeconomic or health status. • Participation in nonvigorous activity was associated with high psychological and somatic symptoms on Malaise Inventory.

mental health is defined as positive mood, general well-being, and relatively infrequent symptoms of anxiety and depression. This relationship is independent of the effects of education and physical health status, and is stronger for women and those age 40 years and over than for men and those age under 40. The robustness of this conclusion derives from the varied sources of evidence: four population samples in two countries over a 10-year period, four different methods of operationalizing physical activity and six different mental health scales. (pp. 41-42)

Evidence from population surveys, therefore, supports a relationship between exercise (or at least PA) and mood and affect, but allows us to conclude only that participation in exercise, or the quantity of PA, is associated with PWB over time. Acute effects of exercise cannot be studied in this way. Similarly, experimental trials are required to show whether this relationship is causal.

Experimental Trials

There have been few controlled experimental trials investigating effects of exercise on affect and mood. Five British studies (table 12.4) show that exercise intensity is important in determining exercise effects on mood—something not suggested in other types of studies. Three studies by Steptoe and colleagues (Steptoe & Bolton, 1988; Steptoe & Cox, 1988; Moses, Steptoe, Mathews, & Edwards, 1989) show that moderate but not high-intensity exercise enhances mood. Similarly, Parfitt, Markland, and Holmes (1994) reported that feeling states in exercise are significantly worse at a higher intensity for less active individuals, and Hardy and Rejeski (1989) reported more negative moods after higher-intensity exercise than after less intensive activity. Consequently, "moderate-intensity exercise appears to have the best potential to impact on participant mood states" (Leith, 1994, p. 146).

Raglin (1997) suggests that high-intensity activity may delay rather than eliminate postexercise anxiety reductions. The increases in negative mood after high-intensity exercise reported in Steptoe's research may be due to the higher exertion, but studies have shown that positive mood is still enhanced some time later. The temporal characteristics of mood changes after different intensities of exercise require further investigation. However, even if the postexercise negative mood effect is transitory, it may be enough to affect adherence and reduce PA participation.

Boutcher, McAuley, and Courneya (1997) reported greater positive affect after aerobic treadmill exercise in trained runners as compared to matched untrained participants, suggesting that training status may account for postexercise affective responses. Since Steptoe's research involved primarily untrained participants it may not be surprising, and is consistent with the work of Boutcher et al. (1997), that exercise of only moderate intensity produces positive affective responses.

Finally, in a controlled trial of healthy American adults, participants in a six-month PA intervention showed significant improvements in body appearance satisfaction, perceived physical fitness, and satisfaction with weight in comparison to controls (King, Taylor, Haskell, & DeBusk, 1989). No differences were found for depressed mood, tension/anxiety, or confidence/well-being. These results suggest that psychological changes are more likely if closely linked to the physical changes associated with an exercise program.

Factors Moderating the Relationship Between Mood, Affect, and Exercise

Although PA seems to produce more positive affect in women and in persons over age 40, the picture is not clear for specific aspects of affect such as depression. Studies involving people of both genders and all ages have shown positive mood effects; but again, whether specific forms of exercise are more beneficial than others is unknown. As mentioned earlier, however, training status may be important (Boutcher et al., 1997).

Table 12.4 Controlled Experimental Trials From Britain Investigating Physical Activity, Exercise, and Psychological Well-Being

Study	Sample	Design and treatment	Results and conclusions
Steptoe & Cox (1988)	Female students (N = 32)	• Single-session experiment testing effects of exercise intensity and music on mood. • All participants exercised for four periods: at both low and moderate intensity with music and metronome.	• Moderate-intensity exercise produced more negative mood states (increased tension-anxiety, reduced vigor and exhilaration). • Low-intensity exercise produced favorable mood state changes. • Ratings of Perceived Exertion were slightly lower during exercise with music than with a metronome. No mood effects for music.
Steptoe & Bolton (1988)	Female students (N = 40)	• Replication and extension of Steptoe & Cox (1988). • Exercised for 15 min at either moderate or low intensity.	• Immediately after higher-intensity exercise, participants reported higher tension-anxiety and mental fatigue than those in low-intensity condition. • Both groups showed a decline in these states during the exercise recovery period.
Moses et al. (1989)	Sedentary adults (N = 109)	• An experimental study of the effects of exercise training on mental well-being. • Participants assigned to either high-intensity aerobic exercise, moderate-intensity aerobic exercise, attention-placebo, or wait list control. • 10-week training period undertaken.	• Only the moderate-intensity exercise group showed reductions on the tension-anxiety and confusion mood scales and a measure of coping deficits.
Steptoe et al. (1993)	Sedentary adults (N = 33) within borderline or "definite" range for anxiety	• Experimental study of effects of exercise on psychological stress and mood responses (only mood effects reported here). • Participants assigned to either moderate exercise or attention-placebo control conditions.	• Exercise group showed significant reduction in confusion and improvement in perceived stress coping. • These trends not shown in attention-placebo group.

(continued)

Table 12.4	(continued)		
Study	**Sample**	**Design and treatment**	**Results and conclusions**
Parfitt et al. (1994)	Students (N = 80)	• Experimental test on affective reactions to exercise as a function of exercise intensity and exercise history. • High- and low-active participants reported psychological affect in the last 30 sec and 5 min after exercising at 60% and 90% of $\dot{V}O_2$ max.	• High-active participants reported greater positive affect in the high-intensity condition than the low-active group. • No differences at the lower intensity.

One popular area of sport psychology research may shed light on contextual factors influencing exercise emotion. People's approach to some physical activities (goals) and the perceived environment (climate) may be important. We have studied two main achievement goals in PA. A task goal orientation defines success primarily in terms of self-improvement and task mastery. This correlates highly with the belief that effort will bring success. An ego goal orientation defines success in terms of winning and demonstrating superiority, and this correlates highly with the belief that ability is necessary for success (see Duda, 1993).

We conducted a meta-analysis of 36 studies, with a total of 39 independent samples (N = 7649), on the relationship between task and ego goals and positive (PA) and negative affect (NA) (Ntoumanis & Biddle, in press-a). The correlation between task orientation and positive affect was moderate to high (.55). Other correlations were generally small: task-NA = −.18; ego-PA = .09; ego-NA = .04. These results suggest that a task goal orientation for physical activity will lead to more positive affective reactions, perhaps because of greater perceptions of control and higher intrinsic motivation.

In another review, we calculated ESs for the relationship between task and ego climates in physical activity and positive and negative affect (Ntoumanis & Biddle, in press-b). Climates refer to the perception of contextual cues (e.g., in an exercise class) that may emphasize either a task or an ego climate. In the former, group members perceive greater involvement in decision making; success is defined and evaluated in terms of individual effort and improvement; and new learning strategies are encouraged. In an ego climate, interpersonal comparison is emphasized and evaluation is based on normative standards.

Calculations from 14 studies revealed that a task climate was associated quite strongly with positive affective and motivational outcomes, such as satisfaction and intrinsic motivation (ES = .71); an ego climate was associated with positive outcomes in a negative direction (ES= −.30). Negative outcomes, such as worry, were negatively associated with a task climate (ES = –.26) and positively with an ego climate (ES = .46). A task climate appears to be associated with greater positive and less negative affect.

Mood and Affect: Summary

The evidence reviewed suggests the following summary statements:

▶ Participation in PA is consistently associated with positive affect and mood.

▶ Quantified trends indicate that aerobic exercise has a small-to-moderate effect on vigor (+), fatigue (–), and confusion (–) and a small effect on anger (–).

▶ Several large population surveys, using different measures of activity and well-being, confirm the relationship between PA and PWB.

▶ Experimental trials support a positive effect for moderate-intensity exercise on PWB.

▶ The effect for high-intensity exercise on affect and mood is less clear, although it may occur after postexercise recovery.

▶ Quantified trends support an association between a task-oriented (self-referenced) goal in PA and positive affect.

▶ Quantified trends support an association between a mastery motivational climate in PA settings and positive motivational and affective reactions.

EXERCISE AND ANXIETY

The proposed anxiety-reducing effects of exercise have long interested researchers and are still much studied (Biddle, 1997). Typically, anxiety is defined in both state and trait terms, and sometimes with reference to both cognitive and somatic elements (see chapters 3, 4, and 7). Researchers have also examined the psychophysiological stress reactions of participants differing in fitness levels (see Crews & Landers, 1987, for a meta-analysis).

Given the volume of research on anxiety, I have separated anxiety from mood and affect. Although many mood and affect studies deal with tension and anxiety, separate treatment is conceptually clearer.

Since other chapters cover anxiety extensively (see chapters 3, 4, and 7), I will not dwell on the issue of measurement. I note only that most studies of exercise and anxiety have assessed state anxiety using either the state scale of the State-Trait Anxiety Inventory (STAI; Spielberger, Gorsuch, & Lushene, 1970), the POMS tension subscale (McNair et al., 1971), or the MAACL anxiety subscale (Zuckerman & Lubin, 1965). Studies assessing trait anxiety have almost exclusively used the trait scale of the STAI.

Meta-Analytic Findings

This review draws extensively on results from several meta-analyses (Long & van Stavel, 1995; McDonald & Hodgdon, 1991; Petruzzello et al., 1991; Schlicht, 1994b). Landers and Petruzzello (1994) have also reported some updating of their 1991 meta-analysis.

Schlicht (1994b) located 22 samples from between 1980 and 1990 and found a small and nonsignificant ES of –.15, concluding that exercise had little effect on anxiety. However, strongly criticizing this paper, Petruzzello (1995) pointed out that Schlicht had not located all the studies (see Schlicht, 1995, for his response). Whereas Schlicht (1994b) analyzed 22 samples from 20 studies, the meta-analysis of Petruzzello et al. (1991) covered 50 studies for Schlicht's time period, and 104 studies overall. Schlicht was unable to conduct moderator analyses, and his meta-analysis lacked statistical power (see Schlicht, 1995).

Petruzzello et al. (1991) have conducted the most comprehensive meta-analysis to date. I review their studies alongside the more focused meta-analyses of McDonald and Hodgdon (1991) and Long and van Stavel (1995). While caution is always warranted in interpreting the results of any review, I believe that appropriate use of meta-analysis will lead to greater understanding of exercise effects on anxiety (see Morgan, 1997b; Raglin, 1997).

Petruzzello et al. (1991) analyzed data in 124 studies published between 1960 and 1989, as well as in unpublished studies, investigating state anxiety, trait anxiety, and psychophysiological indicators of anxiety. Coding for methodological variables allows testing for the effect for methodological adequacy. McDonald and Hodgdon (1991) analyzed studies investigating the effects of aerobic fitness training on psychological outcomes, including anxiety. This yielded 36 ESs from 22 studies. The authors reported no date limitation but omitted unpublished studies, abstracts, and dissertations, and included only studies using standardized anxiety measures as well as fitness and pre- and posttest measures. Long and van Stavel (1995) restricted their meta-analysis to quasi-experimental or experimental training studies using standardized anxiety measures in adults. Clinical studies (psychiatric and Type A) were omitted, leaving 40 studies and 76 ESs for analysis.

The main findings from these meta-analyses (table 12.5) show that exercise has a significant small-to-moderate effect on anxiety. Petruzzello et al. (1991) found that in state anxiety studies, no-treatment control and motivational control groups both showed a significant ES, but the ES was larger for the pre-post within-subjects design. However, McDonald and Hodgdon (1991) found that survey studies produced a lower ES than experimental studies. These results suggest that a study's internal validity may not influence ES but that anxiety change can occur when motivational factors are controlled. Additionally, Petruzzello et al. found that exercise was as effective as other anxiety-reducing treatments. This last finding may be particularly important given the low cost of exercise.

Aerobic exercise showed greater effects than nonaerobic exercise, but caution is warranted concerning this result since Petruzzello et al. (1991) used

Table 12.5 Summary Results From Three Meta-Analyses on Exercise and Anxiety

Study	Outcome variables	Activity/fitness measure	N of ESs	Mean ES
McDonald & Hodgdon (1991)	State anxiety	Aerobic fitness training	13	0.28
	Trait anxiety	Aerobic fitness training	20	0.25
Petruzzello et al. (1991)	State anxiety	Exercise	207	0.24
	Trait anxiety	Exercise	62	0.34
	Psychophysiological indicators	Exercise	138	0.56
Long & van Stavel (1995)	Within-group pre-post studies	Exercise training	26	0.45
	Contrast group studies	Exercise training	50	0.36

Note: All ESs are significantly different from zero.

only 13 ESs to calculate the effects of nonaerobic exercise. They found no differences between types of aerobic exercise, in agreement with McDonald and Hodgdon (1991).

Interestingly, exercise length might be related to anxiety. Petruzzello et al. (1991) showed superior effects for exercise lasting 21-30 min in comparison to shorter sessions. However, with elimination of the ESs in the 0-20 min category calculated from comparisons with other anxiety-reducing treatments, the ES increased from .04 to .22, and was not significantly different from the .41 for the 21-30 min duration.

As noted earlier, higher-intensity exercise may not produce such positive effects as more moderate exercise. However, for state anxiety, Petruzzello et al. (1991) found that ESs for exercise intensity were homogeneous. For psychophysiological indexes of anxiety, though, the highest ES was for 40-59% of maximal heart rate or $\dot{V}O_2$max (ES = 1.06; N = 13), and this was significantly different from the 70-79% intensity effect (ES = .41; N = 24). However, all four intensity categories, including 80% and above, showed ESs significantly different from zero. The results indicate that while moderate-intensity exercise may be particularly beneficial for anxiety reduction, higher intensities can be beneficial also.

Population Surveys

The extensive secondary analysis by Stephens (1988) includes evidence on anxiety. In over 10,000 adults in Canada, more active individuals were less likely to report symptoms of anxiety. This held for men under and over age 40 and for women over age 40, but not for younger women. While Steptoe and Butler (1996) did not use anxiety-specific measures in their study of 5061 adolescents, they did report that "greater participation in vigorous sports and activities was associated with lower risk of emotional distress, independently of sex, social class, illness during the previous year, and use of hospital services" (p. 1791).

Experimental Trials

In a qualitative review, Leith (1994) identified 20 experimental studies; 14 (70%) showed reduced anxiety from exercise, and the rest no change. A series of experimental trials in the United Kingdom by Steptoe and colleagues provides a useful framework for conclusions concerning experimental work in this area (see table 12.4).

Steptoe and Cox (1988) examined psychological responses of 32 female medical students to both high (cycle ergometry exercise of 50 rpm against 2 kg/ 100 W) and low (0.5 kg/25 W) intensities. For POMS anxiety-tension subscale scores, they found a significant level × time interaction showing a significant increase in anxiety from pre- to posttest for the high-intensity condition and a nonsignificant decrease for low-intensity exercise. Steptoe and Bolton (1988) reported similar results, with anxiety increasing during high-intensity exercise and declining postexercise. Anxiety levels in the lower-intensity condition showed a clear decline from pre- to posttest, including anxiety reported during the activity.

Moses et al. (1989), testing sedentary adults across high-intensity, moderate-intensity, attention-placebo, and waiting list conditions, also observed anxiety reduction in the moderate- but not the high-intensity group. In fact, those exercising at a higher intensity reported increases in anxiety from pre- to posttest. Moderate-intensity exercise in low-active anxious adults in the study by Steptoe, Moses, Edwards, and Mathews (1993) was also associated with anxiety reduction as compared to no change in an attention-placebo condition.

This research illustrates an association between exercise and anxiety reduction under experimental conditions. However, Steptoe's data (e.g., Steptoe & Bolton, 1988) are particularly striking in suggesting that it is moderate rather high-intensity exercise that produces anxiety reduction, although anxiety also decreased postexercise as seen earlier in the wider context of mood and affect.

Factors Moderating the Relationship Between Anxiety and Exercise

Moderators of the exercise-anxiety relationship were alluded to earlier. In summary, exercise-induced anxiety reduction is evident across all ages and both genders; any differences identified have not been consistently observed across studies. Data are lacking on differences between groups varying by ethnicity and education.

Anxiety: Summary

The preceding evidence suggests several summary statements concerning exercise and anxiety:

► Meta-analytic findings indicate that exercise is associated with a significant small-to-moderate reduction in anxiety.

► This holds for acute and chronic exercise, state and trait anxiety, psychophysiological indexes of anxiety, and groups differing by gender and age.

► Evidence concerning different effects for aerobic and nonaerobic exercise is unclear.

► Experimental studies support an anxiety-reducing effect for exercise—mainly for moderate exercise during activity, but also for both moderate and high-intensity exercise postactivity.

► Large-scale epidemiological surveys support an anxiety-reducing effect for exercise.

EXERCISE AND DEPRESSION

According to Paykel and Priest (1992), 20% of those seeking consultation in primary health care settings in the United Kingdom have some degree of depressive symptomology. Another estimate is that 5-10% of the population of developed countries are affected by clinical depression at some time (Weismann & Klerman, 1992). Dunn and Dishman (1991) provide additional epidemiological data on depression. In short, if exercise can reduce depression it will constitute an important area of mental health. Consequently, much research exists in this area, although many studies are cross-sectional and have poor internal validity or other methodological problems.

Measuring Depression in Exercise Research

Defining depression has been notoriously difficult, and some fail to agree on diagnosis, classification, and measurement (North, McCullagh, & Tran, 1990). Typically, depression is defined in terms of bipolar and depressive disorders. According to Dunn and Dishman (1991), bipolar disorders require "the presence of one or more manic or hypomanic episodes intermixed or alternating with at least one full day of major depression" (p. 45). Depressive disorders include "major depression," defined as "a change of mood that has been present at least two weeks and is marked by symptoms of depressed mood or a loss of pleasure or interest" (p. 45).

Many studies on exercise and depression fail to define depression clearly, use inappropriate measures, or involve participants who have not reached clinically defined levels of depression. For example, many studies report "depression" scores from the POMS rather than from clinical assessment tools such as the Beck Depression Inventory (BDI; Beck, 1967).

Meta-analyzing aerobic training studies, McDonald and Hodgdon (1991) identified five measures of depression: the BDI, the Centre for Epidemiological Studies Depression Scale (CES-D; Radloff, 1977), Lubin's (1965) Depression Adjective Check List (DACL), the Symptom Check List 90 (SCL-90; Derogatis, Lipman, & Covi, 1973), and Zung's (1965) Self-Rating Depression Scale. The POMS depression subscale has been used (see Leith, 1994), although McDonald and Hodgdon classified this under mood rather than depression per se.

Meta-Analytic Findings

Two meta-analyses deal with exercise and depression (table 12.6). McDonald and Hodgdon (1991), referred to in the sections on mood and anxiety, also meta-analyzed depression as an outcome variable for their study of aerobic fitness training. Additionally, North et al. (1990) reported a meta-analysis of 80 studies yielding 290 ESs on exercise and depression.

The conclusions from these meta-analyses are optimistic, although the optimism is not universal (e.g., see Dishman, 1994, 1995; Dunn & Dishman, 1991). North et al. (1990), for example, conclude that both acute and chronic exercise are associated with depression reduction; that this is also the case in follow-up; and that the ESs are mainly moderate in strength. Similarly, the aerobic fitness training studies in McDonald and Hodgdon's (1991) review provided evidence for a moderate effect of exercise on depression. Additionally, when logical clusters of ESs were calculated, the depression cluster was higher than those for anxiety, self-esteem, and "adjustment" (McDonald & Hodgdon, 1991).

Although these meta-analyses probably constitute the best evidence to date, a number of issues—many argued well by Dunn and Dishman (1991) and Dishman (1995)—caution against overconfidence. For example, some studies may have included individuals experiencing depression with a primary anxiety component. To argue this, Dunn and Dishman point to evidence that many people who meet DSM-II-R criteria for agoraphobia and panic attacks also have depression or a history of depression; hence exercise may reduce state anxiety and elevate mood, which could then produce changes in depression. The meta-analysis of North et al. (1990) also raises questions in that depression is not uniformly defined and the meta-analytic results differ from those of other studies. According to Dunn and Dishman (1991), the meta-analytic finding of an association between acute bouts of exercise and depression reduction is not consistent with effects observed for tricyclic antidepressant drugs: the authors comment that "it is difficult to explain this discrepancy in terms of pharmacological and neurobiological pathways" (p. 49). Similarly, Dishman (1994) argues that study of exercise and mental health must involve greater integration of biological and behavioral methods.

Table 12.6 Summary Results From Two Meta-Analyses on Exercise and Depression

Study	Outcome variables	Activity/fitness measure	N of ESs	Mean ES[1]
North et al. (1990)	Depression	Exercise	290	0.53
	Depression	Exercise programs	226	0.59
	Depression	Follow-up	38	0.50
	Depression	Single exercise sessions	26	0.31
	Depression	Exercise for initially non-depressed	143	0.59
	Depression	Exercise for initially depressed	120	0.53
	Depression	Weight training	7	1.78
	Depression	Various aerobic	54	0.67
	Depression	Walk and/or jog	89	0.55
	Depression	Aerobic class	13	0.56
	Depression	Jogging	66	0.48
McDonald & Hodgdon (1991)	Depression	Aerobic fitness training	17	0.97
	Depression "cluster"[2]	Aerobic fitness training	Mean of 7 combined ES	0.55
	SDS	Aerobic fitness training	7	0.66[3]
	BDI[4]	Aerobic fitness training	5	1.22[3]
	DACL[4]	Aerobic fitness training	3	1.54[3]
	CES-D	Aerobic fitness training	2	0.73[3]
	SCL-90	Aerobic fitness training	1	1.02

[1]All ESs are significantly different from zero unless stated (or with ES N = 1); signs disregarded (all ES scores reflect a decrease in depression with exercise).

[2]Cluster comprised depression scores from the MAACL, POMS, MMPI, and other "mixed tests"; POMS confusion scale; POMS vigor scale (reversed); POMS fatigue scale.

[3]No significance levels reported.

[4]BDI and DACL were used together in one study.

Population Surveys

The large-scale survey analysis by Stephens (1988) again provides epidemiological evidence. Specifically concerning depression assessed with the CES-D, results for over 3000 North American adults from the first National Health and Nutrition Examination Survey (NHANES-I) showed that depression was highest for those in the "little/no exercise" categories compared to the "moderate" and "much" categories. Interestingly, this suggests that moderate exercise may be sufficient for antidepressant effects, with additional activity yielding no additional benefit. Follow-up data in NHANES-II provided further support (Farmer et al., 1988).

These data can be persuasive for reasons of generalizability and large sample sizes. However, many individuals in these surveys are not depressed in the first place, so measurement may be capturing simply transient mood or general well-being. Also, measures of PA are weak, often using single-item self-report measures in a cross-sectional rather than prospective design.

Experimental Trials

Leith (1994) reported 42 studies investigating exercise and depression, 81% showing antidepressant effects. Of the 13 Leith classified as experimental, 9 (69%) showed changes in depression, although not all involved clinically depressed individuals. More recently, Mutrie (in press) reported 10 randomized controlled trials on exercise and depression involving people at clinical levels of depression. She concludes that exercise, aerobic as well as anaerobic, does decrease depression in a manner similar to that with other treatments. Evidence also suggests that exercise can produce long-term effects, at least up to one year. These trials all lasted between 8 and 12 weeks but included only adults; more work is required with young people.

The work of Martinsen and colleagues in Norway has been particularly influential in demonstrating antidepressant effects of exercise. For example, Martinsen, Medhus, and Sandvik (1985) randomly allocated psychiatric hospital patients to an aerobic exercise group, who underwent three 1-hr aerobic training sessions at 50-70% of aerobic capacity for nine weeks, and a control group, who underwent occupational therapy. Increases in aerobic fitness and decreases in depression were greater in the exercise group; changes in depression, however, did not relate to fitness changes. While recognizing the difficulties of experimentation in hospital settings, Martinsen et al. concluded that "a training programme had a substantial antidepressant effect in psychiatric patients up to 60 years old in hospital" (p. 109).

Factors Moderating the Relationship Between Depression and Exercise

The results from all the types of studies reviewed suggest that exercise is associated with reduced depression. However, the evidence does not strongly indicate clear differences between groups (e.g., men and women) or across ages. Evidence could not be located in groups differing by socioeconomic status or ethnicity, although some researchers have controlled for these factors and still found antidepressant effects for exercise (e.g., Farmer et al., 1988, for socioeconomic status). Common sense dictates, however, that the greatest effects are likely for those with higher initial levels of depression. Nondepressed individuals cannot become "more nondepressed" in any meaningful way as a result of exercise!

In searching for moderators for exercise and depression, it is important to recognize factors identified by O'Connor, Aenchbacher, and Dishman (1993) in their review of exercise and depression in elderly persons. For example, age is confounded by health status such that factors likely to lead to depression (e.g., poor health status) will be disproportionately represented in elderly groups. Thus any correlations between PA and depression in elderly people could be explained by many factors often uncontrolled for.

O'Connor et al. (1993) suggest that assessing depression is more difficult in elderly people and that age may be confounded by inactivity. The latter point concerns cohort effects for activity; evidence shows, for example, that exercise is less acceptable in older than in younger adults. Therefore, age per se may not be the factor accounting for age differences in PA in elderly people. Finally, assessing PA is particularly problematic in elderly persons. The four issues identified by O'Connor et al. (1993) highlight the potential problems in locating moderators of the exercise-depression relationship, at least in this group.

In looking for moderators, we are attempting to identify our level of confidence in concluding that exercise or PA *causes* a reduction in depression. Some have suggested adoption of criteria used in epidemiological research for this purpose (see Dishman, 1995; Mutrie, in press). Although the exact criteria differ slightly (e.g., Hill, 1965; Mausner & Kramer, 1985), there is considerable overlap. The main criteria entail demonstrating the following:

▶ **Consistency.** The exercise-depression association has been demonstrated over several decades and countries, in different populations (e.g., psychiatric inpatients, mildly depressed people) and ages, in both genders, and through different designs. For these reasons, Mutrie (in press) is satisfied that the literature meets the criterion of consistency. Dishman (1995), less convinced, highlights some inconsistent findings for age and gender. Overall, however, the evidence seems to support a consistent relationship.

▶ **Strength.** Undisputed evidence, obtained in many studies including meta-analysis, shows a moderate relationship between exercise and depression. The strength is shown by an ES of approximately 0.5, or higher for those with clinical depression (Craft & Landers, 1998).

▶ **Temporal sequence.** To strengthen the case that exercise reduces depression, one must show that exercise precedes depression change; cross-sectional studies cannot do this. However, Mutrie (in press) suggests that prospective population studies strengthen our confidence in the temporal sequence. Additionally, the ADNFS (Sports Council & Health Education Authority, 1992) showed the same relationships between PA and well-being (not just depression) for people in poor health and those in better health. In short, although some evidence for this temporal sequence exists, this area needs additional work.

▶ **Dose response.** Evidence for amounts of exercise and depression is mixed. Data from the meta-analysis of North et al. (1990) suggest a dose-response curve. Less than 16 weeks of exercise training (ES = 0.30) had less effect than 17-20 weeks (ES = 0.97), which in turn had less effect than 21 weeks or more (ES = 2.25). However, experimental evidence is weak because few studies have directly tested the issue. Also, the large-scale population data reported by Stephens (1988) shows a "threshold" effect (active or inactive) rather than a dose-response relationship.

▶ **Biological plausibility.** Identifying *why* exercise reduces depression is an important step in demonstrating cause and effect. There are many "plausible" mechanisms, both biological (see Dishman, 1994, 1995; Dunn & Dishman, 1991) and nonbiological (see Biddle & Mutrie, 1991; Morgan, 1997a). However, as we are not at the stage of identifying these mechanisms (see later section), getting there is a major research priority.

▶ **Specificity.** Depression is affected not only by exercise; therefore the specificity condition cannot be supported. However, this does not preclude a real effect.

▶ **Experimental support.** Experimental evidence supports the depression-reducing effect of exercise. This conclusion is also supported by Mutrie (in press) and Dishman (1995) and adds to the claim of a causal link.

In summary, according to criteria used to test cause and effect in epidemiological research, evidence points in the direction of exercise causing depression change. However, the criteria are not supported unequivocally, and further refinement is required.

Depression: Summary

The following summary statements can be made concerning exercise and depression:

▶ Meta-analytic findings suggest that exercise is associated with a significant moderate reduction in depression.

▶ This holds for acute and chronic exercise, different exercise modalities, and groups differing by gender and age.

▶ Experimental studies support an antidepressant effect for exercise.

▶ Large-scale epidemiological surveys indicate that a physically active lifestyle is associated with lower depression.

▶ With use of epidemiological research criteria for establishing cause and effect, evidence supports a relationship between exercise and depression with respect to consistency, strength of association, and experimental support.

▶ Although some evidence exists, it is more difficult to substantiate an appropriate temporal sequence, a dose-response effect, or biological plausibility.

▶ On balance, some support exists for a causal relationship between exercise and depression.

EXERCISE-INDUCED EMOTION: MECHANISMS

The review has suggested that PA is associated with mood/affect, anxiety, and depression. However, this is not enough. We need to know more about *why* and *how* such effects occur.

Mechanisms for exercise effects on emotion have not been clearly identified. Several are plausible, including biochemical, physiological, and psychological mechanisms (see Biddle & Mutrie, 1991; Boutcher, 1993; Morgan, 1997a). Possible biochemical and physiological mechanisms include changes associated with increased core body temperature during exercise (thermogenic hypothesis; see Koltyn, 1997), increased endorphin production following exercise (endorphin hypothesis; see Hoffmann, 1997), changes in central serotonergic systems from exercise (serotonin hypothesis; see Chaouloff, 1997), and exercise effects on neurotransmitters (e.g., norepinephrine hypothesis; see Dishman, 1997). Additionally, the "feel better" effect may result from changes in self-esteem due to mastering new tasks, from an increased sense of personal control, or from time away from negative aspects of our lives.

In an elegant analysis of possible mechanisms and their interaction with exercise experience, Boutcher (1993) proposes that for people just starting exercise (i.e., in the "adoption phase"), emphasis on psychological mechanisms should be greater since physiological adaptation has not begun. In the maintenance phase, both psychological and physiological mechanisms are likely to be important; and in the final habituation phase, emphasis should be on physiological mechanisms and the influence of behavioral conditioning. These ideas are appealing because they integrate the context and experience of exercise with likely underpinning mechanisms. However, they require further testing.

SUMMARY

This chapter has reviewed the emotional correlates of involvement in exercise. While many exercisers testify to the emotional "uplift" of involvement in PA, researchers have struggled with methodological and conceptual issues. Nevertheless, the evidence clearly favors a relationship between exercise involvement and several aspects of emotion. Specifically, one can conclude that

▶ participation in exercise and PA is associated with positive affect and mood;

▶ exercise has small-to-moderate anxiety-reduction effects; and

▶ exercise has a moderate effect on depression, and evidence points to the link as causal.

Concluding Remarks

Where to From Here?

Yuri L. Hanin
Finland

Since most previous writing on emotions and sport has focused on stress and anxiety (Apitzsch, 1983; Hanin, 1983a, 1983b; Jones & Hardy, 1990; Kerr, 1997), it may be premature to predict the future of work in the area. However, the preceding chapters suggest some answers to at least three questions regarding conceptual, methodological, and application aspects of emotion-performance relationships:

1. What do we know about emotion-performance relationships?
2. What are the promising research directions?
3. How can we go about this work?

The effort in this book was not to summarize the entire field. Rather, emphasis was on the individualized approach to studying the role of subjective emotional experiences in the field setting of high-achievement sport.

Progress has been significant mainly in the study of single, basic emotion clusters such as precompetition anxiety. Research on anxiety and athletic performance, closely related to developments in mainstream psychology, is perhaps the strongest area in sport and exercise psychology. However, whether much has been added to knowledge derived from educational and clinical settings, for instance, is not clear, primarily because the methods and models applied to sport have come mainly from non-sport settings. It is fine to borrow from other settings as long as this limitation is clearly acknowledged. In fact, testing borrowed models can be beneficial if we recognize the need to develop sport-specific approaches.

CONCEPTUAL ISSUES

Important conceptual aspects concern terminology, issues of multidimensionality, a shift from anxiety to emotions and further to performance-related states, and models and tentative explanations of emotion-performance relationships.

Terminology

Terminology and concepts describing emotions remain a serious problem. There is still confusion regarding the terms emotions, feelings, affect, affective states, emotional states, emotional response, emotional reactions, emotional behavior, emotional (affective) experiences, and so on. These terms are often used interchangeably, and we need to define them more precisely for use in applied research. *Subjective emotional experiences* seems to be a general term referring to the phenomenology of emotions. Another problem is that when such terms as emotional response, emotional state, mood, and affect are used, differences in temporal patterns are implied but usually disregarded.

Achieving consensus about these differences and subtleties appears to be an important task. One may expect more efforts to integrate concepts as the emotion database increases. However, recently formulated conceptual frameworks to integrate the current terminology in anxiety and arousal research (e.g. Gould & Krane, 1992), for example, indicate that the task remains a challenge. The term *state*, or condition (affective, emotional, feeling, performance and exercise related, pre-performance, post-performance, in- or mid-task, as well as experienced, perceived, and reported), may be another useful generic term that will allow conceptualization of emotional experience as a component of performance-related states.

The Multidimensionality of Emotion-Performance Relationships

Multidimensionality is a central issue in conceptualizing the basic parameters for emotion-performance relationships. As an example, an earlier debate in sport psychology emphasized the need to overcome the limitations of a unidimensional conception of anxiety or arousal. Consequently, two labels (cognitive anxiety and somatic anxiety) borrowed from test-anxiety research came into use in sport to account for the multidimensional nature of anxiety (Gould & Krane, 1992; Hardy, 1990; Martens, Vealey, & Burton, 1990). However, some have recently expressed serious doubts about the adequacy of these two dimensions (see chapters 3, 4; Gould & Tuffey, 1996), and four components of state anxiety have been proposed. Moreover, it seems strange that cognitive and somatic labels have rarely, if ever, been used to describe emotions other than anxiety, such as anger, joy, or frustration (Hanin, 1992, 1996). This calls into question the generalizability of the cognitive-somatic distinction for describing positive and negative emotions.

Two future directions appear possible. One is to search for more dimensions within a given emotion, such as test anxiety, based on factor-analytical studies (Hodapp & Benson, 1997). The other is to use a systems approach as proposed in the Individual Zones of Optimal Functioning (IZOF) model. The aim of this approach is to describe the structure, dynamics, and function of performance-related states. Therefore, different emotions are seen as components of performance-related psychobiosocial state that can be described using the same framework of basic dimensions (see chapters 4-7, 9-11).

This approach serves as an open system for conceptualizing and measuring performance-related experiences, and also makes it increasingly clear what dimensions require more research attention. For instance, among seven basic components (modalities) in the form dimension, the most studied in sport are somatic, cognitive, and negative affective. Situational motivation and motor-behavioral, performance, and communication components (chapters 3 and 5) are the least studied. Additionally, IZOF-based multidimensionality provides a framework for examining intermodal interactions (cognitive, affective, motivational, etc.) and the total joint effect of emotions on the quality of athletic performance and its outcomes.

Finally, future research in sport psychology should entail at least two important shifts: first, from stress-related emotions to a wide range of positive and negative emotions (Hanin, 1993, 1997a; Lazarus, 1993); second, from positive and negative emotions to performance-related psychobiosocial states. Remarkably, in the early 1970s, European sport psychology emphasized holistic psychological precompetition states. However, a lack of reliable self-report measures and overemphasis on the bodily-somatic component did not allow holistic examination of emotion-performance relationships.

Performance-Related Optimal Emotion Patterns

Most of the preceding chapters, on emotion clusters (chapters 4-6) as well as emotional responses (chapters 7-12), emphasized the need to identify optimal performance-related emotion patterns. It has become increasingly clear that optimal, less-than-optimal, and dysfunctional intensity is the critical factor for understanding of emotion-performance relationships (chapter 7; Morgan, 1997b). In contrast to earlier research, future work needs to address less-than-optimal zones related to typical, customary, or average performance. Moreover, these qualitatively different performance categories should be clearly distinguished at the individual level. Finally, examining the whole working range of intensity in selected emotions and in the total psychobiosocial state would seem valuable.

New to emotion study, both conceptually and empirically, is the notion of optimal and dysfunctional emotion content. Qualitatively, performance-enhancing or -impairing emotion content is as important as emotion intensity. Athletes use idiosyncratic emotion vocabularies to describe their optimal and dysfunctional emotions; the content of these words reflects the available resources and the individual ways athletes recruit and use them. Thus, the notion of optimal content not only extends the notion of optimal intensity but also accords with earlier research describing somatic stereotypy (Lacey, 1967). The finding of no significant correlations between various physiological markers in between-subject comparisons has not been yet fully appreciated. Since people have individually sensitive markers of their physiological functioning, it is also important to identify these indicators and to develop appropriate measures. This will present great conceptual and methodological challenges.

Research using the IZOF-emotion model has identified individually relevant emotion content and compared this content with that in group-oriented scales. Individually relevant content and optimal and dysfunctional zones represent a characteristic similar to what Lacey (1967) called individual stereotypy. However, zones as well as content specificity are related to subjective emotional experiences rather than to somatic functioning. The findings on content further indicate the potential value of identifying optimal markers in dimensions other than intensity or emotion content, for instance, temporal patterns and context.

Finally, researchers thus far have examined emotion patterns primarily on the assumption that they are relatively stable. Future research should address the dynamics of these patterns to see whether and how they change over time. Another task is to clarify the accuracy of situational attributions of facilitating or debilitating effects of emotion (Jones, 1995a) in predicting individual performance.

METHODOLOGICAL ISSUES

The following sections deal with several lessons we have learned in using individualized and normative measures of emotions and performance.

Self-Report Measures of Subjective Emotional Experiences

At least three aspects of subjective emotional experiences should be considered in the measurement of performance-related emotions:

1. Actually experienced emotions
2. Subjectively perceived emotions
3. Verbally reported emotions (or performance states)

Not all actually experienced emotions are subjectively perceived, and even less of emotion content can be verbally reported. The key issue is an athlete's awareness and acceptance of performance-related subjective experiences. Large interindividual differences should exist between athletes of differing sporting experience, skill, and achievement level. Thus, the extent of overlap between experienced and perceived (awareness) and between perceived and reported (accuracy) subjective experiences can vary greatly.

Indications are that self-report measures will be used increasingly in studies of performance-related subjective experiences (Duda, 1998). This will occur as the advantages and limitations of self-reports are fully recognized. The distinction between nomothetic (group-oriented) and individualized (see chapter 7) self-report scales should be acknowledged. Nomothetic scales describe general group tendencies using a limited number of content categories, such as optimal anxiety, anger and joy, with an implied similarity of personal meaning across participants. Individualized scales focus on individual growth and change rather than on interindividual differences.

Another issue, revealed in comparative studies of emotion scales, concerns general versus sport-specific scales (chapter 7; Hanin, Jokela, & Syrjä, 1998; Syrjä & Hanin, 1997a, 1997b). The emotion content in most general scales developed in non-sport settings is only partially adequate in sport, since it does not include several functional aspects specific to sport. Developers of sport-specific measures should consider the relevancy of individual emotional content, for instance, by aggregating athlete-generated items from individualized scales across sports, tasks, and samples.

Generating Individualized Emotion Items and Metaphors

Individualized scaling of emotion content is especially well suited for skilled athletes. However, future research should seek to determine the best age at which to start emotion profiling using recall. It appears that repeated measurement enhances an athlete's awareness and accuracy in recalls and predictions (Hanin & Syrjä, 1996). Additionally, individualized emotion profiling is clearly indicated for individualized interventions and self-regulation of emotions (chapter 7).

However, generating emotion items and describing one's state in terms of individually relevant optimal and dysfunctional emotions is an analytical procedure requiring verbal skills. Therefore, a more holistic and action-oriented approach complementary to individualized emotion profiling might be warranted in future research and applications. A possible solution to this methodological challenge is metaphoric description. Studies in mainstream (Averill, 1990; McReynolds, 1990; Weiner, 1991) and sport psychology (Hanin, 1999c; Stelter, 1998) have suggested the benefits of this approach assessing performance-related states.

Metaphoric description was used to identify individualized performance states in several unpublished studies conducted in Finland (N = 18 male Olympic-level soccer players; N = 80 male young skilled ice-hockey players) and Russia (N = 20 males and 22 females in track and field and team sports) (Hanin, Heliskoski, & Syrjä, 1997; Hanin & Lukkarila, 1998; Hanin & Stambulova, 1998). After being given examples of metaphors for emotional states, athletes were asked to think about their best- and worst-ever competitions and find metaphors that would accurately describe their states before, during, and after those competitions. Preliminary results indicate the feasibility and potential of this approach for holistically describing a performance-related state. Athletes described performance states using "strong" (e.g., a growling lion, a tiger ready to jump, an eagle) and "weak" images (a fish on the shore, a reindeer, an overconfident fox, a trapped wolf, an angry cat, a piece of melting butter). Metaphors also helped trigger more precise emotion phrases or other individual markers. But perhaps most importantly, such metaphors are more action oriented than conventional descriptors. They can help athletes not only in describing states but also in evaluating their overall readiness to perform well, and can help trigger this readiness. More research is needed to determine how analytical and holistic action-oriented descriptions can be combined. Preliminary content analysis suggests that individualized metaphors can serve as indirect indicators of the functional meaning of particular states related to successful and less-than-successful performances. Future research will clarify how these metaphors compare across athletes, sporting tasks, and settings.

Performance Process and Performance Outcome Measures

Sport psychologists increasingly agree on the importance of developing both performance outcome and performance process measures (chapter 7; Gould & Krane, 1992; Gould & Tuffey, 1996; Hanin, 1993, 1995, 1996, 1997a; Butler & Hardy, 1992; Raglin, 1992). Future research should focus more on individualized performance profiling and development of specific performance indicators. As with emotion intensity and content, we need to develop ranges corresponding to typical, successful, and individually poor performance ranges under best possible, average, and worst possible conditions (Hanin, 1993, 1995). Also promising are attempts to incorporate individual strengths and limitations in performance process as individualized performance profiles (chapter 7; Hanin, 1999b). Individualized performance and performance-emotion contingencies may be another promising area.

In addition to previous attempts to identify psychomotor markers of performance process in electromyograms, as well as movement sequence patterns and quality of movement, new work suggests other promising areas. For instance, a typical study of performance-emotion relationships compares various markers of psychobiosocial state with performance outcomes. Such relationships are not clear partly because the measures of subjective emotional experiences are not individualized and partly because athletes' ratings are not accurate due to a lack of full awareness. However, so-called objective measures also provide equivocal results. For instance, Konttinen, Lyytinen, and Viitasalo (1998) recorded cardiac activity in six elite and nonelite male shooters during the 6 sec before trigger pull. The athletes' preparatory heart rate patterns were not associated with performance outcomes: that is, heart rate deceleration was not associated with task efficiency as indexed by the shooting result. This might have important implications for future research. For instance, individualized markers of some modality of the psychobiosocial state should be related to specific components (movement sequences) of performance process which is contrasted with the performance outcome. Thus, in shooting, heart rate should be compared not with final shooting scores but with the components of shooting performance that lead to particular results: specifically, heart rate patterns should be compared with the quality of balancing performance (rifle hold), aiming, and triggering. Therefore, emotion patterns can better predict the quality of performance process components, whereas the outcome score should be predicted based on these performance process components.

Owing to the complicated and probabilistic relationships between performance process and performance outcomes, not all successful performance processes lead to excellent performance outcomes, and an average performance process can sometimes produce outstanding outcomes. In other words, emotion-performance relationships can be better examined if intermediate factors (moderators) in the performance process are also considered. Whereas sport psychologists typically focus on pre-performance state measures and the total outcome, the relationships between performance process and total outcome scores should receive more emphasis.

Most sport psychology research is still unidirectional; that is, it focuses mainly on how pretask emotions impact performance. The dynamics of emotion change during performance, and more research should address the impact of intermediate performance results and performance process. This aspect of emotion-performance research will depend to a great extent on further development of recalls and performance process measures. Finally, productivity measures and performance contingencies used in organizational settings (Pritchard, 1990) could be helpful for developing individual- and team-relevant components of performance process.

FUTURE IZOF-BASED APPLICATIONS

The results described in earlier chapters suggest additional worthwhile areas for future IZOF-based research. The remaining sections present some examples.

Prediction of Burnout, Staleness, and Maladaptive Fatigue

An issue that has emerged from research on repeated physical overload (chapters 8-10) is the prediction of early markers of staleness. In all cases, emotional disturbances, usually measured on standardized scales, were among the earliest and most informative signals of staleness. This suggests that individualized emotion scaling might aid in describing both healthy and maladapted functioning. Until quite recently, individually selected emotion descriptors with individualized optimal and dysfunctional zones were used mainly to predict performance, with less emphasis on post-performance recovery from physical and psychological stresses.

Data such as those described in preceding chapters will make it possible to fill this void. For instance, individualized emotion-performance profiles could be used to indicate the effectiveness of post-performance procedures in recuperation of resources. A minimum intensity of dysfunctional emotions in this case would indicate an efficient quality of recovery. On the other hand, it would be possible to identify early signs of underrecovery (excessive intensity of negative dysfunctional emotions) or amotivation (pleasant dysfunctional emotions following big successes). Individualized emotion profiles could then be used to evaluate recovery. This is a new and promising focus in application of the in-out of the zone notion, with more emphasis on general well-being and enhancement of situational working capacity. Analogously to the approach for developing individually optimal and dysfunctional emotions, each athlete might have a specific constellation of emotions, varying in content and intensity, that could be effective or ineffective for recovery after demanding work. A challenge would be to identify these recovery zones and compare them with performance-related optimal and dysfunctional states. This kind of comparison of exercise-induced and performance-induced emotions appears worthwhile.

Emotion-Based Prediction of Injury

At present, most injury research in sport concerns the development of strategies to facilitate rehabilitation, and emotion response is considered critical (chapter 11). However, researchers pay less attention (Kreider, Fry, & O'Toole, 1998) to the role of situational factors, such as specific performance-related states, in the occurrence of injuries. Are there in fact emotions that increase the probability of—or even lead to—serious injuries? Preliminary data on optimal and dysfunctional emotions demonstrate that some emotions, such as complacency following success (feeling satisfied, content, pleasant), often result in less alertness, inefficient focus, and diminished effort due to underestimation of performance-related risks. Analysis of preinjury emotional experiences could serve to empirically test such hypotheses.

Clearly there are several interesting avenues for the study of emotion-performance relationships, especially from the individualized perspective. The approach described in this book would seem useful for examining and explaining other components of psychobiosocial state (cognitive, motivational, somatic, motor-behavioral, performance, and communicative) and their interrelationships. Furthermore, research comparing exercise-induced emotions and patterns of response in a major non-sport activity might offer useful insights into the role of optimal and dysfunctional states across settings and tasks. Finally, it would appear worthwhile to use the IZOF model as a basis for teaching self-regulation skills and introducing multimodal interventions in sport and other high-achievement settings.

APPENDIX A
Introduction to the IZOF-Based Individualized Emotion-Profiling Forms

On the following pages are forms that may be used to gather data for applying the IZOF model to individual athletes. You may copy it and use it as often as you like. The form will be most useful if copied at 130%. Use the form only after you have studied and absorbed the material in this book on how to use the IZOF model to help athletes improve their performance. Below are some important reminders about the use of the model. Do not use the forms until the content of these reminders is second nature to you.

1. It is important to emphasize at the beginning of practical work with an athlete that the IZOF-based assessment and monitoring program is a step-wise self-regulation empowering program requiring full commitment of all involved: athlete, coach, and the IZOF practitioner. Everyone should understand that the development of emotion profiles is just the first step in this combined effort.

2. The core of the IZOF model is individual strengths leading to performing up to one's potential. Thus successful performances are central to identifying both the potential and the factors that help realize it. Listing most important competitions helps one look into past performance history: Were successes recent experiences, or was there a long spell of average and less-than-successful performance? How does an athlete describe his or her performance (results)? Is it easy to identify these successful experiences?

3. Details of these competitions can be very important in future, more detailed work with the athlete. Prompt him or her to include references to environment, opponents, his or her own activity, and the like, as well as any cues to situational factors that affected performance processes or outcomes.

4. In identifying successful and poor performance it is crucial to think not only about the best and worst results in the most memorable competitions, but also about the best and worst performance processes. Thus it could be that results were average or above average, but performance quality was outstanding. The opposite might also be the case: personally best results with average performance process. Furthermore, realize that the first step in the assessment form should alert an athlete to discriminate between the quality of performance in terms of individual success and individual failure ranges. A minimum of three successful and three poor competitions, rather than unique situations, are recommended for identifying patterns. However, in the steps described later, only BEST EVER and WORST EVER competitions are used to illustrate the procedures.

5. The step-wise assessment procedure helps an athlete to (a) identify individually relevant emotion content, (b) relate these feelings to specific contexts (successful and poor competitions), (c) visualize emotional states (interaction effects), (d) validate and refine emotion profiles, and (e) extend emotion profiles to other dimensions and tasks.

6. Please note that in some cases content descriptors are not exactly emotion words. For instance, "quick," "rapid," and "fast" are related more to the motor component of emotional state than to feelings. However, since these descriptors were selected from available mood scales and are translations from those scales, they are acceptable for description of emotional states.

7. Immediate recalls after successful and poor performances can be used not only for validation and refinement of initially developed emotion profiles but also as a part of post-performance analysis aimed at enhancing an athlete's and coach's awareness of important subjective experiences. Ratings for several successful and poor competitions help to identify possible variability of emotion intensities across performance situations. Thus initial recall can be useful for identifying patterns and zones (ranges) of intensities for each individual emotion.

8. In some cases it is useful to start developing emotion profiles to enhance the quality of performance in practices, and then to develop emotion profiles in competitions. If an athlete is also sensitive to other modalities of psychobiosocial state (bodily-somatic signals, or motivational and cognitive markers), then his or her emotion profile can be extended by including these individually important descriptors.

In the following pages is an individualized assessment program to identify subjective emotional experiences helpful and harmful to one's performance. Before beginning the program, make copies of forms B.1 (p. 310), B.2 (p. 311), and B.3 (p. 312). Their use will be explained in the next section. The following are the steps in developing emotion profiles:

1. Identify individually successful and unsuccessful (poor) performance.
2. Identify positive and negative emotions that are helpful for performance.
3. Identify negative and positive emotions that are harmful for performance.
4. Establish optimal emotion intensities for each emotion related to the best ever performance.
5. Establish dysfunctional emotion intensities for each emotion related to the worst ever performance.
6. Visualize emotional states in your best ever competition.
7. Visualize emotional states in your worst ever competition.
8. Validate and refine the individualized emotion scale and emotion profile.
9. Extend emotion profiles to other dimensions and modalities.

The forms begin on the following page.

APPENDIX B
IZOF-Based Emotion-Profiling: Step-Wise Procedures and Forms

Before using these forms, please read the introduction to them on the preceding pages.

Step 1: Identify BEST EVER and WORST EVER Performances.

Concentrate on your own best ever and worst ever performances: do not compare yourself with other athletes.

Indicate the date, place, and results of your BEST EVER competition:

_____

_____

Provide any important details about this competition and your performance during it.

_____

_____

_____

_____

Indicate the date, place, and results of your WORST EVER competition:

_____

_____

Provide any important details about this competition and your performance during it.

_____

_____

_____

_____

_____

From *Emotions in Sport* by Yuri L. Hanin, 2000, Champaign, IL: Human Kinetics.

Step 2: Identify HELPFUL-Positive and HELPFUL-Negative Emotions.

Go over the list of HELPFUL-positive (pleasant) emotions below and select from the list up to five (5) words that describe the emotions you felt before your best ever competition in the past. Each line in the list consists of several synonyms; you may select only one word on the same line. Circle the words that you select. If you don't find a word describing an emotion that is important to you, you may add your own word at the end of the list.

Follow the same procedure for HELPFUL-negative (unpleasant) emotions.

HELPFUL-POSITIVE EMOTIONS (P+):

active, dynamic, energetic, vigorous

relaxed, comfortable, easy

calm, peaceful, unhurried, quiet

cheerful, merry, happy

confident, certain, sure

delighted, overjoyed, exhilarated

determined, set, settled, resolute

excited, thrilled

brave, bold, daring, dashing

glad, pleased, satisfied, contented

inspired, motivated, stimulated

lighthearted, carefree

nice, pleasant, agreeable

quick, rapid, fast, alert

Your own emotion: _____

HELPFUL-NEGATIVE EMOTIONS (N+):

afraid, fearful, scared, panicky

angry, aggressive, furious, violent

annoyed, irritated, distressed

anxious, apprehensive, worried

concerned, alarmed, disturbed, dissatisfied

discouraged, dispirited, depressed

doubtful, uncertain, indecisive, irresolute

helpless, unsafe, insecure

inactive, sluggish, lazy

intense, fierce

jittery, nervous, uneasy, restless

sorry, unhappy, regretful, sad, cheerless

tense, strained, tight, rigid

tired, weary, exhausted, worn out

Your own emotion: _____

From *Emotions in Sport* by Yuri L. Hanin, 2000, Champaign, IL: Human Kinetics.

Step 3: Identify HARMFUL-Negative and HARMFUL-Positive Emotions.

Follow the same procedure as for step 2, selecting up to five (5) words to describe the HARMFUL-negative and HARMFUL-positive emotions you felt before your WORST EVER competition. Circle the words that you selected. Again, you can add words of your own to the ends of the lists.

HARMFUL-NEGATIVE EMOTIONS (N–):

afraid, fearful, scared, panicky

angry, aggressive, furious, violent

annoyed, irritated, distressed

anxious, apprehensive, worried

concerned, alarmed, disturbed, dissatisfied

discouraged, dispirited, depressed

doubtful, uncertain, indecisive, irresolute

helpless, unsafe, insecure

inactive, sluggish, lazy

intense, fierce

jittery, nervous, uneasy, restless

sorry, unhappy, regretful, sad, cheerless

tense, strained, tight, rigid

tired, weary, exhausted, worn out

Your own emotion: _____

HARMFUL-POSITIVE EMOTIONS (P–):

active, dynamic, energetic, vigorous

relaxed, comfortable, easy

calm, peaceful, unhurried, quiet

cheerful, merry, happy

confident, certain, sure

delighted, overjoyed, exhilarated

determined, set, settled, resolute

excited, thrilled

brave, bold, daring, dashing

glad, pleased, satisfied, contented

inspired, motivated, stimulated

lighthearted, carefree

nice, pleasant, agreeable

quick, rapid, fast, alert

Your own emotion: _____

From *Emotions in Sport* by Yuri L. Hanin, 2000, Champaign, IL: Human Kinetics.

Step 4: Describe Emotion Intensity in Your BEST EVER Competition.

On form B.1, "Emotions in Your BEST EVER Competition," write the words you chose as helpful emotions for your most successful competition (P+N+) and those you chose as harmful emotions experienced in your worst ever competition (N– P–). Make sure that emotions in each category are entered correctly under the appropriate subheadings: helpful-positive (P+), helpful-negative (N+), harmful-negative (N–), and harmful-positive (P–). This is your individualized scale with the content of emotions important for your performance. The intensity of these emotions is measured by the CR-10 scale (chapter 3) ranging from 0 to 10 and • maximal possible.

Now think about *the intensity of your emotions before your most successful competition that you identified* in step 1. Circle one number (0-10) on the intensity scale in form B.1 for each emotion you wrote indicating the MAGNITUDE of the emotion you felt just before this competition. The intensity scale is defined immediately below. By connecting the circled numbers on your personal emotional scale (form B.1), you will get your emotional profile describing the content and intensity of your feelings before your best ever competition. Provided below are both the original Borg CR10 scale and our modified version (CR-10 scale). Note that the modified version is a standard format to measure emotion intensity (chapter 7, page 163). The original Borg CR10 scale to measure different perceptual continua (perceived exertion, pain, loudness, taste) is described in Borg 1998.

Borg CR10 Scale			**Modified Borg CR10 Scale (CR-10 Scale)**	
0	Nothing at all		0	Nothing at all
0.5	Extremely weak	(just noticeable)	0.5	Very, very little
1	Very weak		1	Very little
2	Weak	(light)	2	Little
3	Moderate		3	Moderate
4			4	
5	Strong	(heavy)	5	Much
6			6	
7	Very strong		7	Very much
8			8	
9			9	
10	Extremely strong	(almost max)	10	Very, very much
•	Maximal		•	Maximal possible

Borg CR10 scale
© Gunnar Borg 1981, 1982

Adapted, by permission of the publisher, from Borg, 1998, p. 41.

From *Emotions in Sport* by Yuri L. Hanin, 2000, Champaign, IL: Human Kinetics.

Step 5: Describe Emotion Intensity in Your WORST EVER Competition.

Now, rewrite the emotion descriptors from form B.1 onto form B.2, "Emotions in Your WORST EVER Competition." Rate your feelings before your worst ever competition (identified in step 1) following exactly the same procedure as you did for your best ever competition (step 4): circle one number for each emotion.

Step 6: Visualize Your Emotional States in Your BEST EVER Competition.

Feedback and functional interpretation of emotion profiles are crucial in the IZOF assessment program. Therefore, to enhance an athlete's awareness of the interaction effects of optimal and dysfunctional emotions on performance and to facilitate the interpretation of emotion scores, it is useful to visualize the self-ratings by developing IZOF profiles (chapter 3) shaped in a way that facilitates the interpretation of emotion scores.

First, select the emotion of highest intensity from the P+ category list (form B.1, step 4, "Emotions in Your BEST EVER Competition). Enter it under the 1P+ subheading, in the middle of a copy of form B.3. Plot the intensity of this emotion. Then, take the second highest intensity emotion descriptor from the same P+ category, enter it on the graph under subheading 2P+, and plot its intensity. Do the same for the other emotions in this category (3P+, 4P+, 5P+). Thus emotions in this category are ranked from the highest (1) to the lowest (5) in intensity.

Following this procedure, do the same for the emotion descriptors in other categories (N+, N–, and P–) by again ranking them (from form B.1) on the intensity from the highest (1) to the lowest (5) within each category and plotting intensity scores for the BEST EVER competition. Note that in form B.3 optimal emotion categories (N+ and P+) are located in the middle, whereas dysfunctional emotions (N– and P–) are located by the sides.

Connect the emotion intensity scores of all emotion descriptors across the four categories to derive the IZOF optimal emotion profile for your BEST EVER competition.

Note that the IZOF optimal emotion profile usually is bell-shaped and looks like an iceberg (peak, mountain). This shape reflects the optimal interaction effects: an elevated intensity in HELPFUL (P+N+) emotions (located in the middle) and a low intensity in HARMFUL (P–N–) emotions (located by the sides). (See figure C.1, p. 315.)

From *Emotions in Sport* by Yuri L. Hanin, 2000, Champaign, IL: Human Kinetics.

Step 7: Visualize Your Emotional States in Your WORST EVER Competition.

Now, contrast your optimal emotion profile for the BEST EVER competition with emotion intensities experienced in your WORST EVER competition. Plot the emotion intensities of your WORST EVER competition (form B.2) on form B.3 with emotions ranked for the BEST EVER competitions. Make sure you plot the intensities for each emotion within the P+ category (located in the middle) under appropriate headings. Do the same for emotion words within each of the other categories: N+, P–, and N– according to their location in form B.3. Again, make sure that you plot the intensities for each emotion on the graph under the appropriate subheadings. Connect the intensity scores for all emotions to derive a dysfunctional emotion profile for your WORST EVER competition.

Note that emotion profile for the WORST EVER competition is shaped differently from the optimal "iceberg" emotion profile. This shape reflects less-than-optimal interaction effects: a low intensity in HELPFUL (N+P+) emotions (located in the middle) and an elevated intensity in HARMFUL (either P– and/or N–) emotions (located by the sides). Usually there are two types of dysfunctional profiles: (a) the N– -skewed profile with an elevation in the intensity of negative dysfunctional emotions, and (b) the P– -skewed profile with an elevation in the intensity of positive dysfunctional emotions. In both cases, the intensity of optimal emotions (P+N+) is below individually optimal zones. (See figure C.2, p. 316.)

Step 8: Validate and Refine Emotion Profiles.

Recalled emotion profiles and intensity zones are based on past experiences and on awareness about these experiences, and may vary among athletes. Therefore, it is important to validate these tentative individualized scales by repeated assessments of emotional states in successful and less successful performance situations. Three to five repeated assessments are usually sufficient to show if the emotion descriptors and intensities (optimal and dysfunctional) identified by recalls are working well for you, or if you need to make revisions or refinements. You may change one to two items in each emotion category by selecting synonyms or more accurate descriptors. This indicates your increased awareness of your emotional states related to performance. With more assessments and experience, idiosyncratic emotion descriptors remain more stable.

Step 9: IZOF-Based Extended Emotion Profiling.

So far there have been two basic forms to use for individualized emotion profiling: a self-rating scale with optimal and dysfunctional emotions (forms B.1 and B.2) and the IZOF optimal and dysfunctional emotion profiles plotted on form B.3. However, for self-enhancement, consulting, and research purposes, it is possible to extend emotion profiling based on the notion of multidimensionality (chapter 3) by changing the standard instructions. Therefore, after repeated assessments as previously described, validated and refined emotion profiles—initially developed only for competitions—can be further developed, modified, and extended. Listed on the next page are other important dimensions that should guide the modification and extension of assessment procedures.

From *Emotions in Sport* by Yuri L. Hanin, 2000, Champaign, IL: Human Kinetics.

1. Emotion Intensity Dimension

   ▶ Optimal intensity levels and zones

   ▶ Dysfunctional intensity levels and zones

   ▶ Typical, customary intensity (in competitions and practices)

   ▶ Working range of intensity (min-max range)

   ▶ Emotion contingencies along the working range of intensity (chapter 7)

   ▶ Interaction between different emotion intensities

2. Emotion Content and Intensity: Setting/Context Dimension

   ▶ Emotions in different levels of competition (local, national, international; difficult-easy)

   ▶ Emotions in different practices (technical skills, high-intensity workouts, precontest)

   ▶ Emotions in different tasks (single task-multitask, well-learned tasks-new tasks)

   ▶ Emotions outside sports (in other major activities vs. leisure)

3. Emotion Content and Intensity: Time Dimension

   ▶ Current (actual—right now) emotion content and intensity

   ▶ Recalled emotion content and intensity

   ▶ Predicted (anticipated) emotion content and intensity

   ▶ Task execution-related emotion content and intensity (pre-, mid-, post-performance)

   ▶ Emotion content and intensity across one competition (tournament)

   ▶ Emotion content and intensity across one (several) season(s)

   ▶ Emotion content and intensity across a four-year Olympic cycle

   ▶ Emotion content and intensity across one's sport career

The basic (and extended) emotion profiles described above provide a useful tool for the IZOF-based assessment and monitoring of performance-related emotions in competitions (chapter 7) and in practices (chapters 8, 9, 10). They can also be useful for evaluating the effectiveness of different interventions, recovery procedures, and exercise programs (chapters 9, 11, 12). Use the self-rating forms (form B.4) and the profiles visualizing interaction effects of optimal and dysfunctional emotions (form B.3) in your standard assessments.

It is important to realize that these step-wise emotion profiling procedures are also instrumental for individualized profiling of other modalities (form dimension) of the psychobiosocial state (chapter 3): cognitive, motivational, somatic, motor-behavioral, performance process, and communicative. As of today, both self-rating forms and iceberg/precipice visualization profiles have been successfully used for individualized performance profiling (individual strengths vs. weaknesses) and motivational states (Hanin, 1999b, 1999c).

From *Emotions in Sport* by Yuri L. Hanin, 2000, Champaign, IL: Human Kinetics.

Form B.1 Emotions in Your BEST EVER Competition

Name _____ **Date** _____ **Before/During/After** _____

Circle the number from 0 to 10 to indicate the intensity of your emotions.

Intensity of emotions

(P+) _____	0	0.5	1	2	3	4	5	6	7	8	9	10	•
(P+) _____	0	0.5	1	2	3	4	5	6	7	8	9	10	•
(P+) _____	0	0.5	1	2	3	4	5	6	7	8	9	10	•
(P+) _____	0	0.5	1	2	3	4	5	6	7	8	9	10	•
(P+) _____	0	0.5	1	2	3	4	5	6	7	8	9	10	•
(N+) _____	0	0.5	1	2	3	4	5	6	7	8	9	10	•
(N+) _____	0	0.5	1	2	3	4	5	6	7	8	9	10	•
(N+) _____	0	0.5	1	2	3	4	5	6	7	8	9	10	•
(N+) _____	0	0.5	1	2	3	4	5	6	7	8	9	10	•
(N+) _____	0	0.5	1	2	3	4	5	6	7	8	9	10	•
(N–) _____	0	0.5	1	2	3	4	5	6	7	8	9	10	•
(N–) _____	0	0.5	1	2	3	4	5	6	7	8	9	10	•
(N–) _____	0	0.5	1	2	3	4	5	6	7	8	9	10	•
(N–) _____	0	0.5	1	2	3	4	5	6	7	8	9	10	•
(N–) _____	0	0.5	1	2	3	4	5	6	7	8	9	10	•
(P–) _____	0	0.5	1	2	3	4	5	6	7	8	9	10	•
(P–) _____	0	0.5	1	2	3	4	5	6	7	8	9	10	•
(P–) _____	0	0.5	1	2	3	4	5	6	7	8	9	10	•
(P–) _____	0	0.5	1	2	3	4	5	6	7	8	9	10	•
(P–) _____	0	0.5	1	2	3	4	5	6	7	8	9	10	•

From *Emotions in Sport* by Yuri L. Hanin, 2000, Champaign, IL: Human Kinetics.

Form B.2 Emotions in Your WORST EVER Competition

Name _____ **Date** _____ **Before/During/After** _____

Circle the number from 0 to 10 to indicate the intensity of your emotions.

<u>Intensity of emotions</u>

(P+) _____	0 0.5 1 2 3 4 5 6 7 8 9 10 •
(P+) _____	0 0.5 1 2 3 4 5 6 7 8 9 10 •
(P+) _____	0 0.5 1 2 3 4 5 6 7 8 9 10 •
(P+) _____	0 0.5 1 2 3 4 5 6 7 8 9 10 •
(P+) _____	0 0.5 1 2 3 4 5 6 7 8 9 10 •
(N+) _____	0 0.5 1 2 3 4 5 6 7 8 9 10 •
(N+) _____	0 0.5 1 2 3 4 5 6 7 8 9 10 •
(N+) _____	0 0.5 1 2 3 4 5 6 7 8 9 10 •
(N+) _____	0 0.5 1 2 3 4 5 6 7 8 9 10 •
(N+) _____	0 0.5 1 2 3 4 5 6 7 8 9 10 •
(N−) _____	0 0.5 1 2 3 4 5 6 7 8 9 10 •
(N−) _____	0 0.5 1 2 3 4 5 6 7 8 9 10 •
(N−) _____	0 0.5 1 2 3 4 5 6 7 8 9 10 •
(N−) _____	0 0.5 1 2 3 4 5 6 7 8 9 10 •
(N−) _____	0 0.5 1 2 3 4 5 6 7 8 9 10 •
(P−) _____	0 0.5 1 2 3 4 5 6 7 8 9 10 •
(P−) _____	0 0.5 1 2 3 4 5 6 7 8 9 10 •
(P−) _____	0 0.5 1 2 3 4 5 6 7 8 9 10 •
(P−) _____	0 0.5 1 2 3 4 5 6 7 8 9 10 •
(P−) _____	0 0.5 1 2 3 4 5 6 7 8 9 10 •

From *Emotions in Sport* by Yuri L. Hanin, 2000, Champaign, IL: Human Kinetics.

Form B.3 Profiling Performance-Related Emotions

Name _____ Date _____ Context: competition/practice/leisure _____

Time: before/during/after _____

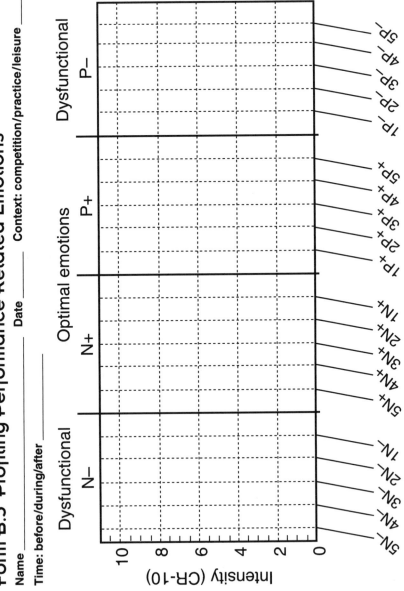

Circle (O) intensities for BEST EVER performances. Cross (X) intensities for WORST EVER performances.
From *Emotions in Sport* by Yuri L. Hanin, 2000, Champaign, IL: Human Kinetics.

Form B.4 Emotions in Competitions / Practices / Leisure

Name _____ Age _____ Date _____

Time: before/during/after _____

Intensity scale		Emotion intensity

Intensity scale	Emotion intensity
0 – nothing at all	(P+) _____ 0 0.5 1 2 3 4 5 6 7 8 9 10 •
0.5 – very, very little	(P+) _____ 0 0.5 1 2 3 4 5 6 7 8 9 10 •
1 – very little	(P+) _____ 0 0.5 1 2 3 4 5 6 7 8 9 10 •
2 – little	(P+) _____ 0 0.5 1 2 3 4 5 6 7 8 9 10 •
3 – moderate	(P+) _____ 0 0.5 1 2 3 4 5 6 7 8 9 10 •
4	(N+) _____ 0 0.5 1 2 3 4 5 6 7 8 9 10 •
5 – much	(N+) _____ 0 0.5 1 2 3 4 5 6 7 8 9 10 •
6	(N+) _____ 0 0.5 1 2 3 4 5 6 7 8 9 10 •
7 – very much	(N+) _____ 0 0.5 1 2 3 4 5 6 7 8 9 10 •
8	(N+) _____ 0 0.5 1 2 3 4 5 6 7 8 9 10 •
9	(N–) _____ 0 0.5 1 2 3 4 5 6 7 8 9 10 •
10 – very, very much	(N–) _____ 0 0.5 1 2 3 4 5 6 7 8 9 10 •
• – maximal possible	(N–) _____ 0 0.5 1 2 3 4 5 6 7 8 9 10 •
	(N–) _____ 0 0.5 1 2 3 4 5 6 7 8 9 10 •
	(N–) _____ 0 0.5 1 2 3 4 5 6 7 8 9 10 •
	(P–) _____ 0 0.5 1 2 3 4 5 6 7 8 9 10 •
	(P–) _____ 0 0.5 1 2 3 4 5 6 7 8 9 10 •
	(P–) _____ 0 0.5 1 2 3 4 5 6 7 8 9 10 •
Adapted, by permission of the publisher, from Borg, 1998, p. 41.	(P–) _____ 0 0.5 1 2 3 4 5 6 7 8 9 10 •
	(P–) _____ 0 0.5 1 2 3 4 5 6 7 8 9 10 •

Performance rating

My performance was:	Poor	Average	Good
Quality	0 0.5 1	2 3 4 5 6 7	8 9 10 •

Comments: _____
_____
_____
_____
_____

From *Emotions in Sport* by Yuri L. Hanin, 2000, Champaign, IL: Human Kinetics.

APPENDIX C
Practical Example of IZOF Profiles

Figures C.1 and C.2 provide illustrations of emotion profiles for successful and poor performances, respectively. Using an individualized emotion scale, a top javelin thrower—rated after each performance—recalls how he felt before each of six throws in a major competition. As shown in the profile in figure C.1, four throws were very good. Two other throws, shown in figure C.2, were less than successful. Several aspects of these figures are important to note.

1. Emotion words selected by this athlete included from two to five descriptors. For P+ emotions, such terms as *eager, sure,* and *determined* were used; for N+ emotions, *tense* and *furious;* for P– emotions, *nice, calm, pleasant,* and *content;* and for N– emotions, *tired, slack, lazy,* and *unwilling.*

2. This athlete's best performance profiles in all four cases are bell- or iceberg-shaped with high intensities of optimal emotions (P+ and N+) and lower (minimum) intensities of dysfunctional emotions (P– and N–). Thus, the profile shape clearly reflects the optimal interactive effects of different emotion categories.

3. Emotion intensity scores across the four throws in figure C.1 are very similar for pleasant, content, lazy, unwilling, slack, and tired feelings, whereas

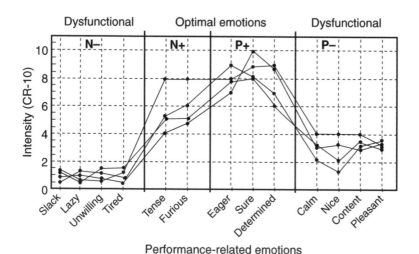

Figure C.1   IZOF emotional profiles before successful javelin throws.

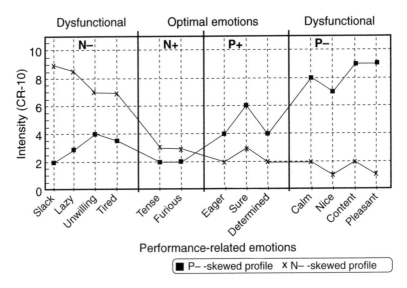

Figure C.2   IZOF emotion profiles before poor javelin throws.

for tense, furious, eager, sure, and determined feelings there is some variability in intensity scores. This variability of emotion intensity is best described as a range, or *zone*, of optimal emotional intensity, representing a minimum and a maximum intensity for a particular emotion that is helpful for performance.

4. A recall (indirect) method and an actual or empirical (direct) assessment method are used for establishing optimal intensity zones (see chapter 7, pp. 163-164, and chapter 4, pp. 100-102).

Figure C.2, illustrating two unsuccessful performances, displays deviations from the optimal emotion profile (and zones). Emotion profiles for poor throws are either P– -skewed or N– -skewed. P– -skewed emotion profiles show elevated intensity levels of positive dysfunctional (P–) emotions and low levels of optimal emotions (P+ and N+). This type of profile usually occurs when an athlete mentally discontinues his or her performance after successfully beginning task execution.

N– -skewed emotion profiles show elevated intensity levels of negative dysfunctional (N–) emotions accompanied by low intensity levels of optimal emotions. This type of profile usually occurs when an athlete, for such reasons as failure in a previous competition or lack of recovery, is not able to meet the demands of the task at hand. In such cases, one can predict a high probability of poor performance.

References

Abele, A., & Brehm, W. (1993). Mood effects of exercise versus sports games: Findings and implications for well-being and health. *International Review of Health Psychology, 2*, 53-80.

Abernethy, B. (1993). Attention. In R.N. Singer, M. Murphey, & L.K. Tennant (Eds.), *Handbook of research on sport psychology* (pp. 127-170). New York: Macmillan.

Adler, N., & Matthews, K. (1994). Health psychology: Why do some people get sick and some stay well? *Annual Review of Psychology, 45*, 229-259.

Aldercreutz, H., Harkonen, M., Kuoppasalmi, K., Naveri, H., Hutaniemi, I., Tikkanen, H., Remes, K., Dessypris, A., & Karvonen, J. (1986). Effect of training plasma anabolic and catabolic steroid hormones and their response during exercise. *International Journal of Sports Medicine, 7*, 27-28.

Aleksejev, A.V. (1969). *Psihoregulirujutshaja trenirovka: Mobilizatsiya* [Psycho-regulation training: Mobilization]. Part II. Moscow: VNIIFK.

Alexander, F. (1950). *Psychosomatic medicine: Its principles and applications.* New York: Norton.

Allard, F., Brawley, L.R., Deakin, J., & Elliot, D. (1989). The effect of exercise on visual attention performance. *Human Performance, 2*, 131-145.

Allport, G. (1960). The open system in personality theory. *Journal of Abnormal and Social Psychology, 61* (3), 301-310.

Alpert, R., & Haber, R.N. (1960). Anxiety in academic achievement situations. *Journal of Abnormal and Social Psychology, 61*, 207-215.

Ames, C. (1992). Achievement goals, motivational climate, and motivational processes. In G.C. Roberts (Ed.), *Motivation in sport and exercise* (pp. 161-176). Champaign, IL: Human Kinetics.

Ananjev, B.G. (1968). *Chelovek kak predmet poznaniya* [Person as a subject of study]. Leningrad: Leningrad University Press.

Andersen, C.L. (1985). *Treatment of anger: A review of current literature.* Doctor of Psychology paper, Biola University, La Mirada, California.

Andersen, M.B., & Williams, J.M. (1988). A model of stress and athletic injury: Prediction and prevention. *Journal of Sport and Exercise Physiology, 10*, 294-306.

Anderson, K.J. (1990). Arousal and the inverted-U hypothesis: A critique of Neiss's "reconceptualizing arousal." *Psychological Bulletin, 107*, 96-100.

Annesi, J.J. (1997). Three-dimensional state anxiety recall: Implications for individual zone of optimal functioning research and application. *The Sport Psychologist, 11*, 43-52.

Annesi, J.J. (1998). Applications of the individual zones of optimal functioning model for the multimodal treatment of precompetitive anxiety. *The Sport Psychologist, 12* (3), 300-316.

Apitzsch, E. (Ed.). (1983). *Anxiety in sport*. Magglingen, Switzerland: FEPSAC.

Apter, M.J. (1982). *The experience of motivation: The theory of psychological reversals.* London and New York: Academic Press.

Apter, M.J. (1989). *Reversal theory: Motivation, emotion, and personality.* London: Routledge.

Aristotle. (1941). Rhetoric. In R. McKeon (Ed.), *The basic works of Aristotle.* New York: Random House.

Arnold, M.B. (1960). *Emotion and personality* (Vols. 1 & 2). New York: Columbia University Press.

Arnold, M.B. (1968). *The nature of emotion.* Baltimore: Penguin Books.

Arnold, M.B. (1970a). Brain function in emotion: A phenomenological analysis. In P. Black (Ed.), *Physiological correlates of emotion.* New York: Academic Press.

Arnold, M.B. (1970b). Perennial problems in the field of emotion. In M.B. Arnold (Ed.), *Feelings and emotion.* New York: Academic Press.

Arnold, M.B., & Gasson, J.A. (1954). *The human person: An approach to an integral theory of personality.* New York: Ronald Press.

Aronson, T.A., Carasiti, I., McBane, D., & Whitaker-Axmitia, P. (1989). Biological correlates of lactate sensitivity in panic disorder. *Biological Psychiatry, 26,* 463-477.

Averill, J.R. (1980). A constructivist view of emotion. In R. Plutchik & H. Kellerman (Eds.), *Theories of emotion: Theory, research, and experience* (Vol. 1, pp. 305-339). San Diego: Academic Press.

Averill, J.R. (1982). *Anger and aggression: An essay on emotion.* New York: Springer-Verlag.

Averill, J.R. (1983). Studies on anger and aggression: Implications for theories of emotion. *American Psychologist, 38,* 1145-1160.

Averill, J.R. (1990). Inner feelings, works of flesh, the beast within, diseases of the mind, driving force, and putting on a show: Six metaphors of emotion and their theoretical extensions. In D.E. Leary (Ed.), *Metaphors in the history of psychology* (pp. 104-132). Cambridge: Cambridge University Press.

Ax, A.F. (1953). The physiological differentiation between fear and anger in humans. *Psychosomatic Medicine, 15,* 433-442.

Bahrick, R.E., & Watson, J.S. (1985). Detection of intermodal proprioceptive-visual contingency as a potential basis of self-perception in infancy. *Developmental Psychology, 21,* 963-973.

Bak, P. (Per). (1996). *How nature works.* New York: Springer-Verlag.

Baldwin, K.M., Klinderfuss, G.H., Terjung, R.L., Mole, P.A., & Holloszy, J.O. (1972). Respiratory capacity of white, red, and intermediate muscle: Adaptive response to exercise. *American Journal of Physiology, 222,* 373-378.

Bandura, A. (1973). *Aggression: A social learning analysis.* Englewood Cliffs, NJ: Prentice Hall.

Bandura, A. (1978). The self-system in reciprocal determinism. *American Psychologist, 33,* 344-358.

Bandura, A. (1983). Temporal dynamics and decomposition of reciprocal determinism: A reply to Phillips and Orton. *Psychological Review, 90,* 166-170.

Bandura, A. (1986). *Social foundations of thought and action: A social cognitive theory.* Englewood Cliffs, NJ: Prentice Hall.

Bandura, A. (1991). Social cognitive theory of self-regulation. *Organizational Behavior and Human Decision Processes, 50,* 248-287.

Bandura, A. (1997). *Self-efficacy: The exercise of control.* New York: Freeman.

Bandura, A., & Walters, R.H. (1963). *Social learning and personality development.* New York: Holt, Reinhart & Winston.

Banks, R. (1997). An afrocentric approach to group social skills training with inner-city African-American adolescents. (ERIC Document Reproduction Service No. ED 4100333).

Bar-Eli, M. (1985). Arousal-performance relationship: A transactional view on performance jags. *International Journal of Sport Psychology, 16,* 193-209.

Bar-Eli, M. (1997). Psychological performance crisis in competition: 1984-1996. *European Yearbook of Sport Psychology, 1,* 73-112.

Bar-Eli, M., Taoz, E., Levy-Kolker, N., & Tennebaum, G. (1992). Performance quality and behavioral violations as crisis indicators in competition. *International Journal of Sport Psychology, 23,* 325-342.

Bard, P. (1928). A diencephalic mechanism for the expression of rage with special reference to the sympathetic nervous system. *American Journal of Physiology, 84,* 490-513.

Baron, R.M., & Kenny, D.A. (1986). The moderator-mediator variable distinction in social psychological research: Conceptual, strategic, and statistical considerations. *Journal of Personality and Social Psychology, 51,* 1173-1182.

Barron, J.L., Noakes, T.D., Levy, W., Smith, C., & Millar, R.P. (1985). Hypothalamic dysfunction in overtrained athletes. *Journal of Clinical Endocrinology and Metabolism, 60,* 803-806.

Batson, D.C., Shaw, L.L., & Oleson, K.C. (1992). Differentiating affect, mood, and emotion. In M.S. Clark (Ed.), *Emotion* (pp. 294-326). Newbury Park, CA: Sage.

Beck, A.T. (1967). *Depression: Clinical, experimental, and theoretical aspects.* New York: Harper & Row.

Beecher, H.K. (1956-1957). The measurement of pain, prototype for the quantitative study of subjective responses. *Pharmacological Reviews, 8-9,* 60-209.

Beidleman, B.A., Muza, S.R., Rock, P.B., Fulco, C.S., Lyons, T.P., Hoyt, R.W., & Cymerman, A. (1997). Exercise responses after altitude acclimatization are retained during reintroduction to altitude. *Medicine and Science in Sports and Exercise, 12,* 1588-1595.

Bejek, K., & Hagtvet, K.A. (1996). The content of pre-competitive state anxiety in top and lower level female gymnasts. *Anxiety, Stress, and Coping, 9,* 19-31.

Bennett, P., & Murphy, S. (1997). *Psychology and health promotion.* Buckingham: Open University Press.

Berger, B.G. (1996). Psychological benefits of an active lifestyle: What we know and what we need to know. *Quest, 48,* 330-353.

Berger, B.G., & McInman, A. (1993). Exercise and the quality of life. In R.N. Singer, M. Murphey, & L.K. Tennant (Eds.), *Handbook of research on sport psychology* (pp. 729-760). New York: Macmillan.

Berglund, B., & Säfström, H. (1994). Psychological monitoring and modulation of training load of world-class canoeists. *Medicine and Science in Sports and Exercise, 26,* 1036-1040.

Berkowitz, L. (1962). *Aggression: A social psychological analysis.* New York: McGraw-Hill.

Berkowitz, L. (1964). Aggressive cues in aggressive behaviour and hostility catharsis. *Psychological Review, 71,* 104-122.

Berkowitz, L. (1989). Frustration-aggression hypothesis: Examination and reformulation. *Psychological Bulletin, 106,* 59-73.

Betancourt, H. (1990). An attribution-empathy model of helping behavior: Behavioral intentions and judgements of help-giving. *Personality and Social Psychology Bulletin, 16,* 573-591.

Beuter, A., & Duda, J.L. (1985). Analysis of the arousal/motor performance relationship in children using movement kinematics. *Journal of Sport Psychology, 7,* 229-243.

Beuter, A., Duda, J.L., & Widule, C.L. (1989). The effects of arousal on joint kinematics and kinetics in children. *Research Quarterly for Exercise and Sport, 13* (3), 227-238.

Biddle, S.J.H. (1993). Attribution research and sport psychology. In R.N. Singer, M. Murphey, & L.K. Tennant (Eds.), *Handbook of research on sport psychology* (pp. 437-464). New York: Macmillan.

Biddle, S.J.H. (1997). Current trends in sport and exercise psychology research. *The Psychologist: Bulletin of the British Psychological Society, 10* (2), 63-69.

Biddle, S.J.H., & Fox, K.R. (1989). Exercise and health psychology: Emerging relationship. *British Journal of Medical Psychology, 62,* 205-216.

Biddle, S.J.H., & Hanrahan, S. (1998). Attributions and attributional style. In J.L. Duda (Ed.), *Advances in sport and exercise psychology measurement* (pp. 3-20). Morgantown, WV: Fitness Information Technology.

Biddle, S.J.H., & Hill, A.B. (1988). Causal attribution and emotional reactions to outcome in sporting contests. *Personality and Individual Differences, 9,* 231-233.

Biddle, S.J.H., & Hill, A.B. (1992a). Attributions for objective outcome and subjective appraisal of performance: Their relationship with emotional reactions in sport. *British Journal of Social Psychology, 31,* 215-226.

Biddle, S.J.H., & Hill, A.B. (1992b). Relationships between attributions and emotions in a laboratory-based sporting contest. *Journal of Sports Sciences, 10,* 65-75.

Biddle, S.J.H., & Mutrie, N. (1991). *Psychology of physical activity and exercise: A health-related perspective.* London: Springer-Verlag.

Bidwell, C., Csikszentmihalyi, M., Hedges, L., & Schneider, B. (in press). *Attitudes and experiences of work for American adolescents.* New York: Cambridge University Press.

Bird, A.M., & Horn, M.A. (1990). Cognitive anxiety and mental errors in sport. *Journal of Sport and Exercise Psychology, 12,* 217-222.

Blanchard, C., & Vallerand, R.J. (1996). [On the relations between situational motivation and situational consequences in basketball]. Unpublished raw data, Université du Québec à Montréal.

Blanchard, C., & Vallerand, R.J. (1998). [On the relations between situational motivation and situational consequences toward exercise]. Unpublished raw data, Université du Québec è Montréal.

Bloom, M. (1997). Making their mark in the record book. *The New York Times*, p. 2.

Blumberg, M.S., & Wasserman, E.A. (1995). Animal mind and the argument from design. *American Psychologist, 50*, 133-149.

Blumenstein, B., Bar-Eli, M., & Tenenbaum, G. (1997). A five-step approach to mental training incorporating biofeedback. *Sport Psychologist, 11* (4), 440-453.

Bompa, T.O. (1983). *Theory and methodology of training: The key to athletic performance.* Dubuque, IA: Kendall/Hunt.

Bond, J., & Nideffer, R.M. (1992, June). Attentional and interpersonal characteristics of elite Australian athletes. *Exel* (Canberra), 101-110.

Bonica, J.J. (1991). Pain management: Past and current states including the role of the anesthesiologist. In T.H. Stanley, M.A. Ashburn, & P.G. Fine (Eds.), *Anesthesiology and pain management.* Boston: Kluwer Academic.

Booth, W. (1987). Arthritis institute tackles sport. *Science, 237*, 846-847.

Borg, G. (1975). Perceived exertion as an indicator of somatic stress. *Scandinavian Journal of Rehabilitational Medicine, 2*, 92-98.

Borg, G. (1982). A category scale with ratio properties for intermodal and interindividual comparisons. In H.-G. Geiss & P. Petzold (Eds.), *Psychophysical judgement and the process of perception* (pp. 25-34). Berlin: VEB Deutscher Verlag der Wissenschaften.

Borg, G. (1998). *Borg's perceived exertion and pain scales.* Champaign, IL: Human Kinetics.

Bortoli, L., Robazza, C., & Nougier, V. (1997). Emotion in hockey and rugby. In R. Lidor & M. Bar-Eli (Eds.), *ISSP IX World Congress of Sport Psychology. Innovations in sport psychology: Linking theory and practice. Proceedings* (Part I, pp. 136-138). Israel: Wingate Institute.

Bortoli, L., Robazza, C., & Nougier, V. (1999a, in press). Emotion, heart rate, and performance in archery: a case study. *The Journal of Sports Medicine and Physical Fitness.*

Bortoli, L., Robazza, C., & Nougier, V. (1999b, in press). Psychological monitoring of emotions in archers during the 1995 World Championships. *International Journal of Sport Psychology.*

Boutcher, S. (1993). Emotion and aerobic exercise. In R.N. Singer, M. Murphey, & L.K. Tennant (Eds.), *Handbook of research on sport psychology* (pp. 799-814). New York: Macmillan.

Boutcher, S.H., McAuley, E., & Courneya, K.S. (1997). Positive and negative affect response of trained and untrained subjects during and after aerobic exercise. *Australian Journal of Psychology, 49*, 28-32.

Bowling, A. (1995). *Measuring health: A review of quality of life measurement scales.* Buckingham: Open University Press.

Bozonian, S., Rejeski, J.W., & McAuley, E. (1994). Self-efficacy influences feeling states associated with acute exercise. *Journal of Sport and Exercise Psychology, 16*, 326-333.

Bramwell, S.T., Masuda, M., Wagner, N.H., & Holmes, T.H. (1975). Psychological factors in athletic injuries: Development and application of the Social and Athletic Readjustment Rating Scale (SARRS). *Journal of Human Stress, 1*, 6-20.

Bredemeier, B.J. (1975). The assessment of reactive and instrumental athletic aggression. In D.M. Landers (Ed.), *Psychology of sport and motor behaviour-II* (pp. 71-83). State College, PA: Penn State HPER Series.

Bredemeier, B.J. (1983). Athletic aggression: A moral concern. In J.H. Goldstein (Ed.), *Sports violence* (pp. 47-81). New York: Springer-Verlag.

Bredemeier, B.J. (1985). Moral reasoning and the perceived legitimacy of intentionally injurious sport acts. *Journal of Sport Psychology, 7*, 110-124.

Bredemeier, B.J. (1994). Children's moral reasoning and their assertive, aggressive, and submissive tendencies in sport and daily life. *Journal of Sport and Exercise Psychology, 16*, 1-14.

Bredemeier, B.J. (1995). Divergence in children's moral reasoning about issues in daily life and sport specific contexts. *International Journal of Sport Psychology, 26* (4), 453-463.

Bredemeier, B., & Shields, D.L. (1985). Values and violence in sports today. The moral reasoning athletes use in their games and in their lives. *Psychology Today, 19* (10), 22-25, 28-29.

Brewer, B.W. (1994). Review and critique of models of psychological adjustment to athletic injury. *Journal of Applied Sport Psychology, 6*, 87-100.

Brewer, B.W., Linder, D.E., & Phelps, C.M. (1995). Situational correlates of emotional adjustment to athletic injury. *Clinical Journal of Sports Medicine, 5*, 241-245.

Brewer, B.W., Linder, D.E., & Phelps, C.M. (1997). False summit. *Outside, 3*, 57-62, 147-149.

Brewer, B.W., Van Raalte, J.L., Linder, D.E., & Van Raalte, N.S. (1991). Peak performance and the perils of retrospective introspection. *Journal of Sport and Exercise Psychology, 8*, 227-238.

Brieère, N.M., Vallerand, R.J., Blais, M.R., & Pelletier, L.G. (1995). Development and validation of an instrument measuring intrinsic, extrinsic, and a motivation in a sport context. The Sport Motivation Scale (French version). *International Journal of Sport Psychology, 26*, 465-489.

Briggs, J.L. (1970). *Never in anger: Portrait of an Eskimo family.* Cambridge: Harvard University Press.

Brown, D.R. (1992). Physical activity, ageing, and psychological well-being: An overview of the research. *Canadian Journal of Sports Science, 17*, 185-193.

Brown, J., & Farber, I.E. (1951). Emotions conceptualized as intervening variables—with suggestions toward a theory of frustration. *Psychological Bulletin, 48*, 465-495.

Buck, R. (1985). Prime theory: An integrated view of motivation and emotion. *Psychological Review, 92*, 389-413.

Burchfield, S.R. (Ed.). (1985). *Stress: Psychological and physiological interactions.* Washington, DC: Hemisphere.

Burisch, M. (1988). *Das Burnout-Syndrom* [The burnout syndrome]. Heidelberg: Springer.

Burke, E.R. (1990, Fall/Winter). Athletes and overtraining: How to spot it, how to avoid it. *American Athletics*, 65-69.

Burke, E.R., Falsetti, H.L., Feld, R.D., Patton, G.S., & Kennedy, C. (1982). Creatine kinase levels in competitive swimmers during a season of training. *Scandinavian Journal of Sports Sciences, 4,* 1-4.

Burton, D. (1988). Do anxious swimmers swim slower? Reexamining the elusive anxiety-performance relationship. *Journal of Sport and Exercise Psychology, 10,* 45-61.

Burton, D. (1990). Multimodal stress management in sport: Current status and future directions. In J.G. Jones & L. Hardy (Eds.), *Stress and performance in sport* (pp. 171-202). Chichester: Wiley.

Burton, D. (1998). Measuring competitive state anxiety. In J.L. Duda (Ed.), *Advances in sport and exercise psychology measurement* (pp. 129-148). Morgantown, WV: Fitness Information Technology.

Bush, L.E. II. (1973). Individual differences multidimensional scaling of adjectives denoting feelings. *Journal of Personality and Social Psychology, 25,* 50-57.

Buss, A.H., & Durkee, A. (1957). An inventory for assessing different kinds of hostility. *Journal of Consulting Psychology, 21,* 343-349.

Buss, A.H., & Perry, M. (1992). The aggression questionnaire. *Journal of Personality and Social Psychology, 63,* 452-459.

Buss, A.H., & Plomin, R. (1984). *Temperament: Early developing personality traits.* Hillsdale, NJ: Erlbaum.

Büssing, A., & Perrar, K.M. (1992). Die Messung von Burnout. Untersuchung einer deutschen Fassung des Maslach Burnout Inventory (MBI-D) [The measurement of burnout. A study on the German version of the MBI-D]. *Diagnostica, 38,* 328-353.

Butler, R.J. (1989). Psychological preparation of Olympic boxers. In J. Kremer & W. Crawford (Eds.), *The psychology of sport: Theory and practice* (pp. 74-84). Leicester, UK: British Psychological Society.

Butler, R.J., & Hardy, L. (1992). The performance profile: Theory and application. *Sport Psychologist, 6,* 253-264.

Buxton, M.J., O'Hanlon, M., & Rushby, J. (1990). A new facility for the measurement of health-related quality of life. *Health Policy, 16,* 199-208.

Buxton, M.J., O'Hanlon, M., & Rushby, J. (1992). EuroQol: A reply and reminder. *Health Policy, 20,* 329-332.

Cacioppo, J.T., Klein, D.J., Berntson, G.C., & Hatfield, E. (1993). The psychophysiology of emotion. In M. Lewis & J. Haviland (Eds.), *Handbook of emotions* (pp. 119-142). New York: Guilford Press.

Callister, R., Callister, R.J., Fleck, S.J., & Dudley, G.A. (1990). Physiological and performance responses to overtraining in elite judo athletes. *Medicine and Science in Sports and Exercise, 22,* 816-824.

Cameron, R., & Meichenbaum, D. (1983). The nature of effective coping and the treatment of stress related problems: A cognitive-behavioral perspective. In L. Goldberger & S. Breznitz (Eds.), *Handbook of stress: Theoretical and clinical aspects* (pp. 695-711). New York: Free Press.

Cannon, W.B. (1927). The James-Lange theory of emotions: A critical examination and an alternative theory. *American Journal of Psychology, 39,* 106-124.

Cannon, W.B. (1939). *The wisdom of the body* (2nd ed.). New York: Simon. (Original work published 1932)

Cannon, W.B., Lewis, J.T., & Britton, S.W. (1927). The dispensability of the sympathetic division of the autonomic system. *Boston Medical and Surgery Journal, 197,* 514-522.

Cantor, N., Mischel, W., & Schwartz, J.C. (1982). A prototype analysis of psychological situations. *Cognitive Psychology, 14,* 45-77.

Capel, S. (1986). Psychological and organizational factors related to burnout. *Research Quarterly for Exercise and Sport, 57,* 321-328.

Carli, M., Delle Fave, A., & Massimini, F. (1988). The quality of experience in the flow channels: Comparison of Italian and US students. In M. Csikszentmihalyi & I. Csikszentmihalyi (Eds.), *Optimal experience: Psychological studies of flow in consciousness* (pp. 288-306). Cambridge: Cambridge University Press.

Carlson, J.H., & Hatfield, E. (1992). *Psychology of emotion.* Orlando, FL: Harcourt Brace Jovanovich.

Carlström, I. (1983). Karlskrona projektet [The Karlskrona project]: Ett försök att påverka barns och ungdomars normer [A trial to influence children's and young people's norms]. Kristianstad: Högskolan [University College of Kristianstad]. *Forum för pedagogisk orientering och debatt* [Forum of educational discussion and debate], Serie B nr 5.

Caruso, C.M., Gill, D.L., Dzewaltowski, D.A., & McElroy, M.A. (1990). Psychological and physiological changes in competitive state anxiety during noncompetition and competitive success and failure. *Journal of Sport and Exercise Psychology, 12,* 6-20.

Carver, R.P. (1974, July). Two dimensions of tests: Psychometric and edumetric. *American Psychologist,* 512-518.

Carver, C.S., & Scheier, M.F. (1998). *On the self-regulation of behavior.* New York: Cambridge University Press.

Cavanaugh, B., & Silva, J. (1980). Spectator perceptions of fan misbehaviour: An attitudinal inquiry. In C.H. Nadeau, W.R. Halliwell, K.M. Newell, & G.C. Roberts (Eds.), *Psychology of motor behaviour and sport* (pp. 189-198). Champaign, IL: Human Kinetics.

Chaouloff, F. (1997). The serotonin hypothesis. In W.P. Morgan (Ed.), *Physical activity and mental health* (pp. 179-198). Washington, DC: Taylor & Francis.

Cherniss, C. (1980). *Staff burnout: Job stress in the human service.* Beverly Hills, CA: Sage.

Clore, G.L., Ortony, A., & Foss, M.A. (1987). The psychological foundations of the affective lexicon. *Journal of Personality and Social Psychology, 53,* 751-766.

Clore, G.L., Schwarz, N., & Conway, M. (1994). Affective causes and consequences of social information processing. In R.S. Wyer & T.K. Srull (Eds.), *Handbook of social cognition* (2nd ed., Vol. 1, pp. 323-417). Hillsdale, NJ: Erlbaum.

Cockerill, I.M., Nevill, A.M., & Lyons, N. (1991). Modelling mood states in athletic performance. *Journal of Sport Sciences, 9* (2), 205-212.

Cogan, K.D., Highlen, P.S., Petrie, T.A., Sherman, M.W., & Simonsen, U. (1991). Psychological and physiological effects of controlled intensive training and diet on collegiate rowers. *International Journal of Sport Psychology, 22* (2), 165-180.

Cohen, S., & Herbert, T. (1996). Health psychology: Psychological factors and physical disease from the perspective of human psychoneuroimmunology. *Annual Review of Psychology, 47,* 113-142.

Cohn, P. (1990). An explanatory study of sources of stress and athlete burnout in youth golf. *Sport Psychologist, 4,* 95-106.

Cohn, P.J. (1991). An exploratory study on peak performance in golf. *The Sport Psychologist, 54* (1), 1-14.

Collins English dictionary (1991). (3rd ed.). Glasglow: Harper Collins.

Collins, D. (1995). Psychophysiology and sport performance. In S.J.H. Biddle (Ed.), *European perspectives on exercise and sport psychology* (pp. 154-178). Leeds, UK: Human Kinetics.

Collis, M.L. (1972). The Collis Scale of Athletic Aggression. *Proceedings of the fourth Canadian Symposium on Psycho-Motor Learning and Sport Psychology* (pp. 366-370). University of Waterloo, Ontario, Canada.

Costill, D.L. (1985). The 1985 C.H. McCloy research lecture: Practical problems in exercise physiology research. *Research Quarterly for Exercise and Sport, 56,* 378-384.

Costill, D.L. (1988). Nutrition and dietetics. In A. Dirix, H. Knuttgen, & K. Tittel (Eds.), *Olympic book of sports medicine.* Oxford: Blackwell Scientific.

Costill, D.L., Flynn, M.G., Kirwan, J.P., Houmard, J.A., Mitchell, J.B., Thomas, R., & Park, S.H. (1988). Effects of repeated days of intensified training on muscle glycogen and swimming performance. *Medicine and Science in Sports and Exercise, 20,* 249-254.

Costill, D.L., King, D.S., Thomas, R., & Hargreaves, M. (1985). Effects of reduced training on muscular power in swimmers. *The Physician and Sportsmedicine, 13,* 94-101.

Counsilman, J.E., & Counsilman, B.E. (1990). No simple answers. *Swimming Technique, 26,* 22-29.

Courneya, K.S., & Chelladurai, P. (1991). A model of performance measures in baseball. *Journal of Sport and Exercise Psychology, 13,* 16-25.

Courneya, K.S., & McAuley, E. (1996). Understanding intentions to exercise following a structured exercise program: An attributional perspective. *Journal of Applied Social Psychology, 26,* 670-685.

Craft, L.L., & Landers, D.M. (1998). The effect of exercise on clinical depression resulting from mental illness: A meta-analysis. *Journal of Sport and Exercise Psychology, 20,* 339-357.

Crane, R.S. (1981). The role of anger, hostility, and aggression in essential hypertension (Doctoral dissertation, University of South Florida, Tampa, 1981). *Dissertation Abstracts International, 42,* 2982B.

Crews, D.J. (1992). Psychological state and running economy. *Medicine and Science in Sports and Exercise, 24,* 275-482.

Crews, D.J., & Landers, D.M. (1987). A meta-analytic review of aerobic fitness and reactivity to psychosocial stressors. *Medicine and Science in Sports and Exercise, 19* (5, supplement), S114-S120.

Crocker, P.R.E. (1995). A confirmatory factor analysis of the Positive Affect Negative Affect Schedule (PANAS) with a youth sport sample. *Journal of Sport and Exercise Psychology, 19,* 91-97.

Crocker, P.R.E., & Bouffard, M. (1992). Perceived challenge in physical activity by individuals with physical disabilities: The relationship between appraisal and affect. *Adapted Physical Activity Quarterly, 9,* 130-140.

Crocker, P.R.E., & Graham, T.R. (1995). Emotion in sport and physical activity: The importance of perceived individual goals. *International Journal of Sport Psychology, 26,* 117-137.

Cryan, P.O., & Alles, E.F. (1983). The relationship between stress and football injuries. *Journal of Sports Medicine and Physical Fitness, 23,* 52-58.

Csikszentmihalyi, M. (1975). *Beyond boredom and anxiety.* San Francisco: Jossey Bass.

Csikszentmihalyi, M. (1990). *Flow: The psychology of optimal sport experience.* New York: Harper & Row.

Csikszentmihalyi, M. (1996). *Creativity: Flow and the psychology of discovery and invention.* New York: Harper Collins.

Csikszentmihalyi, M. (1997). *Finding flow: The psychology of engagement with everyday life.* New York: Harper Collins.

Csikszentmihalyi, M., & Csikszentmihalyi, I. (Eds.). (1988). *Optimal experience: Psychological studies of flow in consciousness.* Cambridge: Cambridge University Press.

Csikszentmihalyi, M., & Larson, R. (1987). Validity and reliability of the experience sampling method. *Journal of Nervous and Mental Disease, 175,* 526-536.

Csikszentmihalyi, M., Rathunde, K., & Whalen, S. (1993). *Talented teenagers: The roots of success and failure.* New York: Cambridge University Press.

D'Andrade, R.G. (1984). Cultural meaning systems. In R.A. Shweder & R.A. LeVine (Eds.), *Culture theory: Essays on mind, self, and emotion* (pp. 88-119). Cambridge: Cambridge University Press.

Dale, J., & Weinberg, R.S. (1990). Burnout in sports: A review and critique. *Journal of Applied Sport Psychology, 2,* 67-83.

Darwin, C. (1965). *The expression of the emotions in man and animal.* Chicago: University of Chicago Press. (Original work published 1872)

Davidson, R.J., & Cacioppo, J.T. (1992). New developments in the scientific study of emotion: An introduction to the special section. *Psychological Science, 3* (1), 21-22.

Davidson, R.J., Ekman, P., Saron, C.D., Senulis, J.A., & Friesen, W.V. (1990). Approach-withdrawal and cerebral asymmetry: I. Emotional expression and brain physiology. *Journal of Personality and Social Psychology, 58,* 330-341.

Davis, M., & Colbert, L.H. (1997). The athlete's immune system, intense exercise, and overtraining. In D.R. Lamb & R. Murray (Eds.), *Perspectives in exercise science and sports medicine: Vol. 10. Optimizing sport performance.* Carmel, IN: Cooper.

Davis, S., & West, J.D. (1991). A theoretical paradigm for performance enhancement: The multimodal approach. *The Sport Psychologist, 6,* 167-174.

Davitz, J.R. (1969). *The language of emotion.* New York: Academic Press.

Debus, G., Erdmann, E., & Kallus, K.W. (Eds.) (1995). *Biopsychologie von Streß und emotionalen Reaktionen* [Biopsychology of stress and emotional reactions]. Göttingen: Hogrefe.

Deci, E.L. (1980). *The psychology of self-determination.* Lexington, MA: Heath, Lexington.

Deci, E.L., & Ryan, R.M. (1985). *Intrinsic motivation and self-determination in human behavior.* New York: Plenum Press.

Deci, E.L., & Ryan, R.M. (1991). A motivational approach to self: Integration in personality. In R. Dienstbier (Ed.), *Nebraska Symposium on Motivation: Vol. 38. Perspectives on motivation* (pp. 237-288). Lincoln, NE: University of Nebraska Press.

Deffenbacher, J.L. (1992). Trait anger: Theory, findings, and applications. In C.D. Spielberger & J.N. Butcher (Eds.), *Advances in personality assessment* (Vol. 9, pp. 177-201). Hillsdale, NJ: Erlbaum.

DeGood, D.E., & Kiernan, B.D. (1997-1998). Pain related cognition as predictors of pain treatment outcome. *Advances in Medical Psychotherapy, 9,* 73-90.

DeHart, J. (1995). Taking DeHart way. *Swimming Technique, 32*(3), 15-17.

Dember, W.N. (1974). Motivation and the cognitive revolution. *American Psychologist, 29,* 161-168.

Demos, E.V. (1995). *Exploring affect: The selected writings of S. S. Tomkins.* Paris: Cambridge University Press, Maison des Sciences de l'Homme.

Department of Health (1991). *The health of the nation: A consultative document for England.* London: HMSO.

Department of Health (1992). *The health of the nation. A strategy for health for England.* London: HMSO.

Department of Health (1993). *The health of the nation: One year on ... A report on the progress of the Health of the Nation.* London: HMSO.

Derogatis, L.R. (1975). *Affect balance scale.* Baltimore: Clinical Psychosomatics Research.

Derogatis, L.R., Lipman, R.S., & Covi, L. (1973). The SCL-90: An outpatient psychiatric rating scale. *Psychopharmacology Bulletin, 9,* 13-28.

Diener, E., & Emmons, R.A. (1984). The independence of positive and negative affect. *Journal of Personality and Social Psychology, 47* (5), 1105-1117.

Diener, E., & Iran-Nejad, A. (1986). The relationship in experience between various types of affect. *Journal of Personality and Social Psychology, 50* (5), 1031-1038.

Diener, E., Sandvik, E., & Pavot, W.G. (1990). Happiness is the frequency not intensity of positive versus negative affect. In F. Strack, M. Argyle, & N. Schwarz (Eds.), *The social psychology of subjective well being* (pp. 119-139). Elmsford, NY: Pergamon Press.

Dishman, R.K. (1994). Biological psychology, exercise, and stress. *Quest, 46,* 28-59.

Dishman, R.K. (1995). Physical activity and public health: Mental health. *Quest, 47,* 362-385.

Dishman, R.K. (1997). The norepinephrine hypothesis. In W.P. Morgan (Ed.), *Physical activity and mental health* (pp. 199-212). Washington, DC: Taylor & Francis.

Dixon, P., Heaton, J., Long, A., & Warburton, A. (1994). Reviewing and applying the SF-36. *Outcomes Briefing, 4,* 3-25.

Dollard, J., Doob, L., Miller, N., Mowrer, O., & Sears, R. (1939). *Frustration and aggression.* New Haven: Yale University Press.

Doyle, J., & Parfitt, G. (1996). Performance profiling and predictive validity. *Journal of Applied Sport Psychology, 8,* 160-170.

Dressendorfer, R.H., Wade, D.E., & Scaff, J.H. Jr. (1985). Increased morning heart rate in runners: A valid sign of overtraining? *The Physician and Sportsmedicine, 131,* 77-86.

Drever, J. (1952). *A dictionary of psychology.* London: Penguin Books.

Duda, J.L. (1992). Motivation in sport settings: A goal perspective approach. In G.C. Roberts (Ed.), *Motivation in sport and exercise* (pp. 57-91). Champaign, IL: Human Kinetics.

Duda, J.L. (1993). Goals: A social-cognitive approach to the study of achievement motivation in sport. In R.N. Singer, M. Murphey, & L.K. Tennant (Eds.), *Handbook of research on sport psychology* (pp. 421-436). New York: Macmillan.

Duda, J.L. (Ed.). (1998). *Advances in sport and exercise psychology measurement.* Morgantown, WV: Fitness Information Technology.

Duda, J.L., Chi, L., & Newton, M. (1990). *Psychometric characteristics of the TEOSQ.* Paper presented at the annual meeting of the North American Society for the Psychology of Sport and Physical Activity, University of Houston, Houston, TX.

Duda, J.L., Chi, L., Newton, M., Walling, M., & Catley, D. (1995). Task and ego orientation and intrinsic motivation in sport. *International Journal of Sport Psychology, 26,* 40-63.

Duda, J.L., & Nicholls, J.G. (1992). Dimensions of achievement motivation in school-work and sport. *Journal of Educational Psychology, 84,* 290-299.

Duda, J.L., Olson, L.K., & Templin, T.J. (1991). The relationship of task and ego orientation to sportsmanship attitudes and the perceived legitimacy of injurious acts. *Research Quarterly for Exercise and Sport, 62,* 79-87.

Duffy, E. (1941). An explanation of "emotional" phenomena without the use of the concept "emotion." *Journal of General Psychology, 25,* 283-293.

Duffy, E. (1951). The concept of energy mobilization. *Psychological Review, 58,* 30-40.

Duffy, E. (1957). The psychological significance of the concept of "arousal" or "activation." *Psychological Review, 66,* 183-201.

Duffy, E. (1962). *Activation and behavior.* New York: Wiley.

Dunn, A.L., & Dishman, R.K. (1991). Exercise and the neurobiology of depression. *Exercise and Sport Sciences Reviews, 19,* 41-98.

Dunn, J. (1988). *The beginnings of social understanding.* Cambridge: Harvard University Press.

Dweck, C.S., & Leggett, E.L. (1988). A social-cognitive approach to motivation and personality. *Psychological Review, 95,* 256-273.

Easterbrook, J.A. (1959). The effect of emotion on cue utilization and the organization of behavior. *Psychological Review, 66,* 183-201.

Ebbeck, V., & Weiss, M.R. (1988). The arousal-performance relationships: Task characteristics and performance measures in track & field athletics. *The Sport Psychologist, 2*, 13-27.

Eichner, E.R. (1989). Chronic fatigue syndrome: How vulnerable are athletes? *The Physician and Sportsmedicine, 17*, 157-160.

Ekman, P. (1977). Biological and cultural contributions to body and facial movement. In J. Blacking (Ed.), *The anthropology of the body* (A.S.A. Monograph no. 15, pp. 39-84). San Diego: Academic Press.

Ekman, P. (1984). Expression and the nature of emotion. In K.R. Scherer & P. Ekman (Eds.), *Approaches to emotion* (pp. 319-343). Hillsdale, NJ: Erlbaum.

Ekman, P. (1989). The argument and evidence about universals in facial expressions of emotion. In H. Wagner & A. Manstead (Eds.), *Handbook of social psychophysiology* (pp. 143-163). New York: Wiley.

Ekman, P. (1994). Strong evidence for universals in facial expressions: A reply to Russell's mistaken critique. *Psychological Bulletin, 115*, 268-287.

Ekman, P., & Davidson, R.J. (Eds.). (1994). *The nature of emotion: Fundamental questions*. New York: Oxford University Press.

Ekman, P., & Friesen, W.V. (1975). *Unmasking the face*. Englewood Cliffs, NJ: Prentice Hall.

Ekman, P., Friesen, W.V., & Ellsworth, P. (1982). Conceptual ambiguities. In P. Ekman (Ed.), *Emotion in the human face* (2nd ed., pp. 7-20). New York: Cambridge University Press.

Ekman, P., Friesen, W.V., & Simons, R.C. (1985). Is the startle reaction an emotion? *Journal of Personality and Social Psychology, 49*, 1416-1426.

Ekman, P., Levenson, R.W., & Friesen, W.V. (1983). Autonomic nervous system activity distinguishes between emotions. *Science, 221*, 1208-1210.

Eksten, F. (1995, Summer). In-season strength and power training for women's basketball. *Coaching Women's Basketball, 9*(5), 22-25.

Endler, N.S. (1975). A person-situation model for anxiety. In C.D. Spielberger & I. Sarason (Eds.), *Stress and anxiety* (Vol. 1, pp. 145-164). Washington, DC: Hemisphere.

Endler, N.S., & Magnusson, D. (1976). Multidimensional aspects of state and trait anxiety: A cross-cultural study of Canadian and Swedish college students. In C.D. Spielberger & R. Diaz-Guerrero (Eds.), *Cross-cultural anxiety* (pp. 143-172). Washington, DC: Hemisphere.

Endler, N.S., & Parker, J.D.A. (1990). Stress and anxiety, conceptual and assessment issues. *Stress Medicine, 6*, 243-248.

Engel, B.T., & Bickford, A.F. (1961). Response specificity. *Archives of General Psychiatry, 5*, 478-489.

Evans, D.R., & Stangeland, M. (1971). Development of the reaction inventory to measure anger. *Psychological Reports, 29*, 412-414.

Eweleit, A. (1998). *Identifizierung von Erholungs-/Belastungsdefiziten, Überlastung und Übertrainingseffekten zur Trainingssteuerung mit Hilfe des Erholungs-Belastungs-Fragebogens für Athleten am Beispiel von Mountainbike-Rennfahrern* [Identification of recovery-stress deficits, of overreaching and overtraining effects for training monitoring with the RESTQ-Sport in mountainbikers]. Unpublished diploma thesis, University of Würzburg.

Eysenck, H.J. (1975). The measurement of emotions: Psychological parameters and methods. In L. Levi (Ed.), *Emotions—their parameters and measurement* (pp. 439-467). New York: Raven Press.

Eysenck, M.W., & Calvo, M.G. (1992). Anxiety and performance: The processing efficiency theory. *Cognition and Emotion, 6* (6), 409-434.

Farmer, M., Locke, B., Moscicki, E., Dannenberg, A., Larson, D., & Radloff, L. (1988). Physical activity and depressive symptoms. The NHANES-I epidemiological follow-up study. *American Journal of Epidemiology, 128,* 1340-1351.

Faulkner, J., Daniels, J., & Balke, B. (1967). Effects of training at moderate altitude on physical performance capacity. *Journal of Applied Physiology, 23* (1), 85-89.

Fazey, J., & Hardy, L. (1988). *The inverted-U hypothesis: A catastrophe for sport psychology?* (BASS Monograph 1). Leeds, UK: White Line Press.

Fehr, B., & Russell, J.A. (1984). Concept of emotion viewed from a prototype perspective. *Journal of Experimental Psychology: General, 113* (3), 464-486.

Fender, L.K. (1989). Athlete burnout: Potential for research and intervention strategies. *Sport Psychologist, 3,* 63-71.

Fenz, W.D., & Epstein, S. (1967). Gradients of physiological arousal in parachutists as a function of an approaching jump. *Psychosomatic Medicine, 29* (1), 33-51.

Ferger, K. (1998). Saisonbegleitende Diagnose der individuellen Belastungs-Erholungsbilanz mit der athletenspezifischen Variante des EBF [The seasonal diagnosis of the individual recovery-stress state with the sport-specific recovery-stress questionnaire]. In D. Teipel, R. Kemper, & D. Heinemann (Eds.), *Sportpsychologische Diagnostik, Prognostik und Intervention* [Sportspsychological diagnosis, prognosis and intervention] (pp. 131-133). Köln: bps.

Ferguson, G.A., & Takane, Y. (1989). *Statistical analysis in psychology and education.* New York: McGraw-Hill.

Ferrario, V.F., Storza, C., Michielon, G., Mauro, F., & Miani, A. (1995). Morphological variation analysis: A new method to quantify the repeatability of sport actions. *Coaching and Sport Science Journal, 1* (3), 29-36.

Feshbach, S. (1964). The function of the aggression and regulation of aggressive drive. *Psychological Review, 71,* 257-272.

Fillingim, R.B., & Blumenthal, J.A. (1993). Psychological effects of exercise among the elderly. In P. Seraganian (Ed.), *Exercise psychology* (pp. 237-253). New York: Wiley.

Fillion, L., Tessier, R., Tawadros, E., & Mouton, C. (1989). Stress et immunité: Étude de validité d'une mesure de stress psychologique [Stress and immunity: A validation study of a measure of psychological stress]. *Canadian Psychology, 30,* 30-38.

Fisher, K.W., & Tangney, J.P. (1995). Self-conscious emotions and the affect revolution: Framework and overview. In J.P. Tangney & K.W. Fisher (Eds.), *Self-conscious emotions: The psychology of shame, guilt, embarrassment, and pride* (pp. 3-22). New York: Guilford Press.

Fleming, D. (1997-1998, December 29-January 5). Wrestling's dirty secret. *Sports Illustrated*, 134.

Flint, F. (1993). Seeing helps in believing: Modeling in injury rehabilitation. In D. Pargman (Ed.), *Psychological bases of sport injuries* (pp. 183-198). Morgantown, WV: Fitness Information Technology.

Folkman, S., & Lazarus, R.S. (1985). If it changes it must be a process: Study of emotion and coping during three stages of a college examination. *Journal Personality and Social Psychology, 48* (1), 150-170.

Folkman, S., & Lazarus, R.S. (1988a). Coping as a mediator of emotion. *Journal of Personality and Social Psychology, 54*, 466-475.

Folkman, S., & Lazarus, R.S. (1988b). The relationship between coping and emotion. *Social Science and Medicine, 26*, 309-317.

Ford, C.B. (1983). *The somatizing disorders: Illness as a way of life*. New York: Elsevier Biomedical.

Fordyce, W.E. (1976). *Behavioral methods for chronic pain and illness*. St. Louis: Mosby.

Fordyce, W.E. (1988). Pain and suffering: A reappraisal. *American Psychologist, 43* (4), 276-283.

Forgas, J.P. (1992). Affect in social judgements and decisions: A multi-process model. In M. Zanna (Ed.), *Advances in experimental social psychology* (Vol. 25, pp. 227-275). New York: Academic Press.

Forgas, J.P. (1995). Mood and judgement: The affect infusion model (AIM). *Psychological Review, 17*, 39-66.

Fox, E.L., Bowers, R.W., & Foss, M.L. (1989). *The physiological basis of physical education and athletics* (4th ed.). Dubuque, IA: Brown.

Frankenhaeuser, M. (1978). Psychoneuroendocrine approaches to the study of emotion as related to stress and coping. In H.E. Howe (Ed.), *Nebraska Symposium on Motivation* (pp. 123-161). Lincoln, NE: University of Nebraska.

Freeman, J.G. (1992). *Anger management for at-risk youth*. Paper presented at the meeting of the National Consultation on Vocational Counselling, January 21-23, Ottawa, Canada.

Frese, M. (1986). Coping as a moderator and mediator between stress at work and psychosomatic complaints. In M. Appley & R. Trumbull (Eds.), *Dynamics of stress* (pp. 183-206). New York: Plenum Press.

Freud, S. (1894). *The neuro-psychoses of defence* (Stand. ed., Vol. 3, pp. 45-61). London: Hogarth.

Freudenberger, H.J. (1974). Staff burnout. *Journal of Social Issues, 30*, 159-165.

Freudenberger, H.J., & Richelson, G. (1981). *Burnout: How to beat the high cost of success*. New York: Bantam Books.

Frijda, N. (1986). *The emotions*. Cambridge: Cambridge University Press.

Frijda, N.H. (1988). The laws of emotion. *American Psychologist, 43*, 349-358.

Frijda, N.H. (1989). Aesthetic emotions and reality. *American Psychologist, 44*, 1546-1547.

Frijda, N.H. (Ed.). (1993a). Appraisal and beyond: The issue of cognitive determinants of emotion. *Cognition and Emotion, 7*, 225-387.

Frijda, N.H. (1993b). Mood, emotion episodes, and emotions. In M. Lewis & J. Haviland (Eds.), *Handbook of emotions* (pp. 381-403). New York: Guilford Press.

Frijda, N.H. (1994). Emotions are functional, most of the time. In P. Ekman & R.J. Davidson (Eds.), *The nature of emotion: Fundamental questions* (pp. 112-123). New York: Oxford University Press.

Frijda, N.H., Kuipers, P., & ter Schure, E. (1989). Relations among emotion, appraisal, and emotional action readiness. *Journal of Personality and Social Psychology, 57*, 212-228.

Frijda, N.H., & Mesquita, B. (1994). The social roles and functions of emotions. In S. Kitayama & H. Markus (Eds.), *Emotion and culture* (pp. 51-87). Washington, DC: American Psychological Association.

Fromm, E. (1976). *Den destruktiva människan* [The destructive human being]. Stockholm: Natur & Kultur.

Fry, R.W., Grove, J.R., Morton, A.R., Zeroni, P.M., Gaudieri, S., & Keast, D. (1994). Psychological and immunological correlates of overtraining. *British Journal of Sports Medicine, 28*, 241-246.

Fry, R.W., Lawrence, S.R., Morton, A.R., Schreiner, A.B., Polglaze, T.D., & Keast, D. (1993). Monitoring training stress in endurance sports using biological parameters. *Clinical Journal of Sport Medicine, 3*, 6-13.

Fry, R.W., Morton, A.W., Garcia-Webb, P., Crawford, G.P.M., & Keast, D. (1992). Biological responses to overload training in endurance sports. *European Journal of Applied Physiology, 64*, 335-344.

Fry, R.W., Morton, A.R., and Keast, D. (1991). Overtraining in athletes. *Sports Medicine, 12* (1), 32-65.

Funkenstein, D.H., King, S.H., & Drolette, M.E. (1954). The direction of anger during a laboratory stress-inducing situation. *Psychosomatic Medicine, 16*, 404-413.

Funkenstein, D.H., King, S.H., & Drolette, M.E. (1957). *Mastery of stress.* Cambridge: Harvard University Press.

Fuqua, D.R., Leonard, E., Masters, M.A., Smith, R.J., Campbell, J.L., & Fischer, P.C. (1991). A structural analysis of the State-Trait Anger Expression Inventory (STAXI). *Educational and Psychological Measurement, 51*, 439-446.

Ganzen, V.A. (1984). *Systemnyje Opisanija v Psikhologii* [Systems descriptions in psychology]. Leningrad: Leningrad University Press.

Garfield, C.A., & Bennett, H.Z. (1984). *Peak performance: Mental training techniques of the world's greatest athletes.* Los Angeles: Tarcher.

Gauvin, L., & Rejeski, W.J. (1993). The Exercise-Induced Feeling Inventory: Development and initial validation. *Journal of Sport and Exercise Psychology, 15*, 403-423.

Gauvin, L., & Spence, J.C. (1998). Measurement of exercise-induced changes in feeling states, affect, mood, and emotions. In J.L. Duda (Ed.), *Advances in sport and exercise psychology measurement* (pp. 325-336). Morgantown, WV: Fitness Information Technology.

Genov, F. (1976). The nature of the mobilization readiness of the sportsman and the influence of different factors upon its formation. In A.C. Fisher (Ed.), *Psychology of sport: Issues and insights* (pp. 145-155). Palo Alto, CA: Mayfield.

Getchell, B. (1992). *Physical fitness: A way of life.* New York: Macmillan.

Gibbs, J.C. (1996). Equipping youth with mature moral judgement. *Journal of Emotional and Behavioral Problems, 5* (3), 156-162.

Gieck, J. (1990). Psychological consideration of rehabilitation. In W.E. Prentice (Ed.), *Rehabilitation techniques in sports medicine* (pp. 107-122). St. Louis: Times Mirror/Mosby.

Gill, D.L. (1994). A sport and exercise psychology perspective on stress. *Quest, 46,* 20-27.

Gill, P. (1985). Idrottsvåld [Sport violence]. Halmstad: *Högskolan* [University College of Halmstad] *rapport* [report], 1.

Gissen, L.D. (1973). *Psihologiya i psyhogigiyena v sporte (Iz opyta raboty v komandah po akademicheskoi greble)* [Psychology and psychohygiene in sport. A summary of experiences of applied work in rowing teams]. Moscow: Fizkultura i sport.

Goldberger, L., & Breznitz, S. (1993). Stress research at a crossroads. In L. Goldberger & S. Breznitz (Eds.), *Handbook of stress* (pp. 3-6). New York: Free Press.

Gordon, S., Milios, D., & Grove, J.R. (1991). Psychological aspects of the injury recovery process from sport injury: The perspective of sport physiotherapists. *Australian Journal of Science and Medicine in Sport, 23* (2), 53-60.

Goss, J.D. (1994). Hardiness and mood in swimmers while overtraining. *Journal of Sport and Exercise Psychology, 6,* 135-149.

Gould, D. (1983). Future directions in youth sports participation research. In L. Wankel & R. Wilberg (Eds.), *Psychology of sports and motor behavior: Research and practice.* Edmonton: University of Alberta.

Gould, D. (1996). Personal motivation gone awry: Burnout in competitive athletes. *Quest, 48,* 275-289.

Gould, D., & Krane, V. (1992). The arousal-athletic performance relationship: Current status and future directions. In T.S. Horn (Ed.), *Advances in sport psychology* (pp. 119-141). Champaign, IL: Human Kinetics.

Gould, D., Pelitchkoff, L., & Weinberg, R. (1984). Antecedents of temporal changes in, and relationships between CSAI-2 subcomponents. *Journal of Sport Psychology, 6,* 289-304.

Gould, D., & Tuffey, S. (1996). Zones of optimal functioning research: A review and critique. *Anxiety, Stress, and Coping, 9* (1), 53-68.

Gould, D., Tuffey, S., Hardy, L., & Lochbaum, M. (1993). Multidimensional state anxiety and middle distance running performance: An exploratory examination of Hanin's (1980) zones of optimal functioning hypothesis. *Journal of Applied Sport Psychology, 5,* 85-95.

Gould, D., Tuffey, S., Udry, E., & Loehr, J. (1996). Burnout in competitive junior tennis players: II. Qualitative analysis. *The Sport Psychologist, 10,* 341-366.

Gould, D., Udry, E., Bridges, D., & Beck, L. (1996). *The psychology of ski racing injury rehabilitation: Final report.* Paper presented as part of U.S. Olympic Committee Sports Science and Technology Grant Project.

Gould, D., Udry, E., Tuffey, S., & Loehr, J. (1996). Burnout in competitive junior tennis players: I. A quantitative psychological assessment. *The Sport Psychologist, 10,* 322-340.

Graham, S. (1984). Communication sympathy and anger to black and white children: The cognitive (attributional) consequences of affective cues. *Journal of Personality and Social Psychology, 47,* 40-54.

Greenspan, M.J., & Feltz, D.L. (1989). Psychological interventions with athletes in competitive situations: A review. *The Sport Psychologist, 3* (3), 219-236.

Greer, D.L. (1983). Spectator booing and the home advantage: A study of social influence in the basketball arena. *Social Psychology Quarterly, 46,* 252-261.

Griffith, C.R. (1926). *Psychology of coaching.* New York: Scribner's.

Guay, F., & Vallerand, R.J. (1998). *On the assessment of situational intrinsic and extrinsic motivation: The Situational Motivation Scale.* Manuscript submitted for publication.

Guttmann, M.C., Pollock, M.L., Foster, C., & Schmidt, D. (1984). Training stress in Olympic speed skaters: A psychological perspective. *The Physician and Sportsmedicine, 12,* 45-57.

Haan, N. (1977). *A manual for interactional morality.* Berkeley: University of California.

Hackfort, D. (1996). The display of emotions in elite athletes. *American Journal of Sports Medicine, 24,* s80-s84.

Hackfort, D., & Schwenkmezger, P. (1989). Measuring anxiety in sports: Perspectives and problems. In D. Hackfort & C.D. Spielberger (Eds.), *Anxiety in sports: An international perspective* (pp. 55-74). New York: Hemisphere.

Hackfort, D., & Schwenkmezger, P. (1993). Anxiety. In R.N. Singer, M. Murphey, & L.K. Tennant (Eds.), *Handbook of research on sport psychology* (pp. 328-364). New York: Macmillan.

Hall, H.K., Kerr, A.K., & Matthews, J. (1998). Precompetitive anxiety in sport: The contribution of achievement goals and perfectionism. *Journal of Sport and Exercise Psychology, 20,* 194-217.

Hamill, G. (1996). *Psychological and physiological correlates of the individual zones of optimal functioning.* Unpublished EdD thesis, Boston University.

Hanin, Y.L. (1977). O srochnoj diagnostike sostojanija lichnosti v gruppe [On immediate diagnostics of personality's state in a group]. *Teoria i Praktika Fizicheskoj Kultury, 8,* 8-11.

Hanin, Y.L. (1978). A study of anxiety in sports. In W.F. Straub (Ed.), *Sport psychology: An analysis of athlete behavior* (pp. 236-249). Ithaca, NY: Mouvement.

Hanin, Y.L. (1980). *Psyhologiya obscheniya v sporte* [Psychology of communication in sport]. Moscow: Fuzkultura i sport.

Hanin, Y.L. (1983a). STAI in sport: Problems and perspectives. In E. Apitzsch (Ed.), *Anxiety in sport* (pp. 129-141). Magglingen, Switzerland: FEPSAC.

Hanin, Y.L. (Ed.). (1983b). *Stress i trevoga v sporte* [Stress and anxiety in sport]. Moscow: FIS. (In Russian; English summary)

Hanin, Y.L. (1985). *Psikhologuija Obshchenia v Sovmestnoj Dejatel'nosti* [Psychology of Communication in Group Activity]. (Unpublished manuscript).

Hanin, Y.L. (1986). State-trait anxiety research in the USSR. In C.D. Spielberger & R. Diaz-Guerrero (Eds.), *Cross cultural anxiety* (Vol. 3, pp. 45-64). Washington, DC: Hemisphere.

Hanin, Y.L. (1989). Interpersonal and intragroup anxiety in sports. In D. Hackfort & C.D. Spielberger (Eds.), *Anxiety in sports: An international perspective* (pp. 19-28). Washington, DC: Hemisphere.

Hanin, Y.L. (1991). Mezhlichnostanaja i vnutrigruppovaja trevoga v uslovijakh znachimoi sovmestnoj dejatel'nosti (Interpersonal and intragroup anxiety in important joint activity). *Voprosy Psykhologuii,* n. 5, pp. 56-64 (English summary).

Hanin, Y.L. (1992). Social psychology and sport: Communication processes in top performance teams. *Sport Science Review, 2,* 13-28.

Hanin, Y.L. (1993). Optimal performance emotions in top athletes. In S. Serpa, J. Alves, V. Ferreira, & A. Paula-Brito (Eds.), *Sport psychology: An integrated approach. Proceedings from the VIII World Congress of Sport Psychology* (pp. 229-232). Lisbon, Portugal: ISSP.

Hanin, Y.L. (1994). Optimization of performance emotions: Individual scaling of performance emotions. *Top performance: Proceedings of the 1st National Congress of Elite Finnish Coaches* (pp. 94-106). Jyväskylä, Finland: KIHU.

Hanin, Y.L. (1995). Individual zones of optimal functioning (IZOF) model: An idiographic approach to performance anxiety. In K. Henschen & W. Straub (Eds.), *Sport psychology: An analysis of athlete behavior* (pp. 103-119). Longmeadow, MA: Mouvement.

Hanin, Y.L. (1996). Performance anxiety in sports: New dimensions. In J. Mohan (Ed.). *Recent advances in sports psychology* (pp. 53-78). Delhi, India: Friends.

Hanin, Y.L. (1997a). Emotions and athletic performance: Individual zones of optimal functioning model. *European Yearbook of Sport Psychology, 1,* 29-72.

Hanin, Y.L. (1997b). Emotions and athletic performance. In *Proceedings, 1st International Meeting on Psychology Applied to Sport and Physical Activity* (pp. 27-48). Braga, Portugal: University of Minho.

Hanin, Y.L. (1997c). Emotions and athletic performance: What is beyond the zones? In *Fourth IOC World Congress on Sport Sciences. Training and care of athletes—current concepts and technologies.* Monte Carlo, October 22-25. Congress Proceedings, Addendum, p. 27.

Hanin, Y.L. (1999a). Sport psychology research and consultancy with elite athletes and coaches. In E. Muller, F. Ludescher, and G. Zallinger (Eds.), *Science in elite sport* (pp. 129-145). London: E & FN Spon/Routledge.

Hanin, Y.L. (1999b, in press). Soccer and emotions: Enhancing or impairing performance. In J. Bangsbo (Ed.), *Soccer and science.* Copenhagen: Copenhagen University Press.

Hanin, Y.L. (1999c, in press). *Sports-specific emotion-motivational profiling: An individualized assessment programme.* A workshop presented at the 10th FEPSAC Congress of Sport Psychology, July 7-11, 1999 Prague, Czech Republic.

Hanin, Y.L., & Bulanova, G.V. (1979). Emotsional'noje sostojanie studentov v sportivnyh i uchebnyh gruppah [Emotional state of students in sports and study groups]. *Teoria i Praktika Fizicheskoj Kultury, 4,* 45-47.

Hanin, Y.L., & Bulanova, G.V. (1981). Status i emotsional'noe samochuvstvie lichnosti v gruppakh raznogo urovnya razvitiya (Status and emotional state of a person in groups of different levels of development). *Voprosy Psykhologuii, 5,* 124-129.

Hanin, Y.L., Heliskoski, J., & Syrjä, P. (1997). Performance related states in skilled soccer players: A metaphoric description. Unpublished raw data. Research Institute for Olympic Sport, Jyväskylä, Finland.

Hanin, Y.L., Jokela, M., & Syrjä, P. (1998). *Emotion correlates of successful and poor performances: A comparison of individualised and group-oriented measures*. Paper presented at the 3rd Annual Congress of European College of Sport Science, July 15-18, Manchester, UK.

Hanin, Y.L., & Kopysov, V.S. (1977). Sostojanie sorevnuyuschegosya sportsmena pri obstchenii s pazlichnymy sekundantami [Athlete's emotional state in communication with different seconds]. *Teoria i Praktika Fizicheskoj Kul'tury, 11,* 37-39.

Hanin, Y.L., & Lukkarila, G. (1998). Emotional states in skilled ice-hockey players: A metaphoric description. Unpublished raw data. Research Institute for Olympic Sport. Jyväskylä, Finland.

Hanin, Y.L., & Stambulova, N.B. (1998). Metaphoric description of performance related states in skilled athletes. Unpublished raw data. Research Institute for Olympic Sport. Jyväskylä, Finland.

Hanin, Y.L., & Syrjä, P. (1995a). Performance affect in junior ice hockey players: An application of the individual zones of optimal functioning model. *The Sport Psychologist, 9,* 169-187.

Hanin, Y.L., & Syrjä, P. (1995b). Performance affect in soccer players: An application of the IZOF model. *International Journal of Sports Medicine, 16* (4), 264-269.

Hanin, Y.L., & Syrjä, P. (1996). Predicted, actual and recalled affect in Olympic-level soccer players: Idiographic assessments on individualized scales. *Journal of Sport and Exercise Psychology, 18* (3), 325-335.

Hanin, Y.L., & Syrjä, P. (1997). Optimal emotions in elite cross-country skiers. In E. Müller, H. Schwameder, E. Kornexl, & C. Raschner (Eds.), *Science and skiing* (pp. 408-419). London: SPON.

Hanne-Paparo, N. (1983). Overtraining in athletes. *Olympic Review, 194,* 829-832.

Hansel, T. (1985). *You gotta keep dancin'*. Elgin, IL: Life Journey Books.

Hanson, S.J., McCullagh, P., & Tonymon, P. (1992). The relationship of personality characteristics, life stress, and coping resources to athletic injury. *Journal of Sports and Exercise Psychology, 14,* 262-272.

Harburg, E., Erfurt, J.C., Hauenstein, L.S., Chape, C., Schull, W.J., & Schork, M.A. (1973). Socioecological stress, suppressed hostility, skin colour, and black-white male blood pressure: Detroit. *Psychosomatic Medicine, 35,* 276-296.

Hardy, C., & Crace, K. (1993). Dimensions of social support in dealing with sport injuries. In D. Pargman (Ed.), *Psychological bases of sport injuries* (pp. 121-144). Morgantown, WV: Fitness Information Technology.

Hardy, C.J., & Riehl, M.A. (1988). An examination of the life stress-injury relationship among noncontact sport participants. *Behavioral Medicine, 14,* 113-118.

Hardy, C.J., & Rejeski, W.J. (1989). Not what, but how one feels: The measurement of affect during exercise. *Journal of Sport and Exercise Psychology, 11,* 304-317.

Hardy, L. (1990). A catastrophe model of performance in sport. In J.G. Jones & L. Hardy (Eds.), *Stress and performance in sport* (pp. 81-106). Chichester: Wiley.

Hardy, L. (1996). Testing the predictions of the cusp catastrophe model of anxiety and performance. *The Sport Psychologist, 10,* 140-156.

Hardy, L., Jones, G., & Gould, D. (1997). *Understanding psychological preparation in sport.* New York: Wiley.

Harger, G.J., & Raglin, J.S. (1994). Correspondence between actual and recalled precompetition anxiety in collegiate track and field athletes. *Journal of Sport and Exercise Psychology, 16,* 206-211.

Harre, D. (1982). *Principles of sports training.* Berlin: Sportverlag.

Hasegawa, E. (1994). An analysis of anger-related aggression in rugby football competition. *Bulletin of Institute of Health and Sport Science* (University of Tsukuba), *17,* 69-82.

Hassmén, P., & Blomstrand, E. (1995). Mood state relationships and soccer team performance. *Sport Psychologist, 9,* 297-308.

Hatfield, E., Cacioppo, J.T., & Rapson, R. (1992). The logic of emotion: Emotional contagion. In M.S. Clark (Ed.), *Review of personality and social psychology: Vol. 14. Emotional and social behavior* (pp. 151-177). Newbury Park, CA: Sage.

Hatfield, E., Cacioppo, J.T., & Rapson, R.L. (1994). *Emotional contagion.* Cambridge: Cambridge University Press.

Hebb, D.O. (1949). *The organization of behavior.* New York: Wiley.

Hebb, D.O. (1976). Physiological learning theory. *Journal of Abnormal Child Psychology, 4* (4), 309-314.

Heil, J. (1993a, Summer). Sport injury risk: A psychological perspective. *Medical Proceedings/Lewis-Gale Clinic,* pp. 8-11.

Heil, J. (1993b). *Psychology of sport injury.* Champaign, IL: Human Kinetics.

Heil, J., Wakefield, C., & Reed, C. (1998). Patient as athlete: A metaphor for injury rehabilitation. *Psychotherapy Patient, 10* (3/4), 21-39.

Henschen, K.P. (1990). Prevention and treatment of athletic staleness and burnout. *Science Periodical on Research and Technology in Sport, 10,* 1-8.

Henschen, K. (1993). Athletic staleness and burnout: Diagnosis, prevention, and treatment. In J. Williams (Ed.), *Applied sport psychology: Personal growth to peak performance* (pp. 328-337). Palo Alto, CA: Mayfield.

Henschen, K.P. (1998). Athletic staleness and burnout: Diagnosis, prevention and treatment. In J.M. Williams (Ed.). *Applied sport psychology: Personal growth to peak performance* (3rd ed., pp. 30-39). Mountain View, CA: Mayfield.

Hess, U., & Kirouac, G. (in press). Emotion expression in groups. In M. Lewis & J. Haviland (Eds.), *Handbook of emotions* (2nd ed.). New York: Guilford Press.

Higgins, E.T. (1987). Self-discrepancy: A theory relating self and affect. *Psychological Review, 94,* 319-340.

Hill, A.B. (1965). The environment and disease: Association or causation? *Proceedings of the Royal Society of Medicine, 58,* 295-300.

Hill, S., Harries, U., & Popay, J. (1996). Is the short form 36 (SF-36) suitable for routine health outcomes assessment in health care for older people? Evidence from preliminary work in community based health services in England. *Journal of Epidemiology and Community Health, 50,* 94-98.

Hirt, E.R., Zillman, D., Erickson, G.A., & Kennedy, C. (1992). Costs and benefits of allegiance: Changes in fan's self-ascribed competencies after team victory versus defeat. *Journal of Personality and Social Psychology, 63,* 724-738.

Hodapp, V., & Benson, J. (1997). The multidimensionality of test anxiety: A test of different models. *Anxiety, Stress, and Coping, 10,* 219-244.

Hoehn-Saric, R., McLeod, D.R., & Zimmerli, W.D. (1989). Psychophysiological response patterns in panic disorder. *Acta Psychiatrica Scandinavica, 83,* 4-11.

Hoffman, M.L. (1985). Affect, cognition, and motivation. In E.T. Higgins & R.M. Sorrentino (Eds.), *Handbook of motivation and cognition: Foundations of social behavior.* New York: Guilford Press.

Hoffmann, P. (1997). The endorphin hypothesis. In W.P. Morgan (Ed.), *Physical activity and mental health* (pp. 163-177). Washington, DC: Taylor & Francis.

Holm, O. (1980). *Attributionsforskning* [Attributional research]. Research paper, HSFR.

Holmes, T.H., & Rahe, R.H. (1967). The social readjustment rating scale. *Journal of Psychosomatic Research, 11,* 213-218.

Hooper, S.L., & Mackinnon, L.T. (1995). Monitoring overtraining in athletes. *Journal of Sports Medicine, 20,* 321-327.

Hooper, S.L., Mackinnon, L.T., & Hanrahan, S. (1997). Mood state as an indication of staleness and recovery. *International Journal of Sport Psychology, 28,* 1-12.

Hooper, S.L., Mackinnon, L.T., Howard, A., Gordon, R.D., & Bachmann, A.W. (1995). Markers for monitoring overtraining and recovery. *Medicine and Science in Sports and Exercise, 27,* 106-112.

Horowitz, M.J., Wilner, M., & Alvarez, W. (1979). Impact of event scale: A measure of subjective stress. *Psychosomatic Medicine, 41,* 209-218.

Houmard, J.A. (1991). Impact of reduced training on performance in endurance athletes. *Sports Medicine, 12,* 380-393.

Hull, C.L. (1943). *Principles of behavior.* New York: Appleton.

Hume, D. (1957). *An inquiry concerning the principles of morals.* New York: Library of Liberal Arts.

Humphreys, M.S., & Revelle, W. (1984). Personality, motivation, and performance: A theory of the relationship between individual differences and information processing. *Psychological Review, 91* (2), 153-184.

Hunt, S.M., McEwan, J., & McKenna, S.P. (1986). *Measuring health status.* London: Croom Helm.

Hutzler, Y., & Bar-Eli, M. (1993). Psychological benefits for sports for disabled people: A review. *Scandinavian Journal of Medicine and Science in Sports, 3,* 217-228.

Hyvönen, A. (1992). *Mielialan Yhteys Kilpailusuoritukseen* [Pre-competition anxiety and performance]. Unpublished master's thesis, Jyväskylä University, Jyväskylä, Finland.

Ievleva, L., & Orlick, T. (1991). Mental links to enhanced healing: An exploratory study. *The Sport Psychologist, 5,* 25-40.

Il'in, E.P. (1980). *Psihofiziologija fizicheskogo vospitaniya* [Psychophysiology of physical education]. Moscow: Prosveschenije.

Imlay, G.J., Carda, R.D., Stanbrough, M.E., & O'Connor, P.J. (1995). Anxiety and performance: A test of optimal function theory. *International Journal of Sport Psychology, 26,* 295-306.

Isberg, L. (1985). Våldet inom idrotten. [Violence in sport]. En teoretisk diskussion och en empirisk analys AV begreppet regelvidrig handling i lagspelet ishockey [A theoretical discussion and empirical analysis of the concept irregular act in ice hockey]. Del I. *Pedagogisk Forskning* [Educational Research] *i Uppsala* nr 61.

Isberg, L. (1986). Studier AV uttalad och tillämpad tolkning AV regler. [Studies of spoken and applied interpretation of the rules]. Den metodologiska ansatsen. [The methodology. Part I, The elite level]. *Arbetsrapporter från Pedagogiska institutionen Uppsala universitet* [Working reports, Department of Education, University of Uppsala] nr 119.

Isberg, L. (1987). Våldet inom idrotten [Violence in sport]. En teoretisk diskussion och empirisk analys AV begreppet medvetenhet om att skada i lagspelet ishockey [A theoretical discussion and an empirical analysis of the concept awareness of injuring in ice hockey]. Del II. *Pedagogisk forskning* [Educational Research] *i Uppsala* nr 77.

Isberg, L. (1989). Våldet inom idrotten [Violence in sport]. En empirisk analys AV begreppen regelvidrig handling och medvetenhet om att skada i lagspelet ishockey [An empirical analysis of the concepts irregular act and awareness of injuring in ice hockey]. Del III. *Pedagogisk forskning* [Educational Research] *i Uppsala* nr 83.

Isen, A.M. (1993). Positive affect and decision making. In M. Lewis & J. Haviland (Eds.), *Handbook of emotions* (pp. 261-278). New York: Guilford Press.

Iso-Ahola, S.E. (1995). Intrapersonal and interpersonal factors in athletic performance. *Scandinavian Journal of Medicine and Science in Sports, 5,* 191-199.

Izard, C.E. (1971). *The face of emotion.* New York: Appleton-Century-Crofts.

Izard, C.E. (1977). *Human emotions.* New York: Plenum Press.

Izard, C.E. (1984). Emotion-cognition relationships and human development. In C.E. Izard, J. Kagan, & R.B. Zajonc (Eds.), *Emotions, cognition, and behavior* (pp. 17-37). New York: Cambridge University Press.

Izard, C.E. (1991). *The psychology of emotions.* New York: Plenum Press.

Izard, C. (1992). Basic emotions, relations among emotions, and emotion-cognition relations. *Psychological Review, 99,* 561-565.

Izard, C. (1993). Four systems for emotion activation: Cognitive and non-cognitive processes. *Psychological Review, 100,* 68-90.

Izard, C. (1994). Cognition is one of four types of emotions activating systems. In P. Ekman & R.J. Davidson (Eds.), *The nature of emotion: Fundamental questions* (pp. 203-207). New York: Oxford University Press.

Izard, C.E., Kagan, J., & Zajonc, R.B. (1984). *Emotions, cognition, and behavior.* Cambridge: Cambridge University Press.

Jackson, S.A. (1992). Athletes in flow: A qualitative investigation of flow states in elite figure skaters. *Journal of Applied Sport Psychology, 4* (2), 161-180.

Jackson, S.A. (1995). Factors influencing the occurrence of flow in elite athletes. *Journal of Applied Sport Psychology, 7* (2), 135-163.

Jackson, S.A. (1996). Toward a conceptual understanding of the flow experience in elite athletes. *Research Quarterly for Exercise and Sport, 67* (1), 76-90.

Jackson, S.A., Kimiecik, J.C., Ford, S., & Marsh, H.W. (1998). Psychological correlates of flow in sport. *Journal of Sport and Exercise Psychology, 4,* 358-378.

Jackson, S.A., & Marsh, H.W. (1996). Development and validation of a scale to measure optimal experience: The Flow State Scale. *Journal of Sport and Exercise Psychology, 18* (1), 17-35.

Jackson, S.A., & Roberts, G.C. (1992). Positive performance states of athletes: Toward a conceptual understanding of peak performance. *Sport Psychologist, 6* (2), 156-171.

Jackson, S.A., Thomas, P., Marsh, H.W., & Smethurst, C. (1999). *Optimal psychological states and strategies for athletic performance.* Unpublished manuscript.

James, W. (1884/1968). What is an emotion? *Mind, 9,* 188-205; reproduced in M.B. Arnold (Ed.), 1968, *The nature of emotions* (pp. 17-36).

Janis, I.L. (1958). *Psychological stress: Psychoanalytic and behavioral studies of surgical patients.* New York: Wiley.

Janke, W., Erdmann, G., & Kallus, K.W. (1985). *Der Streßverarbeitungsfragebogen (SVF)* [The Stress Coping Inventory]. Göttingen: Hogrefe.

Janke, W., & Wolffgramm, J. (1995). Biopsychologie von Stress und emotionalen Reaktionen: Ansätze interdisziplinärer Kooperation von Psychologie, Biologie und Medizin [Nonparametric methods for the provement of emotional reactions]. In G. Debus, G. Erdmann, & K.W. Kallus (Eds.), *Biopsychologie von Stress und emotionalen Reaktionen* [Biopsychology of stress and emotional responses] (pp. 293-347). Göttingen: Hogrefe.

Jenkins, C.D., Zyanski, S.J., & Rosenman, R.H. (1978). Coronary-prone behaviour: One pattern or several? *Psychosomatic Medicine, 40,* 25-43.

Jenkinson, C., Layte, R., Coulter, A., & Wright, L. (1996). Evidence for the sensitivity of the SF-36 health status measure to inequalities in health: Results from the Oxford Healthy Lifestyles Survey. *Journal of Epidemiology and Community Health, 50,* 377-380.

Jeukendrup, A.E., & Hesselinnk, M.K.C. (1994). Overtraining, what do lactate curves tell us? *British Journal of Sports Medicine, 28,* 239-240.

Jex, S.M. (1991). The psychological benefits of exercise in work settings: A review, critique, and dispositional model. *Work and Stress, 5,* 133-147.

Johnson, E. (1984). *Anger and anxiety as determinants of elevated blood pressure in adolescents.* Unpublished doctoral dissertation, University of South Florida, Tampa.

Johnson, J., Anderson, J., AhYee, M., & Makua, G. (1995). *Precompetition emotions in elite junior triathletes.* Paper presented at the Western Psychological Association Convention, March/April, Los Angeles.

Johnson-Laird, P.N., & Oatley, K. (1989). The language of emotions: An analysis of a semantic field. *Cognition and Emotion, 3,* 81-123.

Jokela, M., & Hanin, Y.L. (1997). Does the IZOF model discriminate between successful and less successful athletes? A meta-analysis. *Annual Congress of the European College of Sports Science. Book of abstracts* (Part II, pp. 637-638). Copenhagen: University of Copenhagen.

Jokela, M., & Hanin, Y.L. (in press) Does individual zones of optimal functioning model discriminate between successful and less successful athletes? A meta-analysis. *Journal of Sports Sciences.*

Jones, G. (1991). Recent developments and current issues in competitive state anxiety research. *The Psychologist, 4,* 152-155.

Jones, G. (1993). The role of performance profiling in cognitive behavioral interventions in sport. *The Sport Psychologist, 7,* 160-172.

Jones, G. (1995a). Competitive anxiety in sport. In S.J.H. Biddle (Ed.), *European perspectives on exercise and sport psychology* (pp. 128-153). Leeds, UK: Human Kinetics.

Jones, G. (1995b). More than just a game: Research developments and issues in competitive anxiety in sport. *British Journal of Psychology, 86,* 449-478.

Jones, J.G., & Hardy, L. (Eds.). (1990). *Stress and performance in sport.* Chichester: Wiley.

Kagan, J. (1989). *Unstable ideas: Temperament, cognition, and self.* Cambridge: Harvard University Press.

Kahneman, D. (1973). *Attention and effort.* Englewood Cliffs, NJ: Prentice Hall.

Kallus, K.W. (1995). *Der Erholungs-Belastungs-Fragebogen (EBF)* [The Recovery-Stress-Questionnaire]. Frankfurt: Swets & Zeitlinger.

Kallus, K.W., & Kellmann, M. (1995). The Recovery-Stress-Questionnaire for Coaches. In R. Vanfraechem-Raway & Y. Vanden Auweele (Eds.), *Proceedings of the IXth European Congress on Sports Psychology in Brussels* (Vol. 1, pp. 26-33). Brussels: FEPSAC/Belgian Federation of Sports Psychology.

Kallus, K.W., Kellmann, M., Eberspächer, H., & Hermann, H.-D. (1996). Beanspruchung, Erholung und Streßbewältigung von Trainern im Leistungssport [Strain, recovery, and coping with stress of coaches in elite sports]. *Psychologie und Sport, 3,* 114-126.

Kane, J.E. (1970). Personality and physical abilities. In G.S. Kenyon (Ed.), *Contemporary psychology of sport* (pp. 131-141). Chicago: Athletic Institute.

Karpovich, P.V. (1941). Fatigue and endurance. *Research Quarterly, 12,* 416-422.

Karteroliotis, C., & Gill, D.L. (1987). Temporal changes in psychological and physiological components of state anxiety. *Journal of Sport Psychology, 9,* 261-274.

Kaufmann, H. (1970). *Aggression and altruism.* New York: Holt, Reinhart & Winston.

Keidler, W.J. (1996). The caring classroom. When anger rears its ugly head. *Instructor, 7,* 24-25.

Kelley, B.C., & Gill, D.L. (1993). An examination of personal/situational variables, stress appraisal, and burnout in collegiate teacher-coaches. *Research Quarterly for Exercise and Sport, 64,* 94-102.

Kellmann, M. (1991). *Die Abbildung des Beanspruchungszustandes durch den Erholungs-Belastungs-Fragebogen: Untersuchungen zur Leistungsprädiktion im Sport* [The assessment of the recovery-stress state by the Recovery-Stress-Questionnaire: Studies dealing with performance prediction in sports]. Unpublished diploma thesis, University of Würzburg.

Kellmann, M. (1997). *Die Wettkampfpause als integraler Bestandteil der Leistungsoptimierung im Sport: Eine empirische psychologische Analyse* [The rest period as an integral part for optimizing performance in sports: An empirical psychological analysis]. Hamburg: Dr. Kovac.

Kellmann, M., & Günther, K.-D. (in press). Changes in stress and recovery in elite rowers during preparation for the Olympic Games. *Medicine and Science in Sports and Exercise.*

Kellmann, M., & Kallus, K.W. (1993). The Recovery-Stress-Questionnaire: A potential tool to predict performance in sports. In J.R. Nitsch & R. Seiler (Eds.), *Movement and sports: Psychological foundations and effects* (Vol. 1, pp. 242-247). St. Augustin, Germany: Academia.

Kellmann, M., & Kallus, K.W. (1994). Interrelation between stress and coaches' behavior during rest periods. *Perceptual and Motor Skills, 79,* 207-210.

Kellmann, M., & Kallus, K.W. (1999). Mood, recovery-stress state, and regeneration. In M. Lehmann, C. Forster, U. Gastmann, H. Keizer, & J.M. Steinacker (Eds.), *Overload, fatigue, performance incompetence, and regeneration in sport* (pp. 101-118). New York: Plenum.

Kellmann, M., & Kallus, K.W. (in press). *Der Erholungs-Belastungs-Fragebogen für Sportler; Handanweisung* [The Recovery-Stress-Questionnaire for Athletes; Manual]. Frankfurt: Swetz & Zeitlinger.

Kellmann, M., Kallus, K.W., Günther, K.-D., Lormes, W., & Steinacker, J.M. (1997). Psychologische Betreuung der Junioren-Nationalmannschaft des Deutschen Ruderverbandes [Psychological consultation of the German Junior National Rowing Team]. *Psychologie und Sport, 4,* 123-134.

Kellmann, M., Kallus, K.W., & Kurz, H. (1996). Performance prediction by the Recovery-Stress-Questionnaire. *Journal of Applied Sport Psychology, 8* (Suppl.), S22.

Kellmann, M., Kallus, K.W., Steinacker, J., & Lormes, W. (1997). Monitoring stress and recovery during the training camp for the Junior World Championships in rowing. *Journal of Applied Sport Psychology, 9* (Suppl.), S114.

Kelly, G.A. (1955). *The psychology of personal construct.* New York: Norton.

Kelmar, J.H. (1990). *Measurement of success and failure in small business—a dichotomous anachronism.* Paper presented at the 13th Small Firms Policy and Research Conference, November 14-16, Harrogate, England.

Kemler, D.D. (1988). *Level of athletic, instrumental, and reactive aggression between contact and non-contact, male and female high school athletes under pre- and post testing conditions.* Unpublished master's thesis, University of Oregon, College of Human Development and Performance.

Kemper, T.D. (1981). Social constructionist and positivistic approaches to the sociology of emotions. *American Journal of Sociology, 87,* 337-362.

Kemper, T.D. (1987). How many emotions are there? Wedding the social and the autonomic components. *American Journal of Sociology, 93,* 263-289.

Kenttä, G., & Hassmén, P. (1998). Overtraining and recovery. *Sports Medicine, 26,* 1-16.

Kereszty, A. (1971). Overtraining. In L.A. Larson & D.E. Herrman (Eds.), *Encyclopedia of sport sciences and medicine* (pp. 218-222). New York: Macmillan.

Kerr, J.H. (1989). Anxiety, arousal, and sport performance: An application of reversal theory. In D. Hackfort & C.D. Spielberger (Eds.), *Anxiety in sports: An international perspective* (pp. 137-151). New York: Hemisphere.

Kerr, J.H. (1993). An eclectic approach to psychological interventions in sport: Reversal theory. *The Sport Psychologist, 7,* 400-418.

Kerr, J.H. (1997). *Motivation and emotion in sport: Reversal theory.* East Sussex, UK: Psychology Press.

Kimiecik, J.C., & Harris, A.T. (1996). What is enjoyment: A conceptual/definitional analysis with implications for sport and exercise psychology. *Journal of Sport and Exercise Psychology, 18* (3), 247-263.

King, A.C., Taylor, C.B., Haskell, W.L., & DeBusk, R.F. (1989). Influence of regular aerobic exercise on psychological health: A randomized, controlled trial of healthy middle-aged adults. *Health Psychology, 8,* 305-324.

Kirwan, J.P., Costill, D.L., Flynn, M.G., Mitchell, J.B., Fink, W.J., Neufer, D., & Houmard, J.A. (1988). Physiological responses to successive days of intensive training in competitive swimmers. *Medicine and Science in Sports and Exercise, 20,* 255-259.

Klavora, P. (1978). An attempt to derive inverted-U curves based on the relationship between anxiety and athletic performance. In D.M. Landers & R.W. Christina (Eds.), *Psychology of motor behavior and sport, 1977* (pp. 369-377). Champaign, IL: Human Kinetics.

Klavora, P. (1979). Customary arousal for peak performance. In P. Klavora & J.V. Daniel (Eds.), *Coach, athlete, and sport psychologist* (pp. 155-163). Toronto: University of Toronto.

Kleine, D. (1990). Anxiety and sports performance: A meta-analysis. *Anxiety Research, 2,* 113-131.

Knapp, Guttmann, M., Foster, C., & Pollock, M. (1984). Self motivation among 1984 Olympic speedskating hopefuls and emotional response and adherence to training. *Medicine and Science in Sports and Exercise, 16,* 114.

Koltyn, K.F. (1997). The thermogenic hypothesis. In W.P. Morgan (Ed.), *Physical activity and mental health* (pp. 213-226). Washington, DC: Taylor & Francis.

Konttinen, N., Lyytinen, H., & Viitasalo, J. (1998). Preparatory heart rate patterns in competitive rifle shooting. *Journal of Sport Sciences, 16,* 235-242.

Kowal, J., & Fortier, M.S. (1999). Motivational determinants of flow: Contributions from self-determination theory. *Journal of Social Psychology, 139,* 355-368.

Krahé, B. (1986). Similar perceptions, similar reactions: An idiographic approach to cross-situational coherence. *Journal of Research in Personality, 20,* 349-361.

Krakauer, J. (1997). *Into thin air.* New York: Villard.

Krane, V. (1992). Conceptual and methodological considerations in sport anxiety research: From the inverted-U to catastrophe theory. *Quest, 44,* 72-87.

Krane, V. (1993). A practical application of the anxiety-athletic performance relationships: The zone of optimal functioning hypothesis. *The Sport Psychologist, 7,* 113-126.

Krane, V., Joyce, D., & Rayfeld, J. (1994). Competitive anxiety, situational criticality, and softball performance. *The Sport Psychologist, 8,* 58-72.

Krane, W., & Williams, J.M. (1994). Cognitive anxiety, somatic anxiety, and confidence in track and field athletes: The impact of gender, competitive level, and task characteristics. *International Journal of Sport Psychology, 25,* 203-217.

Krause, M.S. (1961). The measurement of transitory anxiety. *Psychological Review, 68,* 287-294.

Kreider, R.B., Fry, A.C., & O'Toole, M.L. (Eds.). (1998). *Overtraining in sport.* Champaign, IL: Human Kinetics.

Kreiner-Phillips, K. (1990, January). Psyche up for skiing. *Ski Colorado,* 111-114.

Kreiner-Philips, K., & Orlick, T. (1993). Winning after winning: The psychology of ongoing excellence. *The Sport Psychologist, 7,* 31-48.

Kreitler, H., & Kreitler, S. (1976). *Cognitive orientation and behavior.* New York: Springer.

Kubler-Ross, E. (1969). *On death and dying.* New York: Macmillan.

Kuipers, H. (1996). How much is too much? Performance aspects of overtraining. *Research Quarterly for Exercise and Sport, 67,* 65-69.

Kuipers, H., & Keizer, H.A. (1988). Overtraining in elite athletes: Review and directions for the future. *Sports Medicine, 6,* 79-92.

Lacey, J.I. (1959). Psychophysiological approaches to the evaluation of psychotherapeutic process and outcome. In E.A. Rubinstein & M.B. Parloff (Eds.), *Research in psychotherapy* (pp. 160-208). Washington, DC: American Psychological Association.

Lacey, J.I. (1967). Somatic patterning and stress: Some revisions of the activation theory. In M.H. Appley & R. Trumbell (Eds.), *Psychological stress* (pp. 14-37). New York: Appleton-Century-Crofts.

Lacey, J.I., Bateman, D.E., & Van Lehn, R. (1952). Autonomic response specificity and Rorschach color responses. *Psychosomatic Medicine, 14,* 256-260.

Lacey, J.I., & Lacey, B.C. (1958). Verification and extension of the principle of autonomic response stereotypy. *American Journal of Psychology, 71,* 50.

Lai, J.Y., & Linden, W. (1992). Gender, anger expression style, and opportunity for anger release determine cardiovascular reaction to and recovery from anger provocation. *Psychosomatic Medicine, 54* (3), 297-310.

Lakoff, G. (1987). *Women, fire and dangerous things: What categories reveal about mind.* Chicago: University of Chicago Press.

Landers, D.M. (1985). Psychophysiological assessment and biofeedback: Applications for athletes in closed skill sports. In J.J. Sandweiss & S. Wolf (Eds.), *Biofeedback and sport science* (pp. 63-105). New York: Plenum Press.

Landers, D.M. (1994). Performance, stress, and health: Overall reaction. *Quest, 46,* 123-135.

Landers, D.M., & Boutcher, S.H. (1986). Arousal-performance relationships. In J.M. Williams (Ed.), *Applied sport psychology* (pp. 163-184). Palo Alto, CA: Mayfield.

Landers, D.M., & Boutcher, S.H. (1993). Arousal-performance relationships. In J.M. Williams (Ed.), *Applied sport psychology: Personal growth to peak performance* (2nd ed., pp. 170-184). Mountain View, CA: Mayfield.

Landers, D.M., & Boutcher, S.H. (1998). Arousal-performance relationships. In J.M. Williams (Ed.), *Applied sport psychology: Personal growth to peak performance* (3rd ed., pp. 197-218). Mountain View, CA: Mayfield.

Landers, D.M., & Petruzzello, S.J. (1994). Physical activity, fitness and anxiety. In C. Bouchard, R.J. Shephard, & T. Stephens (Eds.), *Physical activity, fitness, and health* (pp. 868-882). Champaign, IL: Human Kinetics.

Lane, A., & Terry, P. (in press). Confirmatory factor analysis of the Competitive State Anxiety Inventory-2. *Journal of Sports Sciences.*

Lane, A., Terry, P., & Karageorghis, L. (1995). Antecedents of multidimensional competitive state anxiety and self-confidence in duathletes. *Perceptual and Motor Skills, 80,* 911-919.

Lang, P.J. (1984). Cognition in emotion: Concept and action. In C. Izard, J. Kagan, & R. Zajonc (Eds.), *Emotions, cognition and behavior* (pp. 192-226). New York: Cambridge University Press.

Lanzetta, J.T., & Orr, S.P. (1986). Excitatory strength of expressive faces: Effects of happy and fear expressions and context on the extinction of a conditioned fear response. *Journal of Personality and Social Psychology, 50,* 190-194.

Laux, L., & Weber, H. (1991). Presentation of self in coping with anger and anxiety: An intentional approach. *Anxiety Research, 3,* 233-255.

Lazarus, R.S. (1966). *Psychological stress and the coping process.* New York: McGraw-Hill.

Lazarus, R.S. (1968). Emotions and adaptations: Conceptual and empirical relations. In W.J. Arnold (Ed.), *Nebraska Symposium on Motivation* (pp. 175-266). New York/ Lincoln, NE: Nebraska University Press.

Lazarus, R.S. (1990). Theory-based stress measurement: With commentaries. *Psychological Inquiry, 1,* 3-51.

Lazarus, R.S. (1991a). Cognition and motivation in emotion. *American Psychologist, 46* (4), 352-367.

Lazarus, R.S. (1991b). *Emotion and adaptation.* New York: Oxford University Press.

Lazarus, R.S. (1991c). Progress on a cognitive-motivational-relational theory of emotion. *American Psychologist, 46,* 819-834.

Lazarus, R.S. (1993). From psychological stress to the emotions: A history of changing outlooks. *Annual Review of Psychology, 44,* 1-21.

Lazarus, R.S. (1994). Appraisal: The long and the short of it. In P. Ekman & R.J. Davidson (Eds.), *The nature of emotion: Fundamental questions* (pp. 181-234). New York: Oxford University Press.

Lazarus, R.S. (1999). *Stress and emotion: A new synthesis.* New York: Springer Publishing Co.

Lazarus, R.S., & Alfert, E. (1964). The short-circuiting of threat. *Journal of Abnormal and Social Psychology, 69,* 195-205.

Lazarus, R.S., & Averill, J.R. (1972). Emotion and cognition: With special reference to anxiety. In C.D. Spielberger (Ed.), *Anxiety: Current trends in theory and research* (Vol. 2, pp. 242-282). San Diego: Academic Press.

Lazarus, R.S., Averill, J.R., & Opton, E.M. Jr. (1970). Toward a cognitive theory of emotions. In M. Arnold (Ed.), *Feelings and emotions* (pp. 207-232). San Diego: Academic Press.

Lazarus, R.S., DeLongis, A., Folkman, S., & Gruen, R. (1985). Stress and adaptational outcomes: The problem of confounded measures. *American Psychologist, 40*, 770-779.

Lazarus, R.S., & Folkman, S. (1984). *Stress, appraisal, and coping.* New York: Springer-Verlag.

Lazarus, R.S., & Folkman, S. (1986). Cognitive theories and the issue of circularity. In M.H. Appley & R. Trumbull (Eds.), *Dynamics of stress* (pp. 63-80). New York: Plenum Press.

Lazarus, R.S., & Folkman, S. (1987). Transactional theory and research on emotions and coping. *European Journal of Personality, 1*, 141-169.

Lazarus, R.S., Kanner, A.D., & Folkman, S. (1980). Emotions: A cognitive-phenomenological analysis. In R. Plutchik & H. Kellerman (Eds.), *Theories of emotion: Vol. 1, Emotion: Theory, research, and experience* (pp. 189-217). San Diego: Academic Press.

Lazarus, R.S., & Smith, C.A. (1988). Knowledge and appraisal in the cognition-emotion relationship. *Cognition and Emotion, 2*, 281-300.

Lebra, T.S. (1983). Shame and guilt: A psychocultural view of the Japanese self. *Ethos, 11*, 192-209.

Ledoux, J.E. (1986). Sensory systems and emotion: A model of affective processing. *Integrative Psychiatry, 4*, 237-248.

Ledoux, J.E. (1989). Cognitive-emotional interactions in the brain. *Cognition and Emotion, 3*, 267-289.

Ledoux, J.E. (1993). Emotional networks in the brain. In M. Lewis & J. Haviland (Eds.), *Handbook of emotions* (pp. 109-118). New York: Guilford Press.

Lefavi, R.G., Reeve, T.G., & Newland, M.C. (1990). Relationship between anabolic steroid use and selected psychological parameters in male bodybuilders. *Journal of Sport Behavior, 13* (3), 157-166.

Lehman, A. (1968). Theory of affectivity. In M.B. Arnold (Ed.), *The nature of emotions* (pp. 37-42). Baltimore: Penguin Books. (Original work published 1914)

Lehmann, M., Foster, C., & Keul, J. (1993). Overtraining in endurance athletes: A brief review. *Medicine and Science in Sports and Exercise, 25*, 854-862.

Lehmann, M., Foster, C., Netzer, N., Lormes, W., Steinacker, J., Liu, Y., Opitz-Gress, A., & Gastmann, U. (1998). Physiological responses to short- and long-term overtraining in endurance athletes. In R.B. Kreider, A.C. Fry, & M.L. O'Toole (Eds.), *Overtraining in sport* (pp. 19-46). Champaign, IL: Human Kinetics.

Leith, L.M. (1994). *Foundations of exercise and mental health.* Morgantown, WV: Fitness Information Technology.

Leith, L.M., & Taylor, A.H. (1990). Psychological aspects of exercise: A decade literature review. *Journal of Sport Behavior, 13*, 219-239.

Lemyre, L., & Tessier, R. (1988). Mesure de stress psychologique (MSO) Se sentir stressée [A measure of psychological stress: To feel stressed out]. *Canadian Journal of Behavioral Science, 20*, 302-321.

Leontjev, A.N. (1975). *Deatel'nost. Soznanie. Lichnost* [Activity. Consciousness. Personality]. Moscow: Politizdat.

LeUnes, A.D., & Nation, J.R. (1996). *Sport psychology: An introduction.* Chicago: Nelson-Hall.

Levenson, R.W. (1988). Emotion and the autonomic nervous system: A prospectus for research on autonomic specificity. In H. Wagner (Ed.), *Social psychophysiology and emotion: Theory and clinical applications* (pp. 17-42). London: Wiley.

Levenson, R.W., Ekman, P., & Friesen, W.V. (1990). Voluntary facial action generates emotion-specific autonomous nervous system activity, *Psychophysiology, 27,* 363-384.

Leventhal, H. (1974). Emotion: A basic problem for social psychology. In C. Nemeth (Ed.), *Social psychology—classic and contemporary integrations* (pp. 1-51). Chicago: Rand McNally.

Leventhal, H. (1982). The integration of emotion and cognition: A view from the perceptual-motor theory of emotion. In M. Clark & S. Fiske (Eds.), *Affect and cognition: The 17th Annual Carnegie Symposium on Cognition* (pp. 123-156). Hillsdale, NJ: Erlbaum.

Leventhal, H. (1984). A perceptual-motor theory of emotion. In K.R. Scherer & P. Ekman (Eds.), *Approaches to emotion* (pp. 271-291). Hillsdale, NJ: Erlbaum.

Levy, R.I. (1973). *Tahitians: Mind and experience in the Society Islands.* Chicago: University of Chicago Press.

Levy, R.I. (1984). Emotion, knowing, and culture. In R.A. Shweder & R.A. LeVine (Eds.), *Culture theory: Essays on mind, self, and emotion* (pp. 214-237). Cambridge: Cambridge University Press.

Lewis, M., & Haviland, J. (1993). *Handbook of emotions.* New York: Guilford Press.

Lewthwaite, R. (1990). Threat perception in competitive trait anxiety: The endangerment of important goals. *Journal of Sport and Exercise Psychology, 12,* 280-300.

Liebert, R.M., & Morris, L.W. (1967). Cognitive and emotional components of test anxiety: A distinction and some initial data. *Psychological Reports, 20,* 975-978.

Liukkonen, J. (1995). Regulation of performance emotions in sports. In J.T. Viitasalo & U. Kujala (Eds.), *The way to win: Proceedings of the International Congress on Applied Research in Sports* (pp. 317-322). Helsinki, Finland: Finnish Society for Research in Sport and Physical Education.

Loehr, J.E. (1982a). *Athletic excellence: Mental toughness training for sport.* Denver, CO: Forum.

Loehr, J.E. (1982b). *Mental toughness training for sports. Achieving athletic excellence.* A Plume Book. New York: Forum.

Loehr, J.E. (1994). *The new toughness training for sports.* New York: Penguin Books.

Lomov, B.F. (1984). *Metodologicheskie i teoreticheskie problemy psyhologii* [Methodological and theoretical problems in psychology]. Moscow: Nauka.

Long, B.C., & van Stavel, R. (1995). Effects of exercise training on anxiety: A meta-analysis. *Journal of Applied Sport Psychology, 7,* 167-189.

Lord, F.M., & Novick, M.R. (1968). *Statistical theories of mental test scores.* Reading, MA: Addison-Wesley.

Lorenz, K. (1969). *Aggression—det så kallade onda* [Aggression—the evil]. Stockholm: Norstedts.

Lorr, M., McNair, D., & Fisher, S. (1982). Evidence for bipolar mood states. *Journal of Personality Assessment, 46*, 432-436.

Lorr, M., McNair, D.M., Weinstein, G.J., Michaux, W.W., & Raskin, A. (1961). Mepbromate and chlorpromazine in psychotherapy. *Archives of General Psychiatry, 4*, 381-389.

Lubin, B. (1965). Adjective checklists for measurement of depression. *Archives of General Psychiatry, 12*, 57-62.

Lutz, C., & White, G.M. (1986). The anthropology of emotions. *Annual Review of Anthropology, 15*, 405-436.

Mace, R., & Baines, C. (1989). Personality characteristics and mood states of females in sport. *Physical Education Review, 12* (2), 158-163.

Machac, M. (1976). *Harmonizing of mental states and performance.* Praha: Univerzita Karlova.

Maddux, J.E. (1997). Habit, health, and happiness. *Journal of Sport and Exercise Psychology, 19*, 331-346.

Mahoney, M.J. (1989). Sport psychology. In I.S. Cohen (Ed.), *The G. Stanley Hall Lectures* (Vol. 9, pp. 101-134). Washington, DC: American Psychological Association.

Mahoney, M.J., & Avener, M. (1977). Psychology of the elite athlete: An exploratory study. *Cognitive Therapy and Research, 1*, 135-141.

Males, J.R., & Kerr, J.H. (1996). Stress, emotion, and performance in elite slalom canoeists. *Sport Psychologist, 10*, 17-36.

Malmo, R.B. (1959). Activation: A neuropsychological dimension. *Psychological Review, 66* (6), 367-385.

Mandler, G. (1984). *Mind and body: Psychology of emotion and stress.* New York: Norton.

Marion, M. (1994). Encouraging the development of responsible anger management in young children. *Journal of Early Child Development and Care, 97*, 155-163.

Markland, D., Emberton, M., & Tallon, R. (1997). Confirmatory factor analysis of the Subjective Exercise Experiences Scale among children. *Journal of Sport and Exercise Psychology, 19*, 418-433.

Markus, H., & Zajonc, R. (1985). The cognitive perspective in social psychology. In G. Lindzey & E. Aronson (Eds.), *Handbook of social psychology* (3rd ed., Vol. 1, pp. 137-230). New York: Random House.

Marris, P. (1975). *Loss and change.* Garden City, NY: Anchor Books.

Marsh, H.W., & Jackson, S.A. (in press). Flow experience in sport: Construct validation of multidimensional, hierarchical state and trait responses. *Structural Equation Modeling.*

Marshall, G.D., & Zimbardo, P.G. (1979). Affective consequences of inadequately explained physiological arousal. *Journal of Personality and Social Psychology, 37*, 970-988.

Martens, R. (1971). Anxiety and motor behavior. *Journal of Motor Behavior, 3*, 151-179.

Martens, R. (1974). Arousal and motor performance. In J.H. Wilmore (Ed.), *Exercise and sport sciences reviews* (Vol. 2, pp. 155-188). New York: Academic Press.

Martens, R. (1977). *Sport Competition Anxiety Test*. Champaign, IL: Human Kinetics.

Martens, R. (1987). *Coaches guide to sport psychology*. Champaign, IL: Human Kinetics.

Martens, R., & Landers, D.M. (1970). Motor performance under stress: A test of the inverted-U hypothesis. *Journal of Personality and Social Psychology, 16,* 29-37.

Martens, R., Vealey, R.S., & Burton, D. (1990). *Competitive anxiety in sport*. Champaign, IL: Human Kinetics.

Martinsen, E.W., Medhus, A., & Sandvik, L. (1985). Effects of aerobic exercise on depression. A controlled study. *British Medical Journal, 291,* 109.

Martinsen, E.W., & Stephens, T. (1994). Exercise and mental health in clinical and free-living populations. In R.K. Dishman (Ed.), *Advances in exercise adherence* (pp. 55-72). Champaign, IL: Human Kinetics.

Maslach, C. (1979). Negative emotional biasing of unexplained arousal. *Journal of Personality and Social Psychology, 37,* 953-969.

Maslach, C. (1982a). *Burnout, the cost of caring*. Englewood Cliffs, NJ: Prentice Hall.

Maslach, C. (1982b). Understanding burnout: Definitional issues in analyzing a complex phenomenon: In W.S. Paine (Ed.), *Job stress and burnout: Research, theory, and intervention perspectives* (pp. 29-40). Beverly Hills, CA: Sage.

Maslach, C., & Jackson, S.E. (1981a). *Maslach Burnout Inventory*. Palo Alto, CA: Consulting Psychologists Press.

Maslach, C., & Jackson, S.E. (1981b). The measurement of experienced burnout. *Journal of Occupational Behavior, 2,* 99-113.

Maslach, C., & Jackson, S.E. (1986). *Maslach Burnout Inventory*. Palo Alto, CA: Consulting Psychologists Press.

Maslach, C., Jackson, S.E., & Leiter, M.P. (1996). *Maslach Burnout Inventory. Manual* (3rd ed.). Palo Alto, CA: Consulting Psychologists Press.

Maslach, C., & Leiter, M.P. (1997). *The truth about burnout*. San Francisco: Jossey-Bass.

Maslow, A. (1968). *Toward a psychology of being* (2nd ed.). New York: Van Nostrand Reinhold.

Mason, J.W. (1975). Emotion as reflected in patterns of endocrine integration. In L. Levi (Ed.), *Emotions: Their parameters and measurement* (pp. 143-181). New York: Raven Press.

Mason, J.W., Maher, J.T., Hartley, L.H., Mougey, E., Perlow, M.J., & Jones, L.G. (1976). Selectivity of corticosteroid and catecholamine responses to various natural stimuli. In G. Serban (Ed.), *Psychopathology of human adaptation* (pp. 147-171). New York: Plenum Press.

Massimini, F., & Carli, M. (1988). The systematic assessment of flow in daily experience. In M. Csikszentmihalyi & I. Csikszentmihalyi (Eds.), *Optimal experience: Psychological studies of flow in consciousness* (pp. 266-287). Cambridge: Cambridge University Press.

Massimini, F., Delle Fave, A., & Bassi, M. (1997). *ESM study of the quality of experience under extreme conditions: A climbing expedition in the Himalayas*. Unpublished manuscript.

Matthews, K.A., Glass, D.C., Rosenman, R.H., & Bortner, R.W. (1977). Competitive drive, Pattern A, and coronary heart disease: A further analysis of some data from the Western Collaborative Group Study. *Journal of Chronic Diseases, 30*, 489-493.

Mausner, J.S., & Kramer, S. (1985). *Epidemiology: An introductory text.* Philadelphia: Saunders.

McAuley, E. (1985). Success and causality in sport: The influence of perception. *Journal of Sport Psychology, 7*, 13-22.

McAuley, E. (1991). Efficacy, attributional, and affective responses to exercise participation. *Journal of Sport and Exercise Psychology, 13*, 382-393.

McAuley, E. (1994). Physical activity and psychosocial outcomes. In C. Bouchard, R.J. Shephard, & T. Stephens (Eds.), *Physical activity, fitness and health* (pp. 551-568). Champaign, IL: Human Kinetics.

McAuley, E., & Courneya, K.S. (1992). Self-efficacy relationships with affective and exertion responses to exercise. *Journal of Applied Social Psychology, 22*, 312-326.

McAuley, E., & Courneya, K. (1994). The Subjective Exercise Experiences Scale (SEES): Development and preliminary validation. *Journal of Sport and Exercise Psychology, 16*, 163-177.

McAuley, E., & Duncan, T.E. (1989). Causal attributions and affective reactions to disconfirming outcomes in motor performances. *Journal of Sport and Exercise Psychology, 11*, 187-200.

McAuley, E., & Duncan, T.E. (1990). Cognitive appraisal and affective reactions following physical achievement outcomes. *Journal of Sport and Exercise Psychology, 12*, 415-426.

McAuley, E., Mihalko, S.L., & Rosengren, K. (1997). Self-efficacy and balance correlates of fear falling in the elderly. *Journal of Aging and Physical Activity, 5*, 329-340.

McAuley, E., Poag, K., Gleason, A., & Wraith, S. (1990). Attrition from exercise programs: Attributional and affective perspectives. *Journal of Social Behavior and Personality, 5*, 591-602.

McAuley, E., & Rudolph, D. (1995). Physical activity, aging, and psychological well-being. *Journal of Aging and Physical Activity, 3*, 67-96.

McAuley, E., Russell, D., & Gross, J.B. (1983). Affective consequences of winning and losing: An attributional analysis. *Journal of Sport Psychology, 5*, 278-287.

McCann, S.C., Murphy, S.M., & Raedeke, T.D. (1992). The effect of performance setting and individual differences on the anxiety-performance relationships for elite cyclists. *Anxiety, Stress, and Coping, 5*, 177-187.

McCarthy, J.F., & Kelly, B.R. (1978). Aggression performance variables and anger self-report in ice hockey players. *Journal of Psychology, 99* (1), 97-101.

McCrae, R.R., & Costa, P.T. Jr. (1987). Validation of a five-factor model of personality across instruments and observers. *Journal of Personality and Social Psychology, 52*, 81-90.

McDonald, D.G., & Hodgdon, J.A. (1991). *Psychological effects of aerobic fitness training: Research and theory.* New York: Springer-Verlag.

McDonald, S.A, & Hardy, C.J. (1990). Affective response patterns of the injured athlete: An exploratory analysis. *The Sport Psychologist, 4*, 261-274.

McFarland, C., & Ross, M. (1982). Impact of causal attributions on affective reactions to success and failure. *Journal of Personality and Social Psychology, 43,* 937-946.

McGowan, R.W., & Schultz, B.B. (1989). Task complexity and affect in collegiate football. *Perceptual and Motor Skills, 69* (2), 671-674.

McNair, D.M., Lorr, M., & Droppleman, L.F. (1971). *Profile of Mood State manual.* San Diego: Educational and Industrial Testing Service.

McNair, D.M., Lorr, M., & Droppleman, L.F. (1981). *Manual for the Profile of Mood State.* San Diego: Educational and Industrial Testing Service.

McNair, D.M., Lorr, M., & Droppleman, L.F. (1992). *Profile of Mood States manual.* San Diego: Educational and Industrial Testing Service.

McReynolds, P. (1990). Motives and metaphors: A study in scientific creativity. In D.E. Leary (Ed.), *Metaphors in the history of psychology* (pp. 133-172). Cambridge: Cambridge University Press.

Mechanic, D. (1962). *Students under stress: A study of the social psychology of adaptation.* New York: Free Press. (Reprinted in 1978 by University of Wisconsin Press)

Mehrabian, A., & Russell, J.A. (1974). *An approach to environmental psychology.* Cambridge, MA: MIT Press.

Meichenbaum, D., & Turk, D. (1987). *Facilitating treatment adherence: A practitioners guidebook.* New York: Plenum Press.

Mellerowicz, H., & Barron, D.K. (1971). Overtraining. In L.A. Larson & D.E. Herrman (Eds.), *Encyclopedia of sport sciences and medicine* (pp. 110-131). New York: Macmillan.

Melzack, R., & Wall, P.D. (1965). Pain mechanisms: A new theory. *Science, 150,* 971-979.

Merskey, H. (1986). *Pain* (Suppl. 3), S1-S226.

Meyer, J.P., & Mulherin, A. (1980). From attribution to helping: An analysis of the mediating effects of affect and expectancy. *Journal of Personality and Social Psychology, 39,* 201-210.

Meyer, W.-V. (1988). Die rolle von überraschung im attributionsprozess [The role of surprise in the process of causal attribution]. *Psychologische Rundschau, 39,* 136-147.

Meyer, W.-V., Niepel, M., Rudolph, U., & Schützwohl, A. (in press). An experimental analysis of surprise. *Cognition and Emotion.*

Mihalko, S., McAuley, E.L., & Bane, S.M. (1996). Self-efficacy and affective responses to acute exercise in middle-aged adults. *Journal of Social Behavior and Personality, 11,* 375-385.

Millenson, J.R. (1967). *Principles and behavioral analysis.* New York: Macmillan.

Moneta, G.B., & Csikszentmihalyi, M. (1996). The effect of perceived challenges and skills on the quality of subjective experience. *Journal of Personality, 64,* 275-310.

Mook, J., Van der Ploeg, H.M., & Kleijn, W.C. (1992). Symptom-positive and symptom-negative items in the state-trait anxiety inventory: A comparison and replication. *Anxiety, Stress, and Coping, 5,* 113-123.

Moger, L.J., & Raglin, J.S. (1998). Mood state and vertical jump during a season of competition in college volleyball players. *Medicine and Science in Sports and Exercise* (abstract).

Morgan, W.P. (1980a, July). Test of champions. *Psychology Today,* 92-99.

Morgan, W.P. (1980b). The trait psychology controversy. *Research Quarterly for Exercise and Sport, 51,* 50-76.

Morgan, W.P. (1985). Selected psychological factors limiting performance: A mental health model. In D.H. Clarke & H.M. Eckert (Eds.), *Limits of human performance* (pp. 70-80). Champaign, IL: Human Kinetics.

Morgan, W.P. (1997a). Methodological considerations. In W.P. Morgan (Ed.), *Physical activity and mental health* (pp. 3-32). Washington, DC: Taylor & Francis.

Morgan, W.P. (1997b). Mind games: The psychology of sport. In D. Lamb & R. Murray (Eds.), *Recent advances in the science and medicine of sports* (pp. 1-31). Carmel, IN: Benchmark Press.

Morgan, W.P. (1997c). *Physical activity and mental health.* Washington, DC: Taylor & Francis.

Morgan, W.P., Brown, D.R., Raglin, J.S., O'Connor, P.J., & Ellickson, K.A. (1987). Psychological monitoring of overtraining and staleness. *British Journal of Sports Medicine, 21,* 107-114.

Morgan, W.P., Costill, D.L., Flynn, M.G., Raglin, J.S., & O'Connor, P.J. (1988). Mood disturbances following increased training in swimmers. *Medicine and Science in Sports and Exercise, 23,* 408-414.

Morgan, W.P., & Ellickson, K.A. (1989). Health, anxiety, and physical exercise. In D. Hackfort & C.D. Spielberger (Eds.), *Anxiety in sports: An international perspective* (pp. 165-182). New York: Hemisphere.

Morgan, W.P., O'Connor, P.J., Ellickson, K.A., & Bradley, P.W. (1988). Personality structure, mood states, and performance in elite male distance runners. *International Journal of Sport Psychology, 19,* 247-263.

Morgan, W.P., O'Connor, P.J., Sparling, P.J., & Pate, R.R. (1987). Psychological characterization of the elite female distance runner. *International Journal of Sports Medicine, 8,* 3124-3131.

Moses, J., Steptoe, A., Mathews, A., & Edwards, S. (1989). The effects of exercise training on mental well-being in the normal population: A controlled trial. *Journal of Psychosomatic Research, 33,* 47-61.

Muldoon, M.F., Barger, S.D., Flory, J.D., & Manuck, S.B. (1998). What are quality of life measurements measuring? *British Medical Journal, 316,* 542-545.

Murphy, M., & White, R. (1995). *In the zone.* New York: Penguin Books.

Murphy, S.M., Fleck, S.J., Dudley, G., & Callister, R. (1990). Psychological and performance concomitants of increased volume training in elite athletes. *Journal of Applied Sport Psychology, 2,* 34-50.

Mutrie, N. (in press). The relationship between physical activity and clinically defined depression. In S.J.H. Biddle, K. Fox, & S. Boutcher (Eds.). *Physical activity and psychological well-being.* London: Routledge.

Mutrie, N., & Biddle, S.J.H. (1995). The effects of exercise on mental health in nonclinical populations. In S.J.H. Biddle (Ed.), *European perspectives on exercise and sport psychology* (pp. 50-70). Champaign, IL: Human Kinetics.

Näätänen, R. (1973). The inverted-U relationship between activation and performance: A critical review. In S. Kornblum (Ed.), *Attention and performance IV*. New York: Academic Press.

Neiss, R. (1988). Reconceptualizing arousal: Psychobiological states in motor performance. *Psychological Bulletin, 103* (3), 345-366.

Neufer, P.D. (1989). The effect of detraining and reduced training volume on the physiological adaptations to aerobic exercise training. *Sports Medicine, 8,* 302-321.

Newcomer, R.R., Roh, J.L., Perna, F.M., & Etzel, E.F. (1998, September). Injury as a traumatic experience: Intrusive thoughts and avoidance behavior associated with injury among college student athletes. Paper presented at the Annual Conference of the Association for the Advancement of Applied Sport Psychology, Hyannis, MA.

Newton, M., & Duda, J.L. (1993). The relationship of task and ego orientation to performance: Cognitive content, affect, and attributions in bowling. *Journal of Sport Behavior, 16,* 209-220.

Nicholls, J. (1984). Achievement motivation: Conceptions of ability, subjective experience, task choice, and performance. *Psychological Review, 91,* 328-346.

Nideffer, R.M. (1978). *Predicting human performance: A theory and test of attentional and interpersonal style.* San Diego: Enhanced Performance Associates.

Niedenthal, P.M., & Setterlund, M.B. (1994). Emotion congruence in perception. *Personality and Social Psychology Bulletin, 20,* 401-411.

Nisbett, R.E., & Wilson, T.D. (1977). Telling more than we know: Verbal reports on mental processes. *Psychological Review, 84,* 231-259.

Nitsch, J.R. (1975). Sportliches Handeln als Handlungsmodell [Sports actions as action model]. *Sportwissenschaft, 5* (1), 39-55.

North, T.C., McCullagh, P., & Tran, Z.V. (1990). Effect of exercise on depression. *Exercise and Sport Sciences Reviews, 18,* 379-415.

Novaco, R.W. (1975). *Anger control: The development and evaluation of an experimental treatment.* Lexington, MA: Heath, Lexington.

Ntoumanis, N., & Biddle, S.J.H. (in press-a). Affect and achievement goals in physical activity: A meta-analysis. *Scandinavian Journal of Medicine and Science in Sports.*

Ntoumanis, N., & Biddle, S.J.H. (in press-b). A review of motivational climate in physical activity. *Journal of Sports Sciences.*

O'Connor, P.J. (1997). Overtraining and staleness. In W.P. Morgan (Ed.), *Physical activity and mental health* (pp. 149-160). Washington, DC: Taylor & Francis.

O'Connor, P.J., Aenchbacher, L.E., & Dishman, R.K. (1993). Physical activity and depression in the elderly. *Journal of Aging and Physical Activity, 1,* 34-58.

O'Connor, P.J., Morgan, W.P., & Raglin, J.S. (1991). Psychobiological effects of 3 days of increased training in female and male swimmers. *Medicine and Science in Sports and Exercise, 23,* 1055-1061.

O'Connor, P.J., Morgan, W.P., Raglin, J.S., Barksdale, C.N., & Kalin, N.H. (1989). Mood state and salivary cortisol levels following overtraining in female swimmers. *Psychoneuroendocrinology, 14,* 303-310.

O'Toole, M.L. (1998). Overreaching and overtraining in endurance athletes. In R.B. Kreider, A.C. Fry, & M.L. O'Toole (Eds.), *Overtraining in sport* (pp. 3-17). Champaign, IL: Human Kinetics.

Oatley, K., & Jenkins, J.M. (1992). Human emotions: Functions and dysfunction. *Annual Review of Psychology, 43*, 55-85.

Oatley, K., & Jenkins, J.M. (1996). *Understanding emotions.* Cambridge, MA: Blackwell Scientific.

Ogilvie, B.C., & Tutko, T.A. (1966). *Problem athletes and how to handle them.* London: Pelham Books.

Orlick, T. (1986). *Psyching for sport.* Champaign, IL: Human Kinetics.

Orlick, T. (1990). *In pursuit of excellence.* Champaign, IL: Leisure Press.

Ortony, A., & Clore, G.L. (1981). Disentangling the affective lexicon. *Proceedings of the Third Annual Conference of the Cognitive Science Society, 3*, 90-95.

Ortony, A., & Clore, G.L. (1989). Emotions, moods, and conscious awareness: Comment on Johnson-Laird and Oatley's "The language of emotions: An analysis of a semantic field." *Cognition and Emotion, 3*, 125-137.

Ortony, A., Clore, G.L., & Collins, A. (1988). *The cognitive structure of emotions.* Cambridge: Cambridge University Press.

Ortony, A., Clore, G.L., & Foss, M.A. (1987). The referential structure of emotions. *Cognitive Science, 11*, 341-364.

Ostrow, A.C. (1996). *Directory of psychological tests in the sport and exercise sciences* (2nd ed.). Morgantown, WV: Fitness Information Technology.

Oxendine, J.B. (1970). Emotional arousal and motor performance. *Quest, 13*, 23-32.

Oxford English reference dictionary (1996). (2nd ed.) Oxford: Oxford University Press.

Papousek, H., & Papousek, M. (1974). Mirror-image and self-recognition in young human infants: A new method of experimental analysis. *Developmental Psychobiology, 7*, 149-157.

Parfitt, G., Markland, D., & Holmes, C. (1994). Responses to physical exertion in active and inactive males and females. *Journal of Sport and Exercise Psychology, 16*, 178-186.

Pargman, D. (Ed.). (1993). *Psychological bases of sport injuries.* Morgantown, WV: Fitness Information Technology.

Parkinson, B. (1997). Untangling the appraisal-emotion connection. *Personality and Social Psychology Review, 1*, 62-79.

Parmenter, D.C. (1923). Some medical aspects of the training of college athletes. *The Boston Medical and Surgical Journal, 189*, 45-50.

Paykel, E.S., & Priest, R.G. (1992). Recognition and management of depression in general practice: A consensus statement. *British Medical Journal, 305*, 1198-1202.

Pedersen, P. (1986). The grief response and injury: A special challenge for athletes and athletic trainers. *Athletic Training, 21*, 312-314.

Pelletier, L.G., Vallerand, R.J., Green-Demers, I., Brière, N.M., & Blais, M.R. (1995). Loisirs et santé mentale: Les relations entre la motivation pour la pratique des loisirs et le bien-être psychologique [Leisure and mental health: Relationships between leisure involvement and psychological well-being]. *Canadian Journal of Behavioral Science, 27*, 214-225.

Pennebaker, J.W. (Ed.). (1995). *Emotion, disclosure, and health.* Washington, DC: American Psychological Association.

Pennebaker, J.W., & Beall, S.K. (1986). Confronting a traumatic event: Toward an understanding of inhibition and disease. *Journal of Abnormal Psychology, 95*, 274-281.

Peronnet, F., & Tribault, G. (1989). Mathematical analysis of running performance and world running records. *Journal of Applied Physiology, 67*, 453-465.

Perreault, S., Vallerand, R.J., Guay, F., Chantal, Y., & Richer, S. (1998). *Hockey, a parade, and subjective well-being inferences: Taking a second look at the effects of affect on judgments of life satisfaction.* Manuscript submitted for publication.

Pesonen, T. (1995). *Tunteiden yhteys suoritukseen juniorijalkapalloilijoilla* [Emotion-performance relationship in junior soccer players]. Unpublished master's thesis, Jyväskylä University, Jyväskylä, Finland.

Peterson, K., Durtschi, S., & Murphy, S. (1990). *Cognitive patterns and conceptual schemes of elite distance runners during submaximum and maximum running effort.* Paper presented at the annual meeting of the Association for the Advancement of Applied Sport Psychology, September, San Antonio, TX.

Petrie, G. (1993). Injury from the athlete's point of view. In J. Heil (Ed.), *Psychology of sport injury* (pp. 17-23). Champaign, IL: Human Kinetics.

Petruzzello, S.J. (1995). Does physical exercise reduce anxious emotions? A reply to W. Schlicht's meta-analysis. *Anxiety, Stress, and Coping, 8*, 353-356.

Petruzzello, S.J., Landers, D.M., Hatfield, B.D., Kubitz, K.A., & Salazar, W. (1991). A meta-analysis on the anxiety-reducing effects of acute and chronic exercise: Outcomes and mechanisms. *Sports Medicine, 11*, 143-182.

Pines, A. (1993). Burnout. In L. Goldberger & S. Breznitz (Eds.), *Handbook of stress* (pp. 386-402). New York: The Free Press.

Pines, A., Aronson, E., & Kafry, D. (1981). *Burnout: From tedium to personal growth.* New York: Free Press.

Plutchik, P. (1980). *Emotion: A psychobioevolutionary synthesis.* New York: Harper & Row.

Plutchik, P. (1993). Emotions and their vicissitudes: Emotions and psychopathology. In M. Lewis & J. Haviland (Eds.), *Handbook of emotions* (pp. 53-66). New York: Guilford Press.

Podilchak, W. (1991). Establishing the fun in leisure. *Leisure Sciences, 13*, 123-136.

Pons, D.C. (1994). *Un estudio sobre la relacion entre ansiedad y rendimiento en jugadores de golf* [A study of relationship between anxiety and performance in golf players]. Unpublished PhD thesis, Universitat de Valencia, Valencia.

Prapavessis, H., & Carron, A. (1996). The effect of group cohesion on competitive state anxiety. *Journal of Sport and Exercise Psychology, 18*, 64-74.

Prapavessis, H., & Grove, J.R. (1991). Precompetitive emotions and shooting performance: The mental health and zone of optimal function models. *The Sport Psychologist, 5*, 223-234.

Pritchard, R.D. (1990). *Measuring and improving organizational productivity: A practical guide*. New York: Praeger.

Pritchard, R.D., Jones, S.D., Roth, P.L., Stuebing, K.K., & Ekeberg, S.E. (1989). The evaluation of integrated approach to measuring organizational productivity. *Personnel Psychology, 42* (1), 69-115.

Privette, G. (1981). Dynamics of peak performance. *Journal of Humanistic Psychology, 21* (1), 57-67.

Privette, G., & Bundrick, C.M. (1991). Peak experience, peak performance, and flow: Personal descriptions and theoretical constructs. *Journal of Social Behavior and Personality, 6* (5), 169-188.

Puni, A.C. (1969). *Psikhologicheskaja podgotovka k sorevnovaniyu v sporte* [Psychological preparation for the competition in sport]. Moscow: Fizkultura i Sport.

Quinn, A.M. (1997). *The psychological factors involved in the recovery of elite athletes from long-term injury.* Paper presented at the Association for the Advancement of Applied Sport Psychology, September, San Diego, CA.

Radcliffe, J. & Farentinos, R. (1985). *Plyometrics: Explosive power training.* Champaign, IL: Human Kinetics.

Radloff, L.S. (1977). The CED-D scale: A self-report depression scale for research in the general population. *Applied Psychological Measurement, 1,* 385-401.

Raglin, J.S. (1992). Anxiety and sport performance. In J.O. Holloszy (Ed.), *Exercise and sport sciences reviews* (Vol. 20, pp. 243-274). New York: Williams & Wilkins.

Raglin, J.S. (1993). Overtraining and staleness: Psychometric monitoring of endurance athletes. In R.B. Singer, M. Murphey, & L. K. Tennant (Eds.), *Handbook of research on sport psychology* (pp. 840-850). New York: Macmillan.

Raglin, J.S. (1997). Anxiolytic effects of physical activity. In W.P. Morgan (Ed.), *Physical activity and mental health* (pp. 107-126). Washington, DC: Taylor & Francis.

Raglin, J.S. (1999). Psychological factors in sport performance. In R. Maughan (Ed.). *Basic and applied sciences for sports medicine* (pp. 260-289). Boston: Butterworth-Heinemann.

Raglin, J.S., Eksten, F., & Garl, T. (1995). Mood state response to a pre-season conditioning program in male collegiate basketball players. *International Journal of Sport Psychology, 26,* 214-225.

Raglin, J.S., Koceja, D.M., Stager, J.M., & Harms, C.A. (1996). Mood, neuromuscular function, and performance during training in female swimmers. *Medicine and Science in Sports and Exercise, 28,* 372-377.

Raglin, J.S., & Morgan, W.P. (1988). Predicted and actual levels of pre-competition state anxiety in swimmers. *Journal of Swimming Research, 4,* 5-8.

Raglin, J.S., & Morgan, W.P. (1994). Development of a scale for use in monitoring training-induced distress in athletes. *International Journal of Sports Medicine, 15,* 84-88.

Raglin, J.S., Morgan, W.P., & Luchsinger, A.E. (1990). Mood and self-motivation in successful and unsuccessful female rowers. *Medicine and Science in Sports and Exercise, 22,* 849-853.

Raglin, J.S., Morgan, W.P., & O'Connor, P.J. (1991). Changes in mood states during training in female and male college swimmers. *International Journal of Sports Medicine, 12,* 585-589.

Raglin, J.S., Morgan, M.P., & Wise, K.J. (1990). Pre-competition anxiety and performance in female high school swimmers: A test of optimal function theory. *International Journal of Sports Medicine, 11,* 171-175.

Raglin, J.S., & Morris, M.J. (1994). Precompetition anxiety in women volleyball players: A test of ZOF theory in a team sport. *British Journal of Sports Medicine, 28,* 47-52.

Raglin, J.S., & Turner, P.E. (1992). Predicted, actual, and optimal precompetition anxiety in adolescent track and field athletes. *Scandinavian Journal of Exercise and Science in Sports, 2,* 148-152.

Raglin, J.S., & Turner, P.E. (1993). Anxiety and performance in track and field athletes: A comparison of the inverted-U hypothesis with zone of optimal function theory. *Personality and Individual Differences, 14,* 163-171.

Raglin, J.S., Wise, K., & Morgan, W.P. (1990). Predicted and actual pre-competition anxiety in high school girl swimmers. *Journal of Swimming Research, 6,* 5-8.

Rainey, D.W. (1986). A gender difference in acceptance of sport aggression: A classroom activity. *Teaching of Psychology, 13* (3), 138-140.

Randle, S., & Weinberg, R. (1997). Multidimensional anxiety and performance: An exploratory examination of the zone of optimal functioning hypothesis. *Sport Psychologist, 11,* 160-174.

Ravizza, K. (1977). Peak experiences in sport. *Journal of Humanistic Psychology, 17* (4), 35-40.

Ravizza, K. (1984). Qualities of the peak experience in sport. In J.M. Silva & R.S. Weinberg (Eds.), *Psychological foundations of sport* (pp. 452-462). Champaign, IL: Human Kinetics.

Reisenzein, R. (1986). A structural equation analysis of Weiner's attribution-affect model of helping behavior. *Journal of Personality and Social Psychology, 50,* 1123-1133.

Rejeski, W.J., Brawley, L.R., & Schumaker, S.A. (1996). Physical activity and health-related quality of life. *Exercise and Sport Sciences Reviews, 24,* 71-108.

Renger, R. (1993). A review of the Profile of Mood States (POMS) in the prediction of athletic success. *Journal of Applied Sport Psychology, 5,* 78-84.

Rice, T.S., Ostrow, A.C., Ramsburg, J.D., & Brooks, D.D. (1989). A reactive aggression measure for baseball: A pilot investigation (abstract). In *Psychology of motor behavior and sport.* Kent, OH: *Proceedings of the North American Society for the Psychology of Sport and Physical Activity annual convention.*

Robazza, C., Bortoli, L., & Nougier, V. (1998). Performance-related emotions in skilled athletes: Hedonic tone and functional impact. *Perceptual and Motor Skills, 87,* 547-564.

Robazza, C., Bortoli, L., Zadro, I., & Nougier, V. (1998). Emotions in track and field athletes: A test of the individual zones of optimal functioning model. *European Yearbook of Sport Psychology, 2,* 94-123.

Robbins, T.W. (1997). Arousal systems and attentional processes. *Biological Psychology, 45,* 57-71.

Roberts, G.C. (1992). *Motivation in sport and exercise*. Champaign, IL: Human Kinetics.

Roberts, G.C., & Treasure, D.C. (1995). Achievement goals, motivation climate, and achievement strategies and behaviors in sport. *International Journal of Sport Psychology, 26,* 64-80.

Robinson, D.W., & Howe, B.L. (1989). Appraisal variable/affect relationships in youth: A test of Weiner's attributional model. *Journal of Sport and Exercise Psychology, 11,* 431-444.

Rosaldo, M.Z. (1983). The shame of headhunters and the autonomy of self. *Ethos, 11,* 135-151.

Roseman, I.J. (1984). Cognitive determinants of emotion: A structural theory. In P. Shaver (Ed.), *Review of personality and social psychology: Vol. 5. Emotions, relationships, and health* (pp. 11-36). Beverly Hills, CA: Sage.

Rowland, T.W. (1986). Exercise fatigue in adolescents: Diagnosis of athlete burnout. *The Physician and Sportsmedicine, 14,* 69-77.

Rowley, A.J., Landers, D., Kyllo, L.B., & Etnier, J.L. (1995). Does the Iceberg Profile discriminate between successful and less successful athletes? A meta analysis. *Journal of Sport and Exercise Psychology, 17* (2), 185-199.

Rozniak, L., Blanchard, C., & Koestner, R. (1998). *Mood changes and exercise behavior.* Manuscript submitted for publication.

Rubinstein, S.L. (1946). *Osnovy obtshej psykhologuii* [Foundations of general psychology]. Moscow: Uchpedgiz.

Rushall, B.S. (1978). Environment specific behavior inventories: Developmental procedures. *International Journal of Sport Psychology, 9,* 97-110.

Russell, D. (1982). The Causal Dimension Scale: A measure of how individuals perceive causes. *Journal of Personality and Social Psychology, 42,* 1137-1145.

Russell, J.A. (1979). Affective space is bipolar. *Journal of Personality and Social Psychology, 37,* 345-356.

Russell, J.A. (1980). A circumplex model of affect. *Journal of Personality and Social Psychology, 39,* 1161-1178.

Russell, J.A., Weiss, A., & Mendelsohn, G.A. (1989). Affect grid: A single-item scale of pleasure and arousal. *Journal of Personality and Social Psychology, 57* (3), 493-502.

Russell, S.F. (1981). *The factor structure of the Buss-Durkee hostility inventory.* Unpublished master's thesis, University of South Florida, Tampa.

Ryan, A.J. (1983). Overtraining of athletes: A round table. *The Physician and Sportsmedicine, 11,* 93-110.

Ryan, J. (1995). *Little girls in pretty boxes.* New York: Warner Books.

Ryan, R.M., Deci, E.L., & Grolnick, W.S. (1995). Autonomy, relatedness, and the self: Their relation to development and psychopathology. In D. Cicchetti & D.J. Cohen (Eds.), *Developmental psychology: Vol. 1. Theory and methods* (pp. 618-655). New York: Wiley.

Saarnio, J. (1995). *Performance affect in competitive swimmers.* Unpublished master's thesis, University of Jyväskylä, Jyväskylä, Finland.

Salminen, S., Liukkonen, J., Hanin, Y., & Hyvönen, A. (1995). Anxiety and athletic performance of Finnish athletes: An application of zone of optimal functioning model. *Personality and Individual Differences, 19*, 725-729.

Scanlan, T.K., Carpenter, P.J., Lobel, M., & Simons, J.P. (1993). Sources of enjoyment for youth sport athletes. *Pediatric Exercise Science, 5*, 275-285.

Scanlan, T.K., & Simons, J.P. (1992). The construct of sport enjoyment. In G.C. Roberts (Ed.), *Motivation in sport and exercise* (pp. 199-216). Champaign, IL: Human Kinetics.

Scanlan, T.K., Stein, G.L., & Ravizza, K. (1989). An in-depth study of former elite figure skaters II: Sources of enjoyment. *Journal of Sport and Exercise Psychology, 11*, 65-83.

Schachter, S. (1964). The interaction of cognitive and physiological determinants of emotional state. In L. Berkowitz (Ed.), *Advances in experimental social psychology* (Vol. 1, pp. 49-80). New York: Academic Press.

Schachter, S., & Singer, J.E. (1962). Cognitive, social, and physiological determinants of emotional state. *Psychological Review, 69*, 379-399.

Schachter, S., & Singer, J.E. (1979). Comments on the Maslach and Marshall-Zimbardo experiments. *Journal of Personality and Social Psychology, 37*, 989-995.

Schedrovitsky, G.P. (1964). *Problemy metodologii systemnogo issledovaniya* [Methodological problems of the systems research]. Moscow: Uchpedgiz.

Scherer, K.R. (1984a). Emotion as a multicomponent process: A model and some cross-cultural data. In P. Shaver (Ed.), *Review of personality and social psychology: Vol. 5. Emotions, relationships, and health* (pp. 37-63). Beverly Hills, CA: Sage.

Scherer, K.R. (1984b). On the nature and function of emotion: A components process approach. In K.R. Scherer & P. Ekman (Eds.), *Approaches to emotion* (pp. 293-317). Hillsdale, NJ: Erlbaum.

Schlicht, W. (1994a). Does physical exercise reduce anxious emotions? A meta-analysis. *Anxiety, Stress, and Coping, 6*, 275-288.

Schlicht, W. (1994b). Sport und seelische Gesundheit: Eine Meta-Analyse. In J. Nitsch & R. Seiler (Eds.), *Health sport-movement therapy: Proceedings of the 8th European Congress of Sport Psychology 1991* (Vol. 4, pp. 57-63). Saint Augustin, Germany: Academia Verlag.

Schlicht, W. (1995). Does physical exercise reduce anxious emotions? A retort to Steven J. Petruzzello. *Anxiety, Stress, and Coping, 8*, 357-359.

Schlosberg, H. (1954). Three dimensions of emotion. *Psychological Review, 61*, 81-88.

Schmidt, G., & Weiner, B. (1988). An attribution-affect-action theory of behavior: Replications of judgments of help-giving. *Personality and Social Psychology Bulletin, 14*, 610-621.

Schmidt, G.W., & Stein, G.L. (1991). Sports commitment: A model integrating enjoyment, dropout, and burnout. *Journal of Sports & Exercise Psychology, 8*, 254-265.

Scholtz, G.J., Willemse, J.W. (1991). Antecedents of aggression in sport. *Journal for Research in Sport, Physical Education and Recreation, 14* (1), 51-62.

Schönpflug, W. (1983). Coping efficiency and situational demands. In R. Hockey (Ed.), *Stress and fatigue in human performance* (pp. 299-326). Chichester: Wiley.

Schultheis, R. (1984). *Bone games*. New York: Breakaway Books.

Schutz, R.W. (1998). Assessing the stability of psychological traits and measures. In J.L. Duda (Ed.), *Advances in sport and exercise psychology measurement* (pp. 393-408). Morgantown, WV: Fitness Information Technology.

Schwartz, G.E., Davidson, R.J., & Goleman, D.J. (1978). Patterning of cognitive and somatic processes in the self-regulation of anxiety: Effects of meditation versus exercise. *Psychosomatic Medicine, 40,* 321-328.

Schwarz, N. (1990). Feelings as information: Information and motivational functions of affective states. In R. Sorrentino & E.T. Higgins (Eds.), *Handbook of motivation and cognition* (Vol. 2, pp. 527-561). New York: Guilford Press.

Schwarz, N., & Bohner, G. (1996). Feelings and their motivational implications: Mood and the action sequence. In P.M. Gollwitzer & J.A. Bargh (Eds.), *The psychology of action* (pp. 119-145). New York: Guilford Press.

Schwarz, N., & Strack, F. (1991). Evaluating one's life: A judgment model of subjective well-being. In F. Strack, M. Argyle, & N. Schwarz (Eds.), *Subjective well-being: An interdisciplinary perspective* (pp. 27-47). Oxford: Pergamon Press.

Schwarz, N., Strack, F., Kommer, D., & Wagner, D. (1987). Soccer, rooms and the quality of your life: Mood effects on judgments of satisfaction with life in general and with specific life domains. *European Journal of Social Psychology, 17,* 69-79.

Seheult, C. (1997). Freud on fencing: The role of unconscious psychological defenses. In R.J. Butler (Ed.), *Sports psychology in performance* (pp. 217-247). Oxford: Butterworth-Heinemann.

Seligman, M.E.P. (1998, October). What is the "good life"? *APA Monitor, 2.*

Selye, H. (1976). *The stress of life.* New York: McGraw-Hill. (Original work published 1956)

Shapiro, K.L., & Lim, A. (1989). The impact of anxiety on visual attention to central and peripheral visual stimuli. *Behavioral Research and Therapy, 27,* 345-351.

Shaver, P., Schwartz, J., Kirson, D., & O'Connor, C. (1987). Emotion knowledge: Further exploration of a prototype approach. *Journal of Personality and Social Psychology, 52,* 1061-1086.

Shepard, R.N. (1984). Ecological constraints on internal representation: Resonant kinematics of perceiving, imaging, thinking, and dreaming. *Psychological Review, 91,* 417-447.

Shuer, M.L., & Dietrich, M.S. (1997). Psychological effects of chronic injury in elite athletes. *Western Journal of Medicine, 166,* 104-109.

Shweder, R.A., & LeVine, R.S. (1984). (Eds.). *Culture theory: Essay on mind, self, and emotion.* Cambridge: Cambridge University Press.

Silva, J.M. (1978). Understanding aggressive behavior and its effects upon athletic performance. In W.F. Straub (Ed.), *Sport psychology.* Ithaca, NY: Mouvement.

Silva, J. (1979). Changes in the effective state of guilt as a function of exhibiting proactive assertion or hostile aggression. In C.G. Roberts & K.M. Newell (Eds.), *Psychology of motor behavior and sport* (pp. 98-108). Champaign, IL: Human Kinetics.

Silva, J.M. (1990). An analysis of the training stress syndrome in competitive athletics. *Journal of Applied Sport Psychology, 2,* 5-20.

Simonov, P.V. (1970). *Teoria otrazhenia i psykhofisiologia emotsij* [Reflection theory and psychophysiology of emotions]. Moscow: Medgiz.

Smith, A.P., & Jones, D.M. (1992). *Handbook of human performance, 2.* New York: Academic Press.

Smith, C.A., & Ellsworth, P.C. (1985). Patterns of cognitive appraisal in emotion. *Journal of Personality and Social Psychology, 52,* 475-488.

Smith, C.A., & Lazarus, R.S. (1990). Emotion and adaptation. In L. Pervin (Ed.), *Handbook of personality* (pp. 609-637). New York: Guilford Press.

Smith, M.D. (1971, January/February). Aggression in sport: Toward a role approach. *Journal of the Canadian Association for Health, Physical Education and Recreation, 371,* 22-25.

Smith, M.D. (1977). An evaluation of aggression in minor hockey players. In B. Kerr (Ed.), *Human performance and behavior. Proceedings of the Canadian Psycho-Motor Learning and Sports Psychology Symposium,* Annual Conference (IX), 185-190.

Smith, M.D. (1983a). *Violence and sport.* Toronto: Butterworth.

Smith, M.D. (1983b). What is sport violence? A sociological perspective. In J.H. Goldstein (Ed.), *Sports violence* (pp. 33-45). New York: Springer-Verlag.

Smith, R.E. (1986). Toward a cognitive-affective model of athletic burnout. *Journal of Sports Psychology, 8,* 36-50.

Smith, R.E. (1996). Performance anxiety, cognitive interference, and concentration enhancement strategies in sports. In I.G. Sarason, G.R. Pierce, & B.R. Sarason (Eds.), *Cognitive interference: Theories, methods, and findings* (pp. 261-284). Hillsdale, NJ: Erlbaum.

Smith, R.E., Smoll, F.L., & Hunt, E. (1977). A system for the behavioral assessment of athletic coaches. *Research Quarterly, 48,* 401-407.

Smith, R.E., Smoll, F.L., & Ptacek, S.T. (1990). Conjunctive moderator variables in vulnerability and resiliency: Life stress, social support, coping skills, and adolescent sport injuries. *Journal of Personality and Social Psychology, 58,* 360-370.

Smith, R.E., Smoll, F.L., & Schultz, R.W. (1990). Measurement and correlates of sport-specific cognitive and somatic trait anxiety: The Sport Anxiety Scale. *Anxiety Research, 2,* 263-280.

Smith, R.S., Smoll, F.L., & Wiechman, S.A. (1998). Measuring trait anxiety in sport. In J.L. Duda (Ed.), *Advances in sport and exercise psychology measurement* (pp. 105-127). Morgantown, WV: Fitness Information Technology.

Smoll, F.L., & Smith, R.E. (1984). Leadership research in youth sports. In J.M. Silva & R.S. Weinberg (Eds.), *Psychological foundations of sport.* Champaign, IL: Human Kinetics.

Snyder, E.E. (1990). Emotion and sport: A case study of collegiate women gymnasts. *Sociology of Sport Journal, 7,* 254-270.

Solomon, R.C. (1993). The philosophy of emotions. In M. Lewis & J. Haviland (Eds.), *Handbook of emotions* (pp. 3-16). New York: Guilford Press.

Sonstroem, R.J. (1986). An overview of anxiety in sport. In J.M. Silva & R.S. Weinberg (Eds.), *Psychological foundations of sport psychology* (pp. 104-117). Champaign, IL: Human Kinetics.

Sonstroem, R.J., & Bernardo, P. (1982). Individual pregame state anxiety and basketball performance: A re-examination of the inverted-U curve. *Journal of Sport Psychology, 4,* 235-245.

Spencer, H. (1890). *The principles of psychology* (Vol. 1). New York: Appleton. (Original work published 1855)

Spielberger, C.D. (1966a). *Anxiety and behavior.* New York: Academic Press.

Spielberger, C.D. (1966b). Theory and research in anxiety. In C.D. Spielberger (Ed.), *Anxiety and behavior* (pp. 1-17). New York: Academic Press.

Spielberger, C.D. (1972). Anxiety as an emotional state. In C.D. Spielberger (Ed.), *Anxiety: Current trends in theory and research* (Vol. 1). New York: Academic Press.

Spielberger, C.D. (1988). *Manual for the State-Trait Anger Expression Inventory (STAXI).* Odessa, FL: Psychological Assessment Resources.

Spielberger, C.D. (1989). Stress and anxiety in sports. In D. Hackfort & C.D. Spielberger (Eds.), *Anxiety in sports: An international perspective* (pp. 3-17). New York: Hemisphere.

Spielberger, C.D., Gorsuch, R.L., & Lushene, R.E. (1970). *Manual for the State-Trait Anxiety Inventory (STAI).* Palo Alto, CA: Consulting Psychologists Press.

Spielberger, C.D, Gorsuch, R.L., Lushene, R.E., Vagg, P.R., & G.A. Jacobs (1983). *Manual for the State-Trait Anxiety Inventory: STAI (Form Y).* Palo Alto, CA: Consulting Psychologists Press.

Spielberger, C.D., Jacobs, G., Russell, S., & Crane, R. (1983). Assessment of anger: The State-Trait Anger Scale. In J.N. Butcher & C.D. Spielberger (Eds.), *Advances in personality assessment* (Vol. 2, pp. 159-187). Hillsdale, NJ: Erlbaum.

Spielberger, C.D., Johnson, E.H., Russell, S.F., Crane, R.J., Jacobs, G.A., & Worden, T.J. (1985). The experience and expression of anger: Construction and validation of an anger expression scale. In M. A. Chesney & R. H. Rosenman (Eds.), *Anger and hostility in cardiovascular and behavioral disorders* (pp. 5-30). New York: Hemisphere.

Spielberger, C.D., Krasner, S.S., & Solomon, E.P. (1988). The experience, expression, and control of anger. In M.P. Janisse (Ed.), *Health psychology: Individual differences and stress* (pp. 89-108). New York: Springer-Verlag.

Spielberger, C.D., & London, P. (1990, January/February). Blood pressure and injustice. *Psychology Today, 48,* 50-51.

Spielberger, C.D., Reheiser, E.C., & Sydeman, S.J. (1995). Measuring the experience, expression, and control of anger. In H. Kassinove (Ed.), *Anger disorders: Definitions, diagnosis, and treatment* (pp. 49-67). Washington, DC: Taylor & Francis.

Spielberger, C.D., & Sydeman, S.J. (1994). State-Trait Anxiety Inventory and State-Trait Anger Expression Inventory. In M.E. Maurish (Ed.), *The use of psychological tests for treatment planning and outcome assessment* (pp. 292-321). Hillsdale, NJ: Erlbaum.

Sports Council & Health Education Authority (1992). *Allied Dunbar National Fitness Survey: Main findings.* London: Author.

Spriet, L.L. (1997). Erogenic aids: Recent advances and retreats. In D.R. Lamb & R. Murray (Eds.), *Perspectives in exercise science and sports medicine: Vol. 10. Optimizing sport performance.* Carmel, IN: Cooper.

Stambulova, N.B. (1994). Developmental sports career investigations in Russia: A post-perestroika analysis. *Sport Psychologist, 8*, 221-237.

Stanford, S.C., & Salmon, P. (Eds.). (1993). *Stress: From synapse to syndrome.* London: Academic Press.

Steadman, J.R. (1993). A physician's approach to the psychology of injury. In J. Heil (Ed.), *Psychology of sport injury* (pp. 25-32). Champaign, IL: Human Kinetics.

Stein, G.L., Kimiecik, J.C., Daniels, J., & Jackson, S.A. (1995). Psychological antecedents of flow in recreational sport. *Personality and Social Psychology Bulletin, 21* (2), 125-135.

Stelter, R. (1998). The body, self, and identity. Personal and social constructions of the self through sport and movement. *European Yearbook of Sport Psychology, 2*, 1-32.

Stenberg, C.R., & Campos, J.J. (1990). The development of anger expressions in infancy. In N. Stein, B. Leventhal, & T. Trabasso (Eds.), *Psychological and biological approaches to emotion* (pp. 247-282). Hillsdale, NJ: Erlbaum.

Stephens, D.E., & Light-Bredemeier, B.J. (1996). Moral atmosphere and judgements about aggression in girls' soccer: Relationship among moral and motivational variables. *Journal of Sport and Exercise Psychology, 18* (2), 158-173.

Stephens, T. (1988). Physical activity and mental health in the United States and Canada: Evidence from four population surveys. *Preventive Medicine, 17*, 35-47.

Steptoe, A. (1992). Physical activity and psychological well-being. In N. Norgan (Ed.), *Physical activity and health* (pp. 207-229). Cambridge: Cambridge University Press.

Steptoe, A., & Bolton, J. (1988). The short-term influence of high and low intensity physical exercise on mood. *Psychology and Health, 2*, 91-106.

Steptoe, A., & Butler, N. (1996). Sports participation and emotional well-being in adolescents. *Lancet, 347*, 1789-1792.

Steptoe, A., & Cox, S. (1988). Acute effects of aerobic exercise on mood. *Health Psychology, 7*, 329-340.

Steptoe, A., Moses, J., Edwards, S., & Mathews, A. (1993). Exercise and responsivity to mental stress: Discrepancies between the subjective and physiological effects of aerobic training. *International Journal of Sport Psychology, 24*, 110-129.

Stone, M.H., Keith, R.E., Kearney, J.T., Fleck, S.J., Wilson, G.D., & Triplett, N.T. (1991). Overtraining: A review of the signs, symptoms and possible causes. *Journal of Applied Sport Science Research, 5*, 35-50.

Storm, C., & Storm, T. (1987). A taxonomic study of the vocabulary of emotions. *Journal of Personality and Social Psychology, 53*, 805-816.

Story, D., & Deffenbacher, J.L. (1985). *General anger and personality.* Paper presented at Rocky Mountain Psychological Association, Tucson, AZ.

Striegel, D. (1993). Anger in tennis: Part 1—The developmental years, the expression of anger and the causes of anger. *Contemporary Thought on Performance Enhancement, 2* (2), 54-81.

Strongman, K.T. (1973). *The psychology of emotion.* New York: Wiley.

Suls, J., & Mullen, B. (1983). From the cradle to the grave: Comparison and self-evaluation across the life-span. In J. Suls (Ed.), *Psychological perspectives on the self* (Vol. 1, pp. 97-128). Hillsdale, NJ: Erlbaum.

Syrjä, P. (1993). *Suoritustunteet juniorijääkiekkoilijoilla* [Performance emotions in junior ice-hockey players]. Unpublished master's thesis, University of Jyväskylä, Jyväskylä, Finland.

Syrjä, P. (1997). Emotion in junior ice-hockey players: A comparative study. *Annual Congress of the European College of Sports Science. Book of abstracts.* Part II, pp. 657-658. Copenhagen: University of Copenhagen.

Syrjä, P., & Hanin, Y.L. (1997a). Individualised and group-oriented measures of emotion in sport: A comparative study. *Annual Congress of the European College of Sports Science. Book of abstracts* (Part II, pp. 641-642). Copenhagen: University of Copenhagen.

Syrjä, P., & Hanin, Y.L. (1997b). Measurement of emotion in sport: A comparison of individualized and normative scales. In R. Lidor & M. Bar-Eli (Eds.), *ISSP IX World Congress of Sport Psychology. Proceedings* (Part 2, pp. 682-684). Netanya, Israel: Wingate Institute.

Syrjä, P., Hanin, Y., & Pesonen, T. (1995). Emotion and performance relationship in soccer players. In R. Vanfraechem-Raway & Y. Vanden Auweele (Eds.), *Proceedings of the IXth European Congress on Sport Psychology: Integrating laboratory and field studies* (Part 1, pp. 191-197). Brussels: Belgian Federation of Sport Psychology.

Syrjä, P., Hanin, Y., & Tarvonen, S. (1995). Emotion and performance relationship in squash and badminton players. In R. Vanfraechem-Raway & Y. Vanden Auweele (Eds.), *Proceedings of the IXth European Congress on Sport Psychology: Integrating laboratory and field studies* (Part 1, pp. 183-190). Brussels: Belgian Federation of Sport Psychology.

Tarvonen, S. (1995). *Suoritustunteiden ja suorituksen välinen yhteys squash-ja sulkapallopelaajilla* [Emotion-performance relationships in squash and badminton players]. Unpublished master's thesis, Jyväskylä University, Jyväskylä, Finland.

Tate, A.K., Petruzzello, S.J., & Lox, C.L. (1995). Examination of the relationship between self-efficacy and affect at varying levels of aerobic exercise intensity. *Journal of Applied Social Psychology, 25,* 1922-1936.

Taylor, A.H., Daniel, J.V., Leith, L., & Burke, R.J. (1990). Perceived stress, psychological burnout and paths to turnover intentions among sport officials. *Journal of Applied Social Psychology, 2,* 84-97.

Taylor, J. (1996). Intensity regulation and athletic performance. In J.L. Van Raalte & B.W. Brewer (Eds.), *Exploring sport and exercise psychology.* Washington, DC: American Psychological Association.

Taylor, S.E. (1981). The interface of cognitive and social psychology. In J. Harvey (Ed.), *Cognition, social behavior, and the environment* (pp. 189-211). Hillsdale, NJ: Erlbaum.

Taylor, S.E., Repetti, R.L., & Seeman, T. (1997). Health psychology: What is an unhealthy environment and how does it get under the skin? In J.T. Spence, J.M. Darley, & D.J. Foss (Eds.), *Annual Review of Psychology, 48,* 411-447.

Teigen, K.H. (1994). Yerkes-Dodson: A law for all seasons. *Theory & Psychology, 4,* 525-547.

Tellegen, A. (1985). Structures of mood and personality and their relevance to assessing anxiety, with an emphasis on self-report. In A.H. Tuma & J.D. Maser (Eds.), *Anxiety, and the anxiety disorders* (pp. 681-706). Hillsdale, NJ: Erlbaum.

Tellegen, A. (1991). Personality traits: Issues of definition, evidence, and assessment. In D. Cicchetti & W.M. Grove (Eds.), *Personality and psychopathology* (pp. 10-35). Minneapolis: University of Minnesota Press.

Terry, P. (1995). The efficacy of mood state profiling with elite performers: A review and synthesis. *The Sport Psychologist, 9*, 309-324.

Terry, P., & Slade, A. (1995). Discrimination effectiveness of psychological state measures in predicting performance outcome in karate competition. *Perceptual and Motor Skills, 81* (1), 275-286.

Tessier, R., Fillion, L., Muckle, G., & Gendron, M. (1990). Quelques mesures-critères de stress et la prédiction de l'état de santé physique. Une étude longitudinale [Some criterion-measures of stress and the prediction of physical health. A longitudinal study]. *Canadian Journal of Behavioral Science, 22*, 271-281.

Thayer, R.E. (1978). Toward a psychological theory of multidimensional activation (arousal). *Motivation and Emotion, 2* (1), 1-34.

Thirlaway, K., & Benton, D. (1996). Exercise and mental health: The role of activity and fitness. In J. Kerr, A. Griffiths, & T. Cox (Eds.), *Workplace health, employee fitness and exercise* (pp. 69-82). London: Taylor & Francis.

Thompson, M. (1989). The development of a sport aggression questionnaire for the study of acts of aggression (abstract). *Proceedings of the Association for the Advancement of Applied Sport Psychology* (p. 104). Seattle, WA.

Tomkins, S.S. (1962). *Affect, imagery, consciousness: Vol. I. The positive affects.* New York: Springer-Verlag.

Tomkins, S.S. (1963). *Affect, imagery, consciousness: Vol. II. The negative affects.* New York: Springer-Verlag.

Tomkins, S.S. (1970). A theory of motivation. In P. Suefeld & H. Schroeder (Eds.), *Information processing and motivation.* New York: Ronald Press.

Tomkins, S.S. (1991). *Affect, imagery, consciousness: Vol. 3. The negative affects: Anger and fear.* New York: Springer-Verlag.

Treasure, D.C., & Newbery, D.M. (1998). Relationships between self-efficacy, exercise intensity, and feeling states in a sedentary population during and following an acute bout of exercise. *Journal of Sport and Exercise Psychology, 20*, 1-11.

Trevarthen, C. (1979). Communication and cooperation in early infancy: A description of primary intersubjectivity. In M. Bullowa (Ed.), *Before speech: The beginnings of human communication.* London: Cambridge University Press.

Trevarthen, C., & Hubley, P. (1978). Secondary intersubjectivity: Confidence, confining acts of meaning in the first year. In A. Lock (Ed.), *Action, gesture and symbol: The emergence of language.* San Diego: Academic Press.

Turner, P.E., & Raglin, J.S. (1996). Variability in precompetition anxiety and performance in college track and field athletes. *Medicine and Science in Sports and Exercise, 28* (3), 378-385.

Tuson, K.M., & Sinyor, D. (1993). On the affective benefits of acute aerobic exercise: Taking stock after twenty years of research. In P. Seraganian (Ed.), *Exercise psychology* (pp. 80-121). New York: Wiley.

Udry, E. (1997). Coping and social support among injured athletes following surgery. *Journal of Sport and Exercise Psychology, 19,* 71-90.

Uneståhl, L.-E. (1981). *Inner mental training.* Örebro, Sweden: Veje.

Uneståhl, L.-E. (1986). The ideal performance. In L.-E. Uneståhl (Ed.), *Sport psychology in theory and practice* (pp. 21-38). Örebro, Sweden: Veje.

Urhausen, A., Gabriel, H.H.W., & Kindermann, W. (1998). Impaired pituitary hormonal response to exhaustive exercise in overtrained endurance athletes. *Medicine and Science in Sports and Exercise, 30,* 407-414.

U.S. Department of Health and Human Services (1996). *Physical activity and health: A report of the Surgeon General.* Washington, DC: Author.

Vallacher, R.R., & Nowak, A. (1997). The emergence of dynamical social psychology. *Psychological Inquiry, 8* (2), 73-99.

Vallerand, R.J. (1981). *Une analyse des déterminants de la motivation intrinsèque en contexte sportif* [An analysis of determinants of intrinsic motivation in sport]. Unpublished doctoral dissertation, Université de Montréal.

Vallerand, R.J. (1983). On emotion in sport: Theoretical and social psychological perspectives. *Journal of Sport Psychology, 5,* 197-215.

Vallerand, R.J. (1984). Emotion in sport: Definitional, historical, and social psychological perspectives. In W. Straub & J. Williams (Eds.), *Cognitive sport psychology* (pp. 65-78). Lansing, NY: Sport Science Associates.

Vallerand, R.J. (1987). Antecedents of self-related affects in sport: Preliminary evidence on the intuitive-reflective appraisal model. *Journal of Sport Psychology, 9,* 161-182.

Vallerand, R.J. (1997). Towards a hierarchical model of intrinsic and extrinsic motivation. In M.P. Zanna (Ed.), *Advances in experimental social psychology* (Vol. 29, pp. 271-360). San Diego: Academic Press.

Vallerand, R.J. (in press). A hierarchical model of intrinsic and extrinsic motivation in sport and exercise. In G. Roberts (Ed.), *Advances in motivation in sport and exercise.* Champaign, IL: Human Kinetics.

Vallerand, R.J., & Losier, G.F. (in press). Intrinsic and extrinsic motivation in sport. *Journal of Applied Sport Psychology.*

Vallerand, R.J., & Reid, G. (1988). On the relative effects of positive and negative verbal feedback on males and females' intrinsic motivation. *Canadian Journal of Behavioral Sciences, 20,* 239-250.

Vanden Auweele, Y., Cuyper, B.D., Mele, V.V., & Rzewnicki, R. (1993). Elite performance and personality: From description and prediction to diagnosis and intervention. In R.N. Singer, M. Murphey, & L.K. Tennant (Eds.), *Handbook of research on sport psychology* (pp. 257-289). New York: Macmillan.

Van Handel, P.J., Katz, A., & Troup, J.P. (1988). Oxygen consumption and blood lactic acid response to training and taper. In R. Ungerechts, K. Wilke, and K. Reischle (Eds.), *Swimming Science V, International Series on Sports Sciences* (Vol. 18). Champaign, IL: Human Kinetics.

Vealey, R.S., & Campbell, J.L. (1988). Achievement goals of adolescent figure skaters: Impact on self-confidence, anxiety, and performance. *Journal of Adolescent Research, 3,* 227-243.

Vealey, R.S., Udry, E.M., Zimmerman, V., & Soliday, J. (1992). Intrapersonal and situational predictors of coaching burnout. *Journal of Sports and Exercise Psychology, 14*, 40-58.

Verde, T., Thomas, S., & Shepard, R. (1992). Potential markers of heavy training in highly trained distance runners. *British Journal of Sports Medicine, 26*, 167-175.

Vlachopoulos, S., Biddle, S., & Fox, K. (1996). A social-cognitive investigation into the mechanism of affect generation in children's physical activity. *Journal of Sport and Exercise Psychology, 18*, 174-193.

von Bertalanffy, L. (1952). Theoretical models in biology and psychology. In D. Krech & G.S. Klein (Eds.), *Theoretical models and personality theory*. Durham, NC: Duke University Press.

Vygotsky, L.S. (1926). *Pedagogicheskaja psyhologiya* [Pedagogical psychology]. Moscow: Rabotnik Prosveschenija.

Wagman, D., & Khelifa, M. (1996). Psychological issues in sport injury rehabilitation: Current knowledge and practice. *Journal of Athletic Training, 31*, 257-261.

Wall, B.R., & Gruber, J.J. (1984). *Relationship between aggression and anxiety in women's intercollegiate basketball*. Paper presented at Pre-Olympic Scientific Congress, Eugene, OR.

Walters, K.S. (1989). Aesthetic emotions and reality. *American Psychologist, 44*, 1545-1546.

Wankel, L.M. (1997). "Strawpersons," selective reporting, and inconsistent logic: A response to Kimiecik and Harris's analysis of enjoyment. *Journal of Sport and Exercise Psychology, 19* (1), 98-109.

Wankel, L.M., & Berger, B.G. (1990). The psychological and social benefits of sport and physical activity. *Journal of Leisure Research, 22*, 167-182.

Wankel, L.M., & Kreisel, P.J.J. (1985). Factors underlying enjoyment of youth sport. *Journal of Sport Psychology, 7*, 51-64.

Wankel, L.M., & Sefton, J.M. (1989). A season-long investigation of fun in youth sports. *Journal of Sport and Exercise Psychology, 11*, 355-366.

Wann, D.L., Dolan, T.J., McGeorge, K.K., & Allison, J.A. (1994). Relationships between spectator identification and spectators' perceptions of influence, spectators' emotions, and competition outcome. *Journal of Sport and Exercise Psychology, 16*, 347-364.

Warr, P., Barter, J., & Brownbridge, G. (1983). On the independence of positive and negative affect. *Journal of Personality and Social Psychology, 44* (3), 644-651.

Watson, D., & Clark, L.A. (1992). On traits and temperament: General and specific factors of emotional experience and their relation to the five-factor model. *Journal of Personality, 60*, 441-476.

Watson, D., & Clark, L.A. (1994). Emotion, moods, traits, and temperaments: Conceptual distinctions and empirical findings. In P. Ekman & R.J. Davidson (Eds.), *The nature of emotion: Fundamental questions* (pp. 89-93). New York: Oxford University Press.

Watson, D., Clark, L.A., & Tellegen, A. (1985). Towards a consensual structure of mood. *Psychological Bulletin, 98*, 219-235.

Watson, D., Clark, L.A., & Tellegen, A. (1988). Development and validation of brief measures of positive and negative affect: The PANAS scales. *Journal of Personality and Social Psychology, 54,* 1063-1070.

Watzlawick, P. (1976). *How real is real?* New York: Random House.

Weinberg, R.S. (1978). The effects of success and failure on patterning of neuromuscular energy. *Journal of Motor Behavior, 10,* 53-61.

Weinberg, R.S. (1989). Anxiety, arousal, and motor performance: Theory, research, and applications. In D. Hackfort & C.D. Spielberger (Eds.), *Anxiety in sports: An international perspective* (pp. 95-112). New York: Hemisphere.

Weinberg, R.S. (1990). Anxiety and motor performance: Where to from here? *Anxiety Research, 2,* 227-242.

Weinberg, R.S., & Hunt, V.V. (1976). The interrelationships between anxiety, motor performance, and electromyography. *Journal of Motor Behavior, 8,* 219-224.

Weiner, B. (1972). *Theories of motivation: From mechanism to cognition.* Chicago: Rand McNally.

Weiner, B. (1977). Attribution and affect: Comments on Sohn's critique. *Journal of Educational Psychology, 69,* 506-507.

Weiner, B. (1979). A theory of motivation for some classroom experiences. *Journal of Educational Psychology, 71,* 33-25.

Weiner, B. (1980). A cognitive (attribution)-emotion-action model of motivated behavior: An analysis of judgments of help-giving. *Journal of Personality and Social Psychology, 39,* 186-200.

Weiner, B. (1981). The role of affect in sport psychology. In G.C. Roberts & D.M. Landers (Eds.), *Psychology of motor behavior and sport, 1980* (pp. 37-48). Champaign, IL: Human Kinetics.

Weiner, B. (1985a). An attributional theory of achievement motivation and emotion. *Psychological Review, 92,* 548-573.

Weiner, B. (1985b). "Spontaneous" causal thinking. *Psychological Bulletin, 97,* 74-84.

Weiner, B. (1986). *An attributional theory of motivation and emotion.* New York: Springer-Verlag.

Weiner, B. (1991). Metaphors in motivation and attribution. *American Psychologist, 46* (9), 921-930.

Weiner, B. (1995). *Judgments of responsibility: A foundation for a theory of social conduct.* New York: Guilford Press.

Weiner, B., Amirkhan, J., Folkes, V.S., & Verette, J.A. (1987). An attributional analysis of excuse giving: Studies of a naive theory of emotion. *Journal of Personality and Social Psychology, 52,* 316-324.

Weiner, B., Russell, D., & Lerman, D. (1978). Affective consequences of causal ascriptions. In J.H. Harvey, W. Ickes, & R.F. Kidd (Eds.), *New directions in attribution research* (Vol. 2, pp. 59-90). Hillsdale, NJ: Erlbaum.

Weiner, B., Russell, D., & Lerman, D. (1979). The cognition-emotion process in achievement-related contexts. *Journal of Personality and Social Psychology, 37,* 1211-1220.

Weiner, H., Florin, I., Murrison, R., & Hellhammer, D. (Eds.). (1989). *Frontiers of stress research. Neuronal control of bodily function* (Vol. 3). Lewiston, NY/Bern: Huber.

Weismann, M.M., & Klerman, G.L. (1992). Depression: Current understanding and changing trends. *Annual Review of Public Health, 13,* 319-339.

Wheeler, K. (1989). Sports nutrition for the primary care physician: The importance of carbohydrates. *The Physician and Sportsmedicine, 17,* 106-117.

White, S.A., & Duda, J.L. (1991). *The interdependence between goal perspectives, psychological skills, and cognitive interference among elite skiers.* Paper presented at the annual meeting of the Association for the Advancement of Applied Sport Psychology, Savannah, GA.

Wiese-Bjornstal, D.M., Smith, A.M., & LaMott, E.E. (1995). A model of psychological response to athletic injury and rehabilitation. *Athletic Training: Sports Health Care Perspectives, 1,* 17-30.

Williams, D.A. (1997). Acute procedural and postoperative pain: Patient related factors in its undermanagement. *American Pain Society Bulletin, 4,* 8-10.

Williams, J.M., & Roepke, N. (1993). Psychology of injury and injury rehabilitation. In R.N. Singer, M. Murphey, & L.K. Tennant (Eds.), *Handbook of research on sport psychology.* New York: Macmillan.

Willimczik, K., & Rethorst, S. (1995). Cognitions and emotions in sport achievement situations. In S.J.H. Biddle (Ed.), *European perspectives on exercise and sport psychology* (pp. 218-241). Exeter, UK: Human Kinetics.

Wilson, G.S., & Raglin, J.S. (1997). Optimal and predicted anxiety in 9-12 year old track and field athletes. *Scandinavian Journal of Medicine and Science in Sports, 2,* 148-152.

Wilson, G.S., Raglin, J.S., & Harger, G. (1999). Training practices, mood state and staleness in adolescent distance runners. *Medicine and Science in Sports and Exercise, 31*(Suppl.), S216.

Wilson, V.E., & Bird, E. (1984). *Teacher-coach burnout.* Paper presented at the District AAHPERD Convention, Eugene, OR.

Winton, W.M. (1987). Do introductory textbooks present the Yerkes-Dodson law correctly? *American Psychologist, 42,* 202-203.

Wittig, A.F., Houmard, J.A., & Costill, D.L. (1989). Psychological effects during reduced training in distance runners. *International Journal of Sports Medicine, 10,* 97-100.

Woodman, T., Albinson, J., & Hardy, L. (1996). An investigation of the zone of optimal functioning (ZOF) hypothesis within a multidimensional framework. In P. Marconnet, J. Gaulard, I. Margaritis, & F. Tessier (Eds.), *First Annual Congress of the ECSS. Frontiers in sport science. The European perspective. Book of abstracts* (pp. 66-67). Nice, France: University of Nice Sophia-Antipolis.

Woodman, T., Albinson, J.G., & Hardy, L. (1997). An investigation of the zones of optimal functioning hypothesis within a multidimensional framework. *Journal of Sport and Exercise Psychology, 19,* 131-141.

Woodworth, R.S., & Schlosberg, H.S. (1954). *Experimental psychology.* New York: Holt.

Wooten, I.L. (1997-1998). Positively winning: The story of Linda Bunker. *Association for the Advancement of Applied Sport Psychology Newsletter, 12* (3), 16.

World Health Organization (1986). *Targets for health for all*. Copenhagen: WHO.

Worrell, G.L., & Harris, D.V. (1986). The relationship of perceived and observed aggression of ice hockey players. *International Journal of Sport Psychology, 17* (1), 34-40.

Wundt, W. (1905). *Grundriss der psychologie* [Outline of psychology] (7th rev. ed.). Leipzig: Engelman.

Wykoff, W. (1993). The psychological effects of exercise on non-clinical and clinical populations of adult women: A critical review of the literature. *Occupational Therapy in Mental Health, 12* (3), 69-106.

Yarnold, P.R. (1988). Classical test theory methods for repeated measures N=1 research designs. *Educational and Psychological Measurement, 48*, 913-919.

Yeadon, M.R., & Challis, J.H. (1992). *Future directions for performance related research in sport biomechanics*. London: Sports Council.

Yerkes, R.M., & Dodson, J.D. (1908). The relation of strength of stimulus to rapidity of habit-formation. *Journal of Comparative Neurology and Psychology, 18*, 459-482.

Young, P.T. (1959). The role of affective processes in learning and motivation. *Psychological Review, 66* (2), 104-125.

Young, P.T. (1973). *Emotion in man and animal*. New York: Krieger.

Yukelson, D., & Heil, J. (1998). Psychological considerations in working with injured athletes (pp. 45-49). In P.K. Canavan (Ed.), *Rehabilitation in sports medicine: A comprehensive guide*. Stamford, CT: Appleton & Lange.

Zaichkowski, L., Hamill, G., & Dallis, B. (1994). *Physiological correlates of the zone of optimal functioning*. Poster session presented at the annual meeting of the Association for the Advancement of Applied Sport Psychology, October, Lake Tahoe, NV.

Zaichkowski, L., & Takenaka, K. (1993). Optimizing arousal level. In R.N. Singer, M. Murphey, & L.K. Tennant (Eds.), *Handbook of research on sport psychology* (pp. 511-527). New York: Macmillan.

Zajonc, R.B. (1998). Emotions. In D.T. Gilbert, S.T. Fiske, & G. Lindzey (Eds.), *The handbook of social psychology* (4th ed., Vol. 1, pp. 591-632). New York: McGraw-Hill.

Zajonc, R.B., Murphy, S.T., & McIntosh, D.N. (1993). Brain temperature and subjective emotional experience. In M. Lewis & J. Haviland (Eds.), *Handbook of emotions* (pp. 209-222). New York: Guilford Press.

Zedeck, S. (1971). Problems with the use of "moderator" variables. *Psychological Bulletin, 76*, 295-310.

Zelin, M.L., Adler, G., & Myerson, P.G. (1972). Anger self-report: An objective questionnaire for the measurement of aggression. *Journal of Consulting and Clinical Psychology, 39*, 340.

Zevon, M.A., & Tellegen, A. (1982). The structure of mood change: An idiographic/nomothetic analysis. *Journal of Personality and Social Psychology, 43* (1), 111-122.

Zillman, D. (1978). Attribution and misattribution of excitatory reactions. In J.H. Harvey, W. Ickes, & R.F. Kidd (Eds.), *New directions in attribution research* (Vol. 2, pp. 335-368). Hillsdale, NJ: Erlbaum.

Zillman, D., Johnson, R.C., & Day, K.D. (1974). Attribution of apparent arousal and proficiency of recovery from sympathetic activation affecting excitation transfer to aggressive behavior. *Journal of Experimental Social Psychology, 10,* 503-515.

Zuckerman, M., & Lubin, B. (1965). *Manual for the Multiple Affect Adjective Checklist.* San Diego: Educational and Industrial Testing Service.

Zung, W.W.K. (1965). A self-rating depression scale. *Archives of General Psychiatry, 12,* 63-70.

Additional Resources

Akiskal, H.S., & Mckinney, W.T. (1975). Overview of recent research in depression: Integration of ten conceptual models into a comprehensive clinical frame. *Archives of General Psychiatry, 32,* 285-305.

American College of Sports Medicine. (1990). The recommended quantity and quality of exercise for developing and maintaining cardiorespiratory and muscular fitness in healthy adults. *Medicine and Science in Sports and Exercise, 22,* 265-274.

Balke, B., Nagle, F., & Daniels, J. (1965). Altitude and maximum in work and sports activity. *Journal of the American Medical Association, 194,* 646-649.

Bendig, A.W. (1962). Factor analytic scale of covert and overt hostility. *Journal of Counselling Psychology, 26,* 200.

Boyle, G.J. (1987). A cross validation of the factor structure of the Profile of Mood States: Were the factors correctly identified in the first instance? *Psychological Reports, 60,* 343-354.

Budgett, R. (1990). Overtraining syndrome. *British Journal of Sports Medicine, 24,* 231-236.

Cameron, C.A. (1996). *Creating peaceful learning environments.* Paper presented at the International Congress of Psychology, August 16-21, Montreal, Canada.

Duda, J.L. (1987). Toward a developmental theory of achievement motivation in sport. *Journal of Sport Psychology, 9,* 130-145.

Enoka, R.M. (1997). Neural adaptations with chronic physical activity. *Journal of Biomechanics, 30,* 447-455.

Gill, P. (1979). *Moral judgements of violence among Irish and Swedish adolescents.* Göteborg: Acta Universitatis Gothoburgensis.

Goldiamond, I. (1965). Stuttering and fluency as manipulable operand behavioral classes. In L. Krasner & L.P. Ullman (Eds.), *Research in behavior modification: New developments and implications* (pp. 106-156). New York: Holt, Reinhart & Winston.

Gondola, J.C., & Tuckman, B.W. (1982). Psychological mood state in "average" marathon runners. *Perceptual and Motor Skills, 55,* 1295-1300.

Kane, T.D., Marks, M.A., Zaccaro, S.J., & Blair, V. (1996). Self-efficacy, personal goals, and wrestler's self-regulation. *Journal of Sport and Exercise Psychology, 18,* 36-48.

Kling, M.A., Perini, G.I., Demitrack, M.A., Geracioti, T.D., Linnoila, M., Chrousos, G.P., & Gold, P.W. (1989). Stress-responsive neurohormonal systems and the symptom complex of affective illness. *Psychopharmacology Bulletin, 25,* 312-318.

Lochman, J.E. (1987). *Teacher consulting and cognitive-behavioral interventions with aggressive boys.* Paper presented at the Annual Convention of the American Psychological Association, August 28-September 1, New York.

Lumsden, L. (1994). Class teaches students to cope with anger. *OSSC Report, 34* (2), 1-6.

Macera, C.A., Pate, R.R., Powell, K.E., Jackson, K.L., Kendric, J.S., & Craven, T.E. (1989). Predicting lower extremity injuries among habitual runners. *Archives of Internal Medicine, 149,* 2565-2568.

Madak, P.R., & Bravi, G.D. (1992). *"Second-Step: A Violence Prevention Curriculum" in a Western Canadian elementary school.* Committé for Children. Seattle: 20th Avenue.

McWhirter, B.T., & Page, G.L. (1996). *An evaluation of psychoeducational groups for alternative high school students.* Paper presented at the Annual Meeting of the American Psychological Association, August 9-13, Toronto.

Morgan, W.P., & Costill, D.L. (1996). Selected psychological characteristics and health behaviors of aging marathon runners: A longitudinal study. *International Journal of Sports Medicine, 17,* 305-312.

Morgan, W.P., & Goldston, S.E. (1987). *Exercise and mental health.* New York: Hemisphere.

Morgan, W.P., & Pollock, M.C. (1977). Psychological characterization of the elite distance runner. *Annals of the New York Academy of Science, 301,* 382-405.

Moyer, K.E. (1976). *The psychobiology of aggression.* New York: Harper & Row.

Norcross, J.C., Guadognoli, E., & Prochaska, J.O. (1984). Factor structure of the Profile of Mood States (POMS): Two partial replications. *Journal of Clinical Psychology, 40,* 1270-1277.

Novaco, R.W. (1977). Stress inoculation: A cognitive therapy for anger and its application to a case of depression. *Journal of Consulting and Clinical Psychology, 45* (4), 600-607.

Orlick, T. (1982). *The second cooperative sports and games book.* New York: Pantheon Books.

Parfitt, G., & Hardy, L. (1993). The effects of competitive anxiety on memory span and rebound shooting tasks in basketball players. *Journal of Sport Sciences, 11,* 517-524.

Pasternak, G.W. (1988). Multiple morphine and enkephalin receptors and the relief of pain. *Journal of the American Medical Association, 259,* 1362-1367.

Phillips, H.E., & Kanagy, B. (1996). Teaching students to manage personal anger constructively. *Elementary School Guidance and Counselling, 30* (3), 229-236.

Plutchik, R. (1962). *The emotions: Facts, theories, and a new model.* New York: Random House.

Pollans, C.H. (1983). *The psychometric properties and factor structure of the Anger Expression (AX) Scale.* Unpublished master's thesis, University of South Florida, Tampa.

Raglin, J.S. (1990). Exercise and mental health: Beneficial and detrimental effects. *Sports Medicine, 9,* 323-329.

Reddon, J.R., Marceau, R., & Holden, R.R. (1985). A confirmatory evaluation of the Profile of Mood States: Convergent and discriminant item validity. *Journal of Psychopathology and Behavioral Assessment, 7,* 243-259.

Reid, R.M., & Hay, D. (1978). Aggression in rugby and soccer players. *British Journal of Physical Education, 9* (2), 45-46.

Ryan, R.M., Vallerand, R.J., & Deci, E.L. (1984). Intrinsic motivation in sport: A cognitive evaluation theory interpretation. In W. Straub & J. Williams (Eds.), *Cognitive sport psychology* (pp. 231-244). Lansing, NY: Sport Science Associates.

Smith, A.M., Scott, S.G., O'Fallon, W., & Young, M. (1990). Emotional responses of athletes to injury. *Mayo Clinic Proceedings, 65,* 38-50.

Snyder, M. (1974). Self-monitoring of expressive behavior. *Journal of Personality and Social Psychology, 30* (4), 526-537.

Stephens, D.E., Light-Bredemeier, B.J., & Shields, D.L.L. (1997). Construction of a measure designed to assess players' descriptions and prescriptions for moral behavior in youth sport soccer. *Journal of International Psychology of Sport, 28,* 370-390.

Udry, E., Gould, D., Bridges, D., & Beck, L. (1997). Down but not out: Athlete responses to season ending injuries. *Journal of Sport and Exercise Psychology, 19,* 229-248.

Udry, E., Gould, D., Bridges, D., & Tuffey, S. (1997). People helping people? Examining the social ties of athletes coping with burnout and injury stress. *Journal of Sport and Exercise Psychology, 19* (4), 368-395.

Vallerand, R.J., Deci, E.L., & Ryan, R.M. (1987). Intrinsic motivation in sport. In K.B. Pandolf (Ed.), *Exercise and sport sciences reviews* (pp. 389-425). New York: Macmillan.

Warr, P. (1990). The measurement of well-being and other aspects of mental health. *Journal of Occupational Psychology, 63,* 193-210.

Watson, D., Clark, L.A., & Carey, G. (1988). Positive and negative affectivity and their relation to anxiety and depressive disorders. *Journal of Abnormal Psychology, 97,* 346-353.

Zillman, D., Bryant, J., & Zapolsky, B.S. (1989). Enjoyment from sports spectatorship. In J.H. Goldstein (Ed.), *Sports, games, and play: Social and psychological viewpoints* (2nd ed., pp. 241-278). Hillsdale, NJ: Erlbaum.

Zillman, D., & Paulus, P.B. (1993). Spectators: Reactions to sports events and effects on athletic performance. In R. Singer, M. Murphey, & L.K. Tennant (Eds.), *Handbook of research on sport psychology* (pp. 600-619). New York: Macmillan.

Index

About the Editor

Internationally renowned sport psychologist Yuri L. Hanin, PhD, is Professor and Senior Researcher at the Research Institute for Olympic Sports in Jyväskylä, Finland. He has been a university-level teacher and researcher in the field of sport psychology for more than 30 years.

The author of three books as well as numerous book chapters and journal articles related to optimizing sports performance, Dr. Hanin has carried out extensive research, teaching, training, and consulting activities with national, international, and Olympic teams, athletes, and coaches. In addition, he has been a speaker at conferences throughout the United States, Canada, Europe, and Australia.

Dr. Hanin has served as an associate editor of the *European Yearbook of Sport Psychology*. He is also a newsletter editor for the International Association of Applied Psychology (Division 12—Sport Psychology) and a member of the editorial board for the *International Journal of Sport Psychology, The Sport Psychologist, Revista de Psicologia del Deporte,* and *Coaching and Sport Science.*

Dr. Hanin holds PhD (1970) and Doctor of Psychological Sciences (1986) degrees in Social Psychology from Leningrad University. He received the 1998 Visiting Scholar Award from the Australian College of Sport Psychologists and the 1999 Distinguished International Scholar Award from the Association for the Advancement of Applied Sport Psychology (AAASP).

Dr. Hanin lives with his wife Muza in Jyväskylä, Finland. In his leisure time he enjoys downhill skiing and swimming.

About the Contributors

Stuart Biddle, PhD, is a Professor of Exercise and Sport Psychology at Loughborough University, United Kingdom. He received his PhD in Psychology from the University of Keele, United Kingdom, and his MSc in Sport Psychology from Pennsylvania State University. He serves as the Chair of the Scientific Committee of the European College of Sport Science and has served two terms as President of the European Federation of Sport Psychology from 1991-1999. He is a Chartered Psychologist and Chartered Health Psychologist for the British Psychological Society. A member of the editorial board of *The Sport Psychologist* and the *European Physical Education Review,* he also serves as a reviewer for numerous other psychology journals. He served as the editor for the book *European Perspectives on Exercise and Sport Psychology* (Human Kinetics, 1995) and is the author of numerous book chapters and journal articles in the subject areas of motivation and emotion in sport and exercise and the psychology of health-related exercise. In 1998, he received the Distinguished International Scholar Award from the Association for the Advancement of Applied Sport Psychology.

Céline M. Blanchard, PhD, completed her dissertation at the Université du Québec à Montréal. She received her BA in Psychology from University of Ottawa, Canada, and her BA in Psychology with honors from Carleton University, Canada. She is a member of the American Psychological Association, the American Psychological Society, and the Canadian Psychological Association. Her research interests include motivation, emotions, sport, exercise, passionate interests, and health. She has made several scientific presentations and has recently published articles in the *International Journal of Sport Psychology* and the *Journal of Sport and Exercise Psychology.*

John Heil, DA, specializes in pain & behavioral medicine and sport psychology at the Lewis-Gale Clinic in Roanoke, Virginia. He received his master's degree in clinical psychology from St. Louis University and his Doctorate in Health Psychology from Lehigh University. He completed his postdoctoral training in pain and behavioral medicine at the University of Utah School of Medicine. He is the author of *Psychology of Sport Injury* (Human Kinetics, 1993) and numerous book chapters and papers on sport psychology, pain management, and injury rehabilitation. Heil is the sport psychology consultant and chair of the sport science, safety, and technology committee of the United States Fencing Association, director of sportsmedicine for the Commonwealth Games of Virginia, and the Vice President of the Board of Directors for Virginia Amateur Sports.

Keith Henschen, PED, is a Professor in the Exercise and Sport Science Department at the University of Utah. He received his PED from Indiana University in 1976. Henschen has 30 years of professional experience in the field of Applied Sport Psychology. He has published more than 190 articles, 20 book chapters, 3 books, 7 monographs, and has made over 350 presentations on sport psychology. A member of the American Psychological Association and the Association for the Advancement of Applied Sport Psychology, Henschen has worked with numerous national governing bodies of sport and with world-class and professional athletes. He is Vice President of the International Society of Sport Psychology and was President of the American Alliance for Health, Physical Education, Recreation and Dance from 1997-1998.

Leif Isberg, PhD, is a Professor in the Department of Physical Education and Health at the University of Örebro, Sweden, and a Guest Professor at Norwegian University of Sport and Physical Education, Oslo. He received his PhD from Uppsala University, Sweden, specializing in the pedagogical and psychological areas of sport. A frequent lecturer at numerous international conferences, he is well-known for his research and developing work in teacher education. He is a former elite player in soccer and ice hockey; and since 1978, Isberg has been working in three areas of sport: violence in sport, leadership and coaching, and referee problems, publishing several book chapters and scientific articles on those subjects. He was responsible for the first coach education program in Sweden and is currently Director of the program. He has been a member of the editorial board of the International Society of Sport Psychology and an Expert at the National Swedish Board of Universities and Colleges.

Susan A. Jackson, PhD, is a Lecturer in Sport and Exercise Psychology at Queensland University of Technology, Australia. She received her PhD from the University of North Carolina, Greensboro. She is a researcher of flow states in sport and exercise emphasizing the application of flow theory to sport and has published and presented numerous papers in this area. Jackson has recently published, with coauthor Mihaly Csikszentmihalyi, *Flow in Sports: The Key to Optimal Experiences and Performances* (Human Kinetics,1999). She is also the author of several book chapters and research articles. She is an International Affiliate of the American Psychological Association, a member of the College of Sport Psychologists with the Australian Psychological Society, and a member of International Relations Committee with the Association for the Advancement of Applied Sport Psychology.

K. Wolfgang Kallus, PhD, is a Professor for Applied Psychology at the Institute of Psychology at the Karl-Franzens University in Graz, Austria. He received his Diploma in Psychology and his Doctorate in Psychology from the University of Düsseldorf, and his second doctorate (habilitation) from the University of Würzburg. He has conducted experimental research on stress, coping, and recovery, and applied research in field settings. He has published on initial state and stress, on reactivity, and on recovery. Kallus is coauthor of the German Coping Questionnaire and author of the Recovery Stress Questionnaire. He founded a small research enterprise, which conducts applied research such as cognitive task analysis of air control in Europe. He is a member of the German Psychological Association (Deutsche Gesellschaft für Psychologie), the German Psychophysiological Association (Deutsche Gesellschaft für Psychophysiologie und ihre Anwendungen), the New York Academy of Sciences, and the International Biometric Society.

Dr. Michael Kellmann, is a Hochschulassistent (equivalent to assistant professor, nontenured) for Sport Psychology at University of Potsdam, Institute of Sport Science, Germany. He received his Doctored degree and Diploma in Psychology from the University of Würzburg, Germany. He has been a consultant to the German Junior National Rowing Team since 1995 and is a member of the German Association for Sport and the Association for the Advancement of Sport Psychology. Kellmann is on the editorial review board of *The Sport Psychologist*, an editorial assistant and reviewer for *Psychologie und Sport* (German Journal of Sport Psychology), and has authored or coauthored several publications in sport psychology.

Richard S. Lazarus, PhD, is Professor Emeritus of Psychology at the University of California, Berkeley. Lazarus has published over 200 scientific articles and 25 books, both monographs and textbooks in personality and clinical psychology. In 1966, he published *Psychological Stress and Coping* (McGraw-Hill), which is now considered a classic. In 1991, he published *Emotion and Adaptation* (Oxford University Press), which presents a cognitive-motivational-relational theory of emotions. His theoretical and research efforts have contributed substantially to what has been called the "cognitive revolution" in psychology. In 1989, he was awarded the Distinguished Scientific Contribution Award by the American Psychological Association. Lazarus also has two honorary degrees, one received in July 1988 from the Johannes Gutenberg University in Mainz, Germany, the other received in June 1995 from Haifa University in Israel. He continues to write and publish research on stress, coping, and the emotions.

John S. Raglin, PhD, is an Associate Professor in the Department of Kinesiology at Indiana University, Bloomington and was a Visiting Research Fellow at Stockholm University, Sweden in 1998. He received his PhD in Sport Psychology from the University of Wisconsin-Madison. He is a Fellow of the American Psychological Association, the American College of Sports Medicine, and the American Academy of Kinesiology and Physical Education. He has also been an invited speaker at conferences throughout the United States, Europe, and Asia. Raglin is an associate editor of the *Journal of Swimming Research,* and has published 11 book chapters and over 40 articles.

Robert J. Vallerand, PhD, is full Professor and Director of the Laboratoire de Recherche sur le Comportement Social in the Department of Psychology at the Université du Quèbec à Montréal where he teaches experimental social psychology and human motivation. Dr. Vallerand has written 3 books and more than 100 articles and book chapters. He has served as Chair of the Psychology Department, President of the Quebec Society for Research in Psychology, Chair of both the Social Psychology and the Sport Psychology sections of the Canadian Psychological Association, Associate Editor of the *Canadian Journal of Behavioural Sciences,* and editorial board member of several journals including the *Journal of Applied Sport Psychology* and the *Journal of Personality and Social Psychology*. His current research interests focus on the hierarchical model of intrinsic and extrinsic motivation as well as on passions and their consequences for people's lives. He is a Fellow of the Canadian Psychological Association, and he received the Sport Science Award from the International Olympic Committee in 1995.

Gregory S. Wilson, PED, is an Assistant Professor in the Department of Human Kinetics and Sport Studies at the University of Evansville, Indiana. He received his Doctorate of Physical Education from Indiana University, Bloomington. Two recently published articles in *Educational Research Quarterly* and the *International Sports Journal* have focused on his primary research interest of the examination of effects of personality and anxiety on performance in both athletic and academic settings. Wilson's secondary research interest is in the area of overtraining and staleness in athletes. He is a member of the American Alliance for Health, Physical Education, Recreation & Dance, the American College of Sports Medicine, and the American Psychological Association.

Related Books from Human Kinetics

Sport Psychology Interventions
Shane M. Muphy, PhD, Editor
1995 • Hardback • 392 pp • ISBN 0-87322-659-3
$45.00 ($67.50 Canadian)

Sport Psychology Interventions shows professionals how to help athletes get the most out of their sport experience and maintain a healthy lifestyle. This practical guide explains how to assist athletes at all levels in facing the special challenges and unique problems that are common in today's sport world.

Sports Slump Busting
10 Steps to Mental Toughness and Peak Performance
Alan S. Goldberg, EdD
1998 • Paperback • 288 pp • ISBN 0-88011-653-6
$16.95 ($24.95 Canadian)

In *Sports Slump Busting*, Dr. Alan Goldberg presents a 10-step program that's benefited hundreds of coaches and slumping athletes and teams in a wide variety of sports, at every level of competition. Each step in the program includes real-life examples and self-evaluation exercises to apply training or competition to ensure success.

Alcohol and Sport
Robert D. Stainback
1997 • Hardback • 232 pp • ISBN 0-87322-531-7
$30.00 ($44.95 Canadian)

Alcohol mixes with athletics no better than it does with driving. Robert Stainback's *Alcohol and Sports* reveals the extent of the sport and alcohol relationship and how professionals can help prevent and treat alcohol abuse in sport. This book is an essential reference for the entire support team who help athletes perform and cope with life's problems.

To request more information or to order, U.S. customers call 1-800-747-4457, e-mail us at **humank@hkusa.com**, or visit our web site at **http://www.humankinetics.com**. Persons outside the U.S. can contact us via our web site or use the appropriate telephone number, postal address, or e-mail address shown in the front of this book.

HUMAN KINETICS
The Information Leader in Physical Activity